S0-BJN-378

WILLIAM SHAKESPEARE AND ROBERT BURTON

Printed by Bradley & Son Limited
at The Crown Press, Caxton Street, Reading
1960

William Shakespeare
and
Robert Burton

By

A. BROWNLEE

In memory of my mother from
whom I inherited a love of
poetic literature

"*Stylus virum arguit*, our style bewrays us, and as hunters find their game by the trace, so is a man's genius descried by his works." B. p. 8

PREFACE

I DEAL in strong probabilities not certainties. I cite extensive evidence which indicates that at least two authors contributed to the writing of the works at present generally attributed to William Shakespeare alone. It is claimed that, of these two, Shakespeare was the inferior and that the great poet and dramatist was Robert Burton, author of *The Anatomy of Melancholy*. In the past many have questioned the authenticity of authorship of these works mainly on the ground that Shakespeare could not possibly have been well enough educated to be able to write so learnedly, and have attributed the works to contemporaries such as Francis Bacon, Lord Oxford and others. Other critics, noticing great inequality within the canon, consider that Shakespeare must have had collaborators. Nearest to the view taken in this present work is that held by an American, Mr. M. L. Horr, who believed that Burton was "Shakespeare"; apparently, however, he credited Burton with all the "Shakespeare" works, a proposition which I strongly reject. Another person to find similarities between "*Shakespeare's*" *Works* and *The Anatomy of Melancholy* was Ignatius Donnelly*, who, however, was of the opinion that the explanation of them was that Francis Bacon wrote both works.

Burton is known to have been a poet, and a dramatist; in this book over a thousand quotations from the *great* work of "Shakespeare" are placed in juxtaposition with parallel quotations from *The Anatomy of Melancholy* to show the remarkable similarity in thought and mode of expression in these two works; passages from "Shakespeare" are autobiographical when applied to Burton. All such evidence strongly supports my claim. Should it be without foundation I beg pardon of the shades of William Shakespeare and of Robert Burton for misrepresenting them.

Any reader, who does not find satisfactory my evidence in favour of Burton's authorship of "Shakespeare" and who is unacquainted with *The Anatomy of Melancholy*, may still find something of value when examining the Burton quotations given in Chapters VI, VII, VIII, IX, XI and XII and thereby be introduced to the great

---

* *The Great Cryptogram*; Sampson Low, Marston, Searle & Rivington; Vol. II, p. 968.

discrepancy that "Shakespeare's" plays are known throughout the world while this most profound, entertaining, instructive, comforting, all-embracing, poetic *Anatomy of Melancholy* dealing, as it does, with the same theme as the great plays, namely the science of man and its practical application to day-to-day life, is comparatively unheard-of at the present time.

Should any of my colleagues object that I would have been better employed concentrating on study more nearly related to my professional requirements, I would reply that Burton was the scientist's poet *par excellence* and that his observations on psychosomatic medicine, psychology and ecology are still of great value to the catholic mind.

A. Brownlee

ACKNOWLEDGMENTS AND REFERENCES

FOR a general account of the life of Shakespeare I am indebted to Sir Sidney Lee's *A Life of William Shakespeare*, John Murray, 1925, and to Mr. F. E. Halliday's *Shakespeare and His Critics*, Gerald Duckworth & Co., Ltd., London, 1950. I am particularly indebted to Mr. Halliday and his publishers for permission to quote the passage given on page 2 of this book, also to Messrs. John Murray for permission to quote the passage from *Is It Shakespeare* by 'A Graduate of Cambridge', given in Chapter XII, and to Professor Peter Alexander and Messrs. Collins for permission to use the book *William Shakespeare: The Complete Works*, edited by Peter Alexander; Collins, London and Glasgow, 1951, in giving references to the many passages quoted from it. The Edition of *The Anatomy of Melancholy* used for most of my study was that of Chatto & Windus, London, 1883, and the references given as "B. p. . ." refer to this edition, as does the "Key" given on pages 335-6 and referred to on page 129; from this edition also I have extracted much of the data given in my Chapter II. The Reverend A. R. Shilleto's edition of *The Anatomy of Melancholy*, George Bell and Sons, 1893, pointed out references and possible references to Shakespeare, some of which I had previously overlooked; details are given in Chapter IV. Mrs. Cowden Clarke's *The Complete Concordance to Shakespeare*, Bickers & Son, 1881, was of great value to me when looking up references. D. H. Lambert's *Shakespeare's Documents*, George Bell and Sons, 1904, I have found of much help, so also *Holinshed's Chronicle as used in Shakespeare's Plays* edited by Prof. Allardyce Nicoll and Josephine Nicoll; to these latter editors and their publishers, Messrs. J. M. Dent and Sons, I am indebted also for permission to publish extracts from their book. I have taken short quotations from *Plutarch's Lives of Coriolanus, Cæsar, Brutus and Antonius in North's Translation*, edited by R. H. Carr; Oxford, at the Clarendon Press, 1906. For the checking of the instances, given in this book, of Shakespeare referring to *Ovid's Metamorphoses*, I have used *A New Translation* by Mary M. Innes, The Penguin Classics. To George Sampson's edition of *Much Ado About Nothing*, Pitt Press Shakespeare, I am indebted for its analysis of the plot and for the Bandello story translated by Mrs. Sampson. I have quoted from F. S. Boas' edition of *The Taming of a Shrew*. G. G. Greenwood in his book, *The Shakespeare Problem Restated*, John Lane, The Bodley Head, 1908, drew my attention to certain errors in Shakespeare's natural-history lore and to Shakespeare's daughters' lack of education. Mention of other sources of information is given in the text. Other unnamed writers on Shakespeare, including editors of editions of single plays and of quarto facsimiles, doubtless influenced my thought and to them I am grateful. I can think of no better way of expressing my indebtedness to previous writers in my attempted build up of knowledge of Shakespeare and Burton than by quoting humbly the latter—"He that comes last is commonly best". B. p. 8.

An index of authors is to be found at the end.

CONTENTS

Chapter I

A SHORT ACCOUNT OF SHAKESPEARE'S LIFE

William Shakespeare was born at Stratford-on-Avon in 1564. There is no recorded evidence to show whether or not he attended school. According to Aubrey (see Sidney Lee, p. 25, and Halliday, p. 16) he assisted his father, who was a butcher. At the age of eighteen he married. A daughter was born in 1583 and twins, son and daughter, in 1585; the son died when eleven years of age. It would appear that all alone he left Stratford about 1585 and no further record of him is extant until in 1592 he is the subject of a bitter attack by Robert Greene, a dramatist, who, in his *Groatsworth of Wit bought with a Million of Repentance*, wrote "There is an upstart crow, beautified with our feathers, that, with his *Tygers heart wrapt in a Players hide*, supposes he is as well able to bumbast out a blanke verse as the best of you; and being an absolute *Johannes Factotum*, is in his owne conceit the onely Shake-scene in a countrie."* The Tygers heart wrapt in a Players hide is accepted as being a parody on "O tiger's heart wrapp'd in a woman's hide" to be found in *Part* 2 of *The Contention* and in *King Henry VI*, pt. 3, I, 4, 137. Henry Chettle, Greene's publisher, later in 1592 apologized for publishing, unmodified, Greene's attack—"I am as sory as if the originall fault had beene my fault, because myselfe have seene his demeanor no lesse civill, than he exelent in the qualitie he professes;—besides, divers of worship have reported his uprightnes of dealing, which argues his honesty, and his facetious grace in writing, that aprooves his art."†

In 1593 and 1594 respectively were published the poems *Venus and Adonis* and *The Rape of Lucrece* with a dedication, made to Lord Southampton and signed "William Shakespeare," prefacing each poem. A number of plays (the quartos) were published from 1594 onwards, only some with their title page showing that William Shakespeare was their author. It is unlikely that these were prepared for publication by Shakespeare as Heminge and Condell (see below) claimed that they had been surreptitiously copied.

He made a number of visits to Oxford and he stood as godfather to Sir William Davenant at his baptism in 1606.‡

---

* Lambert, p. 16.

† Lambert, p. 9.

‡ *The Historical Handbook and Guide to the City and University of Oxford* by Jas. J. Moore; Shrimpton and Son, Oxford, 1871.

His career as actor, playwright and shareholder in the theatre brought him considerable wealth, enabling him to purchase property in Stratford and London. Records of, and references to, business transactions, legal procedures and lastly his Will constitute the most of what is authentically known of his activities apart from references to him as actor and writer of plays and poems. (The text of these records is given in Lambert's book.) He returned to Stratford about 1611 and during the last five years or so of his life he appears to have written little if anything. F. E. Halliday (pp. 69-70) writes:—

> "We think of Keats's fear of death before his pen had gleaned his teeming brain, of the blind Milton dictating *Paradise Lost* for which he received ten pounds, of the deaf Beethoven composing his celestial last quartets and full of projects for a tenth symphony, of the crippled Michelango dying in his ninetieth year in the middle of vast schemes and responsibilities, of the aged Renoir painting up to the last with his brush strapped into position between his contorted finger and thumb, of Virgil, Dante, Bach, Goethe, Cézanne, and the other great creative spirits of the world, and there seems to be no parallel. Perhaps he did write something and it has been lost? Perhaps he turned again to his first love, to the pure poetry of the *Sonnets* and lyrics—and there are indications in the later plays that he might well have done so—and perhaps his puritanical son-in-law destroyed his work? Or perhaps in 1612 he was a very sick man? Who knows? But the man who wrote the *Sonnets*, *Romeo and Juliet*, *Henry IV*, *Twelfth Night*, *Hamlet*, *King Lear*, and *The Tempest*, though he might cease writing for the stage, could scarcely cease writing altogether and sink into what for him must have been the living death of a country gentleman pottering about his estate, unless he were too ill to think and too weak to write."

There is no record of his having given any attention to his daughters' education. Apart from signatures, no handwriting of his is extant. In his Will there is no reference to books or to any writings. He died in 1616, survived by his wife and two daughters, and was buried at Stratford.

In 1623 two of his fellow actors, John Heminge and Henrie Condell, published in the 1st Folio thirty-six plays ascribing them to William Shakespeare; *Pericles*, a thirty-seventh play now usually attributed to Shakespeare, was not included. In their dedication of the folio to Earls Pembroke and Montgomery, these two actors write "We have but collected them, and done an office to the dead, to procure his orphanes guardians; without ambition either of selfe-profit or fame, onely to keepe the memory of so worthy a friend and fellow alive, as was our Shakespeare, by humble offer of his playes, to your most noble patronage."* And *To The Great Variety of Readers* they write "... so to have publish'd them, as where (before) you were abus'd with diverse stolne and surreptitious copies, maimed and deformed by the frauds and stealthes of injurious impostors that expos'd them; even those are now offer'd to your view cur'd, and perfect of their limbes, and all the rest absolute in their numbers as he conceived them; who, as he was a happie imitator of Nature, was a most gentle expresser of it. His mind and hand went together; and what he thought, he uttered with that easinesse that wee have scarse received from him a blot in his papers."† Ben Jonson in a poem *To The Memory of My Beloved, The Author Mr. William Shakespeare and What He Hath Left Us*, which was included in the preface to the first folio, writes in high praise, saying amongst other eulogies:—

"He was not of an age, but for all time!"

Jonson also wrote in the same poem:—

"And though thou hadst small Latine and lesse Greeke."

In his *Discoveries* Jonson wrote "I remember the players have often mentioned it as an honour to Shakespeare, that in his writings (whatsoever he penn'd) he never blotted out a line. My answer had been, Would he had blotted a thousand!"‡

---

* Lambert, p. 94.
† Lambert, p. 96.
‡ Copied from *Bacon and Shakespeare* by W. H. Smith; John Russell Smith, London, 1857, p. 26.

CHAPTER II

A SHORT ACCOUNT OF BURTON'S LIFE

Robert Burton was born of an ancient and genteel family at Lindley in Leicestershire on the 8th February, 1577. He received his early education at Sutton Coldfield or Nuneaton or both, then went to Brazenose College, Oxford, in 1593; was elected student of Christ Church, Oxford, in 1599, and graduated B.A. in 1602*; was admitted to the reading of the Sentences in 1614. He became vicar of St. Thomas, Oxford in 1616 and rector of Seagrave, Leicestershire in 1636 (or 1630 or 1631†). He resided during all his adult life at Christ Church. He says of himself in his book, *The Anatomy of Melancholy*, "I would not willingly be known" (B. p. 1); "I have lived a silent, sedentary, solitary, private life, *mihi et musis* in the University, as long almost as Xenocrates in Athens, *ad senectam ferè* to learn wisdom as he did, penned up most part in my study" (B. p. 2); "I have no wife nor children good or bad to provide for" (B. p. 3); "I never travelled but in map or card, in which my unconfined thoughts have freely expatiated, as having ever been especially delighted with the study of Cosmography" (B. p. 3); "When I first took this task in hand, *et quod ait ille, impellente genio negotium suscepi*, this I aimed at; *vel ut lenirem animum scribendo*, to ease my mind by writing; for I had *gravidum cor, fœtum caput*, a kind of imposthume in my head, which I was very desirous to be unladen of, and could imagine no fitter evacuation than this. Besides, I might not well refrain, for *ubi dolor, ibi digitus*, one must needs scratch where it itches" (B. p. 5).

The subject of his book was man himself:—

"No Centaurs here, or Gorgons look to find,
My subject is of man and human kind.
Thou thyself art the subject of my discourse.
Whate'er men do, vows, fears, in ire, in sport,
Joys, wand'rings, are the sum of my report." B. p. 1

"I will spend my time and knowledge, which are my greatest fortune, for the common good of all." B. p. 5

He left a library of over a thousand books (listed in Vol. I, Proceedings and Papers, Oxford Bibliographical Society 1922-26, p. 163). From a Memoir of the Author prefacing the Chatto and

---

* From *Proceedings and Papers*, Oxford Bibliographical Society, Vol. I, p. 160.
† *Ibid*

Windus edition of *The Anatomy* the following six passages are extracted:—

1. Wood's character of him is, that "he was an exact mathematician, a curious calculator of nativities, a general read scholar, a thorough-paced philologist, and one that understood the surveying of lands well. As he was by many accounted a severe student, a devourer of authors, a melancholy and humorous person; so by others, who knew him well, a person of great honesty, plain dealing and charity. I have heard some of the ancients of Christ Church often say, that his company was very merry, facete, and juvenile; and no man in his time did surpass him for his ready and dexterous interlarding his common discourses among them with verses from the poets, or sentences from classic authors; which being then all the fashion in the University, made his company the more acceptable." He appears to have been a universal reader of all kinds of books, and availed himself of his multifarious studies in a very extraordinary manner. From the information of Hearne, we learn that John Rouse, the Bodleian librarian, furnished him with choice books for the prosecution of his work. The subject of his labour and amusement, seems to have been adopted from the infirmities of his own habit and constitution. Mr. Granger says, "He composed this book with a view of relieving his own melancholy, but increased it to such a degree, that nothing could make him laugh, but going to the bridge-foot and hearing the ribaldry of the bargemen, which rarely failed to throw him into a violent fit of laughter. Before he was overcome with this horrid disorder, he, in the intervals of his vapours, was esteemed one of the most facetious companions in the University."

2. "Burton's *Anatomy of Melancholy*," he (Dr. Johnson) said, "was the only book that ever took him out of bed two hours sooner than he wished to rise." *Boswell's Life of Johnson*, Vol. I, p. 580, 8vo. edit.

3. "Burton's *Anatomy of Melancholy* is a valuable book," said Dr. Johnson. "It is, perhaps, overloaded with quotation. But there is great spirit and great power in what Burton says when he writes from his own mind." *Ibid*, Vol. II, p. 325.

4. "He was capable of writing excellent poetry, but he seems to have cultivated this talent too little. The English verses prefixed to his book, which possess beautiful imagery, and great sweetness of versification, have been frequently published. His Latin elegiac verses addressed to his book, shew a very agreeable turn for raillery." *Ferriar's Illustrations of Sterne*, p. 58.

5. "When the force of the subject opens his own vein of prose, we discover valuable sense and brilliant expression. Such is his account of the first feelings of melancholy persons, written probably, from his own experience." (See p. 161 of the present edition.) *Ibid*, p. 60.

6. "During a pedantic age, like that in which Burton's production appeared, it must have been eminently serviceable to writers of many descriptions. Hence the unlearned might furnish themselves with appropriate scraps of Greek and Latin, whilst men of letters would find their inquiries shortened, by knowing where they might look for what both ancients and moderns have advanced on the subject of human passions. I confess my inability to point out any other English author who has so largely dealt in apt and original quotation." *Manuscript note of the late George Steevens, Esq., in his copy of* The Anatomy of Melancholy.

The first edition of his *The Anatomy of Melancholy* was published in 1621. Four subsequent editions were published during his lifetime. Burton worked at his book until his death in 1640 and left additions with his publisher, Henry Cripps, to be incorporated in a sixth edition, as is indicated by the following note, which was printed at the end of the sixth edition published in 1651-52:

TO THE READER

"Be pleased to know (Courteous Reader) that since the last Impression of this Book, the ingenuous Author of it is deceased, leaving a Copy of it exactly corrected, with several considerable Additions by his own hand; this copy he committed to my care and custody, with directions to have those Additions inserted in the next Edition; which in order to his command, and the Publicke Good, is faithfully performed in this last Impression." H.C.

Shilleto (Introduction, p. viii) drew my attention to the footnote in Part. 1, Sec. 2, Mem. 3, Subs. 15 (B. p. 213), which refers to the acting of Burton's Latin play, *Philosophaster*, at Christ Church on February 16th, 1617.

Lines written by Burton form his epitaph in Christ Church:—

Paucis notus, paucioribus ignotus,
Hic jacet *Democritus* Junior
Cui vitam dedit et mortem
Melancholia.

B. p. xi

CHAPTER III

THE BEGINNINGS OF THIS PRESENT BOOK

By September 1950 the idea began to develop that the thought and manner of expression in *The Anatomy of Melancholy* and in the plays attributed to Shakespeare were very similar and therefrom arose the concept that Burton was "Shakespeare". Some months later this idea obtained support when I read the section on Robert Burton in the *Selected Writings of Sir William Osler*.* Here Osler gives reference (Bodleian Quarterly Record (1917), Vol. II, p. 108) to a short account by Mr. "E.G.P." of the investigations that were made by Mr. M. L. Horr in collaboration with E.G.P.'s father, Mr. George Parker of the Bodleian library. Mr. M. L. Horr was an American who came to England about 1891 to obtain further evidence in support of his theory that Burton wrote Shakespeare. Horr considered that Hamlet's character was Burton's own. He stressed, as evidence for Burton's authorship, a note "His work" written by John Rous (elected Bodley's librarian in 1620) in the margin opposite the entry, *Venus and Adonis*, in the list of books bequeathed by Burton to the Bodleian library. Mr. George Parker appears to have been impressed by Horr's views and Osler, also, did not consider them at all far-fetched. Referring to the Bacon-Shakespeare controversy Osler writes:"Is it not just as reasonable to suppose, as Mr. [George] Parker of Oxford suggested, that Burton himself wrote the plays of Shakespeare? Does he not quote him several times, and are there not fine original editions of *Venus and Adonis* and *The Rape of Lucrece* among his books in the Bodleian?"

Early in my studies on this subject, I also would have subscribed vaguely to the view that Burton wrote *all* the works of"Shakespeare." On further study of the subject, however, I came to the conclusion that the evidence against such a contention was far too strong to permit of it being accepted in its entirety. After all, Shakespeare's contemporaries, including Greene, Chettle, Ben Jonson, Heminge and Condell, did credit him with being a writer of plays and it is unlikely that they were wholly wrong. My opinion is that Shakespeare wrote only some of the works, wholes or parts, generally attributed to him and that Burton wrote most of the remainder and I now proceed to give evidence which, I consider, does justify the holding of this opinion.

---

* Oxford University Press, 1951, p. 77.

CHAPTER IV

BURTON REFERS TO SHAKESPEARE

In *The Anatomy of Melancholy*, a book in which there are literally thousands of quotations from, and references to, other works, Burton refers to Shakespeare by name on two occasions only:—

1. On B. p. 511 he writes "When Venus ran to meet her rose-cheeked Adonis, as an elegant poet of ours [footnote, "Shakspeare"] sets her out,

'the bushes in the way
Some catch her neck, some kiss her face,
Some twine about her legs to make her stay,
And all did covet her for to embrace.' "

2. On B. p. 531 he writes "And many times those which at the first sight cannot fancy or affect each other, but are harsh and ready to disagree, offended with each other's carriage, like Beatrice and Benedict in the comedy, [footnote, "Shakspeare"] and in whom they find many faults, by this living together in a house, conference, kissing, colling, and such like allurements, begin at last to dote insensibly one upon another."

Thus Burton concurs with the present-time orthodox belief that Shakespeare wrote *Venus and Adonis* and *Much Ado About Nothing* and I think Horr must be wrong in attributing *Venus and Adonis* to Burton as it is extremely unlikely that he deliberately attributed to another what he himself had written. Moreover, *Venus and Adonis* was published in 1593, when Burton was only sixteen years of age and therefore most unlikely to be publishing under another living person's name.

There occur also in *The Anatomy* quotations which are undoubtedly from Shakespeare but his name is not mentioned in connection with them. These are now given along with what Shilleto says in his edition of *The Anatomy*, which is given *verbatim*.

(I) On B. p. 583 Burton gives:—

"Whoever heard a story of more woe
Than that of Juliet and her Romeo."

Shilleto, Vol. III, p. 216, gives "(Last lines of Shaks. R. & J. quoted *memoriter*)."

(II) On B. p. 624 Burton quotes:—

"Tomorrow is St. Valentine's day."

Shilleto, Vol. III, p. 291, remarks "(No doubt Burton took this from Hamlet A. IV. Sc. V. 48)."

(III) On B. p. 600 Burton quotes:—

"Young men will do it when they come to it."

Shilleto, Vol. III, p. 246, gives "(Hamlet A. IV. Sc. V. 60)."

(IV) On B. p. 46 Burton quotes:—

"For Princes are the glass, the school, the book,
Where subjects' eyes do learn, do read, do look."

Shilleto, Vol. I, p. 91, gives "(Shak. Rape of Lucrece, 615, 616)."

I now give passages from Burton which possibly refer to the following passages from Shakespeare. When Shilleto makes relevant reference his remarks are given *verbatim*.

(I) If fortune my foe were.

The Merry Wives of Windsor III, 3, 55

Sing "Fortune my foe". B. p. 610.

Shilleto, Vol. III p. 265, gives "(The beginning words of a popular Elizabethan ballad. See Malone's Note on Shaksp. Merry Wives, A. III. Sc. III)."

(II) *The Comedy of Errors* [Title of Play].

A new comedy of errors. B. p. 25.

(III) Cry 'Heigh-ho for a husband!'

Much Ado About Nothing, II, 1, 288

Heigh-ho for a husband, cries she. B. p. 602.

Shilleto, Vol. III p. 250, "(Shaksp. Much Ado A. II. Sc. I. 288; cf. A. III. Sc. IV. 47, 48)."

(IV) Vir sapit qui pauca loquitur.

Love's Labour's Lost, IV, 2, 76.

Vir sapit qui pauca loquitor. B. p. 70.

Shilleto, Vol. I p. 134, "(Quoted in Shaks. *Love's Labour's Lost*, IV. 2. The man is wise who speaks little)."

(V) Seeking the bubble reputation
Even in the cannon's mouth.

As You Like It, II, 7, 152.

Void of all fear they run into imminent dangers, cannon's mouth. B. p. 30.

Shilleto, Vol. I p. 63, "(I can't help thinking in this sentence that Burton remembered Shakespeare's *As You Like It*, A. II. Sc. VII. 152, 153 'Seeking the bubble reputation Even in the cannon's mouth')."

(VI) If the cat will after kind.

As You Like It, III, 2, 93.

Cat to her kind. B. p. 657.

Shilleto, Vol. III p. 352, "(Cf Shak. As You Like It, Act III. Sc. II. 91)."

(VII) What, man! more water glideth by the mill
Than wots the miller of.

Titus Adronicus, II, 1, 85.

And yet, *Non omnem molitor quæ fluit undam videt*, "the miller sees not all the water that goes by his mill."

B. p. 647.

.(VIII) Ira furor brevis est.

Timon of Athens, I, 2, 28.

Ira furor brevis est. B. p. 177.

Shilleto, Vol. I p. 311, "(Hor. Epp. I. II. 62. Anger is temporary madness)." Shilleto does not mention Shakespeare.

(IX) The Anthropophagi.

Othello, I, 3, 144.

Those Anthropophagi. B. p. 35.

Shilleto, Vol. I p. 72, gives "(Cannibals. See Shakespeare, Othello, I. III. 144)."

(X) Shilleto, Vol. II p. 91, (B. p. 343) enters a footnote to Burton's—"The *Greeks* had their *Olympian*, *Pythian*, *Isthmian*, *Nemean*, Games, in honour of *Neptune*, *Jupiter*, *Apollo*; *Athens* her's: some for Honour, Garlands, Crowns; [some] for beauty, dancing, running, leaping, like our silver games"—"Does Shakespeare's Tempest, Act ii, Sc. ii, explain this passage? 'Were I in England now, as once I was, and had but this fish painted, not a holiday fool there but would give a piece of silver'."

(XI) Shilleto, Vol. II p. 162, (B. p. 384) to Burton's footnote "*Corpore sunt et animo fortiores spurii, plerumque ob amoris vehementiam, seminis crass. etc.*" adds "[De Subtilitate, Lib. xii. Cf. Shak. K.L. A. i. Sc. ii]."

When we consider "Shakespeare's" great store of purple passages admirably suited for quotation, the most surprising feature of the above is that not a single great passage is quoted. Nor can this be explained with any degree of assurance on the grounds that Burton did not know of them. Of *Hamlet* he almost certainly knew, for besides quoting the two passages given above, which were probably taken from *Hamlet*, we have the evidence that *Hamlet* was performed at Oxford. The title page of the 1603 quarto says:—

"As it hath beene diverse times acted by his Highnesse servants in the Cittie of London: as also in the two Universities of Cambridge and Oxford, and else-where."

As Burton went to Oxford in 1593 and lived there most of his life thereafter, he was almost certain to have heard of this play being acted in Oxford, and therefore likely to be all the more interested in it. If he did not actually see the play himself he still would have had the opportunity of hearing of it from his colleagues. Burton's frequent references in his *Anatomy* to players and theatres indicate interest and the probability is that he would have taken the opportunity to see the play.

Moreover a study of the "parallel quotations" section of this book

(Chapter XI) will show clearly that many of the themes dealt with in *Hamlet* are also dealt with by Burton in his *Anatomy* and the obvious question is—why did Burton not use quotations from *Hamlet* to illustrate his points? Horr was of the opinion that Hamlet's character was Burton's own; Bradley* (p. 152) considered that Hamlet's character was close to Shakespeare's. As Bradley (p. 102) believed that the cause of Hamlet's irresolution was a state of profound melancholy, then it follows that Bradley would not have been averse to a view that the author of *Hamlet* suffered from melancholy. Thus this could agree with what is contended in this book, namely that Burton was joint-author of *Hamlet*, as Burton suffered from melancholy. He writes "I was not a little offended with this malady, shall I say my Mistress 'Melancholy'," (B. p. 5). Also, in the *Memoir of the Author* given at the beginning of *The Anatomy*, Mr. Granger is quoted as saying, "He composed this book with a view of relieving his own melancholy, but increased it to such a degree, that nothing could make him laugh, but going to the bridge-foot and hearing the ribaldry of the bargemen, which rarely failed to throw him into a violent fit of laughter." (B. p. x). These facts make it all the more puzzling why Burton did not quote the purple passages in *Hamlet* and the most satisfactory explanation appears to me to be that Burton himself wrote them and deliberately refrained from quoting his own work. Why does he mention "Chaucer's neat poem of Troilus and Cresseide" (B. p. 537) and omit *Troilus and Cressida*? Similar questions arise when we find that Burton mentions Macbeth, Banquo, Coriolanus, Timon, Cæsar, Antony, Cleopatra without referring to Shakespeare. (See below, Chapter XI).

* *Shakespearean Tragedy*; Macmillan & Co., London, 1912.

Chapter V

AT LEAST TWO AUTHORS CONTRIBUTED TO THE WRITING OF THE "SHAKESPEARE" WORKS

General

This is a long chapter and necessarily so as the questions raised by the chapter heading are not easily answered; yet they are crucial. It is my opinion that if one author alone wrote the whole of "Shakespeare" then that author was indeed William Shakespeare and most emphatically not Robert Burton, in which case the later chapters in this book with their many quotations from *The Anatomy of Melancholy* would be valueless so far as the intended purpose of their presentation here is concerned. However, I do not believe that one author wrote all "Shakespeare". As others also have found, (this will be dealt with more fully shortly) there is too much variation in the quality of the work to be compatible with single authorship. Admittedly the subject is difficult and if I were asked to adjudicate on a short passage, I might be uncertain, especially so when I recall that the subject matter and even the phraseology used may have been borrowed from other works, but with long passages and whole plays it is my opinion that they can be allocated to a superior or to an inferior author. The question of borrowing will be dealt with later in this chapter.

It is important for me to make clear early in this chapter that I do not hold Durning-Lawrence's* view that Shakespeare "could not write so much as his own name" or Bormann's† that his signatures represent almost or quite the extent of Shakespeare's calligraphic powers; I believe that Shakespeare did write extensively. It is most unlikely that Heminge and Condell, who were fellow actors with Shakespeare and must have known his capabilities, would have attributed the plays to a man who could not write; nor would Ben Jonson have said "would he had blotted a thousand" if he could not write one; nor, also, would Greene have said that Shakespeare "supposes he is as well able to bumbast out a blanke verse as the best of you" or Burton have referred to Shakespeare as the author of *Venus and Adonis* (B. p. 511) and *Much Ado About Nothing* (B. p. 531).

These preliminaries over, I shall begin by giving a short review of what some others have said that has a bearing upon the present

---

* *Bacon is Shakespeare*; Gay & Hancock, p. 30.
† *Francis Bacon's Cryptic Rhymes*; Siegle, Hill & Co., p. 46.

discussion. Ben Jonson gave praise to "Shakespeare" saying he was "for all time" but he also dispraised him saying "would he had blotted a thousand". Dryden noticed the varying quality of "Shakespeare's" works, saying in his essay on *The Dramatic Poetry of the Last Age**, "Shakespeare, who many times has written better than any poet, in any language, is yet so far from writing wit always, or expressing that wit according to the dignity of the subject, that he writes, in many places, below the dullest writer of ours, or any precedent age. Never did any author precipitate himself from such height of thought to so low expressions, as he often does. He is the very Janus of poets; he wears almost everywhere two faces; and you have scarce begun to admire the one, ere you despise the other." Hazlitt, an admirer of Shakespeare, also found inequalities. Of *Titus Adronicus* he writes† "*Titus Andronicus* is certainly as unlike Shakespear's usual style as it is possible," and on p. 264 he writes "The two poems of Venus and Adonis and of Tarquin and Lucrece appear to us like a couple of ice-houses. They are about as hard, as glittering, and as cold. The author seems all the time to be thinking of his verses, and not of his subject—not of what his characters would feel, but of what he shall say; and as it must happen in all such cases, he always puts into their mouths those things which they would be the last to think of, and which it shews the greatest ingenuity in him to find out. The whole is laboured, up-hill work. The poet is perpetually singling out the difficulties of the art to make an exhibition of his strength and skill in wrestling with them. He is making perpetual trials of them as if his mastery over them were doubted. The images, which are often striking, are generally applied to things which they are the least like." John Bailey writes‡ "The truth is that Shakespeare of all writers is least equal."

Thus early and modern critics have observed great inequality in the works attributed to William Shakespeare. Other critics observing this feature seek to explain it by postulating that Shakespeare must have had one or more collaborators. The view taken in this present book is that William Shakespeare, himself, was the "collaborator" and that the great dramatic poet was Robert Burton. The features which distinguish these two authors are:—

1. Shakespeare was in the main a narrative poet, while Burton was mainly contemplative. Thus Shakespeare wrote *Venus and Adonis* and *The Rape of Lucrece* and Burton wrote *The Sonnets;* Burton wrote most of *Hamlet* and *Macbeth*, while Shakespeare wrote *The Merry Wives of Windsor* and *Much Ado About Nothing*.

---

* *Dramatic Essays*; Dent, p. 103.
† *Characters of Shakespeare's Plays*; Dent, p. 261.
‡ *Shakespeare*; Longmans, Green & Co., 1929, p. 51.

2. Quite often Shakespeare was content to borrow material from other authors and merely repeat the theme in much the same or in other words without adding anything of value, while Burton, when he borrowed, used the original for the most part as a framework which he clothed with his own thought. Thus Shakespeare repeated long passages from Holinshed without even trying to add anything of importance as in *King Henry V*, Act I, Sc. 2, *King Henry VI*, pt. 2, Act II, Sc. 2, and in *King Henry VIII*, Act IV, Sc. 1. Also he borrowed plots from old plays without improving them in any worthwhile fashion as in *The Taming of the Shrew* borrowed from *The Taming of a Shrew* and *King John* borrowed from *The Troublesome Raigne*. I hasten to add that, in the case of both these plays, I refer to the Shakespeare parts as Burton, in my opinion, contributed to both; for example, *The Induction* and Act I of *The Shrew* and Act IV of *King John* are Burton's.
3. Shakespeare dealt mainly with the material and the physical, Burton with the intellectual and the spiritual.
4. Shakespeare wrote much verbose, non-subtle, tedious, commonplace, descriptive detail, while Burton avoided the commonplace, was concise and appealed to the reader's imagination to fill in detail for itself. Furthermore, a feature of Shakespeare's detailed descriptions is that they often fail to convey the impression of a unified whole, as in his description of the horse (*Venus and Adonis* 289-300), that of the picture (*The Rape of Lucrece* 1366-1582), or that of Queen Mab's waggon (*Romeo and Juliet* I, 4, 53). In all three what appears to my mind's eye is a mere jumble of parts. By contrast how apt, concise, illuminating and complete are Burton's descriptions of Spring and Winter (at end of *Love's Labour's Lost*), of the wedding night scene (at beginning of *A Midsummer's Night's Dream*) and of Macbeth's castle (at the beginning of Act I, Sc. 6)!
5. Shakespeare concerned himself solely with the present requirements of the play: Burton created a residuum of thought.

Let us, however, study some of Shakespeare's work in more detail, beginning with *Venus and Adonis*, one of the works which Burton ascribed to Shakespeare. It was published in 1593 when Shakespeare was twenty-nine years of age and begins thus:—

Even as the sun with purple-coloured face
Had ta'en his last leave of the weeping morn,
Rose-cheek'd Adonis hied him to the chase;
Hunting he lov'd, but love he laugh'd to scorn.
Sick-thoughted Venus makes amain unto him,
And like a bold-fac'd suitor gins to woo him.

About this first verse there are several points to be noticed:—(i) its narrative character, (ii) its clear expression and lack of any subtlety gives the reader no difficulty in following what the author wishes to convey and, if one passes quickly on to the next verse, all is well, (iii) closer inspection shows lack of exactitude and other flaws: (a) it is a very rare phenomenon for the sun to have a purple-coloured face, (b) as the rising of the sun is a process, not an event, "had ta'en" should have read "was taking", (c) as we read on through the poem we realize that Venus was indeed a "bold-fac'd suitor" so that it was pointless for the poet thus to compare her, (d) to use the line endings "unto him": "to woo him" necessitating the stressing of the first "-to" and unstressing the second shows clearly that the poet had a poor ear for rhyme. These characteristics of Shakespeare's verse will be dealt with again later. We pass on to lines 11-12:—

> Nature that made thee, with herself at strife,
> Saith that the world hath ending with thy life.

and note that nature saith no such thing so the words are quite meaningless. Next we examine lines 43-48:—

> So soon was she along as he was down,
> Each leaning on their elbows and their hips;
> Now doth she stroke his cheek, now doth he frown,
> And gins to chide, but soon she stops his lips,
> And kissing speaks, with lustful language broken:
> 'If thou wilt chide, thy lips shall never open.'

We note the profusion of purely physical and quite trivial detail; we note the ungrammatical second line and that the thought of the last line merely repeats that of the fourth. As we read on we soon find that the poem drags on with verses filled with physical detail time after time. At line 223 we read:—

> Sometime she shakes her head, and then his hand;
> Now gazeth she on him, now on the ground;
> Sometime her arms infold him like a band;
> She would, he will not in her arms be bound;
> And when from thence he struggles to be gone,
> She locks her lily fingers one in one.

and some 200 lines further we still find no progress:—

> You hurt my hand with wringing; let us part,
> And leave this idle theme, this bootless chat;
> Remove your siege from my unyielding heart;
> To love's alarms it will not ope the gate.
> Dismiss your vows, your feigned tears, your flatt'ry;
> For where a heart is hard they make no batt'ry.

Lines 421-426

then again:—

> But all in vain; good queen, it will not be.
> She hath assay'd as much as may be prov'd;
> Her pleading hath deserv'd a greater fee;
> She's Love, she loves, and yet she is not lov'd.
> 'Fie, fie,' he says, 'you crush me; let me go;
> You have no reason to withhold me so.' Lines 607-612

Ben Jonson was right: Shakespeare should have "blotted a thousand".

Leaving *Venus and Adonis* and passing on to *The Rape of Lucrece* which was published in 1594 when Shakespeare was thirty years of age, we find again elaborate description of the physical and commonplace. Subtlety is again absent. Much unnecessary repetition appears and few elevated thoughts are expressed in the whole long poem though, admittedly, there are some good lines, e.g. 330-333 and 848-854. The author loves to deal with the material and avoids the intellectual and spiritual; perhaps the best example of this is to be found in the following verse which is one of a number describing the scenes which Lucrece views on a canvas depicting the siege of Troy:—

> There pleading might you see grave Nestor stand,
> As 'twere encouraging the Greeks to fight,
> Making such sober action with his hand
> That it beguil'd attention, charm'd the sight.
> In speech, it seem'd, his beard all silver white
> Wagg'd up and down, and from his lips did fly
> Thin winding breath, which purl'd up to the sky.
> Lines 1401-1407

Nestor could have made some worthwhile comment on the ageless scene, but the whole concern of the poet is to inform the reader that Nestor made sober action with his hand, that his beard wagged up and down and his breath purled up to the sky. On contrasting the young Keats' *Ode on a Grecian Urn* (a very similar subject), we wonder how it could happen that, at thirty years of age, the man, who in orthodox opinion is the world's greatest poet, could write in such commonplace fashion on such a grand theme. Moreover, could it be really possible or probable that the author, who made Nestor, when at Troy, virtually dumb, would be so metamorphosed within ten years or less as to be able to give the following profoundly intellectual speech to that same Nestor while at the same Troy?

> *Nest.* In the reproof of chance
> Lies the true proof of men. The sea being smooth,
> How many shallow bauble boats dare sail
> Upon her patient breast, making their way
> With those of nobler bulk!

But let the ruffian Boreas once enrage
The gentle Thetis, and anon behold
The strong-ribb'd bark through liquid mountains cut,
Bounding between the two moist elements
Like Perseus' horse. Where's then the saucy boat,
Whose weak untimber'd sides but even now
Co-rivall'd greatness? Either to harbour fled
Or made a toast for Neptune. Even so
Doth valour's show and valour's worth divide
In storms of fortune; for in her ray and brightness
The herd hath more annoyance by the breese
Than by the tiger; but when the splitting wind
Makes flexible the knees of knotted oaks,
And flies fled under shade—why, then the thing of courage,
As rous'd with rage, with rage doth sympathise,
And with an accent tun'd in self-same key
Retorts to chiding fortune.

Troilus and Cressida, I, 3, 33.

I believe this passage was written by Burton and that *The Rape of Lucrece* was written by Shakespeare. Orthodox opinion would have us believe that the hand which wrote the trivial and commonplace:—

So soon was she along as he was down,
Each leaning on their elbows and their hips.

Venus and Adonis, 43-44

did in fact, some eight years later, write the profound lines:—

Who would these fardels bear,
To grunt and sweat under a weary life,
But that the dread of something after death—
The undiscover'd country, from whose bourn
No traveller returns—puzzles the will,
And makes us rather bear those ills we have
Than fly to others that we know not of?

Hamlet, III, 1, 76.

What is the explanation of the many discrepancies such as these two just given? Sir Edmund Chambers wrote*:—"the secret of his [Shakespeare's] genius lies in its power of development" and this is without doubt true of the great works—Burton's works. Of himself Burton wrote (B. p. 11) "Many things I disallow at this present, which when I writ, *Non eadem est ætas non mens;* I would willingly retract much, etc., but 'tis too late, I can only crave pardon now for what is amiss." The stumbling-block to a theory that mental evolution explains the above discrepancies is that much work, written later

* *Encyclopaedia Brit.*, 1946, Vol. 20, p. 446.

than *Troilus and Cressida* and *Hamlet*, is imbued with the same commonplace and physical detail and repetitions that we find in *Venus and Adonis* and *The Rape of Lucrece* and my studied opinion is that one contributor to the canon (Burton) did evolve while the other (Shakespeare) did not. As examples of writings, later than *Hamlet*, showing lack of any appreciable mental evolution, I give five, one from *Cymbeline*, one from *The Winter's Tale*, one from *Othello* and two from *King Henry VIII*:—

1. In *Cymbeline* the writer (Shakespeare) waxes eloquent in describing what Iachimo sees in Imogen's bedroom (Act II, Sc. 2) and it is worthy of note that, in so doing, Shakespeare's thoughts go back to the Tarquin of his own poem, *The Rape of Lucrece*—

Our Tarquin thus
Did softly press the rushes ere he waken'd
The chastity he wounded. II, 2, 12—

for what follows is reminiscent of the description of what Tarquin saw in Lucrece's bedroom. The Cymbeline description may be livelier than the Lucrece one, but the level of thought is no higher and thus there is no evidence of any mental evolution having occurred during that quite long period of years. In Act II, Sc. 4, Iachimo is allowed to redescribe to Posthumous what he had seen and, to make sure that the audience has not forgotten, a third brief reference is made in the last scene of the play. In Iachimo's account to Posthumous we read:—

A piece of work
So bravely done, so rich, that it did strive
In workmanship and value; which I wonder'd
Could be so rarely and exactly wrought,
Since the true life on't was— II, 4, 72.

and

The cutter
Was as another nature, dumb; outwent her,
Motion and breath left out. II, 4, 83.

Can one say that these two quotations show any advance over:—

Look when a painter would surpass the life
In limning out a well-proportion'd steed,
His art with nature's workmanship at strife,
As if the dead the living should exceed;
So did this horse excel a common one
In shape, in courage, colour, pace, and bone.

Venus and Adonis, 289-294?

The reader should also observe the padding in Shakespeare's Cymbeline passages particularly:—

Never saw I figures
So likely to report themselves. II, 4, 82.

which, as padding, is very similar to:—

A thousand lamentable objects there,
In scorn of nature, art gave lifeless life.

The Rape of Lucrece, 1373-4.

For much imaginary work was there.

The Rape of Lucrece, 1422.

2. *The Winter's Tale* was clearly intended in the early parts to be a sad tale, best for winter, yet in Act V, Scs. 2 and 3, all is turned topsy-turvy and a more joyous ending would hardly be imagined; Hermione, thought dead, is restored alive to Leontes; Perdita, thought dead, is restored to her father and mother; Florizel and Perdita presumably are to be married with their parents' blessing; Camillo at the command of Leontes is to marry Paulina. I may be too severe a moraler but what point has the play with such an ending for the author of *Macbeth?* Florizel had disobeyed his father. Camillo had deceived Leontes and also had instructed Florizel in the art of deceiving, yet neither offender is reproved in these last two scenes. Moreover, much of Act V, Sc. 2 is mere repetition of what is already known—the storm, the wreck, the bear; and the whole scene is filled with physical and commonplace detail—the mantle, the jewel, handkerchief, rings, bleed tears, wept blood, swooned, sorrowed. Padding again abounds:—

Beseech you, sir, were you present at this relation? Line 1.

I would gladly know the issue of it. Line 8.

I make a broken delivery of the business. Line 9.

There was speech in their dumbness, language in their very gesture. Line 14.

A notable passion of wonder appeared in them. Line 16.

Such a deal of wonder is broken out within this hour that ballad-makers cannot be able to express it. Line 24.

Then have you lost a sight which was to be seen, cannot be spoken of . . . I never heard of such another encounter, which lames report to follow it and undoes description to do it. Lines 41-56.

Note: "cannot be able" in the sixth quotation.

It is hard to believe that the writer of the intellectual, profound and concise floral scene (Act IV, Sc. 4) could, on a sudden, descend from the heights and, with all these discrepancies occurring together, one cannot escape considering whether or not two authors contributed to this play.

3. My example from *Othello* is especially valuable as the purely physical treatment of the subject can be compared with the spiritual treatment of a scene in *Macbeth* dealing with similar circumstances. In *Macbeth*, Duncan has been murdered in the dark and the author

(Burton) probes to the very depths of the murderer's soul:—

Mac. I have done the deed. Didst thou not hear a noise?
Lady M. I heard the owl scream and the crickets cry.

. . . .

Mac. But wherefore could not I pronounce 'Amen'?
I had most need of blessing and 'Amen'
Stuck in my throat. *Macbeth*, II, 2, 14-33

In *Othello*, Roderigo and Cassio have both been stabbed in the dark and this author (Shakespeare) begins by attempting to borrow from *Macbeth* and then fills in the remainder of the scene with purely physical, commonplace and repetitive detail of his own:—

Iago. Who's there? Whose noise is this that cries on murder?
Lod. We do not know.
Iago. Did not you hear a cry?

. . . .

Cas. My leg is cut in two.
Iago. Marry, heaven forbid!
Light, gentlemen. I'll bind it with my shirt.
Bian. What is the matter, ho? Who is't that cried?
Iago. Who is't that cried!
Bian. O my dear Cassio!
My sweet Cassio! O Cassio, Cassio, Cassio!
Iago. O notable strumpet! Cassio, may you suspect
Who they should be that have thus mangled you?
Cas. No.
Gra. I am sorry I find you thus; I have been to seek you.
Iago. Lend me a garter. So.
O, for a chair, to bear him easily hence!
Bian. Alas, he faints! O Cassio, Cassio, Cassio!
Iago. Gentlemen all, I do suspect this trash
To be a party in this injury.
Patience awhile, good Cassio. Come, come;
Lend me a light. Know we this face or no?
Alas, my friend and my dear countryman
Roderigo? No—yes, sure; O heaven! Roderigo.
Gra. What, of Venice?
Iago. Even he, sir; did you know him?
Gra. Know him! Ay.
Iago. Signior Gratiano? I cry your gentle pardon;
These bloody accidents must excuse my manners,
That so neglected you.
Gra. I am glad to see you.
Iago. How do you, Cassio?—O, a chair, a chair!
Gra. Roderigo!
Iago. He, he, 'tis he. [*A chair brought in.*

O, that's well said; the chair.
Some good man bear him carefully from hence;
I'll fetch the General's surgeon. *Othello*, V, 1, 48-100

My opinion is that Burton wrote the Macbeth scene and Shakespeare the Othello one.

4 & 5. Still more antagonistic to the mental-evolution explanation are my two examples from *King Henry VIII.* Here we find passages taken almost *verbatim* from Holinshed and rendered into iambic pentameter lines—one cannot say verse for they are certainly not poetry. In Holinshed we read:—

"Wherevpon the *archbishop of Canturburie*, *accompanied with* the bishops of London, Winchester, Bath, Lincolne, and diuers other *learned* men in great number, rode to *Dunstable*, which is *six miles from Ampthill*, *where the princesse* Dowager *laie*; and there *by* one Doctor Lee *she was cited* to appeare before the said archbishop in cause of matrimonie in the said towne of Dunstable, and at the daie of appearance she *appeared not*, but made default; and so she was called peremptorie everie daie fifteen daies togither, *and*, at the last, *for* lacke of *appearance*, *by the assent of all* the *learned men* there present, *she was divorsed* from the king, *and the marriage* declared to be void and *of none effect*."*

In *King Henry VIII* this passage reads (IV, 1, 24-33):—

1 *Gent.* That I can tell you too. The Archbishop
Of Canterbury, accompanied with other
Learned and reverend fathers of his order,
Held a late court at Dunstable, six miles off
From Ampthill, where the Princess lay; to which
She was often cited by them, but appear'd not.
And, to be short, for not appearance and
The King's late scruple, by the main assent
Of all these learned men, she was divorc'd,
And the late marriage made of none effect;
Since which she was removed to Kimbolton,
Where she remains now sick.

Again in Holinshed (p. 202) we read:—

"When she was thus *brought to* the high *place* made *in the* middest of the church, betweene the *queere* and the high altar, she was set *in a rich chaire*. And after that she had *rest*ed *a while*, she descended down *to the* high *altar*, and there prostrate hir selfe while *the archbishop of Canturburie* said certeine collects."

In *King Henry VIII*, IV, 1, 58, we read:—

2 *Gent.* You saw
The ceremony?

---

* Prof. Allardyce Nicoll and Josephine Nicoll edition of Holinshed, p. 201.

3 *Gent.* That I did.
1 *Gent.* How was it?
3 *Gent.* Well worth the seeing.
2 *Gent.* Good sir, speak it to us.
3 *Gent.* As well as I am able. The rich stream
Of lords and ladies, having brought the Queen
To a prepar'd place in the choir, fell off
A distance from her, while her Grace sat down
To rest awhile, some half an hour or so,
In a rich chair of state, opposing freely
The beauty of her person to the people.
Believe me, sir, she is the goodliest woman
That ever lay by man.

If one and the same author wrote the great plays and subsequently wrote these "Holinshed" passages adding "some half an hour or so," I can only say 'all signs fail.' I know that it is considered by many that Fletcher contributed to the writing of *King Henry VIII* but I think it unlikely that Fletcher wrote these two passages. After all, such passages could not have been written for any end other than gain and the actor-playwright, Shakespeare, was the person who would gain from them. Moreover, if Shakespeare paid Fletcher for writing what he himself could easily have written, then his known business acumen must have deserted him. For similar reasons we can safely assume that Shakespeare wrote the many other passages which are merely versified Holinshed. So also it is very probable that the same hand, which thus borrowed from Holinshed, perpetrated the crude borrowings from old plays. The following passage from *The Taming of the Shrew* followed by the passage from *The Taming of a Shrew*, from which the former was borrowed, will illustrate how closely this author was prepared to follow other work. I must however be fair and add that, though ideas and words are frequently borrowed from the old plays, the phraseology is seldom so close as in this example:—

Pet. Go, take it up unto thy master's use.
Gru. Villain, not for thy life! Take up my mistress' gown for thy master's use!
Pet. Why, sir, what's your conceit in that?
Gru. O, sir, the conceit is deeper than you think for.
Take up my mistress' gown to his master's use!
O fie, fie, fie!
Pet. Hortensio, say thou wilt see the tailor paid.—
Go take it hence; be gone, and say no more.
Hor. Tailor, I'll pay thee for thy gown tomorrow;
Take no unkindness of his hasty words.
Away, I say; commend me to thy master. [*Exit Tailor.*

Pet. Well, come, my Kate; we will unto your father's
Even in these honest mean habiliments;
Our purses shall be proud, our garments poor;

The Taming of the Shrew, IV, 3, 153-167

Feran. Go, I say, and take it up for your master's use.
San. Souns, villain, not for thy life; touch it not!
Souns, take up my mistress' gown to his master' use!
Feran. Well, sir, what's your conceit of it?
San. I have a deeper conceit in it than you think for.
Take up my mistress' gown to his master' use!
Feran. Tailor, come hither; for this time take it
Hence again, and I'll content thee for thy pains.
Tailor. I thank you, sir. [*Exit Tailor.*
Feran. Come, Kate, we now will go see thy father's house,
Even in these honest mean habiliments;
Our purses shall be rich, our garments plain.

**The Taming of a Shrew*, III, 5, 46-58

We have just seen that Shakespeare borrowed *closely* from Holinshed. Similarly he borrowed closely from Plutarch. In Plutarch (Carr's edition, pp. 177-8) we read:—

"and moreover sent Hirtius and Pansa, then Consuls, to drive Antonius out of Italy. These two Consuls together with Cæsar, who also had an army, went against Antonius that besieged the city of Modena, and there overthrew him in battle: but both the Consuls were slain there. Antonius, flying upon this overthrow, fell into great misery all at once: but the chiefest want of all other, and that pinched him most, was famine. Howbeit he was of such a strong nature, that by patience he would overcome any adversity, and, the heavier fortune lay upon him, the more constant showed he himself. Every man that feeleth want or adversity knoweth by virtue and discretion what he should do: but when indeed they are overlaid with extremity, and be sore oppressed, few have the hearts to follow that which they praise and commend, and much less to avoid that they reprove and mislike. But rather, to the contrary, they yield to their accustomed easy life: and through faint heart, and lack of courage, do change their first mind and purpose. And therefore it was a wonderful example to the soldiers to see Antonius, that was brought up in all fineness and superfluity, so easily to drink puddle water, and to eat wild fruits and roots: and moreover it is reported that, even as they passed the Alps, they did eat the barks of trees, and such beasts as never man tasted of their flesh before."

---

*Boas' Edition, pp. 44-45

Carr (p. 266) draws attention to the close similarity between the above passage and that from *Antony and Cleopatra*, I, 4, 56-68:—

When thou once
Was beaten from Modena, where thou slew'st
Hirtuis and Pansa, consuls, at thy heel
Did famine follow; whom thou fought'st against,
Though daintily brought up, with patience more
Than savages could suffer. Thou didst drink
The stale of horses and the gilded puddle
Which beasts would cough at. Thy palate then did deign
The roughest berry on the rudest hedge;
Yea, like the stag when snow the pasture sheets,
The barks of trees thou brows'd. On the Alps
It is reported thou didst eat strange flesh,
Which some did die to look on.

So also Shakespeare's lines

Eight wild boars roasted whole at a breakfast, and but twelve persons there. *Ant. and Cleo.*, II, 2, 183

are simply a copy of a Plutarch passage (p. 187):—

". . . eight wild boars roasted whole . . . not many guests, nor above twelve in all."

Also the subject matter and many of the actual words used in the Shakespeare lines, II, 2, 195-225, are to be found in Plutarch, pp. 185-6.

In *Timon of Athens* we find close borrowing: V, 1, 203–210 and V, 4, 70–73 have been taken from Plutarch (Carr, pp. 230–1), the latter passage almost word for word.

So also, in *The Tempest*, II, 1, 141-158, we find close borrowing from Florio's translation of Montaigne's Essays* and, in addition, the whole of this scene shows the Shakespeare characteristics—the commonplace, the prosaic, the valueless word-play and the repetitions. These examples show indisputably that Shakespeare was capable of copying closely other work without adding anything worthwhile of his own, whereas the real "Shakespeare" is recognized as one of the world's greatest creators of thought.

In my opinion Shakespeare was a man with comparatively limited ideas and, as we have just seen, he was glad to employ historical passages, old plays and repetitions to help to fill the gap. Another technique he adopted for the same purpose was to play with words which conveyed no points of importance in advancing the action or thought of the play but which did fill in the actors' time. An example of this is to be found in *King Richard III*, IV, 4, 136-431, the subject matter of which passage is practically all already known from the antecedents of the play. The following is an extract (lines 343-365):—

* See *Shakespear* by W. C. Hazlitt; Bernard Quaritch; 1902; pp. 159-60.

K. Rich. Infer fair England's peace by this alliance.
Q. Eliz. Which she shall purchase with still-lasting war.
K.R. Tell her the King, that may command, entreats.
Q.E. That at her hands which the King's King forbids.
K.R. Say she shall be a high and mighty queen.
Q.E. To wail the title, as her mother doth.
K.R. Say I will love her everlastingly.
Q.E. But how long shall that title 'ever' last?
K.R. Sweetly in force unto her fair life's end.
Q.E. But how long fairly shall her sweet life last?
K.R. As long as heaven and nature lengthens it.
Q.E. As long as hell and Richard likes of it.
K.R. Say I, her sovereign, am her subject low.
Q.E. But she, your subject, loathes such sovereignty.
K.R. Be eloquent in my behalf to her.
Q.E. An honest tale speeds best being plainly told.
K.R. Then plainly to her tell my loving tale.
Q.E. Plain and not honest is too harsh a style.
K.R. Your reasons are too shallow and too quick.
Q.E. O, no, my reasons are too deep and dead—
Too deep and dead, poor infants, in their graves.
K.R. Harp not on that string, madam; that is past.
Q.E. Harp on it still shall I till heart-strings break.

Surely such commonplace dialogue was not written by a great artist! When one considers that the subject of these bandyings is Richard's desired marriage to Queen Elizabeth's daughter, can one believe that there is any sincerity in the author? Certainly he did not write from the heart on this occasion. Time-filling passages also occur in *Othello*, IV, 2, 1:—

Oth. You have seen nothing, then?
Emil. Nor ever heard, nor ever did suspect.
Oth. Yes, you have seen Cassio and she together.
Emil. But then I saw no harm, and then I heard
Each syllable that breath made up between them.
Oth. What, did they never whisper?
Emil. Never, my lord.
Oth. Nor send you out o' th' way?
Emil. Never.
Oth. To fetch her fan, her gloves, her mask, nor nothing?
Emil. Never, my lord.
Oth. That's strange.

and in *Othello*, V, 1, 111:—

Emil. 'Las, what's the matter? What's the matter, husband?
Iago. Cassio hath here been set on in the dark
By Roderigo and fellows that are 'scap'd.

He's almost slain, and Roderigo quite dead.
Emil. Alas, good gentleman! Alas, good Cassio!
Iago. This is the fruits of whoring. Prithee, Emilia,
Go know of Cassio where he supp'd tonight—
What, do you shake at that?
Bian. He supp'd at my house; but I therefore shake not.
Iago. O, did he so? I charge you go with me.
Emil. Fie, fie upon thee, strumpet!
Bian. I am no strumpet, but of life as honest
As you that thus abuse me.
Emil. As I! Foh! Fie upon thee!
Iago. Kind gentlemen, let's go see poor Cassio dress'd.

Tedious passages such as these, or the versified Holinshed and Plutarch, or the repetitions or commonplace detail in *Venus and Adonis*, make one draw the conclusion that one of the writers of the canon was capable of waxing eloquent about little and capable of placing together words which were almost or quite of no value or were mere plagiarism—surely strange if this writer be the one whose works are known and esteemed throughout the educated world. This inferior writer contributed to *Hamlet*:—

Last night of all,
When yond same star that's westward from the pole
Had made his course t'illume that part of heaven
Where now it burns . . . I, 1, 35

This passage is astronomically stupid and is valueless except in that it gives Bernardo something to say until the Ghost arrives. Almost valueless also are the lines:—

I have in quick determination
Thus set it down: he shall with speed to England
For the demand of our neglected tribute. *Hamlet*, III, 1, 168

What tribute? Mention of it is not made again, before or after. Let my reader contrast this quite uninspiring reference to historical data with Burton's living message for England which indeed speaks volumes:—

An earnest conjuration from the King,
As England was his faithful tributary,
As love between them like the palm might flourish,
As peace should still her wheaten garland wear
And stand a comma 'tween their amities. *Hamlet*, V, 2, 38

As an example of a verbose, tedious passage from *Hamlet* we have the following:—

King. And now, Laertes, what's the news with you?
You told us of some suit; what is't, Laertes?
You cannot speak of reason to the Dane
And lose your voice. What wouldst thou beg, Laertes,

That shall not be my offer, not thy asking?
The head is not more native to the heart,
The hand more instrumental to the mouth,
Than is the throne of Denmark to thy father.
What wouldst thou have, Laertes?
Laer. My dread lord,
Your leave and favour to return to France;
From whence though willingly I came to Denmark
To show my duty in your coronation,
Yet now, I must confess, that duty done,
My thoughts and wishes bend again towards France,
And bow them to your gracious leave and pardon.
King. Have you your father's leave? What says Polonius?
Pol. 'A hath, my lord, wrung from me my slow leave
By laboursome petition; and at last
Upon his will I seal'd my hard consent.
I do beseech you, give him leave to go.
King. Take thy fair hour, Laertes; time be thine,
And thy best graces spend it at thy will. *Hamlet*, I, 2, 42

Nestor's wagging up and down his beard and saying nothing, referred to above, has its parallel in:—

It lifted up its head and did address
Itself to motion, like as it would speak. *Hamlet*, I, 2, 216

Mere words are:—

Mad call I it; for, to define true madness,
What is't but to be nothing else but mad? *Hamlet*, II, 2, 93

It might be argued that these lines were given to Polonius to illustrate that he was a "foolish, prating knave" but it was far from characteristic of the great "Shakespeare" to waste opportunities of conveying his message. Even Caliban was made to say:—

Remember
First to possess his books; for without them
He's but a sot, as I am. *The Tempest*, III, 2, 87

My reader will find in the opening fourteen lines of Act III of *Hamlet* an example of Shakespeare's art of saying nothing in many words, whereas the author of the great passages was concise and action and thought progressed rapidly. I do not wish, however, to convey the impression that Shakespeare wrote nothing of any value; above I have referred to good lines from *The Rape of Lucrece* and below I shall quote good but unsustained lines from *Much Ado About Nothing*. So also in a Shakespeare contribution to *Hamlet* we find:—

But look, the morn, in russet mantle clad,
Walks o'er the dew of yon high eastward hill.
Hamlet, I, 1, 166

What has been said till now in this chapter is to be regarded as a general account of the problem and I now go on to give more detailed attention to particular aspects. At the end of this chapter I list the works which I attribute to Shakespeare.

Reference by contemporaries

Above, I have indicated that two authors contributed to the writing of "Shakespeare". At least five pieces of evidence can be adduced in favour of believing that William Shakespeare was one of these two:—

(I) Greene's attack and Chettle's apology (see above, Chapter I) point to Shakespeare as author of *The Contention.*

(II) Shakespeare's name appears as signature to the dedications prefacing *Venus and Adonis* and *The Rape of Lucrece.*

(III) Heminge and Condell, his fellow actors, attribute all the plays in the canon (except *Pericles*) to Shakespeare.

(IV) Ben Jonson, who writes in terms indicating that he knew Shakespeare well, credits him with authorship.

(V) Burton refers to Shakespeare by name as author of *Venus and Adonis* and *Much Ado About Nothing.*

In Chapters VI-XI, I give evidence for believing that Burton was the superior of these two authors: here I give evidence for believing that Shakespeare was the inferior:—Greene spoke of Shakespeare being "able to bumbast out a blanke verse." On consulting *Nares' Glossary* I find that in the 16th and 17th centuries 'to bumbast' or 'bombast' implied 'to stuff out' and these words describe exactly what much of Shakespeare's work consists of. When Jonson said "would he had blotted a thousand" it was probably this characteristic of Shakespeare's work which he was condemning. Can one regard as anything but bombast the versified Holinshed passages, or the trivial detail of *Venus and Adonis* or the repetitions in *The Comedy of Errors, Much Ado About Nothing, The Merry Wives of Windsor* and parts of *Twelfth Night* and *Cymbeline*?

Let us examine the particular passage from *The Contention,* which Greene referred to, starting:—

"*Clif.* I, I, so strives the woodcocke with the gin"

and continuing unto:—

"For either that is thine, or else thou wert not his."

which passage corresponds to *King Henry VI* pt. 3, I, 4, 61 –II, 1, 94.

Firstly, the passage contains bombast in the form of re-relation by the *Messenger* of the details of the Duke of York's death and in the duplication as the following show:—

1. "So strives the woodcocke with the gin"

is duplicated in

"So doth the cunnie struggle with the net".

2. "Come make him stand upon this molehill here"
is duplicated in

"And then they set him on a molehill there".

3. "Looke York, I dipt this napkin in the bloud.

. . . .

I give thee this to drie thy cheeks withal".
is duplicated in

"How couldst thou draine the life bloud of the childe
To bid the father wipe his eies withall"
and in

"This cloth thou dipts in bloud of my sweet boy
And loe with tears I wash the bloud awaie"
and in

"The ruthlesse queene perceiving he did weepe
Gave him a handkercher to wipe his eies
Dipt in the bloud of sweet young Rutland."

4. "What, hath thy fierie hart so parcht thine entrailes
That not a teare can fall for Rutland's death?"
is duplicated in

"I cannot weepe, for all my breast's moisture
Scarse serves to quench my furnace burning hart."

Secondly, the whole passage has the characteristics that its theme is outward events and commentaries on events; nothing primary or fundamental, nothing introspective, is allowed, and profound or beautiful thought is almost or quite absent.

It is of the utmost importance that the reader note that a passage with these two sets of characteristics was attributed by a contemporary (Greene) to Shakespeare and that the two works, *Venus and Adonis* (discussed above) and *Much Ado About Nothing* (to be discussed later in this chapter) having these same characteristics, were attributed to Shakespeare by another contemporary, Burton. It is my contention that passages or whole plays, of this same narrative quality as distinguishes these works, are to be found here and there from beginning to end of the "Shakespeare" canon. Shakespeare's technique of discussing outward things relieved him of the task of unfolding his own deepest thought. As indicated by the above mentioned "bombast" and as is shown more clearly in discussing *Venus and Adonis* and *Much Ado About Nothing*, Shakespeare also had the technique of packing into his writings material of little or no importance giving profusion of words and dearth of meaning. The contrast of such work with the introspective, meaningful *Hamlet* or *Macbeth* does not require elaboration; this same contrast will be referred to again later in this chapter when discussing speeches by King John and Falstaff.

Shakespeare did not write to instruct: Burton did

Emerson writes (*Shakespeare; or, the Poet*) "What point of morals, of manners, of economy, of philosophy, of religion, of taste, of the conduct of life, has he not settled? What mystery has he not signified his knowledge of? What office, or function, or district of man's work, has he not remembered? What king has he not taught state, as Talma taught Napoleon? What maiden has not found him finer than her delicacy? What lover has he not outloved? What sage has he not outseen? What gentleman has he not instructed in the rudeness of his behaviour?" So far as I know, no one has lodged any objection to this passage and I would add to Emerson by reminding the reader that Burton's avowed aim in writing was to impart his knowledge for the common good of all (see above, Chapter II). Any reader who questions the didactic nature of the great plays is invited to study carefully the parallel quotations given in Chapter XI. Accepting Emerson's statement and my own addition, I ask the question whether the didactic aim motivated the author of all the so-called Shakespeare works and what follows shows that I reply in the negative.

I begin with the obvious. Can one believe that the versified Holinshed passages were written to teach kings state? Can one believe that *Venus and Adonis* was written to teach a maiden delicacy or that the crude manners of practically every character in *Much Ado About Nothing* give gentlemen instruction in the rudeness of their behaviour? What sage does *The Comedy of Errors* outsee? What mystery does *The Merry Wives of Windsor* show knowledge of?

Shakespeare did endeavour to entertain but not to instruct. *The Comedy of Errors*, *The Merry Wives of Windsor* and *Much Ado About Nothing* show that he could write successful plays. His success comes from his ability to think out clearly a sufficient number of incidents and situations to interest his audience and give his actors plenty to do and talk about. The author then becomes narrator and concerns himself with the immediate, commonplace reactions to these incidents and situations. In *The Comedy of Errors* he cleverly thinks out a number of situations wherein one of each of two sets of twins is mistaken for his twin brother and, each having a different past history, the play is kept going in narrating one such incident after another. Similarly in *The Merry Wives of Windsor*, a play rich in amusing incident and poor in dialogue, Falstaff tries three times to seduce Mrs. Ford and three times is punished for his pains. What an array of incidents there is in the Shakespeare parts of *The Merchant of Venice*! In *Much Ado About Nothing*, the vicarious wooing of Hero for Claudio and the concerted efforts of all the friends to bring together the reluctant lovers, Beatrice and Benedict, give easy scope for ample dialogue; the villainy of Don John and Borachio in conjuring up a situation, wherein Margaret, clandestinely conversing with Borachio, is mistaken for Hero by Don Pedro and Claudio; Borachio's guilt is later uncovered by Dogbery and his watch; this deception of Don Pedro and Claudio leads to the church scene with its slandering of Hero by Claudio. Then begins another plot to pretend that Hero is dead and to bring her later to the altar a second time. Meanwhile the wrongful slandering of Hero serves as a topic for father, uncle and cousin to share in to the full with their repeated bemoanings. Soliloquies are few in these plays and when they do occur their speech is mere commonplace as in Benedict's, Act II, Sc. 3, or in Ford's, *The Merry Wives of Windsor*, end of Act II, Sc. 2. These, which I consider to be by Shakespeare, are for the most part insincere and intended wholly to amuse, not to instruct. In strong contrast Burton's soliloquies, for example those of Hamlet and Macbeth, show great sincerity and, in his plays generally, incident is cut down to a minimum to make room for what he regarded as really worthy of being communicated.

I quite realize that Shakespeare was primarily an actor and a dramatist, not a moralist, philosopher or philologist and therefore strictly it is as a dramatist that he should be judged. Such an approach however would not lead me very far in my present task of distinguishing two authors as it is my belief that the *composition* of the plays was finally in the hands of *one* person, William Shakespeare, who himself wrote plays and who also had liberty to add material of his own to what Burton had written.

Burton (B. p. 5) desired to delight as well as to instruct quoting Horace as his text:—

Simul et jucunda et idonea dicere vitæ,
Lectorem delectando simul atque monendo.

and in my opinion the great plays as well as *The Anatomy of Melancholy* were written with this double purpose. That the plays in the canon, which were written to delight but not at all to instruct, were written by Shakespeare is my contention and for two reasons I select for further attention here *Much Ado About Nothing* as a play of this class:—(i) the play was mentioned by Burton as having been written by Shakespeare and (ii) it was, according to authorities, written about 1599 and thus not an early play.

Shakespeare possibly realized that he was not a great poet and it may be significant that *Much Ado About Nothing* is written largely in prose. Some few snatches of fine poetry do occur, as:—

How still the evening is,
As hush'd on purpose to grace harmony! II, 3, 34
And bid her steal into the pleached bower,
Where honeysuckles, ripened by the sun,
Forbid the sun to enter—like favourites,

Made proud by princes, that advance their pride
Against that power that bred it. III, 1, 7

He could also be very apt:—

It is needful that you frame the season for your own harvest. I, 3, 20

For when rich villains have need of poor ones, poor ones may make what price they will. III, 3, 104

And I see that the fashion wears out more apparel than the man. III, 3, 127

In a false quarrel there is no true valour. V, 1, 120

Having granted these good passages I contend for the following reasons that the great bulk of the play is commonplace stuff indeed and certainly not Burton's:—(i) Failure to show sympathy with the characters presented reveals itself; (ii) Lack of exactitude which we noted in *Venus and Adonis* again appears; (iii) Tediousness is not one jot diminished.

(i) To deal briefly with characterization: Don Pedro, Don John, Claudio and Benedict are entered in the list of *Dramatis Personæ* as Princes and Lords, but no princely or lordly feature is exhibited by any of them. Throughout the whole play Don Pedro does or says practically nothing that is noble. He and Claudio accuse Hero, their host's only daughter, on most unconvincing evidence. Claudio, having publicly termed Hero a "rotten orange", declares his willingness to marry Hero's supposed cousin, though she be an Ethiope. Benedict, the chief male character, does not know his own mind; witness the soliloquy at the beginning of Act II, Sc. 3. Its commonplace chatter certainly does not savour of a Shakespearean soliloquy, where the speaker expresses his inmost thought on a subject of great importance. Beatrice, though obviously intended to be the wittiest, the most kind-hearted and the most level-headed of the female characters, declares that an excellent man would be one midway between Don John, who talks too little, and Benedict, who talks too much. Besides, she is irreverent whereas irreverence is not present in the great works, early or late:—

Leon. So, by being too curst, God will send you no horns.

Beat. Just, if he send me no husband; for the which blessing I am at him upon my knees every morning and evening. II, 1, 22

and again in her imaginary talk with the devil, she says:—

Beat. No; but to the gate, and there will the devil meet me, like an old cuckold, with horns on his head, and say 'Get you to heaven, Beatrice, get you to heaven; here's no place for you maids'. So deliver I up my apes and away to Saint Peter for the heavens; he shows me where the bachelors sit, and there live we as merry as the day is long. II, 1, 37

Margaret is referred to, later, in the "Characterization" section of this chapter. Leonato, governor of Messina, though Hero was his own and only daughter, accepts, without enquiry worthy of the name, the flimsy evidence for her guilt. These failings in not being true to his characters indicate a lack of real sympathy. The imperfections of the plot of this play are detailed by Sampson in an introduction to his edition (Pitt Press Shakespeare). I feel sure that anyone who reads Bandello's story (see Appendix, Sampson's Edition) will agree that Bandello's account is much better than Shakespeare's.

(ii) Unpleasing, inexact diction is a feature of many passages in this play. To take a few:—

Beat. Is it possible disdain should die while she hath such meet food to feed it as Signior Benedick? Courtesy itself must convert to disdain if you come in her presence. I, 1, 102

Claudio. When you went onward on this ended action. I, 1, 259

Ant. As the event stamps them; but they have a good cover; they show well outward. The Prince and Count Claudio, walking in a thick-pleached alley in mine orchard, were thus much overheard by a man of mine: the Prince discovered to Claudio that he loved my niece your daughter, and meant to acknowledge it this night in a dance; and, if he found her accordant, he meant to take the present time by the top, and instantly break with you of it. I, 2, 6

Ant. A good sharp fellow; I will send for him, and question him yourself. I, 2, 15

Note: There should have been a semi-colon after the first "him" and the "and" should have read 'then'.

Beat. Why, he is the Prince's jester, a very dull fool; only his gift is in devising impossible slanders. II, 1, 120

D. John. Sure, my brother is amorous on Hero, and hath withdrawn her father to break with him about it. II, 1, 136

Claud. Farewell, therefore, Hero. II, 1, 161

Bene. What fashion will your wear the garland of? II, 1, 167

Bene. She would have made Hercules have turn'd spit. II, 1, 226

Bene. For certainly, while she is here, a man may live as quiet in hell as in a sanctuary. II, 1, 230

Bene. I will go on the slightest errand now to the Antipodes that you devise to send me on; I will fetch you a toothpicker now from the furthest inch of Asia. II, 1, 234

Note: "Toothpicker" should have read 'toothpick'.

Bene. And now is he turn'd orthography. II, 3, 20

Note: "Orthography" should have read 'orthographer'.

Bene. When I said I would die a bachelor, I did not think I should live till I were married. II, 3, 221

(iii) These examples among many others of inexactitude, weak construction, unpleasing arrangement of words, wrong use of words and mere inanity indicate clearly that the writer of the great plays was not their author. The third very noticeable fault in this play, a fault already pointed out as occurring in *Venus and Adonis* and in *Lucrece*, is its tediousness and the small field of thought covered by the number of words used. Emerson (*Shakespeare; or, The Poet*) writes "He [Shakespeare] was a full man . . . the subtilest of authors . . . nor did he harp on one string." Belying Emerson's verdict, in Act I Sc. 2 this author takes some 215 words to tell his audience that an eavesdropping servant of Antonio had overheard Prince Pedro tell Claudio that he loved Hero and intended, at a dance to be held that evening, to inform her father; not content with this, he takes the second half of the next scene for another eavesdropper to give a slight variation of the same story to Don John. One eavesdropping scene in which Benedict overhears that Beatrice loves him is followed by one in which Beatrice overhears that Benedict loves her. Perhaps the most outstanding example of duplication and padding is the harping on the slandering of Hero:—

Beat. O, on my soul, my cousin is belied! IV, 1, 146

Beat. Is 'a not approved in the height a villain that hath slandered, scorned, dishonoured, my kinswoman? IV, 1, 299

Leon. My soul doth tell me Hero is belied. V, 1, 42

Leon. Thou hast so wrong'd mine innocent child and me. V, 1, 63

Leon. I say thou hast belied mine innocent child;
Thy slander hath gone through and through her heart. V, 1, 67

Leon. Thou hast kill'd my child. V, 1, 78

Ant. And she is dead, slander'd to death by villains. V, 1, 88

Bene. You have kill'd a sweet lady. V, 1, 146

Bene. You have among you kill'd a sweet and innocent lady. V, 1, 183

Bora. The lady is dead upon mine and my master's false accusation. V, 1, 228

Leon. Art thou the slave that with thy breath hast kill'd
Mine innocent child? V, 1, 249

Leon. I thank you, princes, for my daughter's death. V, 1, 254

Urs. It is proved my Lady Hero hath been falsely accus'd. V, 2, 83

Epitaph. 'Done to death by slanderous tongues
Was the Hero that here lies.' V, 3, 3

Taking into consideration the failure to depict consistent characters, the profusion of words, the commonplace theme and the quite superfluous repetitions, it can fairly be concluded that Shakespeare did not write *Much Ado About Nothing* because he had something important to impart. There is nothing didactic in the play and the author was perfectly honest when he gave it its title.

So again, in the very late play, *The Winter's Tale*, Shakespeare, in writing his parts, shows his lack of any didactic aim by that same tendency to repetition. The following illustrates my point:—

1 for 'tis Polixenes
Has made thee swell thus. II, 1, 61
2 She's an adultress. II, 1, 78
3 You have mistook, my lady,
Polixenes for Leontes. II, 1, 81
4 She's an adultress. II, 1, 88
5 that she's
A bed-swerver. II, 1, 92
6 She, th'adultress. II, 3, 4
7 This brat is none of mine;
It is the issue of Polixenes. II, 3, 92
8 The bastard brains with these my proper hands
Shall I dash out. II, 3, 139
9 Shall I live on to see this bastard kneel
And call me father? II, 3, 154
10 To save this bastard's life—for 'tis a bastard,
So sure as this beard's grey—what will you adventure
To save this brat's life? II, 3, 160
11 that thou carry
This female bastard hence. II, 3, 173
12 No, I'll not rear
Another's issue. II, 3, 191
13 . . . in committing adultery with Polixenes. III, 2, 13
14 For Polixenes,
With whom I am accus'd. III, 2, 59
15 You had a bastard by Polixenes. III, 2, 81

This same non-didactic, page-filling author again shows his hand in the questioning of Kent and Oswald in *King Lear*:—

1 *Edm.* What's the matter? II, 2, 40
2 *Glo.* What's the matter here? II, 2, 43
3 *Corn.* What is the matter? II, 2, 45
4 *Corn.* What is your difference? II, 2, 47

5	*Corn.*	Speak yet, how grew your quarrel?	II, 2, 56
6	*Corn.*	Why are you angry?	II, 2, 66
7	*Glo.*	How fell you out?	II, 2, 81
8	*Corn.*	What is his fault?	II, 2, 84
9	*Corn.*	What was th'offence you gave him?	II, 2, 109

and also in the long drawn out theme—the number of knights to be allowed to the king, a hundred, fifty, twenty-five, ten, five, one.

King Lear, II, 4, 200-292

Anomalies in different speeches by one and the same character

A reader would be justified in expecting that the manner of everyday speech of any particular character would be consistent throughout a play or throughout more than one play by the same author and if inconsistencies occur he could suspect dual authorship. This method of distinguishing between Shakespeare's parts and Burton's is adopted here, two characters being selected, (i) King John and (ii) Falstaff. Four of King John's speeches are quoted, followed by Falstaff ones (a) from *King Henry IV* and (b) from *The Merry Wives of Windsor*. Then reasons are given for believing that the first two King John speeches were written by Shakespeare and the second two by Burton and that the first Falstaff speech was by Burton and the second by Shakespeare.

K. John. For our advantage; therefore hear us first.
These flags of France, that are advanced here
Before the eye and prospect of your town,
Have hither march'd to your endamagement;
The cannons have their bowels full of wrath,
And ready mounted are they to spit forth
Their iron indignation 'gainst your walls;
All preparation for a bloody siege
And merciless proceeding by these French
Confront your city's eyes, your winking gates;
And but for our approach those sleeping stones
That as a waist doth girdle you about
By the compulsion of their ordinance
By this time from their fixed beds of lime
Had been dishabited, and wide havoc made
For bloody power to rush upon your peace.
But on the sight of us your lawful king,
Who painfully with much expedient march
Have brought a countercheck before your gates,
To save unscratch'd you city's threat'ned cheeks—
Behold, the French amaz'd vouchsafe a parle;
And now, instead of bullets wrapp'd in fire,

To make a shaking fever in your walls,
They shoot but calm words folded up in smoke,
To make a faithless error in your ears;
Which trust accordingly, kind citizens,
And let us in—your King, whose labour'd spirits,
Forwearied in this action of swift speed,
Craves harbourage within your city walls.

King John, II, 1, 206

K. John. We will heal up all,
For we'll create young Arthur Duke of Britaine,
And Earl of Richmond; and this rich fair town
We make him lord of. Call the Lady Constance;
Some speedy messenger bid her repair
To our solemnity. I trust we shall,
If not fill up the measure of her will,
Yet in some measure satisfy her so
That we shall stop her exclamation.
Go we as well as haste will suffer us
To this unlook'd-for, unprepared pomp.

King John, II, 1, 550

K. John. Good friend, thou hast no cause to say so yet,
But thou shalt have; and creep time ne'er so slow,
Yet it shall come for me to do thee good.
I had a thing to say—but let it go:
The sun is in the heaven, and the proud day,
Attended with the pleasures of the world,
Is all too wanton and too full of gawds
To give me audience. If the mid-night bell
Did with his iron tongue and brazen mouth
Sound on into the drowsy race of night;
If this same were a churchyard where we stand,
And thou possessed with a thousand wrongs;
Or if that surly spirit, melancholy,
Had bak'd thy blood and made it heavy-thick,
Which else runs tickling up and down the veins,
Making that idiot, laughter, keep men's eyes
And strain their cheeks to idle merriment,
A passion hateful to my purposes;
Or if that thou couldst see me without eyes,
Hear me without thine ears, and make reply
Without a tongue, using conceit alone,
Without eyes, ears, and harmful sound of words—
Then, in despite of brooded watchful day,
I would into thy bosom pour my thoughts.

King John, III, 3, 30

K. John. O, when the last account 'twixt heaven and earth
Is to be made, then shall this hand and seal
Witness against us to damnation!
How oft the sight of means to do ill deeds
Make deeds ill done! Hadst not thou been by,
A fellow by the hand of nature mark'd,
Quoted and sign'd to do a deed of shame,
This murder had not come into my mind;
But, taking note of thy abhorr'd aspect,
Finding thee fit for bloody villainy,
Apt, liable to be employ'd in danger,
I faintly broke with thee of Arthur's death;
And thou, to be endeared to a king,
Made it no conscience to destroy a prince.

King John, IV, 2, 216

Fal. . . . If sack and sugar be a fault, God help the wicked! If to be old and merry be a sin, then many an old host that I know is damn'd; if to be fat be to be hated, then Pharaoh's lean kine are to be loved. No, my good lord: banish Peto, banish Bardolph, banish Poins; but, for sweet Jack Falstaff, kind Jack Falstaff, true Jack Falstaff, valiant Jack Falstaff—and therefore more valiant, being, as he is, old Jack Falstaff—banish not him thy Harry's company.

King Henry the Fourth, pt. 1, II, 4, 454

Fal. Hang him, mechanical salt-butter rogue! I will stare him out of his wits; I will awe him with my cudgel; it shall hang like a meteor o'er the cuckold's horns. Master Brook, thou shalt know I will predominate over the peasant, and thou shalt lie with his wife. Come to me soon at night. Ford's a knave, and I will aggravate his style; thou, Master Brook, shalt know him for knave and cuckold. Come to me soon at night.

The Merry Wives of Windsor, II, 2, 248

These passages spoken by the same character either in the same or different plays can be contrasted. The first two by King John are narrative, prosaic and commonplace in theme, and the rate of transference of thought is slow in relation to the number of words used; the verse is monotonous and mechanical in its regular construction. The second two are introspective, the theme is removed from the commonplace, and the thought keeps pace with the words; the verse is more varied and spontaneous. In the case of the Falstaff quotations, both being in prose, there is no verse form to study. The Henry IV one is logically expressed and conveys much food for thought. The Merry-Wives one is disjointed, repetitive and conveys little or no thought of importance; besides, its burden and even some of its very words have already been expressed only a few moments before—"as I am a gentleman, you shall, if you will, enjoy Ford's wife." II, 2, 228, and "for at that time the jealous rascally knave, her husband, will be forth. Come you to me at night," II, 2, 236.

Here then we have what I regard to be an important difference between Shakespeare and Burton. Shakespeare's work is repetitive and conveys little thought with many words while Burton packs in as much meaning as possible, while still complying with dramatic requirements, even to the extent of being elliptical in his expressions as pointed out by the Cowden Clarkes* and others. Ben Jonson said Shakespeare was not of an age but for all time and his words have not been found wanting after three hundred and thirty-six years. The life and death of Falstaff still interests the human mind. It is not however the Falstaff of *The Merry Wives of Windsor* that interests us; this one plays his part well for the performance of the moment and that is the end of him, but Falstaff of whom it was said "The King has kill'd his heart" (*King Henry V*, II, 1, 85), is still to be reckoned with and *it is the absence or the presence of this residuum of thought which enables one to distinguish between Shakespeare's writings and those of Burton respectively*. Looked at in this light, this Falstaff's King-Henry IV quotation is seen to be a fore-warning to Prince Hal of the decision he will have to make one day when he becomes king. So also the first two King-John quotations have no permanent value but the second two are for all time.

This method of contrasting speeches by the same character is especially valuable. However, in this book, most of the passages selected for contrasting are spoken by different characters. In Act II, Sc. 1 of *As You Like It* the speeches of Duke Senior and his Lords have permanent value and their verse form is varied, whereas the following passage has quite no permanent value and shows the strongly narrative theme, the monotonous verse form and the verbosity already noted as characteristic of Shakespeare's work:—

Oli. Orlando doth commend him to you both;
And to that youth he calls his Rosalind
He sends this bloody napkin. Are you he?
Ros. I am. What must we understand by this?
Oli. Some of my shame; if you will know of me
What man I am, and how, and why, and where,
This handkercher was stain'd.
Cel. I pray you, tell it.
Oli. When last the young Orlando parted from you,
He left a promise to return again
Within an hour; and, pacing through the forest,

* Footnote 22 to The Tempest; *The Plays of Shakespeare*; Cassell, Petter and Galpin.

Chewing the food of sweet and bitter fancy,
Lo, what befell! He threw his eye aside,
And mark what object did present itself.
Under an oak, whose boughs were moss'd with age,
And high top bald with dry antiquity,
A wretched ragged man, o'ergrown with hair,
Lay sleeping on his back. About his neck
A green and gilded snake had wreath'd itself,
Who with her head nimble in threats approach'd
The opening of his mouth; but suddenly,
Seeing Orlando, it unlink'd itself,
And with indented glides did slip away
Into a bush; under which bush's shade
A lioness, with udders all drawn dry,
Lay couching, head on ground, with cat-like watch,
When that the sleeping man should stir; for 'tis
The royal disposition of that beast
To prey on nothing that doth seem as dead.
This seen, Orlando did approach the man,
And found it was his brother, his elder brother.
Cel. O, I have heard him speak of that same brother;
And he did render him the most unnatural
That liv'd amongst men.
Oli. And well he might so do,
For well I know he was unnatural.
Ros. But, to Orlando: did he leave him there,
Food to the suck'd and hungry lioness?
Oli. Twice did he turn his back, and purpos'd so;
But kindness, nobler ever than revenge,
And nature, stronger than his just occasion,
Made him give battle to the lioness,
Who quickly fell before him; in which hurtling
From miserable slumber I awak'd.
Cel. Are you his brother?
Ros. Was't you he rescu'd?
Cel. Was't you that did so oft contrive to kill him?

As You Like It, IV, 3, 90

This quotation from *As You Like It* was not intended to instruct. It is quite obvious that the author did spin out his material rather than condense it.

Romeo and Juliet a play of double authorship

Good examples of this dual authorship occur in *Romeo and Juliet*.

Lady M. O, where is Romeo? Saw you him today?
Right glad I am he was not at this fray.

Ben. Madam, an hour before the worshipp'd sun
Peer'd forth the golden window of the east,
A troubled mind drew me to walk abroad;
Where, underneath the grove of sycamore
That westward rooteth from this city side,
So early walking did I see your son.
Towards him I made; but he was ware of me
And stole into the covert of the wood.
I, measuring his affections by my own,
Which then most sought where most might not be found,
Being one too many by my weary self,
Pursu'd my honour, not pursuing his,
And gladly shunn'd who gladly fled from me. I, 1, 114

The jingle of the first two lines of this passage is quite out of keeping with the brawling which has just ended. The Benvolio lines are very markedly of the verbose, narrative type already referred to. Also, the verse form is again prosaic, monotonous and mechanically constructed, and contrasts with the spontaneous lines of Act II, Sc. 2, for example those beginning at line 38:—

'Tis but thy name that is my enemy;
Thou art thyself, though not a Montague.
What's Montague? It is nor hand, nor foot,
Nor arm, nor face, nor any other part
Belonging to a man. O, be some other name!
What's in a name? That which we call a rose
By any other name would smell as sweet.

Having read the sweet and logical second and third scenes of Act II, we are in Scene 4 again confronted with the verbose, the vulgar and the commonplace, beginning:—

Mer. Where the devil should this Romeo be?
Came he not home to-night?
Ben. Not to his father's; I spoke with his man.

We have seen in Chapter IV that in *The Anatomy of Melancholy* Burton quoted only commonplace passages from *Hamlet*; so also we find that, when he quotes from *Romeo and Juliet*, it is from a narrative, commonplace and repetitive passage that the chosen lines had been taken:—

Prince. Give me the letter, I will look on it.
Where is the County's page that rais'd the watch?
Sirrah, what made your master in this place?
Page. He came with flowers to strew his lady's grave;
And bid me stand aloof, and so I did.
Anon comes one with light to ope the tomb;
And by and by my master drew on him;
And then I ran away to call the watch.

Prince. This letter doth make good the friar's words,
Their course of love, the tidings of her death;
And here he writes that he did buy a poison
Of a poor pothecary, and therewithal
Came to this vault to die, and lie with Juliet.
Where be these enemies? Capulet, Montague,
See what a scourge is laid upon your hate,
That heaven finds means to kill your joys with love!
And I, for winking at your discords too,
Have lost a brace of kinsmen. All are punish'd.
Cap. O brother Montague, give me thy hand.
This is my daughter's jointure, for no more
Can I demand.
Mon. But I can give thee more;
For I will raise her statue in pure gold,
That whiles Verona by that name is known,
There shall no figure at such rate be set
As that of true and faithful Juliet.
Cap. As rich shall Romeo's by his lady's lie—
Poor sacrifices of our enmity!
Prince. A glooming peace this morning with it brings;
The sun for sorrow will not show his head.
Go hence, to have more talk of these sad things;
Some shall be pardon'd and some punished;
For never was a story of more woe
Than this of Juliet and her Romeo. V, 3, 277

BURTON APPEALED TO THE IMAGINATION: SHAKESPEARE DID NOT

Hazlitt wrote* "Shakespeare's imagination is of the same plastic kind as his conception of character or passion. 'It glances from heaven to earth, from earth to heaven.' Its movement is rapid and devious. It unites the most opposite extremes; or, as Puck says, in boasting of his own feats, 'puts a girdle round about the earth in forty minutes.' He seems always hurrying from his subject, even while describing it; but the stroke, like the lightning's, is sure as it is sudden." In marked contrast, Hazlitt† dealing with the poems *Venus and Adonis* and *The Rape of Lucrece* writes "A beautiful thought is sure to be lost in an endless commentary upon it. The speakers are like persons who have both leisure and inclination to make riddles on their own situation, and to twist and turn every object or incident into acrostics and anagrams. Everything is spun out into allegory; and a digression is always preferred to the main

* *Lectures on the English Poets*; Everyman, No. 459, p. 53.
† *Characters of Shakespeare's Plays*; Everyman, p. 265.

story." Dowden agrees with this judgement on these two poems. He writes* "Observe his determination to put in accurately the details of each object; to omit nothing. Poor Wat, the hare, is described in a dozen stanzas. Another series of stanzas describes the stallion. . . . In like manner he does not shrink from faithfully putting down each one of the amorous provocations and urgencies of Venus. The complete series of manœuvres must be detailed. In "Lucrece" the action is delayed and delayed that every minute particular may be described, every minor incident recorded." Dowden (p. 59) also gives as one of the characteristics of the early plays "Wit and imagery drawn out in detail to the point of exhaustion." Thus we have an author who, instead of hurrying from his subjects, quite clearly dwells upon them; could any contrast be more striking? An example of this occurs in the early *The Merchant of Venice* where, in Act V, Sc. 1, the rings are referred to some forty-nine times including the "its". However, a most important point, which these two commentators appear to have missed, is that the tendency to elaborate and drag out with detail does not end with the two poems or with the early plays: numerous mere repetitions of antecedents characterize Act V, Sc. 5 of *Cymbeline*; in *King Henry VIII*, Act, IV, Sc. 1, we find detail borrowed from Holinshed eked out with frivolous, physical detail of the author's own invention; in *Othello* there is a never-ending play on the handkerchief theme (on a rough count I find the napkin or handkerchief referred to seventy-one times, including the "its"); no lightning strokes in these scenes, no glancing from earth to heaven; in the late *Antony and Cleopatra* there occurs an example of "spinning out into allegory" as good as any to be found in the early poems:—

> *Agr.* To hold you in perpetual amity,
> To make you brothers, and to knit your hearts
> With an unslipping knot, take Antony
> Octavia to his wife; whose beauty claims
> No worse a husband than the best of men;
> Whose virtue and whose general graces speak
> That which none else can utter. By this marriage,
> All little jealousies, which now seem great,
> And all great fears, which now import their dangers,
> Would then be nothing. Truths would be tales,
> Where now half tales be truths. Her love to both
> Would each to other, and all loves to both,
> Draw after her. Pardon what I have spoke;
> For 'tis a studied, not a present thought,
> By duty ruminated. II, 2, 129

---

* *Shakspere—His Mind and Art*; Kegan Paul, p. 50.

The author is prosaic not poetic, for true poetry is continually appealing to the readers' imagination to fill in the detail for itself. All commentators would agree that the four plays just mentioned were all written after *As You Like It*, yet in this play we find clear examples of this hurrying away. In Act. II, Sc. 1 the questions of man's relationships with his less fortunate brethren, his relationships with the brute creation and animals' relationships with one another have all been raised and the reader is invited to imagine to himself a full scale debate between Duke Senior and Jaques:—

> *Duke S.* And did you leave him in this contemplation?
> 2 *Lord.* We did, my Lord, weeping and commenting
> Upon the sobbing deer.
> *Duke S.* Show me this place;
> I love to cope him in these sullen fits,
> For then he's full of matter.
> 1 *Lord.* I'll bring you to him straight. [*Exeunt.*

Similarly at the end of Act II the reader is invited to fill in for himself the conversation to follow between Duke Senior and Orlando and Adam:—

> Be truly welcome hither. I am the Duke
> That lov'd your father. The residue of your fortune,
> Go to my cave and tell me. Good old man,
> Thou art right welcome as thy master is.
> Support him by the arm. Give me your hand,
> And let me all your fortunes understand. [*Exeunt.*

A third and more typical example is:—

> *Duke S.* Why, how now, monsieur! what a life is this,
> That your poor friends must woo your company?
> What, you look merrily!
> *Jaq.* A fool, a fool! I met a fool i' th' forest [etc.]
> II, 7, 9

These examples are taken from a middle period play. When we come to a late play such as *Macbeth*, we find repeated examples of the sure lightning strokes and the hurrying on as in the following array from Act I—the historical background of the rebellion of Macdonwald; the treason of Cawdor towards Duncan who had put infinite trust in him; the invasion by Norway; the great courage of Macbeth and Banquo; the prophecies of the witches stirring up evil thoughts in Macbeth's receptive mind and the reinforcement of them by Lady Macbeth; the honours bestowed on Macbeth by King Duncan and the promise of further promotion:

> I have begun to plant thee, and will labour
> To make thee full of growing. I, 4, 28

Macbeth's beautiful home inviting him to a holy life:

This castle hath a pleasant seat
. . . . the heaven's breath
Smells wooingly here. I, 6, 1

Duncan's gentle nature:

Besides, this Duncan
Hath borne his faculties so meek. I, 7, 16

Thereby the pros and cons of the situation are briefly but surely given and the reader is invited to imagine for himself the great conflict arising in Macbeth's mind. So also one is invited to consider the full significance of the thoughts stirred up in the mind of Antony as he compares his own past life with Cæsar's—"Yet now—no matter." *Antony and Cleopatra* III, 11, 40.

When we consider these passages we realize that their author (Burton) is full and concise and most unlikely to write the endless repetitions already shown to occur in *Much Ado About Nothing* and other Shakespeare works; also that he is one who is aspiring to the highest thought and therefore unlikely to be the same person as he who wrote, at a probably later date and still apparently with great zest, the trivial descriptions such as the following:—

But my design
To note the chamber. I will write all down:
Such and such pictures; there the window; such
Th' adornment of her bed; the arras, figures—
Why, such and such; and the contents o' th' story.
Ah, but some natural notes about her body
Above ten thousand meaner moveables
Would testify, t' enrich mine inventory. *Cymbeline*, II, 2, 23

Shakespeare is also quite happy composing eloquent lines telling what is already well known to the reader or hearer so that the words are continually dragging behind the thought instead of coinciding with it. Examples of this fault are to be found in his early as well as in the late works, e.g. *The Rape of Lucrece*, lines 1618-1652; *Romeo and Juliet*, V, 3, 215-294; *Twelfth Night*, V, 1, 317-363, and *Cymbeline*, V, 5; to give a few lines from this last:—

Away to Britain
Post I in this design. Well may you, sir,
Remember me at court, where I was taught
Of your chaste daughter the wide difference
'Twixt amorous and villainous. Being thus quench'd
Of hope, not longing, mine Italian brain
Gan in your duller Britain operate
Most vilely; for my vantage, excellent;
And, to be brief, my practice so prevail'd
That I return'd with simular proof enough

To make the noble Leonatus mad,
By wounding his belief in her renown
With tokens thus and thus; averring notes
Of chamber-hanging, pictures, this her bracelet—
O cunning, how I got it!—nay, some marks
Of secret on her person, that he could not
But think her bond of chastity quite crack'd,
I having ta'en the forfeit. *Cymbeline*, V, 5, 191

Such a passage makes no appeal whatever to the imagination; on the contrary, all it has to say is already known from the antecedents of the play. My reader will notice the same type of padding and also the verbal similarities between "with tokens thus and thus" in this passage and "Such and such pictures" and "the arras, figures—why such and such" in the passage just given above. The passage also contains the third reference to the bedroom furnishings and to the mole.

In Burton, on the other hand, we do not find words dragging behind the sense. He is continually delighting the reader's imagination with fresh thought conveyed in words so fitting that words and thought coincide to form one fused whole. As an example of this quality take the following often admired lines in which practically every word conveys fresh thought and cannot be dissociated from that thought:—

Come, seeling night,
Scarf up the tender eye of pitiful day,
And with thy bloody and invisible hand
Cancel and tear to pieces that great bond
Which keeps me pale. Light thickens, and the crow
Makes wing to th' rooky wood;
Good things of day begin to droop and drowse,
Whiles night's black agents to their preys do rouse.

Macbeth, III, 2, 46

Shakespeare's prose rendered in verse form

The passage just quoted is great and real poetry. Yet early and late in the canon are to be found passages which are simply commonplace prose cut up into lines:—

If ever you disturb our streets again,
Your lives shall pay the forfeit of the peace.
For this time all the rest depart away.
You, Capulet, shall go along with me;
And, Montague, come you this afternoon,
To know our farther pleasure in this case,
To old Free-town, our common judgment-place.

Romeo and Juliet, I, 1, 94

Sil. How tall was she?
Jul. About my stature; for at Pentecost,
When all our pageants of delight were play'd,
Our youth got me to play the woman's part,
And I was trimm'd in Madam Julia's gown;
Which served me as fit, by all men's judgments,
As if the garment had been made for me;
Therefore I know she is about my height.

The Two Gentlemen of Verona, IV, 4, 153

Within this hour it will be dinner-time;
Till that, I'll view the manners of the town,
Peruse the traders, gaze upon the buildings,
And then return and sleep within mine inn;
For with long travel I am stiff and weary.

The Comedy of Errors, I, 2, 11

Seb. Shall we go see the reliques of this town?
Ant. To-morrow, sir; best first go see your lodging.
Seb. I am not weary, and 'tis long to night;
I pray you let us satisfy our eyes
With the memorials and the things of fame
That do renown this city. *Twelfth Night*, III, 3, 19

In the south suburbs, at the Elephant,
Is best to lodge. I will bespeak our diet,
Whiles you beguile the time and feed your knowledge
With viewing of the town. *Twelfth Night*, III, 3, 39

or this one:—

Three parts of that receipt I had for Calais
Disburs'd I duly to his Highness' soldiers;
The other part reserv'd I by consent,
For that my sovereign liege was in my debt
Upon remainder of a dear account
Since last I went to France to fetch his queen.

King Richard II, I, 1, 126

Even in so late a play as *Antony and Cleopatra* we still find prose cut into lines:—

Cleo. Sole sir o' th' world,
I cannot project mine own cause so well
To make it clear, but do confess I have
Been laden with like frailties which before
Have often sham'd our sex.
Cæs. Cleopatra, know
We will extenuate rather than enforce.
If you apply yourself to our intents—
Which towards you are most gentle—you shall find

A benefit in this change; but if you seek
To lay on me a cruelty by taking
Antony's course, you shall bereave yourself
Of my good purposes, and put your children
To that destruction, which I'll guard them from,
If thereon you rely. I'll take my leave.

Antony and Cleopatra, V, 2, 119

MEANINGLESS PASSAGES

Emerson writes (*Shakespeare; or, The Poet*) "The thought constructs the tune, so that reading for the sense will best bring out the rhythm," and there can be no doubt that it is the thought or meaning in "Shakespeare" which is so attractive. When therefore we come across lines or even whole verses which are practically meaningless, are we not entitled to question their author's ability to write *Macbeth?* I regard the whole five verses beginning "Since thou art dead" (*Venus and Adonis*, lines 1135-1164) to be meaningless and certainly valueless. The following are examples of meaningless lines:—

Love is all truth: Lust full of forged lies. *Venus and Adonis*, 804

And when the judge is robb'd, the prisoner dies.

The Rape of Lucrece, 1652

The crow doth sing as sweetly as the lark
When neither is attended. *The Merchant of Venice*, V, 1, 102

This night methinks is but the daylight sick;
It looks a little paler; 'tis a day
Such as the day is when the sun is hid.

The Merchant of Venice, V, 1, 124

In nature there's no blemish but the mind.

Twelfth Night, III, 4, 351

She's not well married that lives married long,
But she's best married that dies married young.

Romeo and Juliet, IV, 5, 77

Fathers that wear rags
Do make their children blind;
But fathers that bear bags
Shall see their children kind. *King Lear*, II, 4, 47

She was a charmer, and could almost read
The thoughts of people. *Othello*, III, 4, 57

Her honour is an essence that's not seen;
They have it very oft that have it not. *Othello*, IV, 1, 17

These lines I regard as quite meaningless; others deal with thought so trivial as to be practically meaningless:—

So soon was she along as he was down,
Each leaning on their elbows and their hips.

Venus and Adonis, 43-44

Rain added to a river that is rank
Perforce will force it overflow the bank. *Venus and Adonis*, 71-72
Here one man's hand lean'd on another's head,
His nose being shadowed by his neighbour's ear.
The Rape of Lucrece, 1415-6

Where's Antonio, then?
I could not find him at the Elephant;
Yet there he was; and there I found this credit,
That he did range the town to seek me out.
Twelfth Night, IV, 3, 4

but if we disregard Emerson and concentrate on the verse form rather than on the thought conveyed we shall find that these sets of lines just given are quite as good as:—

Canst thou not minister to a mind diseas'd,
Pluck from the memory a rooted sorrow? *Macbeth*, V, 3, 40

While on the subject of verse form it is necessary to point out that although individual lines may run as smoothly in Shakespeare's verse as in Burton's, there is a difference in the piece. Shakespeare's verse is mechanical and forced; Burton's is apparently effortless and runs in easy numbers. As noticed above, Hazlitt found *Venus and Adonis* and *The Rape of Lucrece* to be laboured, uphill work and such description does apply to much of Shakespeare's parts of the plays. The Holinshed passages are often so:—

Which Salique, as I said, 'twixt Elbe and Sala,
Is at this day in Germany call'd Meisen. *King Henry V*, I, 2, 52

His eldest sister, Anne,
My mother, being heir unto the crown,
Married Richard Earl of Cambridge, who was
To Edmund Langley, Edward the Third's fifth son, son.
By her I claim the kingdom: she was heir
To Roger Earl of March, who was the son
Of Edmund Mortimer, who married Philippe,
Sole daughter unto Lionel Duke of Clarence.
King Henry VI, pt. 2, II, 2, 43

In Shakespeare's contributions to *Macbeth* and *Hamlet*, late plays and therefore ones in which we could expect improvement, we find the same mechanical verse conveying commonplace, prosaic thought:—

I grant him bloody,
Luxurious, avaricious, false, deceitful,
Sudden, malicious, smacking of every sin
That has a name; but there's no bottom, none,
In my voluptuousness. Your wives, your daughters,
Your matrons, and your maids, could not fill up

The cistern of my lust; and my desire
All continent impediments would o'erbear
That did oppose my will. *Macbeth*, IV, 3, 57

Thus much the business is: we have here writ
To Norway, uncle of young Fortinbras—
Who, impotent and bed-rid, scarcely hears
Of this his nephew's purpose—to suppress
His further gait herein, in that the levies,
The lists, and full proportions, are all made
Out of his subject; and we here dispatch
You, good Cornelius, and you, Voltemand,
For bearers of this greeting to old Norway;
Giving to you no further personal power
To business with the King more than the scope
Of these delated articles allow. *Hamlet*, I, 2, 27

A SELECTION OF SHAKESPEARE PASSAGES

I consider that all the following passages were written by Shakespeare. The reader is invited to notice (i) their strongly narrative character, (ii) their almost complete lack of subtlety, (iii) the mechanical construction of the verse and (iv) the fact that they are taken from early, middle and late works:—

1. *Ant. E.* My liege, I am advised what I say;
Neither disturbed with the effect of wine,
Nor heady-rash, provok'd with raging ire,
Albeit my wrongs might make one wiser mad.
This woman lock'd me out this day from dinner;
That goldsmith there, were he not pack'd with her,
Could witness it, for he was with me then;
Who parted with me to go fetch a chain,
Promising to bring it to the Porpentine,
Where Balthazar and I did dine together.
Our dinner done, and he not coming thither,
I went to seek him. In the street I met him,
And in his company that gentleman.
There did this perjur'd goldsmith swear me down
That I this day of him receiv'd the chain,
Which, God he knows, I saw not; for the which
He did arrest me with an officer.
I did obey, and sent my peasant home
For certain ducats; he with none return'd.
Then fairly I bespoke the officer
To go in person with me to my house.
By th' way we met my wife, her sister, and a rabble more

Of vile confederates. Along with them
They brought one Pinch, a hungry lean-fac'd villian,
A mere anatomy, a mountebank,
A threadbare juggler, and a fortune-teller,
A needy, hollow-ey'd, sharp-looking wretch,
A living dead man. This pernicious slave,
Forsooth, took on him as a conjurer,
And gazing in mine eyes, feeling my pulse,
And with no face, as 'twere, outfacing me,
Cries out I was possess'd. Then all together
They fell upon me, bound me, bore me thence,
And in a dark and dankish vault at home
There left me and my man, both bound together;
Till, gnawing with my teeth my bonds in sunder,
I gain'd my freedom, and immediately
Ran hither to your Grace; whom I beseech
To give me ample satisfaction
For these deep shames and great indignities.

The Comedy of Errors, V, 1, 214

2. *Friar.* Hear me a little;
For I have only been silent so long,
And given way unto this course of fortune,
By noting of the lady: I have mark'd
A thousand blushing apparitions
To start into her face, a thousand innocent shames
In angel whiteness beat away those blushes;
And in her eye there hath appear'd a fire
To burn the errors that these princes hold
Against her maiden truth. Call me a fool;
Trust not my reading nor my observations,
Which with experimental seal doth warrant
The tenour of my book; trust not my age,
My reverence, calling, nor divinity,
If this sweet lady lie not guiltless here
Under some biting error. *Much Ado About Nothing*, IV, 1, 155

3. *Jaq. de B.* Let me have audience for a word or two.
I am the second son of old Sir Rowland,
That bring these tidings to this fair assembly.
Duke Frederick, hearing how that every day
Men of great worth resorted to this forest,
Address'd a mighty power; which were on foot,
In his own conduct, purposely to take
His brother here, and put him to the sword;
And to the skirts of this wild wood he came,

Where, meeting with an old religious man,
After some question with him, was converted
Both from his enterprise and from the world;
His crown bequeathing to his banish'd brother,
And all their lands restor'd to them again
That were with him exil'd. This to be true
I do engage my life. *As You Like It*, V, 4, 145

4. *Fab.* Good madam, hear me speak,
And let no quarrel nor no brawl to come
Taint the condition of this present hour,
Which I have wond'red at. In hope it shall not,
Most freely I confess myself and Toby
Set this device against Malvolio here,
Upon some stubborn and uncourteous parts
We had conceiv'd against him. Maria writ
The letter, at Sir Toby's great importance,
In recompense whereof he hath married her.
How with a sportful malice it was follow'd
May rather pluck on laughter than revenge,
If that the injuries be justly weigh'd
That have on both sides pass'd. *Twelfth Night*, V, 1, 342

5. *Boling.* Look what I speak, my life shall prove it true—
That Mowbray hath receiv'd eight thousand nobles
In name of lendings for your Highness' soldiers,
The which he hath detain'd for lewd employments
Like a false traitor and injurious villain.
Besides, I say and will in battle prove—
Or here, or elsewhere to the furthest verge
That ever was survey'd by English eye—
That all the treasons for these eighteen years
Complotted and contrived in this land
Fetch from false Mowbray their first head and spring.
Further I say, and further will maintain
Upon his bad life to make all this good,
That he did plot the Duke of Gloucester's death,
Suggest his soon-believing adversaries,
And consequently, like a traitor coward,
Sluic'd out his innocent soul through streams of blood;
Which blood, like sacrificing Abel's, cries,
Even from the tongueless caverns of the earth,
To me for justice and rough chastisement;
And, by the glorious worth of my descent,
This arm shall do it, or this life be spent.
King Richard II, I, 1, 87

6. *King.* You were about to speak.
North. Yea, my good lord.
Those prisoners in your Highness' name demanded,
Which Harry Percy here at Holmedon took,
Were, as he says, not with such strength denied
As is delivered to your Majesty.
Either envy, therefore, or misprision
Is guilty of this fault, and not my son.
Hot. My liege, I did deny no prisoners.
But I remember when the fight was done,
When I was dry with rage and extreme toil,
Breathless and faint, leaning upon my sword,
Came there a certain lord, neat, and trimly dress'd,
Fresh as a bridegroom, and his chin new reap'd
Show'd like a stubble-land at harvest-home.
He was perfumed like a milliner,
And 'twixt his finger and his thumb he held
A pouncet-box, which ever and anon
He gave his nose and took't away again;
Who therewith angry, when it next came there,
Took it in snuff—and still he smil'd and talk'd—
And as the soldiers bore dead bodies by,
He call'd them untaught knaves, unmannerly,
To bring a slovenly unhandsome corse
Betwixt the wind and his nobility.
With many holiday and lady terms
He questioned me: amongst the rest, demanded
My prisoners in your Majesty's behalf.
I then, all smarting with my wounds being cold,
To be so pest'red with a popinjay,
Out of my grief and my impatience
Answer'd neglectingly I know not what—
He should, or he should not—for he made me mad
To see him shine so brisk, and smell so sweet,
And talk so like a waiting-gentlewoman
Of guns, and drums, and wounds—God save the mark!—
And telling me the sovereignest thing on earth
Was parmaceti for an inward bruise;
And that it was great pity, so it was,
This villainous saltpetre should be digg'd
Out of the bowels of the harmless earth,
Which many a good tall fellow had destroy'd
So cowardly; and but for these vile guns
He would himself have been a soldier.
This bald unjointed chat of his, my lord,

I answered indirectly, as I said;
And I beseech you, let not his report
Come current for an accusation
Betwixt my love and your high Majesty.

King Henry IV, pt. 1, I, 3, 22

7. *West.* Then, my lord,
Unto your Grace do I in chief address
The substance of my speech. If that rebellion
Came like itself, in base and abject routs,
Led on by bloody youth, guarded with rags,
And countenanc'd by boys and beggary—
I say, if damn'd commotion so appear'd
In his true, native, and most proper shape,
You, reverend father, and these noble lords,
Had not been here to dress the ugly form
Of base and bloody insurrection
With your fair honours. You, Lord Archbishop,
Whose see is by a civil peace maintain'd,
Whose beard the silver hand of peace hath touch'd,
Whose learning and good letters peace hath tutor'd,
Whose white investments figure innocence,
The dove, and very blessed spirit of peace—
Wherefore do you so ill translate yourself
Out of the speech of peace, that bears such grace,
Into the harsh and boist'rous tongue of war;
Turning your books to graves, your ink to blood,
Your pens to lances, and your tongue divine
To a loud trumpet and a point of war?
Arch. Wherefore do I this? So the question stands.
Briefly to this end: we are all diseas'd
And with our surfeiting and wanton hours
Have brought ourselves into a burning fever,
And we must bleed for it; of which disease
Our late King, Richard, being infected, died.
But, my most noble Lord of Westmoreland,
I take not on me here as a physician;
Nor do I as an enemy of peace
Troop in the throngs of military men;
But rather show awhile like fearful war
To diet rank minds sick of happiness,
And purge th' obstructions which begin to stop
Our very veins of life. Hear me more plainly.
I have in equal balance justly weigh'd
What wrongs our arms may do, what wrongs we suffer,
And find our griefs heavier than our offences.

We see which way the stream of time doth run
And are enforc'd from our most quiet there
By the rough torrent of occasion;
And have the summary of all our griefs,
When time shall serve, to show in articles;
Which long ere this we offer'd to the King,
And might by no suit gain our audience:
When we are wrong'd, and would unfold our griefs,
We are denied access unto his person,
Even by those men that most have done us wrong.
The dangers of the days but newly gone,
Whose memory is written on the earth
With yet appearing blood, and the examples
Of every minute's instance, present now,
Hath put us in these ill-beseeming arms;
Not to break peace, or any branch of it,
But to establish here a peace indeed,
Concurring both in name and quality.

King Henry IV, pt. 2, IV, 1, 30

8. *Cant.* Then hear me, gracious sovereign, and you peers,
That owe yourselves, your lives, and services,
To this imperial throne. There is no bar
To make against your Highness' claim to France
But this, which they produce from Pharamond:
'In terram Salicam mulieres ne succedant'—
'No woman shall succeed in Salique land';
Which Salique land the French unjustly gloze
To be the realm of France, and Pharamond
The founder of this law and female bar.
Yet their own authors faithfully affirm
That the land Salique is in Germany,
Between the floods of Sala and of Elbe;
Where Charles the Great, having subdu'd the Saxons,
There left behind and settled certain French;
Who, holding in disdain the German women
For some dishonest manners of their life,
Establish'd then this law: to wit, no female
Should be inheritrix in Salique land;
Which Salique, as I said, 'twixt Elbe and Sala,
Is at this day in Germany call'd Meisen.
Then doth it well appear the Salique law
Was not devised for the realm of France;
Nor did the French possess the Salique land
Until four hundred one and twenty years
After defunction of King Pharamond,

Idly suppos'd the founder of this law;
Who died within the year of our redemption
Four hundred twenty-six; and Charles the Great
Subdu'd the Saxons, and did seat the French
Beyond the river Sala, in the year
Eight hundred five. Besides, their writers say,
King Pepin, which deposed Childeric,
Did, as heir general, being descended
Of Blithild, which was daughter to King Clothair,
Make claim and title to the crown of France.
Hugh Capet also, who usurp'd the crown
Of Charles the Duke of Lorraine, sole heir male
Of the true line and stock of Charles the Great,
To find his title with some shows of truth—
Though in pure truth it was corrupt and naught—
Convey'd himself as th' heir to th' Lady Lingare,
Daughter to Charlemain, who was the son
To Lewis the Emperor, and Lewis the son
Of Charles the Great. Also King Lewis the Tenth,
Who was sole heir to the usurper Capet,
Could not keep quiet in his conscience,
Wearing the crown of France, till satisfied
That fair Queen Isabel, his grandmother,
Was lineal of the Lady Ermengare,
Daughter to Charles the foresaid Duke of Lorraine;
By the which marriage the line of Charles the Great
Was re-united to the Crown of France.
So that, as clear as is the summer's sun,
King Pepin's title, and Hugh Capet's claim,
King Lewis his satisfaction, all appear
To hold in right and title of the female;
So do the kings of France unto this day,
Howbeit they would hold up this Salique law
To bar your Highness claiming from the female;
And rather choose to hide them in a net
Than amply to imbar their crooked titles
Usurp'd from you and your progenitors.

King Henry V, I, 2, 33

9. *Cran.* Let me speak, sir,
For heaven now bids me; and the words I utter
Let none think flattery, for they'll find 'em truth.
This royal infant—heaven still move about her!—
Though in her cradle, yet now promises
Upon this land a thousand thousand blessings,
Which time shall bring to ripeness. She shall be—

But few now living can behold that goodness—
A pattern to all princes living with her,
And all that shall succeed. Saba was never
More covetous of wisdom and fair virtue
Than this pure soul shall be. All princely graces
That mould up such a mighty piece as this is,
With all the virtues that attend the good,
Shall still be doubled on her. Truth shall nurse her,
Holy and heavenly thoughts still counsel her;
She shall be lov'd and fear'd. Her own shall bless her:
Her foes shake like a field of beaten corn,
And hang their heads with sorrow. Good grows with her;
In her days every man shall eat in safety
Under his own vine what he plants, and sing
The merry songs of peace to all his neighbours.
God shall be truly known; and those about her
From her shall read the perfect ways of honour,
And by those claim their greatness, not by blood.
Nor shall this peace sleep with her; but as when
The bird of wonder dies, the maiden phœnix,
Her ashes new create another heir
As great in admiration as herself,
So shall she leave her blessedness to one—
When heaven shall call her from this cloud of darkness—
Who from the sacred ashes of her honour
Shall star-like rise, as great in fame as she was,
And so stand fix'd. Peace, plenty, love, truth, terror,
That were the servants to this chosen infant,
Shall then be his, and like a vine grow to him;
Wherever the bright sun of heaven shall shine,
His honour and the greatness of his name
Shall be, and make new nations; he shall flourish,
And like a mountain cedar reach his branches
To all the plains about him; our children's children
Shall see this and bless heaven.
King. Thou speakest wonders.
Cran. She shall be, to the happiness of England,
An aged princess; many days shall see her,
And yet no day without a deed to crown it.
Would I had known no more! But she must die—
She must, the saints must have her—yet a virgin;
A most unspotted lily shall she pass
To th' ground, and all the world shall mourn her.

King Henry VIII, V, 5, 14

10. *Luc.* Then, gracious auditory, be it known to you
That Chiron and the damn'd Demetrius
Were they that murd'red our Emperor's brother;
And they it were that ravished our sister.
For their fell faults our brothers were beheaded,
Our father's tears despis'd, and basely cozen'd
Of that true hand that fought Rome's quarrel out
And sent her enemies unto the grave.
Lastly, myself unkindly banished,
The gates shut on me, and turn'd weeping out,
To beg relief among Rome's enemies;
Who drown'd their enmity in my true tears,
And op'd their arms to embrace me as a friend.
I am the turned forth, be it known to you,
That have preserv'd her welfare in my blood
And from her bosom took the enemy's point,
Sheathing the steel in my advent'rous body.

Titus Andronicus, V, 3, 96

11. *Fri. L.* I will be brief, for my short date of breath
Is not so long as is a tedious tale.
Romeo, there dead, was husband to that Juliet;
And she, there dead, that Romeo's faithful wife.
I married them; and their stol'n marriage-day
Was Tybalt's doomsday, whose untimely death
Banish'd the new-made bridegroom from this city;
For whom, and not for Tybalt, Juliet pin'd.
You, to remove that siege of grief from her,
Betroth'd, and would have married her perforce,
To County Paris. Then comes she to me,
And with wild looks bid me devise some mean
To rid her from this second marriage,
Or in my cell there would she kill herself.
Then gave I her, so tutor'd by my art,
A sleeping potion; which so took effect
As I intended, for it wrought on her
The form of death. Meantime I writ to Romeo
That he should hither come as this dire night
To help to take her from her borrowed grave,
Being the time the potion's force should cease.
But he which bore my letter, Friar John,
Was stay'd by accident, and yesternight
Return'd my letter back. Then all alone
At the prefixed hour of her waking
Came I to take her from her kindred's vault;
Meaning to keep her closely at my cell

Till I conveniently could send to Romeo.
But when I came, some minute ere the time
Of her awakening, here untimely lay
The noble Paris and true Romeo dead.
She wakes; and I entreated her come forth
And bear this work of heaven with patience.
But then a noise did scare me from the tomb,
And she, too desperate, would not go with me,
But, as it seems, did violence on herself.
All this I know, and to the marriage
Her nurse is privy; and if ought in this
Miscarried by my fault, let my old life
Be sacrific'd, some hour before his time,
Unto the rigour of severest law. *Romeo and Juliet*, V, 3, 228

12. *Mar.* Who is't that can inform me?
Hor. That can I;
At least, the whisper goes so. Our last king,
Whose image even but now appear'd to us,
Was, as you know, by Fortinbras of Norway,
Thereto prick'd on by a most emulate pride,
Dar'd to the combat; in which our valiant Hamlet—
For so this side of our known world esteem'd him—
Did slay this Fortinbras; who, by a seal'd compact,
Well ratified by law and heraldry,
Did forfeit, with his life, all those his lands
Which he stood seiz'd of, to the conqueror;
Against the which a moiety competent
Was gaged by our king; which had return'd
To the inheritance of Fortinbras,
Had he been vanquisher; as, by the same comart
And carriage of the article design'd,
His fell to Hamlet. Now, sir, young Fortinbras,
Of unimproved mettle hot and full,
Hath in the skirts of Norway, here and there,
Shark'd up a list of lawless resolutes,
For food and diet, to some enterprise
That hath a stomach in't; which is no other,
As it doth well appear unto our state,
But to recover of us, by strong hand
And terms compulsatory, those foresaid lands
So by his father lost; and this, I take it,
Is the main motive of our preparations,
The source of this our watch, and the chief head
Of this post-haste and romage in the land.
Ber. I think it be no other but e'en so.

Well may it sort, that this portentous figure
Comes armed through our watch; so like the King
That was and is the question of these wars.
Hor. A mote it is to trouble the mind's eye.
In the most high and palmy state of Rome,
A little ere the mightiest Julius fell,
The graves stood tenantless, and the sheeted dead
Did squeak and gibber in the Roman streets;
As, stars with trains of fire, and dews of blood,
Disasters in the sun; and the moist star
Upon whose influence Neptune's empire stands
Was sick almost to doomsday with eclipse;
And even the like precurse of fear'd events,
As harbingers preceding still the fates
And prologue to the omen coming on,
Have heaven and earth together demonstrated
Unto our climatures and countrymen. *Hamlet*, I, 1, 79

13. Be not offended.
I speak not as in absolute fear of you.
I think our country sinks beneath the yoke;
It weeps, it bleeds; and each new day a gash
Is added to her wounds. I think withal
There would be hands uplifted in my right;
And here, from gracious England, have I offer
Of goodly thousands. But, for all this,
When I shall tread upon the tyrant's head,
Or wear it on my sword, yet my poor country
Shall have more vices than it had before;
More suffer, and more sundry ways than ever,
By him that shall succeed. *Macbeth*, IV, 3, 37

14. *Lear.* Resolve me with all modest haste which way
Thou might'st deserve or they impose this usage,
Coming from us.
Kent. My lord, when at their home
I did commend your Highness' letters to them,
Ere I was risen from the place that show'd
My duty kneeling, came there a reeking post,
Stew'd in his haste, half breathless, panting forth
From Goneril his mistress salutations;
Deliver'd letters, spite of intermission,
Which presently they read; on whose contents
They summon'd up their meiny, straight took horse,
Commanded me to follow and attend
The leisure of their answer, gave me cold looks;

And meeting here the other messenger,
Whose welcome I perceiv'd had poison'd mine,
Being the very fellow which of late
Display'd so saucily against your Highness,
Having more man than wit about me, drew.
He rais'd the house with loud and coward cries.
Your son and daughter found this trespass worth
The shame which here it suffers. *King Lear*, II, 4, 24

15. Hear me Queen.
The strong necessity of time commands
Our services awhile; but my full heart
Remains in use with you. Our Italy
Shines o'er with civil swords: Sextus Pompeius
Makes his approaches to the port of Rome;
Equality of two domestic powers
Breeds scrupulous faction; the hated, grown to strength,
Are newly grown to love. The condemn'd Pompey,
Rich in his father's honour, creeps apace
Into the hearts of such as have not thrived
Upon the present state, whose numbers threaten;
And quietness, grown sick of rest, would purge
By any desperate change. My more particular,
And that which most with you should safe my going,
Is Fulvia's death. *Antony and Cleopatra*, I, 3, 41

16. I will tell you.
The barge she sat in, like a burnish'd throne,
Burn'd on the water. The poop was beaten gold;
Purple the sails, and so perfumed that
The winds were love-sick with them; the oars were silver,
Which to the tune of flutes kept stroke, and made
The water which they beat to follow faster,
As amorous of their strokes. For her own person,
It beggar'd all description. She did lie
In her pavilion, cloth-of-gold, of tissue,
O'erpicturing that Venus where we see
The fancy out-work nature. On each side her
Stood pretty dimpled boys, like smiling Cupids,
With divers-colour'd fans, whose wind did seem
To glow the delicate cheeks which they did cool,
And what they undid did. *Antony and Cleopatra*, II, 2, 194

17. *Cym.* Say then to Cæsar,
Our ancestor was that Mulmutius which
Ordain'd our laws—whose use the sword of Cæsar
Hath too much mangled; whose repair and franchise

Shall, by the power we hold, be our good deed,
Though Rome be therefore angry. Mulmutius made our laws,
Who was the first of Britain which did put
His brows within a golden crown, and call'd
Himself a king.
Luc. I am sorry, Cymbeline,
That I am to pronounce Augustus Cæsar—
Cæsar, that hath moe kings his servants than
Thyself domestic officers—thine enemy.
Receive it from me, then: war and confusion
In Cæsar's name pronounce I 'gainst thee; look
For fury not to be resisted. Thus defied,
I thank thee for myself.
Cym. Thou art welcome, Caius.
Thy Cæsar knighted me; my youth I spent
Much under him; of him I gather'd honour,
Which he to seek of me again, perforce,
Behoves me keep at utterance. I am perfect
That the Pannonians and Dalmatians for
Their liberties are now in arms, a precedent
Which not to read would show the Britons cold;
So Cæsar shall not find them. *Cymbeline*, III, 1, 52

18. This is the tenour of the Emperor's writ:
That since the common men are now in action
'Gainst the Pannonians and Dalmatians,
And that the legions now in Gallia are
Full weak to undertake our wars against
The fall'n-off Britons, that we do incite
The gentry to this business. He creates
Lucius proconsul; and to you, the tribunes,
For this immediate levy, he commands
His absolute commission. Long live Cæsar!
Cymbeline, III, 7, 1

The reader will notice that to every one of the eighteen passages there is an introduction "I am advised what I say," "Hear me a little," "Let me have audience for a word or two," "Good Madam, hear me speak," and so on. These are mere padding and conform to the verbose character of Shakespeare's work. That Shakespeare's powers did not evolve to any noteworthy extent is clearly shown by the eighteenth quotation (from a late work) which is quite as good an example of mechanically-constructed verse as is the first (from an early work). Moreover, to my mind, in all these long passages not a single line is worth committing to memory and original illuminating thought and appeal to the reader's imagination are quite absent.

Contrasts in construction

The great poet was a master of concise prose and verse. Typically he used a succession of short, compact phrases:—

> Run when you will; the story shall be chang'd:
> Apollo flies, and Daphne holds the chase;
> The dove pursues the griffin; the mild hind
> Makes speed to catch the tiger—bootless speed,
> When cowardice pursues and valour flies.

A Midsummer Night's Dream, II, 1, 230

> I have neither the scholar's melancholy, which is emulation; nor the musician's, which is fantastical; . . . nor the lover's, which is all these; but it is a melancholy of mine own, compounded of many simples, extracted from many objects, and, indeed, the sundry contemplation of my travels; in which my often rumination wraps me in a most humorous sadness.

As You Like It, IV, 1, 10-18

> If it were done when 'tis done, then 'twere well
> It were done quickly. [etc.]

Macbeth, I, 7, 1

> To be, or not to be—that is the question; [etc.]

Hamlet, III, 1, 56

In contrast, the inferior author contributed, throughout the canon, passages which are unwieldy and clumsily or very loosely constructed. The subject of a sentence may be widely separated from its verb; adverbs, adjectival clauses or qualifying phrases may be separated from the noun or verb to which they refer. Examples of such and similar faults are:—

1. Ceasing their clamorous cry till they have singled
   With much ado the cold fault cleanly out.

   Venus and Adonis, lines 693-4

Note: "Singled" is widely separated from "out".

2. . . . . . . by whose swift aid
   Their mistress, mounted, through the empty skies
   In her light chariot quickly is convey'd.

   Venus and Adonis, lines 1190-92

Note: The sense indicates that "mounted" is qualified by "in her light chariot" and "convey'd" by "through the empty skies"; thus, in both cases these phrases are misplaced.

3. In *The Argument* prefacing *The Rape of Lucrece* we read:—
   Lucius Tarquinius (for his excessive pride surnamed Superbus), after he had caused his own father-in-law, Servius Tullius, to be cruelly murd'red, and, contrary to the Roman laws and customs, not requiring or staying for the people's suffrages, had possessed himself of the kingdom, went, accompanied with his sons and other noble men of Rome, to besiege Ardea; during which siege, the principal men of the army meeting one evening

at the tent of Sextus Tarquinius, the King's son, in their discourses after supper every one commended the virtues of his own wife; among whom Collatinus extolled the incomparable chastity of his wife Lucretia.

Note: It is obvious that the murder of the father-in-law and the possession of the kingdom without staying for the people's suffrage ought to have been treated as quite separate events and their relation not lumped together parenthetically in a sentence telling that Tarquin went to besiege Ardea. Moreover the parentheses have the effect of separating the subject "Lucius Tarquinius" from its predicate "went" by 43 words.

4. Later in *The Argument* we read:—

 She, first taking an oath of them for her revenge, revealed the actor, and whole manner of his dealing, and withal suddenly stabbed herself. Which done, with one consent they all vowed to root out the whole hated family of the Tarquins.

Note: "Which done" refers to the action by Lucrece whereas from the construction one expects the words to refer to an action by "they" (Collatine, Lucretius and their associates) of the sentence to which the words belong.

5. But none where all distress and dolour dwell'd,
 Till she despairing Hecuba beheld,
 Staring on Priam's wounds with her old eyes,
 Which bleeding under Pyrrhus' proud foot lies.

The Rape of Lucrece, 1446

Note: From the sense the last line refers to Priam's wounds but from the construction it refers to Hecuba's eyes.

6. The enmity and discord which of late
 Sprung from the rancorous outrage of your duke
 To merchants, our well-dealing countrymen,
 Who, wanting guilders to redeem their lives,
 Have sealed his rigorous statutes with their bloods,
 Excludes all pity from our threat'ning looks.

The Comedy of Errors, I, 1, 5

Note: The wide separation of subject and verb by the presence of two adjectival clauses makes the whole very unwieldly.

7. *Sec. Mer.* By this, I think, the dial points at five;
 Anon, I'm sure, the Duke himself in person
 Comes this way to the melancholy vale,
 The place of death and sorry execution,
 Behind the ditches of the abbey here.
 Ang. Upon what cause?
 Sec. Mer. To see a reverend Syracusian merchant,
 Who put unluckily into this bay
 Against the laws and statutes of this town,

Beheaded publicly for his offence. *Comedy of Errors*, V, 1, 118

Note: In the second merchant's first speech lines 3 and 5 should have come together as both deal with the description and location of the place of execution. In his second speech "see" is too widely separated from "beheaded".

8. I do much wonder that one man, seeing how much another man is a fool when he dedicates his behaviours to love, will, after he hath laugh'd at such shallow follies in others, become the argument of his own scorn by falling in love.

Much Ado About Nothing, II, 3, 7

Note: The subject ("man"), the verb ("become") and the auxiliary of the verb ("will") are all widely separated.

9. What man was he talk'd with you yesternight
Out at your window, betwixt twelve and one?

Much Ado About Nothing, IV, 1, 82

Note: It is poor construction to separate the two parts of the designation of the time of the episode.

10. she is fall'n
Into a pit of ink, that the wide sea
Hath drops too few to wash her clean again.

Much Ado About Nothing, IV, 1, 139

Note: "That" should have read 'and'.

11. Inquire the Jew's house out. *The Merchant of Venice*, IV, 2, 1

12. Ay, to the proof, as mountains are for winds,
That shake not though they blow perpetually.

The Taming of the Shrew, II, 1, 139

13. I'll bring you to a captain in this town,
Where lie my maiden weeds; by whose gentle help
I was preserv'd to serve this noble Count.

Twelfth Night, V, 1, 246

14. My liege, here is the strangest controversy
Come from the country to be judg'd by you
That e'er I heard. *King John*, I, 1, 44

15. Then God forgive the sin of all those souls
That to their everlasting residence,
Before the dew of evening fall, shall fleet
In dreadful trial of our kingdom's king! *King John*, II, 1, 283

16. Old John of Gaunt, time honour'd Lancaster,
Hast thou, according to thy oath and band,
Brought hither Henry Hereford, thy bold son,
Here to make good the boist'rous late appeal,
Which then our leisure would not let us hear,
Against the Duke of Norfolk, Thomas Mowbray?

King Richard II, I, 1, 1

17. Which blood, like sacrificing Abel's, cries,
Even from the tongueless caverns of the earth,
To me for justice and rough chastisement.

King Richard II, I, 1, 104

18. Mistake me not my lord; 'tis not my meaning
To raze one title of your honour out.

King Richard II, II, 3, 74

Note: Contrast this with "Raze out the written troubles of the brain." *Macbeth*, V, 3, 42

19. Myself—a prince by fortune and by birth,
Near to the king in blood, and near in love
Till you did make him misinterpret me—
Have stoop'd my neck under your injuries.

King Richard II, III, 1, 16

20. So when this thief, this traitor, Bolingbroke,
Who all this while hath revell'd in the night,
Whilst we were wand'ring with the Antipodes,
Shall see us rising in our throne, the east,
His treasons will sit blushing in his face.

King Richard II, III, 2, 47

21. Those prisoners in your Highness' name demanded,
Which Harry Percy here at Holmedon took,
Were, as he says, *not* with such strength *denied*
As is delivered to your Majesty. *King Henry IV*, pt. 1, I, 3, 23

22. And telling me the sovereignest thing on earth
Was parmaceti for an inward bruise.

King Henry IV, pt. 1, I, 3, 57

Note: This should have read 'the sovereignest thing on earth for an inward bruise was parmaceti.'

23. And that it was great pity, so it was,
This villainous saltpetre should be digg'd
Out of the bowels of the harmless earth,
Which many a good tall fellow had destroy'd
So cowardly. *King Henry IV*, pt. 1, I, 3, 59

Note: "Which" plainly refers to "saltpetre" but, from the construction, it refers to "earth".

24. Why, yet he doth deny his prisoners,
But with proviso and exception—
That we at our own charge shall ransom straight
His brother-in-law, the foolish Mortimer;
Who, on my soul, hath wilfully betray'd
The lives of those that he did lead to fight
Against that great magician, damn'd Glendower,
Whose daughter, as we hear, that Earl of March
Hath lately married. *King Henry IV*, pt. 1, I, 3, 77

Note: This tacking on to the end of a sentence of information quite irrelevant to the point under discussion in that sentence is paralleled in *The Argument* prefacing *The Rape of Lucrece* (see above).

25. I cannot blame him; was not he proclaim'd
By Richard that dead is the next of blood?
King Henry IV, pt. 1, I, 3, 145

26. I'll have a starling shall be taught to speak.
King Henry IV, pt. 1, I, 3, 224

27. Hugh Capet also, who usurp'd the crown
Of Charles the Duke of Lorraine, sole heir male
Of the true line and stock of Charles the Great,
To find his title with some shows of truth—
Though in pure truth it was corrupt and naught—
Convey'd himself as th' heir to th' Lady Lingare,
Daughter to Charlemain, who was the son
To Lewis the Emperor, and Lewis the son
Of Charles the Great. *King Henry V*, I, 2, 69

Note: "Hugh Capet" is separated from "conveyed" by 42 words.

28. But I will rule both her, the King, and realm.
King Henry VI, pt. 1, V, 5, 108

29. And, but for Owen Glendower had been king,
Who kept him in captivity till he died.
King Henry VI, pt. 2, II, 2, 41

30. Bring forth that fatal screech-owl to our house.
King Henry VI, pt. 3, II, 6, 56

31. The dismal'st day is this that e'er I saw.
Titus Andronicus, I, 1, 384

32. The birds chant melody on every bush.
Titus Andronicus, II, 3, 12

33. Therefore present to her—as sometimes Margaret
Did to thy father, steep'd in Rutland's blood—
A handkerchief; which, say to her, did drain
The purple sap from her sweet brother's body,
And bid her wipe her weeping eyes withal.
King Richard III, IV, 4, 274

34. Break we our watch up. *Hamlet*, I, 1, 168

35. Therefore our sometime sister, now our queen,
Th' imperial jointress to this warlike state,
Have we, as 'twere with a defeated joy,
With an auspicious and a dropping eye,
With mirth in funeral, and with dirge in marriage,
In equal scale weighing delight and dole,
Taken to wife. *Hamlet*, I, 2, 8

Note: "Taken" is separated from its auxiliary "Have" by 30 words.

36. I have this present evening from my sister
Been well inform'd of them. *King Lear*, II, 1, 101

37. Nay, we must think, men are not gods,
Nor of them look for such observancy
As fits the bridal. *Othello*, III, 4, 149

Note: This should read 'we must not think men are gods' else the reader is led to expect the next line, beginning "Nor", also to be governed by "think", whereas "Nor" begins an entirely independent clause and "look" has status equal to "think".

38. If I do find him fit, I'll move your suit,
And seek to effect it to my uttermost. *Othello*, III, 4, 167

Note: The sense implies that "to my uttermost" qualifies "seek", whereas from the construction it qualifies "effect".

39. Pardon me, Bianca.
I *have* this while with leaden thoughts *been press'd*;
But I *shall* in a more continuate time
Strike off this score of absence. Sweet Bianca,
Take me this work *out*. *Othello*, III, 4, 177

40. Every day thou daff'st me with some device, Iago; and rather, as it seems to me now, keep'st from me all conveniency than suppliest me with the least advantage of hope. I will, indeed, no longer endure it; nor am I yet persuaded to put up in peace what already I have foolishly suffer'd. *Othello*, IV, 2, 176

41. *1st Lord.* What got he by that? You have broke his pate with your bowl.
2nd Lord. If his wit had been like him that broke it, it would have run all out. *Cymbeline*, II, 1, 6

42. He cannot choose but take this service I have done fatherly.
Cymbeline, II, 3, 34

43. some more time
Must wear the print of his remembrance out.
Cymbeline, II, 3, 42

Many passages in Shakespeare are clown parts and it is difficult to know whether or not the poor language was intended. There is no such excuse when one general addresses another on the need for inter-communication; yet what do we find even in a late play?:—

Lep. Tomorrow, Cæsar,
I shall be furnish'd to inform you rightly
Both what by sea and land I can be able*
To front this present time.
Cæs. Till which encounter
It is my business too. Farewell,

* Similarly we find:—
Ballad-makers cannot be able to express it. *The Winter's Tale*, V, 2, 25

Lep. Farewell, my lord. What you shall know meantime
Of stirs abroad, I shall beseech you, sir,
To let me be partaker.
Cæs. Doubt not, sir;
I knew it for my bond. *Antony and Cleopatra*, I, 4, 76

I rewrite this correcting at least some of the mistakes:—

Lep. Tomorrow, Cæsar,
I shall be furnish'd to inform you rightly
What both by sea and land I am able
To front this present time.
Cæs. Till which encounter
This care shall be my business too. Farewell,
Lep. Farewell, my lord. Of what you learn meantime
Of stirs abroad, I do beseech you, sir,
To let me be partaker.
Cæs. Doubt not, sir;
I know it for my bond.

EXAMPLES OF POOR RHYMES

Many of Shakespeare's rhymes fail to please my ear. Not only so, this author is quite prepared to change words or alter tense or number of verbs in the interests of rhyme. As examples:—

1. She sinketh down, still hanging by his neck,
He on her belly falls, she on her back.
Now is she in the very lists of love,
Her champion mounted for the hot encounter.
All is imaginary she doth prove;
He will not manage her, although he mount her.
Venus and Adonis, 593-598

Note: Need to slur the 'h' of "her" in order to rhyme with "encounter".

2. His brawny sides, with hairy bristles armed,
Are better proof than thy spear's point can enter;
His short thick neck cannot be easily harmed;
Being ireful, on the lion he will venter.
The thorny brambles and embracing bushes,
As fearful of him, part; through whom he rushes.
Venus and Adonis, 625-630

Note: 'Venture' has been changed to "venter" in interest of rhyme.

3. But if thou needs wilt hunt, be rul'd by me;
Uncouple at the timorous flying hare,
Or at the fox which lives by subtlety,
Or at the roe which no encounter dare.
Venus and Adonis, 673-676

Note: "Dare" should have read 'dares'.

4. She lifts the coffer-lids that close his eyes
Where, lo, two lamps burnt out in darkness lies.

Note: "Lies" should read 'lie'. *Venus and Adonis*, 1127-1128

5. Beauty itself doth of itself persuade
The eyes of men without an orator;
What needeth then apologies be made
To set forth that which is so singular?
Or why is Collatine the publisher
Of that rich jewel he should keep unknown
From thievish ears, because it is his own?

The Rape of Lucrece, 29-35

Note: Careless rhyming of "-or", "-ar" and "-er".

6. Look as the fair and fiery-pointed sun,
Rushing from forth a cloud, bereaves our sight;
Even so, the curtain drawn, his eyes begun
To wink, being blinded with a greater light;

The Rape of Lucrece, 372-375

Note: "Begun" should have read 'began'.

7. To thee, to thee, my heav'd-up hands appeal,
Not to seducing lust, thy rash relier;
I sue for exil'd majesty's repeal;
Let him return and flatt'ring thoughts retire.

The Rape of Lucrece, 638-641

Note: The necessity to make "retire" a three-syllable word to rhyme with "relier".

8. Grim cave of death! whisp'ring conspirator,
With close-tongu'd treason and the ravisher!

The Rape of Lucrece, 769-770

9. No man inveigh against the withered flow'r,
But chide rough winter that the flow'r hath kill'd.
Not that devour'd, but that which doth devour,
Is worthy blame. O, let it not be hild
Poor women's faults that they are so fulfill'd
With men's abuses! those proud lords to blame
Make weak-made women tenants to their shame.

The Rape of Lucrece, 1254-1360

Note: "hild" should have read 'held' and "fulfill'd" is put in instead of 'fill'd' just to give an extra syllable.

10. And from the strond of Dardan where they fought,
To Simois' reedy banks, the red blood ran,
Whose waves to imitate the battle sought
With swelling ridges; and their ranks began
To break upon the galled shore, and than
Retire again . . . *The Rape of Lucrece*, 1436-1441

Note: Unobtrusively, "than" is inserted instead of 'then'.

11. This we prescribe, though no physic*ian*;
Deep malice makes too deep incisi*on*.
Forget, forgive; conclude and be agr*eed*:
Our doctors say this is no month to bl*eed*.
Good uncle, let this end where it beg*un*;
We'll calm the Duke of Norfolk, you your son.

King Richard II, I, 1, 154

12. When the devout religion of mine eye
Maintains such falsehood, then turn tears to fires;
And these, who, often drown'd, could never die,
Transparent heretics, be burnt for liars!
One fairer than my love! The all-seeing sun
Ne'er saw her match since first the world begun.

Romeo and Juliet, I, 2, 88

Note: "liars" must be made a one-syllable word to rhyme with "fires" and "begun" should have read 'began'.

13. Hark, hark! the lark at heaven's gate sings,
And Phœbus 'gins arise,
His steeds to water at those springs
On chalic'd flow'rs that *lies*.

Cymbeline, II, 3, 20

Such lack of skill or care in the use of rhyme is not consistent with the idea that the author was a great poet. That the true poet of "Shakespeare" did not make such faults is clearly shown by the *Sonnets* (Burton's) in which the rhymes are consistently pleasing and acceptable.

Repetitions

Burton was able to move freely from theme to theme and cover much ground with relatively few words, while, on the other hand, Shakespeare had not a large store of ideas and, besides borrowing from other plays and from Holinshed and Plutarch as already noticed, also borrowed:—

A. from Burton passages in plays written earlier, and

B. from his own passages written earlier.

Examples of A are:—

1. The passage from *Twelfth Night*, V, 1, 357, "Some are born great," etc., which merely repeats what was said by Burton earlier in that play (II, 5, 130) and the passage from *Cymbeline*, V, 5, 435, "When as a lion's whelp," etc., which merely repeats what was said by Burton earlier in the play (V, 4, 138).

2. *Orl.* My fair Rosalind, I come within an hour of my promise.
Ros. Break an hour's promise in love! He that will divide a minute into a thousand parts, and break but a part of the

thousand part of a minute in the affairs of love, it may be said of him that Cupid hath clapp'd him o' th' shoulder, but I'll warrant him heart-whole.

A Burton passage from *As You Like It*, IV, 1, 39

What, keep a week away? seven days and nights?
Eightscore eight hours? and lovers' absent hours,
More tedious than the dial eight score times?
O weary reckoning!

A Shakespeare copy, *Othello*, III, 4, 174

3. A lioness hath whelped in the streets,
And graves have yawn'd and yielded up their dead;
Fierce fiery warriors fight upon the clouds,
In ranks and squadrons and right form of war,
Which drizzled blood upon the Capitol;
The noise of battle hurtled in the air;
Horses did neigh, and dying men did groan,
And ghosts did shriek and squeal about the streets.

A Burton passage from *Julius Cæsar*, II, 2, 17

A little ere the mightiest Julius fell,
The graves stood tenantless, and the sheeted dead
Did squeak and gibber in the Roman streets;
As, stars with trains of fire, and dews of blood,
Disasters in the sun; and the moist star
Upon whose influence Neptune's empire stands
Was sick almost to doomsday with eclipse;
And even the like precurse of fear'd events,
As harbingers preceding still the fates
And prologue to the omen coming on,
Have heaven and earth together demonstrated
Unto our climatures and countrymen.

A Shakespeare copy, *Hamlet*, I, 1, 114

4. If music be the food of love, play on.

From a Burton passage, *Twelfth Night*, I, 1, 1

Give me some music—music, moody food
Of us that trade in love.

A Shakespeare copy, *Antony and Cleopatra*, II, 5, 1

5. Let Rome in Tiber melt!

From a Burton passage, *Antony and Cleopatra*, I, 1, 33

Melt Egypt into Nile!

A Shakespeare copy, *Antony and Cleopatra*, II, 5, 78

6. Our dungy earth.

From a Burton passage, *Antony and Cleopatra*, I, 1, 35

The whole dungy earth.

A Shakespeare copy, *The Winter's Tale*, II, 1, 157

Examples of B are:—

1. Even as an empty eagle, sharp by fast,
   Tires with her beak on feathers, flesh, and bone.

Venus and Adonis, lines 55-56

and like an empty eagle
Tire on the flesh of me and of my son.

King Henry VI, pt. 3, I, 1, 268

2. Were I hard-favour'd, foul, or wrinkled-old,
   Ill-nurtur'd, crooked, churlish, harsh in voice,
   O'er-worn, despised, rheumatic, and cold,
   Thick-sighted, barren, lean, and lacking juice,
   Then might'st thou pause, for then I were not for thee;
   But having no defects, why dost abhor me?

Venus and Adonis, 133-138

If thou that bid'st me be content wert grim,
Ugly, and sland'rous to thy mother's womb,
Full of unpleasing blots and sightless stains,
Lame, foolish, crooked, swart, prodigious,
Patch'd with foul moles and eye-offending marks,
I would not care, I then would be content;
For then I should not love thee; no, nor thou
Become thy great birth, nor deserve a crown.
But thou art fair . . .

King John, III, 1, 43

3. With this, she falleth in the place she stood,
   And stains her face with his congealed blood.

Venus and Adonis, 1121-1122

And then in key-cold Lucrece' bleeding stream
He falls, and bathes the pale fear in his face.

The Rape of Lucrece, 1774-1775

4. Griev'd I I had but one?
   Chid I for that at frugal nature's frame?
   O, one too much by thee! Why had I one?

Much Ado About Nothing, IV, 1, 127

Wife, we scarce thought us blest
That God had lent us but this only child;
But now I see this one is one too much,
And that we have a curse in having her.

Romeo and Juliet, III, 5, 164

5. There is a lady, in Verona here,
   Whom I affect; but she is nice, and coy,
   And naught esteems my aged eloquence.
   Now, therefore, would I have thee to my tutor—
   For long agone I have forgot to court;
   Besides, the fashion of the time is changed—

How and which way I may bestow myself
To be regarded in her sun-bright eye.

The Two Gentlemen of Verona, III, 1, 81

She dwells so securely on the excellency of her honour that the folly of my soul dares not present itself; she is too bright to be look'd against. *The Merry Wives of Windsor*, II, 2, 217

As she is stubborn-chaste against all suit.

Troilus and Cressida, I, 1, 96

6. Nay, more: if any born at Ephesus
Be seen at any Syracusian marts and fairs;
Again, if any Syracusian born
Come to the bay of Ephesus—he dies.

The Comedy of Errors, I, 1, 16

'Tis death for any one in Mantua
To come to Padua. *The Taming of the Shrew*, IV, 2, 81

7. There is a remarkable and, for the purposes of this book, important similarity between Claudio's disavowal of Hero in *Much Ado About Nothing*, Act IV, Sc. 1, and Posthumus' disavowal of Imogen in *Cymbeline*, Act II, Sc. 5:—

(i) I will write against it. *Much Ado*
I'll write against them. *Cymbeline*

(ii) You seem to me as Dian in her orb. *Much Ado*
Yet my mother seem'd
The Dian of that time. *Cymbeline*

(iii) As chaste as is the bud ere it be blown. *Much Ado*
As chaste as unsunn'd snow. *Cymbeline*

(iv) But you are more intemperate in your blood
Than Venus, or those pamp'red animals
That rage in savage sensuality. *Much Ado*
Like a full-acorn'd boar, a German one,
Cried 'O!' and mounted. *Cymbeline*

Wayne* gives 1598-9 as the probable date of composition of *Much Ado About Nothing* and Verity† 1610 for *Cymbeline*. Thus, little or no progress had been made by the author during eleven years or so. It is generally accepted that the works of the real "Shakespeare" testify to a progression through early, middle and late periods. What then are we to make of such a back-water?

Peculiar form of padding

The inferior author appears to have been much attracted to a characteristic page-filling technique by which a character asks a question or makes a demand and then, without any intervening

---

* *Much Ado About Nothing*; Oxford University Press, 1954.
† *Cymbeline*; Cambridge University Press, 1923.

change in the circumstances, he answers the question himself or makes a countermand or an explanation, or a statement is made for the sole purpose of eliciting a contradictory reply. Examples are the following:—

Bene. Boy!
Boy. Signior?
Bene. In my chamber-window lies a book; bring it hither to me in the orchard.
Boy. I am here already, sir.
Bene. I know that; but I would have thee hence and here again. *Much Ado About Nothing*, II, 3, 1

King Philip. Is not the Lady Constance in this troop?
I know she is not; for this match made up
Her presence would have interrupted much.
King John, II, 1, 540

Duch. Lo, this is all—nay, yet depart not so;
Though this be all, do not so quickly go;
I shall remember more. Bid him—ah, what?—
With all good speed at Plashy visit me.
King Richard II, I, 2, 63

Boling. Royally!
Why, it contains no king?
Percy. Yes, my good lord,
It doth contain a king. *King Richard II*, III, 3, 23

Hot. I have forgot the map.
Glend. No, here it is.
King Henry IV, pt. 1, III, 1, 6

Arch. Here stand, my lords, and send discoverers forth
To know the numbers of our enemies.
Hast. We have sent forth already.
Arch. 'Tis well done.
King Henry IV, pt. 2, IV, 1, 3

War. Then Clarence is at hand; I hear his drum.
Som. It is not his, my lord. *King Henry VI*, pt. 3, V, 1, 11

Rat. What, may it please you, shall I do at Salisbury?
K. Rich. Why, what wouldst thou do there before I go?
Rat. Your Highness told me I should post before.
K. Rich. My mind is chang'd. *King Richard III*, IV, 4, 452

Rom. What fray was here?
Yet tell me not, for I have heard it all.
Romeo and Juliet, I, 1, 171

Rom. Whither should they come?
Serv. Up.
Rom. Whither?
Serv. To supper. To our house.

Rom. Whose house?
Serv. My master's.
Rom. Indeed, I should have ask'd you that before.
Serv. Now I'll tell you without asking: my master is the great rich Capulet. *Romeo and Juliet*, I, 2, 72

Lady C. Nurse, give leave awhile.
We must talk in secret. Nurse, come back again.
Romeo and Juliet, I, 3, 8

Par. Give me thy torch, boy; hence and stand aloof;
Yet put it out, for I would not be seen.
Romeo and Juliet, V, 3, 1

Por. I prithee, boy, run to the Senate House.
Stay not to answer me, but get thee gone.
Why dost thou stay?
Luc. To know my errand, madam.
Por. I would have had thee there and here again,
Ere I can tell thee what thou shouldst do there.
Julius Cæsar, II, 4, 1

Macd. See, who comes here?
Mal. My countryman; but yet I know him not.
Macd. My ever gentle cousin, welcome hither.
Mal. I know him now. Good God betimes remove
The means that makes us strangers!
Macbeth, IV, 3, 159

Eno. Hush! Here comes Antony.
Char. Not he; the Queen.
Antony and Cleopatra, I, 2, 74

Cleo. Cut my lace, Charmian, come!
But let it be; I am quickly ill and well—
So Antony loves. *Antony and Cleopatra*, I, 3, 71

Cleo. I have one thing more to ask him yet, good Charmian.
But 'tis no matter; thou shalt bring him to me
Where I will write. *Antony and Cleopatra*, III, 3, 44

Cæs. Where's Dolabella
To second Proculeius?
All. Dolabella!
Cæs. Let him alone, for I remember now
How he's employ'd; he shall in time be ready.
Antony and Cleopatra, V, 1, 69

Clo. Meet thee at Milford Haven! I forgot to ask him one thing; I'll remember't anon. *Cymbeline*, III, 5, 131

Go, get me hither paper, ink and pen—
Yet save that labour, for I have them here.
The Rape of Lucrece, 1289

SHAKESPEARE'S ATTITUDE TO NATURE CONTRASTED WITH BURTON'S

One contributor to the canon (Burton) had great sympathy with nature. We find many examples of this. To take a few:—

The summer's flow'r is to the summer sweet. *Sonnet* 94

From you have I been absent in the spring
When proud-pied April, dress'd in all his trim,
Hath put a spirit of youth in every thing,
That heavy Saturn laugh'd and leap'd with him.
Yet nor the lays of birds, nor the sweet smell
Of different flowers in odour and in hue,
Could make me any summer story tell,
Or from their proud lap pluck them where they grew;
Nor did I wonder at the lily's white,
Nor praise the deep vermilion in the rose. *Sonnet* 98

The ousel cock, so black of hue,
With orange-tawny bill,
The throstle with his note so true,
The wren with little quill.

A Midsummer Night's Dream, III, 1, 114

This shadowy desert, unfrequented woods,
I better brook than flourishing peopled towns
Here can I sit alone unseen of any,
And to the nightingale's complaining notes
Tune my distresses and record my woes.

The Two Gentlemen of Verona, V, 4, 2

Poor jade is wrung in the withers out of all cess.

King Henry IV, pt. 1, II, 1, 6

The turkeys in my pannier are quite starved.

King Henry IV, pt. 1, II, 1, 25

. . . for men, like butterflies,
Show not their mealy wings but to the summer.

Troilus and Cressida, III, 3, 78

Light thickens, and the crow
Makes wing to th' rooky wood. *Macbeth*, III, 2, 50

The noble ruin of her magic, Antony,
Claps on his sea-wing, and like a doting mallard,
Leaving the fight in height, flies after her.

Antony and Cleopatra, III, 10, 19

Another contributor (Shakespeare) had much less sympathy with nature. To take some examples to illustrate the very noteworthy contrast:—

These blue-vein'd violets whereon we lean
Never can blab, nor know not what we mean.

Venus and Adonis, 125-6

The moon being clouded presently is miss'd,
But little stars may hide them when they list.

The Rape of Lucrece, 1007-8

(Our mind contrasts "He made the stars also".)

Gnats are unnoted wheresoe'er they fly,
But eagles gaz'd upon with every eye.

The Rape of Lucrece, 1014-5

(Our mind also contrasts "Then in a wailful choir the small gnats mourn".)

The woods are ruthless, dreadful, deaf, and dull.

Titus Andronicus, II,1, 128

And to the skirts of this wild wood he came.

As You Like It, V, 4, 153

We see from the above quotation from *The Two Gentlemen of Verona* as well as from the woodland scenes of *A Midsummer Night's Dream* that Burton did love woods, whereas from these quotations from *Titus Andronicus* and *As You Like It* we learn that Shakespeare did not. Shakespeare was careless or ignorant when he wrote:—

Or hateful cuckoos hatch in sparrows' nests.

The Rape of Lucrece, line 849

whereas Burton was correct in saying:—

The hedge-sparrow fed the cuckoo . . .

King Lear, I, 4, 214

Greenwood in his chapter, "Shakespeare As Naturalist", draws attention to many errors in Shakespeare's natural history lore. According to my opinion the actual errors were all made by Shakespeare and not by Burton, Greenwood himself being in error in his observations on the dove's golden couplets simile, which I attribute to Burton. Referring to the line

Nightly she sings on yon pomegranate tree

Romeo and Juliet, III, 5, 4

Greenwood rightly comments "Well, Shakespeare could hardly have observed a nightingale on a pomegranate tree. And *she* sings! . . . it is only the male nightingale that sings." He does not refer to Shakespeare's error in saying that the nightingale does not sing by day—*The Merchant of Venice*, V, 1, 104; the passage containing this is worth quoting in full as it blazons forth Shakespeare's utter lack of true sympathy with nature:—

Por. The crow doth sing as sweetly as the lark
When neither is attended; and I think
The nightingale, if she should sing by day,
When every goose is cackling, would be thought
No better a musician than the wren.
How many things by season season'd are
To their right praise and true perfection!

Peace, ho! The moon sleeps with Endymion,
And would not be awak'd.
Lor. That is the voice,
Or I am much deceiv'd, of Portia.
Por. He knows me as the blind man knows the cuckoo,
By the bad voice.

Earlier in this chapter I drew attention to Shakespeare's error in describing the sun as having a "purple-colour'd face"; so also in the same poem we find the anomaly of flies tormenting Adonis' horse (line 316) at the season of violets (line 125) and primroses (line 151). In *The Rape of Lucrece* night-wandering weasels haunt human dwelling-houses (line 307); again the nightingale sings by day (line 1142) and again it is the female bird which sings (line 1080). Another error occurs at *Macbeth*, IV, 2, 9; I am certain no one has ever observed an owl attempting to attack young wrens in the nest.

USE OF IMAGERY CONTRASTED

The real "Shakespeare" is recognized as a master in the apt use of imagery; yet, in the canon, there are passages which show great unaptness in this respect. Had some similes just been ordinarily good and some just ordinarily bad, one might have been prepared to attribute the difference to immaturity or carelessness but the contrast is far too marked to be explained away so lightly. In *Venus and Adonis* Shakespeare writes:—

Look how a bright star shooteth from the sky
So glides he in the night from Venus' eye.

Lines 815-6

There is not the remotest resemblance between a shooting star and a man walking or running by night, whereas the following Burton simile from *Antony and Cleopatra* withstands all criticism:—

Yon ribaudred nag of Egypt—
. . . .
The breese upon her, like a cow in June—
Hoists sails and flies.

III, 10, 14

It is instructive to contrast two sets of similes derived from birds:—

(I) Even as an empty eagle, sharp by fast,
Tires with her beak on feathers, flesh and bone,
Shaking her wings, devouring all in haste,
Till either gorge be stuff'd, or prey be gone;
Even so she kiss'd his brow, his cheek, his chin,
And where she ends she doth anew begin.

From Shakespeare's *Venus and Adonis*, 55-60

There is no real resemblance between Venus kissing Adonis and an eagle tearing and devouring its prey, whereas, to any one who has observed mallard in spring-time, how apt will appear the following!:—

She once being loof'd,
The noble ruin of her magic, Antony,
Claps on his sea-wing, and, like a doting mallard,
Leaving the fight in height, flies after her.

From Burton's *Antony and Cleopatra*, III, 10, 18

(II) Look how a bird lies tangled in a net,
So fasten'd in her arms Adonis lies. *Venus and Adonis*, 67-68

A poorer simile than this would be hard to find (cf. the Hazlitt quotation given early in this chapter) and it contrasts with a Burton one:—

These growing feathers pluck'd from Cæsar's wing
Will make him fly an ordinary pitch,
Who else would soar above the view of men,
And keep us all in servile fearfulness. *Julius Cæsar*, I, 1, 73

Another unapt bird simile is the dive-dapper one in *Venus and Adonis*, lines 85-90.

Quiller-Couch*, referring to the lark's "watch-tower" and to the "dappled dawn" in *L'Allegro*, makes the reader say "Yes, that's just it, now he comes to think." One cannot repeat this in reference to most of the similes in *Venus and Adonis*; yet this poem was published by the world's greatest poet when he was twenty-nine years of age—absurd!

Slaughter-house imagery

One contributor to the works of "Shakespeare" had an intimate knowledge of the work of the butcher. As pointed out in Chapter I above, Shakespeare's father may have been a butcher and the son may have assisted him. Certainly the following quotations lend support to this tradition:—

And from the purple fountain Brutus drew
The murd'rous knife, and, as it left the place,
Her blood, in poor revenge, held it in chase;
And bubbling from her breast, it doth divide
In two slow rivers, that the crimson blood
Circles her body in on every side,
Who like a late sack'd island vastly stood
Bare and unpeopled in this fearful flood.
Some of her blood still pure and red remain'd,
And some look'd black, and that false Tarquin stain'd.

The Rape of Lucrece, 1734-1743

I wish'd your venison better; it was ill kill'd.

The Merry Wives of Windsor, I, 1, 73

---

* *The Art of Reading*, p. 63.

Have I liv'd to be carried in a basket, like a barrow of butcher's offal, and to be thrown in the Thames?

The Merry Wives of Windsor, III, 5, 3

Since I pluck'd geese, play'd truant, and whipp'd top, I knew not what 'twas to be beaten till lately.

The Merry Wives of Windsor, V, 1, 23

If thou embowel me today, I'll give you leave to powder me and eat me too tomorrow. *King Henry IV*, pt. 1, V, 4, 111

No doubt the murd'rous knife was dull and blunt
Till it was whetted on thy stone-hard heart
To revel in the entrails of my lambs.

King Richard III, IV, 4, 226

Weeke weeke!
So cries a pig prepared to the spit. *Titus Andronicus*, IV, 2, 146

This one hand yet is left to cut your throats,
Whiles that Lavinia 'tween her stumps doth hold
The basin that receives your guilty blood.

Titus Andronicus, V, 2, 182

A bump as big as a young cock'rel's stone.

Romeo and Juliet, I, 3, 54

She's e'en setting on water to scald such chickens as you are.

Timon of Athens, II, 2, 72

Such quotations are of great moment to anyone interested in psychology. Burton (footnote B. p. 106) quotes the dictum "*Nihil in intellectu, quod non prius fuerat in sensu*" and the above quotations illustrate this fact, if tradition in this case be indeed true, that Shakespeare could use in his writings only the facts and impressions that had previously reached his mind through his sense organs. Anyone who regards Shakespeare as "an original genius" should have a care to his definition of the term. This, by the way; what concerns us here is that all these quotations come from passages of inferior literature and thus, according to my thesis, were written by Shakespeare.

THE INFERIOR AUTHOR WAS MATERIALLY MINDED

The aim of all is but to nurse the life
With honour, wealth, and ease in waning age.

The Rape of Lucrece, 141-142

Sebastian, I have entertained thee,
Partly that I have need of such a youth
That can with some discretion do my business.

The Two Gentlemen of Verona, IV, 4, 59

Our wealth increas'd
By prosperous voyages I often made
To Epidamnum; till my factor's death,

And the great care of goods at random left,
Drew me from kind embracements of my spouse.

The Comedy of Errors, I, 1, 40

You knew my father well, and in him me,
Left solely heir to all his lands and goods,
Which I have bettered rather than decreas'd.

The Taming of the Shrew, II, 1, 115

Lorenzo, I commit into your hands
The husbandry and manage of my house
Until my lord's return. *The Merchant of Venice*, III, 4, 24

One day shall crown th' alliance on 't, so please you,
Here at my house, and at my proper cost.

Twelfth Night, V, 1, 305

Thou, having made me businesses which none without thee can sufficiently manage, must either stay to execute them thyself, or take away with thee the very services thou hast done. *The Winter's Tale*, IV, 2, 14

This monument five hundred years hath stood,
Which I have sumptuously re-edified. *Titus Andronicus*, I, 1, 350

I am now from home, and out of that provision
Which shall be needful for your entertainment.

King Lear, II, 4, 204

I look'd not for you yet, nor am provided
For your fit welcome. *King Lear*, II, 4, 231

Yea, or so many, sith that both charge and danger
Speak 'gainst so great a number? *King Lear*, II, 4, 238

This house is little: the old man and 's people
Cannot be well bestow'd. *King Lear*, II, 4, 287

Improper use of words

The proper use of words and the exact and pleasing arrangement of words and phrases are characteristic of the great work of "Shakespeare". At school we must commit to memory long or short passages in the hope that "Shakespeare's" manner of expression will influence our own. When therefore we read, within the covers of a book labelled the works of "Shakespeare", passages whose characteristics are often the very reverse of the above, we say to ourselves "Can such work be by the great 'Shakespeare'?" In discussing *Much Ado About Nothing* I gave some examples of improper use of words. Here I give other examples stressing that these are to be found even in late works:—

1. I will predominate over the peasant.

The Merry Wives of Windsor, II, 2, 251

N.B.—All Falstaff intended to do was to outwit Ford, not to be superior to him or exert control over him. Moreover Ford was a "gentleman of Windsor" not a "peasant".

2. Disguised cheaters, prating mountebanks,
And many such-like liberties of sin.

The Comedy of Errors, I, 2, 101

N.B.—"Liberties" presumably was intended for 'libertines'.

3. And here's another
Writ in my cousin's hand, stol'n from her pocket
Containing her affection unto Benedict.

Much Ado About Nothing, V, 4, 88

N.B.—"Stol'n" is too strong a word under the circumstances and should have read 'found in'. "Containing" should have read 'telling of'.

4. They are in the very wrath of love, and they will together.

As You Like It, V, 2, 37

5. Look, York: I stain'd this napkin with the blood
That valiant Clifford with his rapier's point
Made issue from the bosom of the boy.

King Henry VI, pt. 3, I, 4, 79

N.B.—"Valiant" is quite the wrong word here; nor was it used ironically for it was spoken by Queen Margaret whose friend Clifford was.

6. It had been vicious
To have mistrusted her. *Cymbeline*, V, 5, 65

N.B.—"Vicious" is again too strong; 'ungracious' was what he meant.

7. Being so enrag'd, desire doth lend her force
Courageously to pluck him from his horse.

Venus and Adonis, 29-30

N.B.—"Courageously" should have read 'boldly' or some such word as courage was not required for the act done.

8. But having no defects, why dost abhor me?

Venus and Adonis, 138

N.B.—"Abhor" is quite the wrong word but it rhymes with "for" of the previous line.

9. Gazing upon the Greeks with little lust. *The Rape of Lucrece*, 1384

N.B.—"Lust" is quite the wrong word in the context, but it does rhyme with "thrust" of the previous line.

The plea may be advanced that many of these errors are products of their author's youth, but, when we find in a late play (*Othello*) three clear examples of wrong use of words in eleven lines (V, 2, 3–13), another explanation must be sought:—

1. Yet I'll not shed her blood,
Nor scar that whiter skin of hers than snow.

2. I can again thy former light restore,
   Should I repent me.
3. I know not where is that Promethean heat
   That can thy light relume.

In (1) "scar" is the wrong word as scar denotes healed tissue and Othello was determined to kill Desdemona. (Notice also the poor arrangement of words in the second line.)

In (2) "Should I repent me" is obviously intended to mean 'should I change my mind,' quite a different matter.

In (3) "heat" should have read 'fire' or 'flame'.

"Strike up"

It is most interesting to study those passages in which the phrase "strike up" occurs. Following in the main Mrs. Cowden Clarke's *Concordance*, they are:—

Strike up, pipers -	- *Much Ado About Nothing*, V, 4, 124
Come on, strike up	- *The Winter's Tale*, IV, 4, 161
Come, strike up -	- ,, ,, ,, IV, 4, 165
Strike up the drums	- *King John*, V, 2, 164
Strike up our drums	- ,, ,, V, 2, 179
Strike up our drums	- *King Henry IV*, pt. 2, IV, 2, 120
Then strike up drums	- *King Henry VI*, pt. 3, II, 1, 204
Drummer, strike up	- ,, ,, ,, pt. 3, IV, 7, 50
Strike up the drum	- ,, ,, ,, pt. 3, V, 3, 24
Strike up the drum	- *King Richard III*, IV, 4, 179

Phr. & Timan. More counsel and more money, bounteous Timon.

Tim. More whore, more mischief first; I have given you earnest.

Alcib. Strike up the drum towards Athens.

Timon of Athens, IV, 3, 166-168

To me a study of the context of these passages shows that they all were by the inferior writer. Most interesting is that from *The Winter's Tale* where, in the midst of the "floral" scene, Clown, Dorcas and Mopas suddenly break in upon the meditation of Polixenes, Camillo and Shepherd to say:—

Clo. Come on, strike up.
Dor. Mopsa must be your mistress; marry, garlic,
To mend her kissing with!
Mop. Now, in good time!
Clo. Not a word, a word; we stand upon our manners.
Come, strike up.

[*Music.*

Here a dance of Shepherds and Shepherdesses.

When this interruption is over Polixenes resumes his conversation as if nothing has occurred and the passage is probably an interpolation by a collaborator, whom I believe to have been Shakespeare. Further support for this view is the fact that Perdita and Florizel are already dancing, presumably to music, so that there is no point in inviting the pipers to "strike up". The Timon lines may have been interpolated merely to give a longer break in Timon's speech. Such an explanation is supported, also, by the fact that the substance of the interpolation has been given twice previously in the scene at lines 129-132 and 148-149.

CONTRAST IN THEIR INTEREST IN ASTRONOMY
BETWEEN THE TWO AUTHORS

The moon being clouded presently is miss'd,
But little stars may hide them when they list.

The Rape of Lucrece, 1007-8

Venus salutes him [the sun] with this fair good-morrow:
'O thou clear god, and patron of all light,
From whom each lamp and shining star doth borrow
The beauteous influence that makes him bright.'

Venus and Adonis, 859-862

Last night of all,
When yond same star that's westward from the pole
Hath made his course t'illume that part of heaven
Where now it burns, *Hamlet*, I, 1, 35

And the moist star
Upon whose influence Neptune's empire stands
Was sick almost to doomsday with eclipse.

Hamlet, I, 1, 118

We can be quite safe in saying that these four quotations were written by a person with no interest in astronomy. They contrast markedly with:—

Therefore the moon, the governess of floods.

A Midsummer Night's Dream, II, 1, 103

The moon's an arrant thief,
And her pale fire she snatches from the sun.

Timon of Athens, IV, 3, 435

The wind-shak'd surge, with high and monstrous mane,
Seems to cast water on the burning Bear
And quench the guards of th' ever-fixed pole.

Othello, II, 1, 13

But I am constant as the northern star,
Of whose true fix'd and resting quality
There is no fellow in the firmament.
The skies are painted with unnumb'red sparks,

> That are all fire, and every one doth shine;
> But there's but one in all doth hold his place.
>
> *Julius Cæsar*, III, 1, 60

Burton with his great interest in, and his knowledge of, astronomy could well have written the last four passages, but certainly did not write the first four. He wrote quite extensively in *The Anatomy* on astronomy and the following quotation will suffice to show that he would have been very unlikely to say that the stars borrowed their light from the sun as is expressed in the above *Venus and Adonis* quotation:—

> If our world be small in respect, why may we not suppose a plurality of worlds, those infinite stars visible in the firmament to be so many suns, with particular fixed centres; to have likewise their subordinate planets, as the sun hath his dancing still round him? B. p. 327

Burton, moreover, had knowledge of a great variety of subjects and he had also the faculty of bringing together ideas from these to make acceptable and illuminating simile or metaphor. Thus from his knowledge of astronomy, religion and human cupidity he was able to write:—

> As the Moon when she is fuller of light is still farthest from the Sun, the more wealth they have, the farther they are commonly from God. B. p. 389

Anomalies in characterization

In reading the great works of "Shakespeare" one experiences a feeling of trust that the author is sincere in depicting his characters, attributing to them consistent words and deeds, and one is confused when, as does happen, gross inconsistencies appear. Careful reading, however, will show that the offending passages contain also inconsequential and commonplace detail couched often in poorly constructed, dowdy prose or verse and these characteristics occurring together lead one to suspect the presence of two authors. It is noteworthy, moreover, that such flaws occur here and there in late as well as in early works. We read in the early poem *Venus and Adonis* (lines 589-595):—

> 'The boar!' quoth she, whereat a sudden pale,
> Like lawn being spread upon the blushing rose,
> Usurps her cheek; she trembles at his tale,
> And on his neck her yolking arms she throws;
> She sinketh down, still hanging by his neck,
> He on her belly falls, she on her back.
> Now is she in the very lists of love, [etc.]

At one moment Venus is pale and trembles; at the next she is in the very lists of love.

In *The Rape of Lucrece* we find unexpected insincerity in Lucrece's lament (lines 1359-65):—

> But long she thinks till he return again,
> And yet the duteous vassal scarce is gone.
> The weary time she cannot entertain,
> For now 'tis stale to sigh, to weep, and groan;
> So woe hath wearied woe, moan tired moan,
> That she her plaints a little while doth stay,
> Pausing for means to mourn some newer way.

My attention was drawn to this verse by F. J. Furnival, who quotes* "and a curious remark at lines 1364-5 seems to point out the non-spontaneous nature of some of the work." I assume that Furnival would not have objected to my substituting 'insincere' for "non-spontaneous" and then this passage could be compared in its insincerity with that in *King Richard III*, IV, 4, 343-365, quoted earlier in this chapter.

So also it is disconcerting to find near the end of the poem a dispute between Collatine and Lucretius over the newly dead Lucrece:—

> Who should weep most for daughter or for wife. Line 1792

However, it is in the plays that inconsistencies in character, if occurring at all, would be most likely to be found and found they can be. Previous students have commented on at least some of these, though they do not always, as I do, give double authorship as explanation. I shall begin by quoting Arthur Symons on *Titus Andronicus*. He writes†: ". . . his afflicted heroine [Lavinia] fills her mouth with the grossest and vilest insults against Tamora—so gross, so vile, so unwomanly, that her punishment becomes something of a retribution instead of being wholly a brutality. There is every dramatic reason why the victim should not share the villain's soul, every dramatic reason why her situation should be pure pathos. Nothing but the coarseness of nature in the man who first wrote it can explain the absurdity." I agree with this verdict and ask the reader to consider whether or not coarseness of an author is the only explanation for discrepancies such as:—

1. Juliet in *Romeo and Juliet*, according to the nurse's story (Act I, Sc. 3), was a bawdy three-year-old, yet she is chaste when fourteen (Act II, Sc. 2).

2. Mercutio in the same play is as foul-mouthed as Lavinia, yet he is the friend of Romeo and Benvolio.

3. After being coarsely disavowed in church (*Much Ado About Nothing*, IV, 1, 55), Hero, the Governor's daughter, marries her

* Forewords (p. xix), *Shakespeare's Lucrece*, The First Quarto, 1594; Facsimile by Charles Pretorius. Furnival is quoting P. Z. Round.

† Introduction (p. xii) Facsimile, *Titus Andronicus*, 1st Quarto, 1600, by Charles Pretorius.

accuser without demur. This disavowal is closely paralleled by that of Posthumous (*Cymbeline*, II, 5, 1). Posthumous includes his dead father and mother in his diatribe, yet this same father and mother make earnest plea for Posthumous in the dream (*Cymbeline*, V, 4, 30-68).

However it is not only through being coarse that inconsistencies arise: mere lack of interest in characters can be detected. Two outstanding and remarkably similar examples of this are to be found in the characters—Margaret in *Much Ado About Nothing* and Emilia in *Othello*. Presumably devotedly in the case of Margaret and clearly devotedly in the case of Emilia, they each attend a mistress who has been wrongly accused and in each case they are in possession of information which, if disclosed, would show their respective mistress to be guiltless of the charge preferred. Yet neither says one word (at least not at the time that mattered). Had their author allowed them asides to make a plea, such as that of divided loyalty, one would have been satisfied but merely to ignore the situation shows clearly a lack of interest by their author.

Othello himself is peculiarly depicted in that it is not until IV, 1, 44-57 that the unexpected disclosure is made that he suffers from epilepsy. We read in Plutarch (p. 60 of Carr's edition) that Cæsar was "often subject to headache, and otherwhile to the falling sickness . . . but yet therefore yielded not to the disease of his body, to make it a cloak to cherish him withal, but, contrarily, took the pains of war as a medicine to cure his sick body, fighting always with his disease, travelling continually, living soberly, and commonly lying abroad in the field." Othello, like Cæsar, endured great hardships in war (*Othello*, I, 3, 128-170) but no mention of epilepsy is made in the early Acts, which is most strange if we are prepared, foolishly, to allow that the author of *Julius Cæsar* afterwards wrote the worthless Act IV, Sc. 1 of *Othello*.

So also, in Macbeth's characterization, discrepancies occur. He has been depicted very carefully throughout the early Acts, yet Malcolm is allowed to say casually:—

I grant him bloody,
Luxurious, avaricious, false, deceitful,
Sudden, malicious, smacking of every sin
That has a name. *Macbeth*, IV, 3, 57

Bradley* commenting on these lines says "two of these epithets surprise us. Who would have expected avarice and lechery in Macbeth?" I would add, in passing, that the two full lines quoted are both Alexandrines', the first a very poor one, and also that much of this scene is taken from Holinshed and only poorly dramatized.

* *Shakespearean Tragedy*; Macmillan, 1912, p. 363.

Symons (*loc. cit.* p. x) also wrote "Marlowe and Shakspere, it is sad to recollect, alike degraded their art, Marlowe more than once, Shakspere at least once, to please the ears of the groundlings. The intentional debasement of Barabas, in the latter half of *The Jew of Malta*, from a creation into a caricature, is only equalled, but it is equalled, by that similar debasement of Falstaff, in *The Merry Wives of Windsor*, from the prophet and philosopher of this world's cakes and ale into an imbecile buffoon, helpless, witless, and ridiculous."

Another very inconsistent character is that of Richard III. In the early parts of the play he is a man of resource but in Act IV, Sc. 4 he is depicted as an irresolute weakling, as in the passage, lines 440-456, which ends in Richard saying "My mind is chang'd," or lines 508-516 ending in Richard saying to the Messenger:—

I cry thee mercy.
There is my purse to cure that blow of thine.

This is altogether a different Richard from the one who said:—

And buried, gentle Tyrrel? IV, 3, 28

Hazlitt writes* "We should like Jessica better if she had not deceived and robbed her father, and Lorenzo if he had not married a Jewess, though he thinks he has a right to wrong a Jew." I would add to Hazlitt by pointing out that Gratiano and Lorenzo both warmly approve of Jessica's action:—

Jes. I will make fast the doors, and gild myself
With some moe ducats, and be with you straight.
Gra. Now, by my hood, a gentle, and no Jew.
Lor. Beshrew me, but I love her heartily,
For she is wise, if I can judge of her,
And fair she is, if that mine eyes be true,
And true she is, as she hath prov'd herself;
And therefore, like herself, wise, fair, and true,
Shall she be placed in my constant soul.

The Merchant of Venice, II, 6, 49

All good fun, no doubt, but the question to be asked here is whether or not the writer of *A Midsummer Night's Dream* did in fact write, about the same time, stuff such as that. The reward which Jessica and Lorenzo get for their villainy is to be transported into a state of ecstatic bliss (V, 1, 1-88). The sudden consent of Shylock to become a Christian (IV, 1, 382-9) is merely stupid.

Cloten in most of the play *Cymbeline* is depicted as a brute and a braggart but in Act III, Sc. 1 he is brave, modest and pleasantly humorous (lines 11-14, 34-37, 39-44). Thus in early, middle and late plays we have an author who fails to depict consistent characters,

---

* *Characters of Shakespear's Plays*; Dent, p. 209.

and from this can be drawn the conclusion that he was, at least largely, insincere in his writings, a feature to which attention has been drawn twice previously in this chapter.

Shakespeare's wit

Andrew Lang (quoted in *A New Variorum Edition of Shakespeare*, edited by H. W. Furness; *Much Ado About Nothing*, J. B. Lippincott Company, 1904, p. 361) wrote:—

"We cannot be angry with the French for failing to see the point or edge of this lady's wit. It has occasionally no more point or edge than a bludgeon. For example:—

> *Benedict.* God keep your ladyship still in that mind! so some gentleman or other shall 'scape a predestinate scratched face.
>
> *Beatrice.* Scratching could not make it worse, an 'twere such a face as yours.

This kind of merry combat would be thought blunt by a groom and a scullion. There is no possibility of avoiding this distressing truth."

I would add to what Andrew Lang said by quoting the following example of very similar wit from *The Taming of the Shrew*, II, 1, 225:—

> *Pet.* Nay, come, Kate, come; you must not look so sour.
> *Kath.* It is my fashion, when I see a crab.
> *Pet.* Why, here's no crab; and therefore look not sour.
> *Kath.* There is, there is.
> *Pet.* Then show it me.
> *Kath.* Had I a glass I would.
> *Pet.* What, you mean my face?

There is no resemblance between such wit, which I consider to be Shakespeare's, and the implicit wit of Burton's Touchstone or Sir Toby.

An example of how commonplace Shakespeare could be in his attempt at wit is to be found in *The Merchant of Venice*, II, 2, 98:—

> I am famish'd in his service; you may tell every finger I have with my ribs.

A list of the works attributed to Shakespeare

Although I am certain that two authors contributed to the writings discussed in this book, I must confess it has been difficult for me to assign some of the passages to Shakespeare or to Burton and the ability to do so has been an evolving one. Thus the list has been altered in detail quite often. Acts, scenes and lines are inclusive. Although this list implies that Burton wrote Act III, Sc. 2 of *As You Like It*, I consider that the grossly offending lines to be found in this scene must have been interpolated.

The Tempest - - -	II, 1.
The Two Gentlemen of Verona	I, 3, 1-77; II, 7-V, 3.
The Merry Wives of Windsor	All of it.
Measure for Measure - -	V, 1, 1-377.
The Comedy of Errors - -	All of it.
Much Ado About Nothing -	All of it.
A Midsummer Night's Dream	IV, 2.
The Merchant of Venice -	I, 3-II, 8; II, 9, 84-end of play.
As You Like It - - -	II, 2; III, 1; IV, 2-3; V, 2-V, 4, 34; V, 4, 141-end of play.
The Taming of the Shrew -	II-V.
Twelfth Night - - -	II, 1; III, 3; III, 4, 295-356; IV, 3; V, 1, 44-end of play.
The Winter's Tale - -	II, 1, 33-IV, 2; IV, 4, 161-165; V, 1-3.
King John - - -	I-III, 2; V, 1-5.
King Richard II - - -	I, 1-3; II, 2, 86-III, 2, 143; III, 3, 1-126; IV, 1, 1-161.
King Henry IV, pt. 1 - -	I, 3; II, 3; III, 1; IV, 3-end of play.
King Henry IV, pt. 2 - -	IV, 1-3.
King Henry V - - -	I, 2; IV, 8, 71-124.
King Henry VI, pt. 1 - -	All of it.
King Henry VI, pt. 2 - -	I, 1; I, 3; II, 2-3.
King Henry VI, pt. 3 - -	I-II, 4; II, 6; III, 2-3; IV-V, 5.
King Richard III - -	I, 3, 1-338; IV, 4, 132-V, 3, 176; V, 5.
King Henry VIII - -	I-II; IV, 1; V, 5. *N.B.*—It is considered by many that Fletcher contributed to this play.
Troilus and Cressida - -	I, 1-2.
Titus Andronicus - -	All of it.
Romeo and Juliet - -	I-II, 1; II, 4-V, 3, 44; V, 3, 170-309.
Timon of Athens - -	II-III; IV, 3, 166-168; V.
Julius Cæsar - - -	II, 2, 108-II, 4, 45.
Macbeth - - - -	IV, 2-3.
Hamlet - - - -	I, 1-I, 2, 63; I, 2, 160-257; II, 2, 1-169; III, 1, 1-55; III, 1, 162-188; III, 3, 1-35; IV, 1; IV, 3; IV, 5-7; V, 2, 353-395.
King Lear - - -	II-III, 1; III, 3; III, 5.

Othello - - - -	III, 1-3, 75; III, 3, 281-334; III, 4-V, 2, 340.
Antony and Cleopatra - -	I, 2-5; II, 2-6; III, 1-9; V, 1-V, 2, 224; V, 2, 317–363.
Cymbeline - - - -	II-III, 1; III, 5; III, 7; IV, 1; IV, 3; V, 5.
Venus and Adonis - -	All of it.
The Rape of Lucrece - -	All of it.

This massive array of authorship shows that Shakespeare was a man of great energy and purpose and used his poetic and dramatic talents extensively in order to achieve his aim. To him must go the credit for laying the foundations of his own success and I would be grieved if I, mistakenly, have tried to deprive him of the laurels of world's greatest dramatic poet. I do believe he has been awarded insignia, which properly belong to Burton. The evidence for this award, be it noted, was never published in print by Shakespeare. He retired to Stratford without ostentation and his Will makes no mention of any writings. All claim to greatness was thrust upon him by posterity. I now proceed to try to thrust greatness upon Burton, or, more correctly, to try to add to the measure of greatness already accorded to him, by at least a few, for his masterpiece, *The Anatomy of Melancholy*.

Chapter VI

WHY BURTON?

In Chapter V, I endeavoured to show that at least two authors contributed to the "Shakespeare" canon. One of these I have shown, gratuitously perhaps, to be William Shakespeare. The other I have claimed to be Robert Burton but, beyond giving, in my Chapter II, quotations indicating that Burton was a poet and a dramatist and one much esteemed of Johnson and others and pointing out, in my Chapter IV, the important fact that Burton did not quote one single great passage from Shakespeare, I have not yet given my readers data sufficient to warrant such a claim. That the writer of the great plays was an outstanding genius is a truism and therefore I must be able to show that Burton was an outstanding genius and one like to "Shakespeare". There are justifiable objections to such a claim. If Burton contributed to the plays, why did he not say so? The answer might well be in his own words (already quoted), "I would not willingly be known." Johnson did study both Shakespeare and Burton, yet he did not claim that Burton was Shakespeare. Also, though "Shakespeare" still receives universal acclaim, *The Anatomy of Melancholy*, comparatively, is little heard of. Against such objections I place the opinions of Donnelly, Horr, Parker and Osler and what is to follow in this book.

In my succeeding chapters I shall deal more fully with Burton's poetry, his great vocabulary and the great similarity in thought between the author of "Shakespeare" and Burton. Here, lest my reader's interest begin to wane, I show a few highlights to indicate that Burton could have written "Shakespeare".

Burton as poet

Only a man with the mind of a great poet could have written the following:—

1. Constantine *de Agric. lib.* 10. *Cap.* 4 gives an instance out of Florentius his Georgics, of a palm-tree that loved most fervently, "and would not be comforted until such time her love applied herself unto her; you might see the two trees bend, and of their own accords stretch out their boughs to embrace and kiss each other: they will give manifest signs of mutual love". B. p. 492

2. Copernicus, Atlas his successor, is of opinion, the earth is a planet, moves and shines to others, as the moon doth to us. B. p. 43. *Note:* the highly poetic first four words of this quotation.

3. Had he not taken a quill from Cupid's wings, he could never have written so amorously as he did. B. p. 580.

4. The lanthorn in Athens was built by Zenocles, the theatre by Pericles, the famous port Pyræum by Musicles, Pallas Palladium by Phidias, the Pantheon by Callicratidas; but these brave monuments are decayed all, and ruined long since, their builders' names alone flourish by meditation of writers. And as he said of that Marian oak, now cut down and dead, *nullius Agricolæ manu culta stirps tam diuturna quam quæ poetæ versu seminari potest*, no plant can grow so long as that which is *ingenio sata*, set and manured by those ever living wits. Allon Bachuth, that weeping oak, under which Deborah, Rebecca's nurse, died, and was buried, may not survive the memory of such everlasting monuments. Vain glory and emulation . . . B. p. 488.

Note: Speaking personally, no passage in Shakespeare moves me more than does this fourth quotation. Be that as it may, Burton does not make tedious comment on the passage; having written it he passes on to something else—Hazlitt's lightning. "Decayed all and ruined long since" is a clear example of beautiful thought expressed in eminently fitting words, the twin characteristics of the so-called Shakespeare verse. Did two poets with such ability live in the same age or was there but one?

Burton could write both English and Latin verse. His English poems are given in Chapter IX. In Chapter XI I give, in full, parallel passages from *The Tempest*, III, 1, 14 and from *The Anatomy of Melancholy*, B. p. 162. There are in brief:—

Most busy, least when I do it—*The Tempest.*

Never more busy than when he seemed to be most idle—*The Anatomy.*

The importance of these two passages cannot be too strongly emphasized as they show that their author (or authors, if doubters must have it so) was a true poet whose mind was capable of receiving by intuition valuable poetic impressions. A distinctive feature of the works of "Shakespeare" is that the mind of their author must have been sensitized by extensive previous learning else he could not have written:—

1. First for his weeping into the needless stream

As You Like It, II, 1, 46,

borrowed no doubt from:—

"*O me miserum!*

Quis dabit in lacrimas fontem"

quoted by Burton at B. p. 406 and to which Shilleto gives reference—Stroza;

2. I'll go find a shadow and sigh till he comes

As You Like It, IV, 1, 194,

borrowed no doubt from Gerbelius, a version of the relevant passage, along with its reference, being given by Burton at B. p. 579;
3. The beast
With many heads butts me away. *Coriolanus*, IV, 1, 1, adapted from "*bellua multorum capitum*" which Burton quotes at B. p. 678 and to which Shilleto gives reference, Hor. Epp. 1, 1, 76.

These and many other passages, apparently borrowed from previous authors, are quoted, alongside their parallel from Burton, in Chapter XI. Thus Burton had a truly poetic mind and also a learning-sensitized mind, the twin requisites for the author of "Shakespeare's" works.

Burton as genius

Burton gives the following among his reasons for writing *The Anatomy of Melancholy*: "Besides, I might not well refrain, for *Ubi dolor, ibi digitus*, one must needs scratch where it itches. I was not a little offended with this malady, shall I say my Mistress 'Melancholy,' my Ægeria, or my *malus genius*" B. p. 5. I believe that the plays as well as *The Anatomy* are products of this genius. Even to this day it is sometimes said that "Shakespeare" wrote for money, but plays much less subtle than the great works would have served such a purpose equally well, or better, and one can conclude that their author was urged from within to write in the same way as Burton was urged from within to toil till his dying day to compile *The Anatomy*.

Burton (or "Shakespeare") as mathematician

Wood's character of him is that "he was an exact mathematician . . ." B. p. IX (of Introduction). In his Will, Burton's entered the clause:—"I give to John Fell the Dean's Son Student my Mathematical Instruments except my two Crosse Staves which I give to my Lord of Donnol if he be then of the House" and in "Shakespeare" we read:—

O, pardon! since a crooked figure may
Attest in little place a million;
And let us, ciphers to this great accompt,
On your imaginary forces work. *King Henry V*, 1st Prologue.

(See also Chapter XI, below, at *The Winter's Tale*, I, 2, 6.)

Burton (or "Shakespeare") as ecologist

The following example is given as illustrating that the author of "Shakespeare" was profoundly interested in ecology and more particularly in garden ecology:—

Fie on't! Ah, fie! 'tis an unweeded garden,
That grows to seed; things rank and gross in nature
Possess it merely. *Hamlet*, I, 2, 135

The author shows his great sympathy with flowers and that he understood the operation of competition in gardens. He also showed his keen powers of applying the metaphor to human affairs. Exactly similar powers appertain to Burton as exemplified in this passage (B. p. 43):—"This melancholy extends itself not to men only, but even to vegetals and sensibles. I speak not of those creatures which are saturnine, melancholy by nature, as lead, and such like minerals, or those plants, rue, cypress, etc. and hellebore itself, of which Agrippa treats, fishes, birds, and beasts, hares, conies, dormice, etc., owls, bats, nightbirds, but that artificial, which is perceived in them all. Remove a plant, it will pine away, which is especially perceived in date trees, as you may read at large in Constantine's husbandry, that antipathy betwixt the vine and the cabbage, vine and oil. Put a bird in a cage, he will die for sullenness, or a beast in a pen, or take his young ones or companions from him, and see what effect it will cause. But who perceives not these common passions of sensible creatures, fear, sorrow, etc. Of all other, dogs are most subject to this malady, insomuch some hold they dream as men do, and through violence of melancholy run mad; I could relate many stories of dogs that have died for grief, and pined away for loss of their masters, but they are common in every author." Five other very fine illustrations of his interest in ecology are:—(i) As the Reed and Fern in the Emblem averse and opposite in nature. B. p. 604; (ii) The soul is alien to the body, a nightingale to the air, a swallow in a house. B. p. 405; (iii) As some birds hatch eggs by turns. B. p. 633; (iv) Sheep, saith Dion, mend a bad pasture. B. p. 50; (v) Our climes breed lice, Hungary and Ireland *malè audiunt* in this kind; come to the Azores, by a secret virtue of that air they are instantly consumed. B. p. 320. To take some examples from "Shakespeare":—

> The strawberry grows underneath the nettle,
> And wholesome berries thrive and ripen best
> Neighbour'd by fruit of baser quality. *King Henry V*, I, 1, 60

> Now 'tis the spring, and weeds are shallow rooted;
> Suffer them now, and they'll o'ergrow the garden
> And choke the herbs for want of husbandry.
> *King Henry VI*, pt. 2, III, 1, 31

> Anon, as patient as the female dove
> When that her golden couplets are disclos'd,
> His silence will sit brooding. *Hamlet*, V, 1, 280

Burton writes of himself: "I am *verè Saturnus*; no man ever took more delight in springs, woods, groves, gardens, walks, fishponds, rivers, etc." B. p. 343.

N.B.—See also *Addenda*, p. 334.

BURTON (OR "SHAKESPEARE") AS PSYCHOLOGIST

As Dr. Bucknill, a physician especially interested in mental illness, has written a book* showing Shakespeare's great interest in psychology, there is no need for me to elaborate. That Burton was a pre-eminent student of psychology is open for all to read in *The Anatomy of Melancholy*. Thus he was able to write "As the saying is, they dream of that they desire." B. p. 279. I do recommend particularly the sections on *The Anatomy of the Soul* (Part. 1, Sec. 1, Mem. 2, Subs. 5-11 (B. pp. 98-108)). Bergen Evans†, in consultation with George J. Mohr, M.D., points out Burton's great interest in psychology. Those interested in animal psychology are invited to turn to the parallel passages at *Hamlet*, I, 2, 150 in Chapter XI, below.

BURTON (OR "SHAKESPEARE") AS PHYSICIAN

In modern times, when the effect of the mind on the body is becoming increasingly realized, it is illuminating to notice how clearly this aspect of medicine was appreciated by Burton:—"If he desire ought, let him be satisfied; if in suspense, fear, suspicion, let him be secured: and if it may conveniently be, give him his heart's content; for the body cannot be cured till the mind be satisfied. Socrates, in Plato, would prescribe no physic for Charmides' headache, 'till first he had eased his troubled mind; body and soul must be cured together, as head and eyes.' " B. p. 365. My reader will recall:—

> Cure her of that
> Canst thou not minister to a mind diseas'd,
> Pluck from the memory a rooted sorrow. *Macbeth*, V, 3, 39

BURTON (OR "SHAKESPEARE") AS PUZZLE-SETTER

I feel convinced that the author of "Shakespeare" took a delight in writing a line and then saying to his reader, 'Now! tell me, to which passage in literature does that make reference?' My reader will find examples of this on reading Chapter XI. In the following passage Burton sets two puzzles:—"I must for that cause [lack of assistants] do my business myself, and was therefore enforced, as a bear doth her whelps, to bring forth this confused lump; I had not time to lick it into form, as she doth her young ones, but even so to publish it, as it was first written *quicquid in buccam venit*, in an extemporean style, as (Footnote:—*Stans pede in uno*, as he made verses) I do commonly all other exercises, *effudi quicquid dictavit*

---

* *The Psychology of Shakespeare*; Longman, Brown, Green, Longmans & Roberts, 1859.

† *The Psychiatry of Robert Burton*; Columbia University Press, 1944.

genius meus, out of a confused company of notes, and writ with as small deliberation as I do ordinarily speak, without all affectation of big words, fustian phrases, jingling terms, tropes, strong lines, that like Alcesta's arrows caught fire as they flew, strains of wit, brave heats, elogies, hyperbolical exornations, elegancies, etc., which many so much affect. I am (Footnote:—*Non eadem à summo expectes, minimoque poeta**) *aquæ potor*, drink no wine at all, which so much improves our modern wits, a loose, plain, rude writer, *ficum voco ficum, et ligonem ligonem*, and as free, as loose, *idem calamo quod in mente*, I call a spade a spade, *animis hæc scribo, non auribus*, I respect matter not words; remembering that of Cardan, *verba propter res, non res propter verba:* and seeking with Seneca *quid scribam, non quemadmodum*, rather *what* than *how* to write: for as Philo thinks, 'He that is conversant about matter, neglects words, and those that excel in this art of speaking, have no profound learning'." B. p. 11.

The footnote, "*Stans pede in uno*, as he made verses," to the words "As I do commonly all other exercises" is tantalizingly laconic in the same way as are many great passages in "Shakespeare". The words "As I do *commonly* all *other* exercises" may be taken (legitimately I think) to mean that Burton did many exercises other than *The Anatomy of Melancholy* and this may be a reference to his "Shakespeare" plays for his known writings, other than *The Anatomy*, were *Philosophaster* and a number of minor poems which could scarcely justify the use of the word "commonly". The footnote also may be taken to indicate that his "other exercises" were "verses".

The second footnote with its context is, I think, clearer. It brings to my mind a quotation from Emerson's essay, *The Poet*:—"Milton says that the lyric poet may drink wine and live generously, but the epic poet, he who shall sing of the gods, and their descent unto men, must drink water out of a wooden bowl." Carlyle stresses this same point in his essay, *Burns*. Beveridge,† discussing the conditions suitable for the appearance of intuitions, writes "it is notable that only very few consider that they get any assistance from tobacco, coffee or alcohol." Burton touches on this theme again when he writes "Melancholy . . . improves their meditations more than any strong drink or sack." B. p. 257. "Shakespeare" praises "honest water." *Timon of Athens*, I, 2, 57.

Burton set his last puzzle in his epitaph:—

"*Paucis notus, paucioribus ignotus.*"

---

* Shilleto gives ref. Juv. I, 14, but Burton has re-arranged Juvenal's words and added "*non*" so that the meaning conveyed is 'You may not look for these themes to arise even from the most costly, the poet expects them from the most simple.'

† *The Art of Scientific Investigation*; Heinemann, 2nd Edit., 1953, p. 77.

BURTON (OR "SHAKESPEARE") ON EDUCATION

Burton realized the indebtedness of individual man to previous writers and that human thought has evolved through the ages:— "We can say nothing but what has been said, the composition and method is ours only, and shows a scholar. Oribasius, Æsius, Avicenna, have all out of Galen, but to their own method, *diverso stilo, non diversâ fide*. Our poets steal from Homer; he spews, saith Ælian, they lick it up. Divines use Austin's words *verbatim* still, and our story-dressers do as much; he that comes last is commonly best. . . . Though there were many giants of old in Physic and Philosophy, yet I say with Didacus Stella, 'A dwarf standing on the shoulders of a giant may see farther than a giant himself'; I may likely add, alter, and see farther than my predecessors." B. p. 8.

The manner of acquisition of knowledge clearly interested Burton. He realized that "There is nothing in the understanding, which was not first in the sense." B. p. 106. He loved study— "such sweet content there is in study." B. p. 351; "Whosoever he is therefore that is overrun with solitariness, or carried away with pleasing melancholy and vain conceits, and for want of employment knows not how to spend his time, or crucified with worldly care, I can prescribe him no better remedy than this of study." B. p. 352. He did not, however, confine his activities to book learning nor did he advise others to do so, "What more pleasing studies can there be than the mathematics, theoretical or practical parts? as to survey lands, make maps, models, dials, etc., with which I was ever much delighted myself." B. p. 350. "Our modern divines are too severe and rigid against mathematicians; ignorant and peevish, in not admitting their true demonstrations and certain observations." B. p. 327. "If the theory or speculation can so much affect, what shall the place and exercise itself: the practical part do?" B. p. 343. "'*Quid subtilius Arithmeticis inventionibus, quid jucundius Musicis rationibus, quid divinius Astronomicis, quid rectius Geometricis demonstrationibus?* [What is more subtile than arithmetical conclusions? what more agreeable than musical harmonies? what more divine than astronomical? what more certain than geometrical demonstrations? *Shilleto's Translation.*] What vast tomes are extant in law, physic, and divinity, for profit, pleasure, practice, speculation, in verse or prose, etc.!" B. p. 349. "But in all nature what is there so stupendous as to examine and calculate the motion of the planets, their magnitudes, apogees, perigees, eccentricities, how far distant from the earth, the bigness, thickness, compass of the firmament, each star, with their diameters and circumference, apparent area, superficies, by those curious helps of glasses, astrolabes, sextants, quadrants, of which Tycho Brahé in his mechanics, optics (divine optics), arithmetic, geometry, and such like arts and instruments?" B. p. 353.

Burton's emphasis on the practical is well illustrated in the following, to my mind remarkable, passage:—". . . those famous public gardens of Padua in Italy, Nuremburg in Germany, Leyden in Holland, Montpelier in France (and ours in Oxford now in *fieri*, at the cost and charges of the Right Honourable the Lord Danvers, Earl of Danby), are much to be commended, wherein all exotic plants almost are to be seen, and liberal allowance yearly made for their better maintenance, that young students may be the sooner informed in the knowledge of them: which as Fuchsius holds, 'is most necessary for that exquisite manner of curing,' and as great a shame for a physician not to observe them, as for a workman not to know his axe, saw, square, or any tool which he must of necessity use." B. p. 431; and, again, "so much knowledge, so many preachers, so little practice." B. p. 26; and in forthright manner:— "Many poor men, younger brothers, etc., by reason of bad policy and idle education (for they are likely brought up in no calling), are compelled to beg or steal, and then hanged for theft." B. p. 32.

So also in "Shakespeare" we find great stress laid on the value of education, both theoretical and practical:—

1. Knowing I lov'd my books, he furnish'd me
From mine own library with volumes that
I prize above my dukedom. *The Tempest*, I, 2, 166

2. Here in this island we arriv'd; and here
Have I, thy schoolmaster, made thee more profit
Than other princess' can, that have more time
For vainer hours, and tutors not so careful.
The Tempest, I, 2, 171

3. First to possess his books; for without them
He's but a sot, as I am, nor hath not
One spirit to command; they all do hate him
As rootedly as I. Burn but his books.
He has brave utensils—for so he calls them—
The Tempest, III, 2, 88

4. Balk logic with acquaintance that you have,
And practice rhetoric in your common talk;
Music and poesy use to quicken you;
The mathematics and the metaphysics,
Fall to them as you find your stomach serves you.
No profit grows where is no pleasure ta'en;
In brief, sir, study what you most affect.
The Taming of the Shrew, I. 1, 34

5. I say there is no darkness but ignorance.
Twelfth Night, IV, 2, 41

6. *Per.* . . . ., the fairest flow'rs o' th' season
Are our carnations and streak'd gillyvors,
Which some call nature's bastards. Of that kind
Our rustic garden's barren; and I care not
To get slips of them.
. . . .
Pol. Then make your garden rich in gillyvors,
And do not call them bastards.

The Winter's Tale, IV, 4, 81-99

7. I am not taught to make any thing.

As You Like It, I, 1, 27

8. This is Monsieur Parolles, the gallant militarist—that was his own phrase—that had the whole theoric of war in the knot of his scarf, and the practice in the chape of his dagger.

All's Well That Ends Well, IV, 3, 133

9. So that the art and practic part of life
Must be the mistress of this theoric.

King Henry V, I, 1, 51

10. Forsooth, a great arithmetician,
One Michael Cassio, a Florentine,
A fellow almost damn'd in a fair wife,
That never set a squadron in a field,
Nor the division of a battle knows
More than a spinster; unless the bookish theoric,
Wherein the toged consuls can propose
As masterly as he—mere prattle, without practice,
Is all his soldiership. *Othello*, I, 1, 19

11. It must be so; for miracles are ceas'd
And therefore we must needs admit the means
How things are perfected. *King Henry V*, I, 1, 67

These last three lines are among the most profound that "Shakespeare" wrote. That Burton was abreast of the thought contained in them is shown in the words:—"So sweet is the delight of study, the more learning they have (as he that hath a dropsy, the more he drinks the thirstier he is), the more they want to learn, and the last day is *prioris discipulus*." (B. p. 351). [The perfection of today (the last day) is the result of the study and practice (the means) of former (*prioris*) days.]

Having copied out these eleven passages from the works that orthodox opinion attributes to Shakespeare, I digress to re-emphasize that there is no evidence that Shakespeare gave much, if indeed any, attention to the education of his own two daughters. Greenwood writes (p. 196):—"And here we are brought face to face with an astounding fact. Mrs. Hall could at any rate manage to affix her signature to a document, though probably 'this was the extent of her chirographical ability.' But her sister Judith, 'the poet's' younger daughter, was unable to write her name."

Burton's tolerance and catholicism

He was a tolerant person who wrote the great plays as witnessed, for example, in his reference to cakes and ale (see *Twelfth Night*, II, 3, 110 and *Othello*, II, 3, 289 and 298 in Chapter XI below). When one considers the controversy between differing religions and between science and religion that has gone on in the past and is still not at an end, it is interesting to read what Burton wrote over three hundred years ago:—

1 . . . as you may read in the third epistle of Busbequius, "that all those should participate of eternal happiness, that lived a holy and innocent life, what religion soever they professed." B. p. 703.

2. [Burton quotes Seneca and Austin] "What is Nature but God?" call him what thou wilt, Nature, Jupiter, he hath as many names as offices: it comes all to one pass, God is the fountain of all, the first Giver and Preserver, from whom all things depend . . . God is all in all, God is everywhere, in every place. B. p. 708.

3. Others freely speak, mutter, and would persuade the world (as Marinus Marcenus complains) that our modern divines are too severe and rigid against mathematicians; ignorant and peevish, in not admitting their true demonstrations and certain observations, that they tyrannize over art, science, and all philosophy, in suppressing their labours (saith Pomponatius), forbidding them to write, to speak a truth, all to maintain their superstition, and for their profit's sake. B. p. 327.

4. [He appreciates the insignificance of the earth in the vast universe, following Tycho Brahé in saying that] "he will never believe those great and huge bodies [the stars] were made to no other use than this that we perceive, to illuminate the earth, a point insensible in respect of the whole." B. p. 327.

5. Why so many thousand strange birds and beasts proper to America alone, as Acosta demands, *Lib.* 4. *cap.* 36. were they created in six days or ever in Noah's ark? B. p. 319.

Burton's powers of illustration

A most admirable feature of "Shakespeare" is his ability to give concrete illustrations. Burton excelled in this quality. Take for example this one passage among many such:—

Hadst thou Sampson's hair, Milo's strength, Scanderbeg's arm, Solomon's wisdom, Absolom's beauty, Crœsus's wealth, *Pasetis obolum*, Cæsar's valour, Alexander's spirit, Tully's or Demosthenes' eloquence, Gyges' ring, Perseus' Pegasus, and Gorgon's head,

Nestor's years to come, all this would not make thee absolute, give thee content and true happiness in this life, or so continue it. B. p. 182.

By apt use of imagery "Shakespeare" arrests the attention and sets alight the imagination of the reader or hearer, making him pause to think out the full significance of what is being dealt with. Thus the drag of many words is avoided:—

If you can look into the seeds of time
And say which grain will grow and which will not,
Speak then to me. *Macbeth*, I, 3, 58

Look like th' innocent flower,
But be the serpent under 't. *Macbeth*, I, 5, 62

Had he not resembled
My father as he slept, I had done't. *Macbeth*, II, 2, 12

What should be spoken
Here, where our fate, hid in an augur-hole,
May rush and seize us? *Macbeth*, II, 3, 120

Attention has already been drawn by Steevens (see Chapter II above) to the profusion of apt illustration in *The Anatomy*. Here I wish to quote a few only, or as Burton himself would have put it, "Here and there I pull a flower." B. p. 12:—

1. His ruin is a ladder to a third. B. p. 33
2. Frost and fraud come to foul ends. B. p. 208
3. The lightning commonly sets on fire the highest towers. B. p. 388
4. Thou hast enough: he that is wet in a bath, can be no more wet if he be flung into Tiber or into the ocean itself. B. p. 397
5. As a shadow leaves the body when the sun is gone, I am now left and lost, and quite forsaken of the world. B. p. 399
6. Adrian the sixth pope was so highly offended, and grievously vexed with Pasquillers at Rome, he gave command that his statue should be demolished and burned, the ashes flung into the river Tiber, and had done it forthwith, had not Lodovicus Suessanus, a facete companion, dissuaded him to the contrary, by telling him, that Pasquil's ashes would turn to frogs in the bottom of the river, and croak worse and louder than before. B. p. 222 (section dealing with *Scoffs*, *Calumnies*, *Bitter Jests*)
7. I find this reason given by some men, because they have been formerly naught themselves, they think they may be so served by others, they turned up trumps before the cards were shuffled; they shall have therefore *legem talionis*, like for like. B. p. 635 (section dealing with *Causes of Jealousy*)

To have to give the prize for the greater subtlety or the more apt illustration to either set of quotations would incur making a difficult choice. However, it is highly probable that no such decision is necessary, one and the same hand having created them all or, in the case of borrowed material, fitted it into its proper place.

A most remarkable passage occurs near the beginning of *The Merchant of Venice*:—

My wind, cooling my broth,
Would blow me to an ague when I thought
What harm a wind too great might do at sea.
I should not see the sandy hour-glass run
But I should think of shallows and of flats,
And see my wealthy Andrew dock'd in sand,
Vailing her high top lower than her ribs
To kiss her burial. Should I go to church
And see the holy edifice of stone,
And not bethink me straight of dangerous rocks,
Which, touching but my gentle vessel's side,
Would scatter all her spices on the stream,
Enrobe the roaring waters with my silks,
And, in a word, but even now worth this,
And now worth nothing? I, 1, 22

The writer of this passage realized clearly that the human mind has the power to associate ideas nearly, or remotely, similar to one another. This fact was plain to Burton. He writes (B. pp. 101-2) "Phantasy, or imagination, which some call estimative, or cogitative (confirmed, saith Fernelius, by frequent meditation), is an inner sense which doth more fully examine the species perceived by common sense, of things present or absent, and keeps them longer, recalling them to mind again, or making new of his own. In time of sleep this faculty is free, and many times conceives strange, stupend, absurd shapes, as in sick men we commonly observe. His organ is the middle cell of the brain; his objects all the species communicated to him by the common sense, by comparison of which he feigns infinite other unto himself." That Burton was as able as "Shakespeare" to employ this faculty in his writings can be seen from the many comparisons that he makes throughout *The Anatomy*. To add one more to those already given:—

As in Mercury's weather-beaten statue, that was once all over gilt, the open parts were clean, yet there was *in fimbrüs aurum*, in the chinks a remnant of gold: there will be some relics of melancholy left in the purest bodies (if once tainted) not so easily to be rooted out. B. p. 282

Sentences, such as that one, introduce one to realms of thought which, for the most part, are not dealt with in the plays. All that is needed for the purposes of this present book is to emphasize that in *The Anatomy of Melancholy* the range of thought is wider than that of *The Plays of "Shakespeare"* and includes it. There was no possibility that Burton copied "Shakespeare": besides having a thousand books of his own, he had access to books from the Bodleian and he quotes, with references, a multitude of authors, a task not done by "Shakespeare". The plays are a product of his early life, *The Anatomy* of his later when he had a greater build-up of knowledge to draw on.

To return from this short digression; the subject of association of ideas by the imagination was one which greatly interested Burton. He writes:—"As the poet made answer to the husbandman in Æsop, that objected idleness to him; he was never so idle as in his company; or that Scipio Africanus in Tully, *Nunquam minus solus, quàm cum solus; nunquam minus otiosus, quàm quum esset otiosus;* never less solitary, than when he was alone, never more busy, than when he seemed to be most idle. B. p. 162. Beveridge (p. 75) expresses a similar thought when he writes of the intuition becoming active while one is "pottering in the garden."

The following passage is one of the puzzles referred to above:—

And so the Prince obscur'd his contemplation
Under the veil of wildness; which, no doubt,
Grew like the summer grass, fastest by night,
Unseen, yet crescive in his faculty.

King Henry V, I, 1, 63

It appears to me that this passage refers to the continuing activity during sleep ("by night") of the imagination or, in other words, the unconscious ("unseen") part of the mind. On B. p. 101 and again on B. p. 102 Burton says that during sleep the imagination or phantasy is free and it is noteworthy that he also uses the word "faculty". His words on B. p. 101 are "In time of sleep this faculty is free." If my reader wishes to call in Burton to help with the word "crescive" let him turn to B. p. 11, where he can read "*Non eadem est ætas, non mens,*" [The age of a man does not remain the same, nor does his mind]. It is the present author's hope that the parallel passages quoted in Chapter XI, below, will shed light on many passages in "Shakespeare".

Burton's apt arrangement of words

Hazlitt* wrote "Shakspeare's language and versification are like the rest of him. He has a magic power over words: they come winged at his bidding; and seem to know their places." The reader will find in this and the following chapters many examples from *The Anatomy of Melancholy* of words knowing their places; to take a few:—

---

* *Lectures On The English Poets and Spirit Of The Age.* Everyman's Library No. 459, p. 54.

1. Bats, Owls the shady bowers over,
In melancholy darkness hover.

. . . .

Beneath them kneeling on his knee,
A superstitious man you see:
He fasts, prays, on his Idol fixt,
Tormented hope and fear betwixt:
For hell perhaps he takes more pain
Than thou dost heaven itself to gain.
Alas poor soul, I pity thee,
What stars incline thee so to be?

From *The Argument of the Frontispiece*

2. The delight it is, which I aim at, so great pleasure, such sweet content there is in study . . . harsh at first learning is, *radices amaræ*, but *fructus dulces*, according to that of Isocrates, pleasant at last; the longer they live, the more they are enamoured with the Muses. B. p. 351

3. Beyond all hope and expectation many things fall out, and who knows what may happen? B. p. 401

4. Fret not thyself because thou art poor, contemned, or not so well for the present as thou wouldest be, not respected as thou oughtest to be, by birth, place, worth; or that which is a double corrosive, thou hast been happy, honourable, and rich, art now distressed and poor, a scorn of men, a burden to the world, irksome to thyself and others, thou hast lost all.
B. p. 401

5. We must so be gone sooner or later all, and as Calliopeius in the comedy took his leave of his spectators and auditors, *Vos valete et plaudite, Calliopeius recensui*, must we bid the world farewell (*Exit* Calliopeius), and having now played our parts, for ever be gone. B. p. 409

6. Philocharinus, in Aristænetus, met a fair maid by chance, a mere stranger to him, he looked back at her, she looked back at him again, and smiled withal. B. p. 531

7. Witty Lucian in that pathetical love passage, or pleasant description of Jupiter's stealing of Europa, and swimming from Phœnicia to Crete, makes the sea calm, the winds hush, Neptune and Amphitrite riding in their chariot to break the waves before them, the tritons dancing round about, with every one a torch, the sea-nymphs half-naked, keeping time on dolphins' backs, and singing *Hymeneus*, Cupid nimbly tripping on the top of the waters, and Venus herself coming after in a shell, strewing roses and flowers on their heads.
B. p. 577

8. Is it not a man in woman's apparel? is not somebody in that great chest, or behind the door, or hangings, or in some of those barrels? May not a man steal in at the window with a ladder of ropes, or come down the chimney, have a false key, or get in when he is asleep? If a mouse do but stir, or the wind blow, a casement clatter, that's the villain, there he is.

B. p. 641

Yes, there he is! Observe, also, in these passages that succession of short, compact phrases, noticed, in Chapter V under heading "Contrasts in Construction", to be typical of "Shakespeare"!

Chapter VII

BURTON'S VOCABULARY

Sir Edwin Durning-Lawrence in his book* writes as follows:—

> "Max Müller in his 'Science of Language,' Vol. 1, 1899, p. 379, says:—'A well-educated person in England, who has been at a public school and at the University . . . seldom uses more than about 3,000 or 4,000 words. . . . The Hebrew Testament says all that it has to say with 5,642 words, Milton's poetry is built up with 8,000; and Shakespeare, who probably displayed a greater variety of expression than any writer in any language . . . produced all his plays with about 15,000 words'."

Need for a large vocabulary in order to write the works of "Shakespeare" creates no difficulty when one is considering the authenticity of Burton as their author: Burton had an immense vocabulary, as a passage (one of many such) taken from *The Anatomy* (B. p. 3) will illustrate:—

> I hear new news every day, and those ordinary rumours of war, plagues, fires, inundations, thefts, murders, massacres, meteors, comets, spectrums, prodigies, apparitions, of towns taken, cities besieged in France, Germany, Turkey, Persia, Poland, &c., daily musters and preparations, and such like, which these tempestuous times afford, battles fought so many men slain, monomachies, shipwrecks, piracies, and sea-fights; peace, leagues, stratagems, and fresh alarms. A vast confusion of vows, wishes, actions, edicts, petitions, lawsuits, pleas, laws, proclamations, complaints, grievances, are daily brought to our ears. New books every day, pamphlets, currantoes, stories, whole catalogues of volumes of all sorts, new paradoxes, opinions, schisms, heresies, controversies in philosophy, religion, &c. Now come tidings of weddings, maskings, mummeries, entertainments, jubilees, embassies, tilts and tournaments, trophies, triumphs, revels, sports, plays: then again, as in a new shifted scene, treasons, cheating tricks, robberies, enormous villanies in all kinds, funerals, burials, deaths of princes, new discoveries, expeditions, now comical, then tragical matters. To-day we hear of new lords and officers created, to-morrow of some great men deposed, and then again of fresh honours conferred; one is let loose, another

* *Bacon is Shakespeare*; Gay & Hancock, London, 1910, p. 66.

> imprisoned; one purchaseth, another breaketh: he thrives, his neighbour turns bankrupt: now plenty, then again dearth and famine; one runs, another rides, wrangles, laughs, weeps, &c. Thus I daily hear, and such like, both private and public news, amidst the gallantry and misery of the world: jollity, pride, perplexities and cares, simplicity and villany; subtlety, knavery, candour and integrity, mutually mixed and offering themselves.

That passage shows not only evidence of a huge vocabulary but also of an interest in many and widely different subjects so that the oft-referred-to feature of "Shakespeare", namely his multifarious knowledge, is adequately explained by accepting Burton as joint-author. Burton writes of himself (B. p. 2):—

> Something I have done, though by my profession a divine, yet *turbine raptus ingenii*, as he said, out of a running wit, an unconstant, unsettled mind, I had a great desire (not able to attain to a superficial skill in any) to have some smattering in all, to be *aliquis in omnibus, nullus in singulis*, which Plato commends, out of him Lipsius approves and furthers, "as fit to be imprinted in all curious wits, not to be a slave of one science, or dwell together in one subject, as most do, but to rove abroad, *centum puer artium*, to have an oar in every man's boat, to taste of every dish, and sip of every cup," which, saith Montaigne, was well performed by Aristotle, and his learned countryman Adrian Turnebus. This roving humour (though not with like success) I have ever had, and like a ranging spaniel, that barks at every bird he sees, leaving his game, I have followed all, saving that which I should, and may justly complain, and truly, *qui ubique est, nusquam est*, which Gesner did in modesty, that I have read many books, but to little purpose, for want of good method; I have confusedly tumbled over divers authors in our libraries, with small profit for want of art, order, memory, judgment.

The Anatomy shows a knowledge of divinity, medicine, psychology, ecology, law, history, geography, astronomy, astrology, folk lore, sport, agriculture, horticulture and logic. "Shakespeare's" works show a similar range of interests and a merit of both sets of writings is the use of the actual words currently used in practice. On the sport of fowling Burton writes (B. p. 339):—

> Fowling is more troublesome, but all out as delightsome to some sorts of men, be it with guns, lime, nets, glades, gins, strings, baits, pitfalls, pipes, calls, stalking-horses, setting-dogs, decoy-ducks, etc., or otherwise . . . to go abroad with their quail-pipes. . . . The Italians have gardens fitted to such use, with nets, bushes, glades.

So also in "Shakespeare" we find:—

> He uses his folly like a stalking-horse, and under the presentation of that he shoots his wit. *As You Like It*, V, 4, 100
>
> The bird that hath been limed in a bush
> With trembling wings misdoubteth every bush.
> *King Henry VI*, pt. 3, V, 6, 13

Whilst dealing with the subject of language, it is worthy of note that Burton was given high praise by the great philologist Samuel Johnson, who said (see Preface B. p. xiii) that *The Anatomy of Melancholy* was the only book that took him out of bed two hours sooner than he wished to rise. We can assume from this that Burton's command of language did commend itself to Johnson. I have given, in Chapter V, examples of passages, which from the poor diction and wrong use of words were considered to have been written by an inferior writer. They certainly were not written by a great philologist. More proof that parts of Shakespeare were not written by a philologist can usefully be given here; Mercutio in *Romeo and Juliet*, II, 4, 38, says "O flesh, flesh, how art thou fishified!" Is it at all likely that a philologist would have coined such an ugly hybrid word or would he have said that Z is an unnecessary letter as is indicated in *King Lear*, II, 2, 58.

Chapter VIII

BURTON'S STYLE

Burton's extensive and varied reading placed a wide knowledge at his disposal; this, combined with a logical mind and great powers of exact, condensed and yet still poetic expression, enabled him to produce passages like the following one from B. p. 325:—

> Or to omit all smaller controversies, as matters of less moment, and examine that main paradox, of the earth's motion, now so much in question: Aristarchus, Samius, Pythagoras maintained it of old, Democritus and many of their scholars, Didacus Astunica, Anthony Fascarinus, a Carmelite, and some other commentators, will have Job to insinuate as much, *cap.* 9. *ver.* 4. *Qui commovet terram de loco suo*, &c., and that this one place of scripture makes more for the earth's motion than all the other prove against it; whom Pineda confutes most contradict. Howsoever, it is revived since by Copernicus, not as a truth, but a supposition, as he himself confesseth in the preface to Pope Nicholas, but now maintained in good earnest by Calcagninus, Telesius, Kepler, Rotman, Gilbert, Digges, Galileo, Campanella, and especially by Lansbergius, *naturæ, rationi, et veritati consentaneum*, by Origanus, and some others of his followers. For if the earth be the centre of the world, stand still, and the heavens move, as the most received opinion is, which they call *inordinatum cœli dispositionem*, though stiffly maintained by Tycho, Ptolemeus, and their adherents, *quis ille furor?* &c., what fury is that, saith Dr. Gilbert, *satis animosè*, as Cabeus notes, that shall drive the heavens about with such incomprehensible celerity in twenty-four hours, when as every point of the firmament, and in the equator, must needs move (so Clavius calculates) 176,660 in one 246th part of an hour: and an arrow out of a bow must go seven times about the earth whilst a man can say an Ave Maria, if it keeps the same space, or compass the earth 1884 times in an hour, which is *supra humanam cogitationem*, beyond human conceit: *ocyor et jaculo, et ventos æquante sagitta.* A man could not ride so much ground, going 40 miles a day, in 2904 years, as the firmament goes in 23 hours: or so much in 2.03 years, as the firmament in one minute: *quod incredibile videtur:* and the pole-star, which to our thinking, scarce moveth out of its place, goeth a bigger circuit than the sun, whose diameter is much larger than the diameter

of the heaven of the sun, and 20,000 semi-diameters of the earth from us, with the rest of the fixed stars, as Tycho proves.

That is a difficult passage on an erudite theme. For contrast, and to illustrate the wide range of this writer, examine this simple, yet how beautiful, passage from B. p. 367:—

> "It makes a child quiet," the nurse's song, and many times the sound of a trumpet on a sudden, bells ringing, a carman's whistle, a boy singing some ballad tune early in the street, alters, revives, recreates a restless patient that cannot sleep in the night.

or this one from B. p. 396:—

> Let him be my lord, patron, baron, earl, and possess so many goodly castles, 'tis well for me that I have a poor house, and a little wood, and a well by it.

Although well acquainted with academic and technical words Burton did not despise the everyday expression or illustration, as the following examples show:—

> 'Tis pride and vanity that eggs them on. B. p. 6
>
> They [written papers] serve to put under pies, to lap spice in, and keep roast-meat from burning. B. p. 6
>
> Our poets steal from Homer; he spews, saith Ælian, they lick it up. B. p. 8
>
> Heraclitus . . . fell a weeping . . . Democritus on the other side, burst out a laughing. B. pp. 21-22
>
> Teach others to fast, and play the gluttons themselves. B. p. 27
>
> Scarce any conveyance so accurately penned by one, which another will not find a crack in. B. p. 48
>
> How many goodly cities could I reckon up, that thrive wholly by trade, where thousands of inhabitants live singular well by their fingers' ends. B. p. 51
>
> Their poor children are so disheartened and cowed. B. p. 218
>
> Some prescribe a sup of vinegar [Footnote:—*Aceti sorbito*] as they go to bed. B. p. 357
>
> A fat prebend fell void. The carcass scarce cold . . . B. p. 416
>
> And sometimes again, so that it be discreetly and moderately done, it shall not be amiss to make resistance, to take down such a saucy companion, no better means to vindicate himself to purchase final peace: for he that suffers himself to be ridden, or through pusillanimity or sottishness will let every man baffle him, shall be a common laughing stock to flout at. B. p. 423
>
> The first night, having liberally taken his liquor . . . my fine scholar was so fusled . . . B. p. 634
>
> Whether it be a greater sin to kill a man, or to clout shoes upon a Sunday? B. p. 698

They are certainly far gone with melancholy, if not quite mad, and have more need of physic than many a man that keeps his bed. B. p. 700

An old sybil coming to his house, or a holy woman (as that place yields many), took him down for it. B. p. 701

Experience teacheth us, that though many die obstinate and wilful in this malady, yet multitudes again are able to resist and overcome, seek for help and find comfort, are taken *è faucibus Erebi*, from the chops of hell, and out of the devil's paws. B. p. 723

Similarly in "Shakespeare" we find:—

Then slip I from her bum, down topples she,
And 'tailor' cries, and falls into a cough.
A Midsummer Night's Dream, II, 1, 53

They may jowl horns together like any deer i' th' herd.
All's Well That Ends Well, I, 3, 52

Leave thy vain bibble-babble. *Twelfth Night*, IV, 2, 93

I prithee tell me, doth he keep his bed?
King Henry IV, pt. 1, IV, 1, 21

Call me pantler, and bread-chipper.
King Henry IV, pt. 2, II, 4, 304

Pride alone
Must tarre the mastiffs on, as 'twere their bone.
Troilus and Cressida, I, 3, 390

You'll bear me a bang for that. *Julius Cæsar*, III, 3, 18

Till he unseam'd him from the nave to th' chaps.
Macbeth, I, 2, 22

To leave no rubs nor botches in the work.
Macbeth, III, 1, 133

For it hath cow'd my better part of man. *Macbeth*, V, 8, 18

It is generally recognised that a feature of "Shakespeare's" work is the effective use of simile, metaphor and epigram, either original or adapted from sayings of common usage or the writings of others. Burton in his *Anatomy* shows similar powers as illustrated by the following and it is worthy of note that many of Burton's sayings are current today:—

Better do to no end, than nothing. B. p. 5

Magno conatu nihil agimus. B. p. 7

Not valuing the metal, but the stamp that is upon it. B. p. 9

Quot homines, tot sententiæ. B. p. 9

Or had he but observed the common people follow like so many sheep one of their fellows drawn by the horns over the gap. B. p. 27

Such streams of blood able to turn mills. B. p. 27

Prosperum et fœlix scelus, virtus vocatur. B. p. 31

Or some corrupt Judge, that like the Kite in Æsop, while the mouse and frog fought, carried both away. B. p. 33

As that stupid fellow put out the candle because the biting fleas should not find him; he shrouds himself in an unknown habit, borrowed titles, because nobody should discern him. B. p. 37

"And they are the veriest asses that hide their ears most." B. p. 37

As Pliny said, a law and example to himself. B. p. 37

Like Æsop's fox, when he had lost his tail, would have all his fellow foxes cut off theirs. B. p. 37

A fool still begins to live. B. p. 40

Nemo malus fœlix. B. p. 41

Qualis Rex, talis grex. B. p. 46

So that he that goes to law, as the proverb is, holds a wolf by the ears, or as a sheep in a storm runs for shelter to a brier, if he prosecute his cause he is consumed, if he surcease his suit he loseth all; what difference? B. p. 47

Industry is a loadstone to draw all good things. B. p. 50

When a country is overstocked with people, as a pasture is oft overlaid with cattle, they had wont in former times to disburden themselves, by sending out colonies, or by wars, as those old Romans. B. p. 53

We contemn this benefit of carriage by waters, and are therefore compelled in the inner parts of this island, because portage is so dear, to eat up our commodities ourselves, and live like so many boars in a sty, for want of vent and utterance. B. p. 55

He that deserves best shall have best. B. p. 61

Procul à Jove, procul à fulmine. B. p. 65

Ovum prius exstiterit an gallina? B. p. 67

A fool and his money are soon parted. Footnote, B. p. 69

The greatest enemy to man, is man. B. p. 84

Una hirundo non facit æstatem. Footnote, B. p. 92

Perditio tua ex te B. p. 163

By hook and by crook he will obtain it. B. p. 185

Like a hog, or a dog in a manger, he doth only keep it, because it shall do nobody else good. B. p. 188

When they know they come as far short, as a mouse to an elephant, of any such virtues. B. p. 193

"See thou twist not the rope so hard, till at length it break." B. p. 199

They are like grasshoppers, sing they must in summer, and pine in the winter, for there is no preferment for them. B. p. 203

As a dog barks at the moon, to no purpose are your sayings. B. p. 207
Frost and fraud come to foul ends. B. p. 208
No penny, no pater-noster, as the saying is. B. p. 211
The best is always best cheap. B. p. 212
Sed nolo diutius hanc movere sentinam. B. p. 215
Say poor and say all. B. p. 229
Ex musca elephantem. B. p. 257
As the fool thinketh, so the bell clinketh. B. p. 280
Though many times, as Æsop's fishes, they leap from the frying-pan into the fire itself. B. p. 283
Nothing new under the sun. B. p. 330
For as mastication is to meat, so is meditation on that which we read. B. p. 353
Galen, the common master of them all, from whose fountain they fetch water. B. p. 359
Like so many frogs in a puddle. B. p. 373
Make a virtue of necessity. B. p. 376
It is sweet to draw from a great heap. B. p. 388
The lightning commonly sets on fire the highest towers. B. p. 388
As a tree that is heavy laden with fruit breaks her own boughs, with their own greatness they ruin themselves. B. p. 388
And as the Moon when she is fuller of light is still farthest from the Sun, the more wealth they have, the farther they are commonly from God. B. p. 389
He that hath birds, may catch birds. B. p. 398
As a shadow leaves the body when the sun is gone, I am now left and lost, and quite forsaken of the world. B. p. 399
Cut thy coat according to thy cloth. B. p. 402
Monachus in urbe, piscis in arido. B. p. 405
An old fox is not so easily taken in a snare. B. p. 413
Self do, self have, as the saying is. B. p. 419
According to the Dutch proverb, a new physician must have a new church-yard. B. p. 427
Natura non admittit vacuum B. p. 463
Birds of a feather will gather together. B. p. 479
They will stick together like burrs. B. p. 479
Mulus mulum scabit. B. p. 479
Every crow thinks her own bird fairest. B. p. 479
We . . . hold one another's noses to the grindstone hard. B. p. 486
Like the dog in the manger, we neither use it ourselves, let others make use of or enjoy it. B. p. 487
Facilis descensus Averni. B. p. 497

God makes, they say, man shapes. B. p. 524
Their heart is at their mouth. B. p. 552
Ubi amor, ibi oculus. B. p. 554
Drink to him with her eyes. B. p. 554
Pruriens corpus, pruriens anima B. p. 579
Look before ye leap. B. p. 595
But if she be not so to me, what care I how kind she be. B. p. 600
Aliorum naturam ex suâ vitiosâ mente spectavit. B. p. 631
Comparisons are odious. B. p. 632
Stolen waters be more pleasant. B. p. 636
If it be withstood in the beginning, maturely resisted, and as those ancients hold, "the nails of it be pared before they grow too long." B. p. 646
Duci volunt, non cogi. B. p. 650
More irons in the fire. B. p. 676
A silly company of poor souls that follow all and are cluttered together like so many pebbles in a tide. B. p. 677
Fasting . . . The mother of health, key of heaven, a spiritual wing to ereare us, the chariot of the Holy Ghost, banner of faith. B. p. 681
Scold like butter-women. B. p. 684
Ex ungue leonem. B. p. 684
What is Nature but God. B. p. 708
When they are at Rome, they do there as they see done. B. p. 711
Yet it [thy faith] may revive, as trees are dead in winter, but flourish in the spring. B. p. 727
We must live by faith, not by feeling. B. p. 736

The Cowden Clarkes* (Vol. 1, page 19, footnote) write:—"Shakespeare's style is full of this kind of ellipsis. He is so condensed a writer, that we have constantly to bear this in mind, while gathering the full sense of his concise passages." Burton was a very concise author and ellipses often occur as the following examples show:—

Better do to no end, than nothing. B. p. 5
He is a good huntsman, can catch some, not all. B. p. 12
Never a barrel better herring. B. p. 43
Those five outward senses have their object in outward things only and such as are present, as the eye sees no colour except it be at hand, the ear sound. B. p. 100

* "The Plays of Shakespeare". Edited and Annotated by Charles and Mary Cowden Clarke; Cassell, Peter & Galpin, London.

The end is the object, which is desired or eschewed; as in a dog to catch a hare, etc. B. p. 103

If it trouble the mind; as it is diversely mixed, it produceth several kinds of madness and dotage: of which in their place. B. p. 112

Our fathers bad, and we are like to be worse. B. p. 140

Rachel envied her sister, being barren, *Gen.* XXX, Joseph's brethren him, *Gen.* XXXVII. B. p. 175

For I was ever like that Alexander in Plutarch, Crassus his tutor in philosophy, who, though he lived many years familiarly with rich Crassus, was even as poor when from (which many wondered at) as when he first came to him. B. p. 206

Misery and usury do commonly together. B. p. 241

Some laugh, weep; some are mad, some dejected, moped, in much agony, some by fits, other continuate, etc. Some have a corrupt ear, they think they hear music, or some hideous noise as their phantasy conceives, corrupt eyes, some smelling: some one sense, some another. B. p. 264

Scarce the meek, the contentious shall never find. B. p. 264

So say I of land, houses, moveables and money, mine today, his anon, whose tomorrow? B. p. 393

It never was, never will be. B. p. 703

Much of what I have written in this book may give the impression that Burton was devoid of humour and thus incapable of writing "Shakespeare." This is not so, as the following quotations show:—

But see the madman rage downright

. . . .

'Twixt him and thee there's no difference.

Argument of the Frontispiece

Pancreates in Lucian, wanting a servant as he went from Memphis to Coptus in Egypt, took a door bar, and after some superstitious words pronounced (Eucrates the relator was then present) made it stand up like a serving man. B. p. 11

Were it not that they are loath to lay out money on a rope, they would be hanged forthwith, and some die to save charges. B. p. 189

Or that poetic *Infernus*, where Homer's soul was seen hanging on a tree, etc., to which they ferried over in Charon's boat, or went down at Hermione in Greece, *compendiara ad inferos via*, which is the shortest cut, *quia nullum à mortuis naulum eo loci exposcunt* (saith Gerbelius), and besides there are no fees to be paid. B. p. 318

He . . . will admire the effects of art, or that engine of Archimedes, to remove the earth itself, if he had but a place to fasten his instrument. B. p. 349

Carmides in the said Lucian loved Philematium, an old maid of forty-five years; she swore to him she was but thirty-two next December. B. p. 544

And the good abbess in Bocaccio may in some sort witness, that rising betimes, mistook and put on the friar's breeches instead of her veil or hat. B. p. 548

Curl his head, prune his pickitivant, or if he wear it abroad, that the east side be correspondent to the west. B. p. 576

Chapter IX

BURTON'S POETRY

Those who make a case for Francis Bacon as author of Shakespeare's works have the difficulty of proving that Bacon was a poet; with Burton no such difficulty arises. His *Anatomy* contains, besides the two English poems (*The Author's Abstract of Melancholy* and *The Argument of the Frontispiece*) and the Latin poem (*Democritus Junior ad Librum Suum*), large numbers of free translations rendered in poetic form from his beloved Latin. The two English poems are given in full to show Burton's powers of poetic composition and also to allow the reader to observe how closely *The Author's Abstract of Melancholy* resembles the *Sonnets* and how potentially dramatic is *The Argument of the Frontispiece.*

The Author's Abstract of Melancholy

When I go musing all alone,
Thinking of divers things fore-known,
When I build castles in the air,
Void of sorrow and void of fear,
Pleasing myself with phantasms sweet,
Methinks the time runs very fleet.
  All my joys to this are folly,
  Naught so sweet as melancholy.

When I lie waking all alone,
Recounting what I have ill done,
My thoughts on me then tyrannise,
Fear and sorrow me surprise,
Whether I tarry still or go,
Methinks the time moves very slow.
  All my griefs to this are jolly,
  Naught so sad as melancholy.

When to myself I act and smile,
With pleasing thoughts the time beguile,
By a brook side or wood so green,
Unheard, unsought for, or unseen,
A thousand pleasures do me bless.
And crown my soul with happiness.
  All my joys besides are folly,
  None so sweet as melancholy.

When I lie, sit, or walk alone,
I sigh, I grieve, making great moan,
In a dark grove, or irksome den,
With discontents and Furies then,
A thousand miseries at once
Mine heavy heart and soul ensconce,
  All my griefs to this are jolly,
  None as sour as melancholy.

Methinks I hear, methinks I see,
Sweet music, wondrous melody,
Towns, palaces, and cities fine;
Here now, then there; the world is mine,
Rare beauties, gallant ladies shine,
Whate'er is lovely or divine.
  All other joys to this are folly,
  None so sweet as melancholy.

Methinks I hear, methinks I see
Ghosts, goblins, fiends; my fantasy
Presents a thousand ugly shapes,
Headless bears, black men, and apes,
Doleful outcries, and fearful sights,
My sad and dismal soul affrights.
  All my griefs to this are jolly,
  None so damn'd as melancholy.

Methinks I court, methinks I kiss,
Methinks I now embrace my mistress.
O blessed days, O sweet content,
In Paradise my time is spent.
Such thoughts may still my fancy move,
So may I ever be in love.
  All my joys to this are folly,
  Naught so sweet as melancholy.

When I recount love's many frights,
My sighs and tears, my waking nights,
My jealous fits; O mine hard fate
I now repent, but 'tis too late.
No torment is so bad as love,
So bitter to my soul can prove.
  All my griefs to this are jolly,
  Naught so harsh as melancholy.

Friends and companions get you gone,
'Tis my desire to be alone;
Ne'er well but when my thoughts and I

Do domineer in privacy.
No Gem, no treasure, like to this,
'Tis my delight, my crown, my bliss.
  All my joys to this are folly,
  Naught so sweet as melancholy.

'Tis my sole plague to be alone,
I am a beast, a monster grown,
I will no light nor company,
I find it now my misery.
The scene is turn'd, my joys are gone,
Fear, discontent, and sorrows come.
  All my griefs to this are jolly.
  Naught so fierce as melancholy.

I'll not change life with any King,
I ravisht am: can the world bring
More joy, than still to laugh and smile,
In pleasant toys time to beguile?
Do not, O do not trouble me,
So sweet content I feel and see.
  All my joys to this are folly,
  None so divine as melancholy.

I'll change my state with any wretch,
Thou canst from gaol or dunghill fetch;
My pain's past cure, another hell,
I may not in this torment dwell,
Now desperate I hate my life,
Lend me a halter or a knife;
  All my griefs to this are jolly,
  Naught so damn'd as melancholy.

The Argument of the Frontispiece

Ten distinct Squares here seen apart,
Are joined in one by Cutter's art.

I.

Old Democritus under a tree,
Sits on a stone with book on knee;
About him hang there many features,
Of Cats, Dogs and such like creatures,
Of which he makes Anatomy,
The seat of Black Choler to see.
Over his head appears the sky,
And Saturn Lord of Melancholy.

II.

To the left a landscape of Jealousy,
Presents itself unto thine eye.
A Kingfisher, a Swan, an Hern,
Two fighting-Cocks you may discern,
Two roaring Bulls each other hie,
To assault concerning venery.
Symbols are these; I say no more,
Conceive the rest by that's afore.

III.

The next of Solitariness,
A Portraiture doth well express,
By sleeping Dog, Cat: Buck and Doe,
Hares, Conies in the desert go:
Bats, Owls the shady bowers over,
In melancholy darkness hover.
Mark well: If't be not as't should be,
Blame the bad Cutter, and not me.

IV.

I' th' under column there doth stand
Inamorato with folded hand;
Down hangs his head, terse and polite,
Some ditty sure he doth indite.
His lute and books about him lie,
As symptoms of his vanity.
If this do not enough disclose,
To paint him, take thyself by th' nose.

V.

Hypocondriacus leans on his arm,
Wind in his side doth him much harm,
And troubles him full sore, God knows,
Much pain he hath and many woes.
About him pots and glasses lie,
Newly brought from's Apothecary.
This Saturn's aspects signify,
You see them portray'd in the sky.

VI.

Beneath them kneeling on his knee,
A Superstitious man you see:
He fasts, prays, on his Idol fixt,
Tormented hope and fear betwixt:

For hell perhaps he takes more pain,
Than thou dost heaven itself to gain.
Alas poor soul, I pity thee,
What stars incline thee so to be?

VII.

But see the Madman rage downright
With furious looks, a ghastly sight.
Naked in chains bound doth he lie,
And roars amain he knows not why!
Observe him; for as in a glass,
Thine angry portraiture it was.
His picture keep still in thy presence;
'Twixt him and thee, there's no difference.

VIII, IX.

Borage and Hellebor fill two scenes,
Sovereign plants to purge the veins
Of Melancholy, and cheer the heart,
Of those black fumes which make it smart;
To clear the Brain of misty fogs,
Which dull our senses, and Soul clogs.
The best medicine that e'er God made
For this malady, if well assay'd.

X.

Now last of all to fill a place,
Presented is the Author's face;
And in that habit which he wears,
His image to the world appears.
His mind no art can well express,
That by his writings you may guess.
It was not pride, nor yet vain glory,
(Though others do it commonly),
Made him do this: if you must know,
The Printer would needs have it so.
Then do not frown or scoff at it,
Deride not, or detract a whit.
For surely as thou dost by him,
He will do the same again.
Then look upon't, behold and see,
As thou like'st it, so it likes thee.
And I for it will stand in view,
Thine to command, Reader, Adieu.

Not only could Burton write poetry in verse form; he could also write poetic and musical prose as the two following passages show:—

> As a long-winged hawk, when he is first whistled off the fist, mounts aloft, and for his pleasure fetcheth many a circuit in the air, still soaring higher and higher till he be come to his full pitch, and in the end, when the game is sprung, comes down amain, and stoops upon a sudden: so will I, having now come at last into these ample fields of air, wherein I may freely expatiate and exercise myself for my recreation, a while rove, wander round about the world, mount aloft to those ethereal orbs and celestial spheres, and so descend to my former elements again. B. p. 313

> "There is a time to mourn, a time to dance," *Eccles.* iii, 4. Let them take their pleasures then, and as he said of old, "young men and maids flourishing in their age, fair and lovely to behold, well attired, and of comely carriage, dancing a Greek galliard, and as their dance required, kept their time, now turning now tracing, now apart now altogether, now a courtesy then a caper," &c., and it was a pleasant sight to see those pretty knots, and swimming figures. The sun and moon (some say) dance about the earth, the three upper planets about the sun as their centre, now stationary, now direct, now retrograde, now *in apogee*, then *in perigee*, now swift then slow, occidental, oriental, they turn round, jump and trace.
>
> B. p. 542

Chapter X

PASSAGES IN "SHAKESPEARE" AUTOBIOGRAPHICAL OR BIOGRAPHICAL IF ATTRIBUTED TO BURTON

Thus Burton, in all *general* characteristics, resembles "Shakespeare"; Chapter XI of this book deals mainly with pointing out particular instances of circumstance, thought or expression in the *Plays* and *Sonnets* which are found to be paralleled or elucidated in the life and writings of Burton. Before proceeding to give these particulars, I wish to draw the reader's attention to the interesting fact that Shakespeare did visit Oxford presumably quite a number of times, as he appears to have been well known to the Davenants at the Crown Inn. It is generally believed that he stopped there on journeys between London and Stratford. This may have been so but there is no evidence that the visits to Oxford were at all related to visits to Stratford. I submit, by inference, that his visits to Oxford were for the purpose of discussing the plays with Burton. There is, however, no point in trying to elaborate this as I have no factual evidence.

From Oxford to Rome. In Act I, Sc. 1 of *Julius Cæsar* 2nd Citizen says "A trade, sir, that I hope I may use with a safe conscience, which is indeed, sir, a mender of bad soles. . . . I meddle with no tradesman's matters nor women's matter, but with awl." These passages are autobiographical if we accept as author Robert Burton who was a bachelor and a divine. In North's *Plutarch** the following passage occurs (p. 109): "There was one of Cæsar's friends called Cinna, that had a marvellous strange and terrible dream the night before. He dreamed that Cæsar bade him to supper, and that he refused, and would not go: then that Cæsar took him by the hand, and led him against his will. Now Cinna hearing at that time that they burnt Cæsar's body in the market-place, notwithstanding that he feared his dream, and had an ague on him besides: he went into the market-place to honour his funerals. When he came thither, one of the mean sort asked him what his name was? He was straight called by his name. The first man told it to another, and that other unto another, so that it ran straight through them all, that he was one of them that murthered Cæsar (for indeed one of the traitors to Cæsar was also called Cinna

* *Plutarch's Lives of Coriolanus, Cæsar, Brutus, and Antonius in North's Translation*. Edited by R. H. Carr, B.A., Oxford, at the Clarendon Press, 1906.

as himself): wherefore, taking him for Cinna the murtherer, they fell upon him with such fury, that they presently dispatched him in the market-place." Again [*ibid.*, p. 130], a similar account is given with the added information that Cinna was a poet. In the play (Act III, Sc. 3) Plutarch's account is altered; Cinna as poet is retained but he is also described as a bachelor and one who dwelt by the Capitol. Thus in Cinna we have three autobiographical aspects of Burton who was a poet, a bachelor and lived at Christ Church which is only a stonethrow from the Town Hall, the Oxford equivalent of the Roman Capitol.

These possibly autobiographical passages in *Julius Cæsar* are paralleled by a passage in *Twelfth Night*, Act III, Sc. 1:—

> *Viola.* Save thee, friend, and thy music! Dost thou live by thy tabor?
> *Clo.* No, sir, I live by the church.
> *Vio.* Art thou a churchman?
> *Clo.* No such matter, sir: I do live by the church; for I do live at my house, and my house doth stand by the church.
> *Vio.* So thou mayst say the king lies by a beggar, if a beggar dwell near him; or the church stands by thy tabor, if thy tabor stand by the church.

It is not known in which part of Christ Church Burton's chambers were situated but in any case it could have been said that he lived by the church in the sense that his rooms were near Christ Church Cathedral. It may be assumed that at the time *Twelfth Night* was written (around 1601) Burton did not hold office in the Cathedral, as he was not admitted to the reading of the Sentences until 1614.

George Brandes* appears surprised at the author's treatment of the man Julius Cæsar. "Cæsar," he writes, "was diminished and belittled to such a degree, unfortunately, that this matchless genius in war and statesmanship has become a miserable caricature." (Page viii of Introduction.) No surprise, however, need be felt if we allow that Burton wrote *Julius Cæsar*. He says (B. p. 28) "Cæsar killed a million," and (B. p. 406) "Alexander, Cæsar, Trajan, Adrian were as so many land-leapers, now in the east, now in the west, little at home." The freedom-loving, peace-loving Brutus would undoubtedly be Burton's preferred man, rather than the wandering, warmongering Cæsar, so little wonder that it is of Brutus, and not of Cæsar, that he writes:—

> This was the noblest Roman of them all. . . .
> His life was gentle; and the elements
> So mix'd in him that Nature might stand up
> And say to all the world 'This was a man.' V, 5, 68

---

* *Julius Cæsar* with an Introduction by George Brandes; William Heinemann, London, 1904.

In the short account of Burton's life given above (Chapter II) it is stated that Burton was born at Lindley in Leicestershire. A study of a map of this county will show that Lindley is only four miles or so from Bosworth Field, which fact, on the assumption that Robert Burton wrote the relevant part of the play, *King Richard The Third*, would have enabled Charles Knight to get over the difficulty of William Shakespeare possibly not having local knowledge. Knight writes* (p. 57):—"Burton [Knight here refers to William Burton, Robert's brother and author of *The Description of Leicestershire*] goes on to tell two stories connected with the eventful battle. The one was the vision of King Richard, of 'divers, fearful ghosts running about him, not suffering him to take any rest, still crying "Revenge".' Hall relates the tradition thus:—'The fame went that he had the same night a dreadful and a terrible dream, for it seemed to him, being asleep, that he saw divers images like terrible devils, not suffering him to take any quiet or rest.' Burton says, previous to his description of the dream, 'The vision is *reported* to be in this manner,' and certainly his account of the fearful ghosts 'still crying "Revenge" ' is essentially different from that of the chronicler. Shakespeare has followed the more poetical account of the old local historian; which, however, would not have been known to him:—

> 'Methought, the souls of all that I had murder'd
> Came to my tent: and every one did threat
> Tomorrow's vengeance on the head of Richard.'
>
> [K.R. *III*,, V, 3, 204]

Did Shakespeare obtain his notion from the same source as Burton—from 'relation of the inhabitants who have many occurrences and passages yet fresh in memory'."

Robert Burton could quite well have got this account of the dreams from the same source as his brother William.

In this book so far I have made only brief mention of the *Sonnets*; points of similarity between them and passages in *The Anatomy* will be found detailed in the next chapter. Here I wish to make three points only. Firstly, Sir Sidney Lee† and G. B. Harrison‡ consider that the first seventeen sonnets were addressed to a youth advising him to marry. There is no evidence however to show that these seventeen sonnets could not equally well have been addressed, in the second person, to the author himself provided that author were a bachelor, as Burton was. Indeed the last couplet of Sonnet 17—

---

* *A Biography of William Shakespeare*. Imperial Edition of the Works of Shakespeare, edited by Charles Knight; J. S. Virtue & Co., Ltd., London.

† *A Life of William Shakespeare;* John Murray, 1925. p. 166.

‡ *The Sonnets, and A Lover's Complaint;* Penguin, 1949, p. 14.

But were some child of yours alive that time,
You should live twice—in it, and in my rhyme

strongly suggests that this is so as *only* the author can truly be said to *live* in his works. In Sonnet 16, also, the words "pupil pen" suggest a young man as author. It is unlikely that one young man would address to another seventeen sonnets giving gratuitous advice to get married. And, secondly, Sonnet 59 beginning—

If there be nothing new, but that which is
Hath been before, how are our brains beguil'd,
Which labouring for invention bear amiss
The second burthen of a former child!

could hardly have been written but by a widely read, severe student, which Burton was and which on any available evidence Shakespeare was not. And, thirdly, I would agree with Sir Edwin Durning-Lawrence's* interpretation of Sonnet 81—

"Or shall I [Bacon] live your Epitaph to make,
Or you [Shakespeare] survive when I in earth am rotten,
From hence your memory death cannot take,
Although in me each part will be forgotten.
Your name [Shakespeare] from hence immortal life shall have,
Though I [Bacon] once gone to all the world must die,
The earth can yield me but a common grave,
When you entombed in men's eyes shall lie,
Your monument shall be my gentle verse,
Which eyes not yet created shall o'er read,
And tongues to be your being shall rehearse,
When all the breathers of this world are dead,
You [Shakespeare] still shall live, such vertue hath my pen,
Where breath most breathes, even in the mouths of men"

except that in each case of course the name Burton should replace "Bacon".

The line:—

Or as a moat defensive to a house. *King Richard II*, II, 1, 48

is interesting as Lindley Hall, where Burton was born, was a moated house. (See Title Page, *The Description of Leicestershire*, by William Burton, 1622.)

* *Bacon is Shakespeare*; Gay & Hancock, 1910, p. 71.

CHAPTER XI

PARALLEL QUOTATIONS FROM "SHAKESPEARE" AND BURTON

THE TEMPEST

that now he was
The ivy which had hid my princely trunk
And suck'd my verdure out on't. I, 2, 85*

As ivy doth by an oak, embrace it so long, until it hath got the heart out of it . . . B. p. 46†

Me, poor man—my library
Was dukedom large enough—of temporal royalties
He thinks me now incapable. I, 2, 109

how barbarously and basely, for the most part, our ruder gentry esteem of libraries and books, how they neglect and contemn so great a treasure, so inestimable a benefit, as Æsop's cock did the jewel he found in the dunghill. B. p. 351

Good wombs have borne bad sons. I, 2, 120

Wise men beget commonly fools. B. p. 139

I, not remembering how I cried out then,
Will cry it o'er again; I, 2, 133

Things past, present, or to come, the remembrance of some disgrace, loss, injury, abuses, &c. troubles them now being idle afresh, as if it were new done; B. p. 255

Knowing I lov'd my books, he furnish'd me
From mine own library with volumes that
I prize above my dukedom. I, 2, 166

To be at leisure without books is another hell, and to be buried alive. Cardan calls a library the physic of the soul: B. p. 352

---

* This represents Act I Scene 2 Line 85 as given in *William Shakespeare—The Complete Works*, edited by Professor Peter Alexander; Collins, London and Glasgow, 1951.

† This represents page 46 of *The Anatomy of Melancholy*, Chatto & Windus, London, 1883. Burton divides his book into Partitions, Sections, Members and Subsections and, to help the reader, possessing editions other than this one, to find the originals, the page numbers covered by each Part. – Sect. – Mem. – Subsect.– in Chatto & Windus are given on pp. 335-336.

All the infections that the sun sucks up
From bogs, fens, flats, on Prosper fall, and make him
By inch-meal a disease! II, 2, 1

Varro *de re rust. lib.* 1 *cap.* 12 forbids lakes and rivers, marshy and manured grounds, they cause a bad air, gross diseases. B. p. 333
Crato, a German, commends east and south site . . . . free from putrefaction, fens, bogs, and muck-hills. B. p. 334

Then to sea, boys, and let her go hang. II, 2, 52

Or if it be not for his good, as Æneas, forewarned by Mercury in a dream, left Dido's love, and in all haste got him to sea. B. p. 595

Cal. Farewell, master; farewell, farewell!
Trin. A howling monster; a drunken monster!
Cal. No more dams I'll make for fish;
Nor fetch in firing
At requiring,
Nor scrape trenchering, nor wash dish.
'Ban 'Ban, Ca-Caliban,
Has a new master—Get a new man.
Freedom, high-day! high-day, freedom! freedom,
high-day, freedom! II, 2, 167

The most parable and easy, and about which many are employed, is to teach a school, turn lecturer or curate, and for that he shall have falconer's wages, ten pound per annum, and his diet, or some small stipend, so long as he can please his patron or the parish; if they approve him not (for usually they do but a year or two), as inconstant as they that cried "Hosanna" one day, and "Crucify him" the other; serving-man-like, he must go look a new master; . . . If he be a trencher chaplain in a gentleman's house . . . B. p. 202
idleness, love of liberty . . . cause many of us to be backward and remiss. B. p. 210

There be some sports are painful, and their labour
Delight in them sets off; some kinds of baseness
Are nobly undergone, and most poor matters
Point to rich ends. III, 1, 1

James Dubravius, that Moravian, in his book *de pisc.* telleth, how travelling by the highway side in Silesia, he found a nobleman, "booted up to the groins", wading himself, pulling the nets, and labouring as much as any fisherman of them all: and when some belike objected to him the baseness of his office, he excused himself, "that if other men might hunt hares, why should not he hunt carps?" Many gentlemen in like sort with us will wade up to the armholes upon such occasions, and voluntarily undertake that to satisfy their pleasure, which a poor man for a good stipend would scarce be hired to undergo. B. p. 339

This my mean task
Would be as heavy to me as odious, but
The mistress which I serve quickens what's dead,
And makes my labours pleasures. III, 1, 4

Amor mundum fecit, love built cities, *mundi anima*, invented arts, sciences, and all good things, incites us to virtue and humanity, combines and quickens. B. p. 475

Let the burden be never so heavy, love makes it light. B. p. 555

This love is that salt that seasoneth our harsh and dull labours. B. p. 579

But these sweet thoughts do even refresh my labours,
Most busy, least when I do it. III, 1, 14

N.B. The Cowden Clarkes* give the rendering:—
"These sweet thoughts refresh my labours, and make me most busy when I least work."

As the poet made answer to the husbandman in Æsop, that objected idleness to him; he was never so idle as in his company; or that Scipio Africanus in Tully, *Nunquam minus solus, quàm cum solus; nunquam minus otiosus, quàm quum esset otiosus;* never less solitary, than when he was alone, never more busy than when he seemed to be most idle. B. p. 162

For which foul deed
The pow'rs, delaying, not forgetting, have
Incensed the seas and shores. III, 3, 72

Ubi peccatum, ibi procella. [Where the sin, there "The Tempest."] B. p. 82

Nemesis comes after, *serò sed seriò*, stay but a little and thou shalt see God's just judgment overtake him. B. p. 419

Look thou be true; do not give dalliance
Too much the rein; the strongest oaths are straw
To th' fire i' th' blood. Be more abstemious,
Or else good night your vow! IV, 1, 51

---

* *The Plays of Shakespeare;* Cassell, Petter and Galpin.

As "hunger", saith Ambrose, "is a friend of virginity, so is it an enemy of lasciviousness, but fulness overthrows chastity, and fostereth all manner of provocations." B. p. 585

Ceres, most bounteous lady, thy rich leas
Of wheat, rye, barley, vetches, oats, and pease;
Thy turfy mountains, where live nibbling sheep,
And flat meads thatch'd with stover, them to keep;
Thy banks with pioned and twilled brims,
Which spongy April at thy hest betrims,
To make cold nymphs chaste crowns, and thy broom groves,
Whose shadow thy dismissed bachelor loves,
Being lass-lorn; thy pole-clipt vineyard;
And thy sea-marge, sterile and rocky hard,
Where thou thyself dost air—the Queen o' the sky,
Whose wat'ry arch and messenger am I,
Bids thee leave these; and with her sovereign grace,
Here on this grass-plot, in this very place,
To come and sport. IV, 1, 60

Leave your crisp channels. IV, 1, 130

I will not have a barren acre in all my territories, not so much as the tops of mountains; where nature fails, it shall be supplied by art: lakes and rivers shall not be left desolate. All common highways, bridges, banks, corrivations of waters, aqueducts, channels, public works, building, etc., out of a common stock, curiously maintained and kept in repair; no depopulations, engrossings, alterations of wood, arable, but by the consent of some supervisors that shall be appointed for that purpose, to see what reformation ought to be had in all places, what is amiss, how to help it, *et quid quaeque ferat regio, et quid quaeque recuset*, what ground is aptest for wood, what for corn, what for cattle, gardens, orchards, fishponds, etc. with a charitable division in every village. B. p. 58

They that live in the Orcades are registered by Hector Boethius and Cardan, to be of fair complexion, long-lived, most healthful, free from all manner of infirmities of body and mind, by reason of a sharp purifying air, which comes from the sea. B. p. 331

Constantine, *lib*. 2. *cap. de Agricult*. praiseth mountains, hilly, steep places, above the rest by the seaside.
[Chapter on *Air Rectified*] B. p. 333

You sunburnt sicklemen, of August weary,
Come hither from the furrow, and be merry;
Make holiday; your rye-straw hats put on,
And these fresh nymphs encounter every one
In country footing. IV, 1, 134

As all conditions shall be tied to their task, so none shall be over-tired, but have their set times of recreations and holidays, *indulgere genio*, feasts and merry meetings, even to the meanest artificer, or basest servant, once a week to sing or dance. B. p. 61

The cloud-capp'd towers, the gorgeous palaces,
The solemn temples, the great globe itself,
Yea, all which it inherit, shall dissolve,
And, like this insubstantial pageant faded,
Leave not a rack behind. IV, 1, 152

Kingdoms, provinces, towns, and cities, have their periods, and are consumed . . . the world itself must have an end: and every part of it . . . the names are only left, those at length forgotten, and are involved in perpetual night. B. p. 410

The world shall end like a comedy, and we shall meet at last in heaven, and live in bliss together, or else in conclusion, *in nihil evanescere.* B. p. 733

. . . and our little life
Is rounded with a sleep. IV, 1, 157

. . . death is but a perpetual sleep. B. p. 407

Advanc'd thus eyelids, lifted up their noses. IV, 1, 177

"When one [hart] hath driven his co-rival away, he raiseth his nose up into the air, and looks aloft, as though he gave thanks to nature," which affords him such great delight. B. p. 493

As they smelt music; so I charm'd their ears,
That calf-like they my lowing follow'd through
Tooth'd briers, sharp furzes, pricking goss, and thorns,
Which ent'red their frail shins. At last I left them
I' th' filthy mantled pool beyond your cell,
There dancing up to th' chins. IV, 1, 178

. . . so likewise those which Mizaldus called Ambulones, that walk about midnight on great heaths and desert places, which (saith Lavater) "draw men out of the way, and lead them all night a bye-way, or quite bar them of their way;" these have several names in several places; we commonly call them Pucks. B. p. 126

This was well done, my bird. IV, 1, 184

See, below, *Hamlet*, III, 4, 183.

We steal by line and level. IV, 1, 238

A great man in office may securely rob whole provinces, undo thousands, pill and poll, oppress *ad libitum.* B. p. 31

Pro. Go charge my goblins that they grind their joints
With dry convulsions, shorten up their sinews
With aged cramps, and more pinch-spotted make them
Than pard or cat o' mountain.
Ari. Hark, they roar. IV, 1, 257

We roar like bears, and mourn like doves, and want health, etc., for our sins and trespasses. B. p. 82

The diseases of the nerves, cramps, stupor, convulsion, tremor, palsy. B. p. 87

In the line-grove which weather-fends your cell. V. 1, 10

You shall know a village by a tuft of trees at or about it, to avoid those strong winds wherewith the island is infested, and cold winter blasts. B. p. 332

Hast thou, which art but air, a touch, a feeling
Of their afflictions, and shall not myself,
One of their kind, that relish all as sharply,
Passion as they, be kindlier mov'd than thou art? V, 1, 21

Something I can speak out of experience, *ærumnabilis experientia me docuit;* and with her in the poet, *Haud ignara mali miseris succurrere disco;* I would help others out of a fellow-feeling. B. p. 5

You demi-puppets that
By moonshine do the green sour ringlets make,
Whereof the ewe not bites. V, 1, 36

These are they that dance on heaths and greens, as Lavater thinks with Tritemius, and as Olaus Magnus adds, leave that green circle, which we commonly find in plain fields, which others hold to proceed from a meteor falling, or some accidental rankness of the ground, so nature sports herself. B. p. 124

et gramen non pereat. [Footnote to passage just given.] B. p. 124

. . . call'd forth the mutinous winds,
And 'twixt the green sea and the azur'd vault
Set roaring war. To the dread rattling thunder
Have I given fire, and rifted Jove's stout oak
With his own bolt; the strong bas'd promontory
Have I made shake and by the spurs pluck'd up
The pine and cedar. Graves at my command
Have wak'd their sleepers, op'd, and let 'em forth,
By my so potent art. V, 1, 42

Aerial spirits . . . cause many tempests, thunder, and lightnings, tear oaks. B. p. 123

. . . famous magicians . . . make them appear that died long since. B. p. 132

Why do witches and old women fascinate and bewitch children: but as Wierus, Paracelsus, Cardan, Mizaldus, Valleriola, Cæsar Vanninus, Campanella, and many philosophers think, the forcible imagination of the one party moves and alters the spirits of the other. Nay more, they can cause and cure not only diseases, maladies and several infirmities, by this means, as Avicenna *de anim. l.* 4. *sect.* 4. supposeth in parties remote, but move bodies from their places, cause thunder, lightning, tempests. B. p. 169

Mine eyes, ev'n sociable to the show of thine,
Fall fellowy drops. V, 1, 63

How can otherwise blear eyes in one man cause the like affection in another? Why doth one man's yawning make another yawn? One man's pissing provoke a second many times to do the like? B. p. 169

And as the morning steals upon the night,
Melting the darkness, so their rising senses
Begin to chase the ignorant fumes that mantle
Their clearer reason. V, 1, 65

Borage and *Hellebor* fill two scenes,
Sovereign plants to purge the veins
Of Melancholy, and cheer the heart,
Of those black fumes which make it smart;
To clear the brain of misty fogs,
Which dull our senses, and Soul clogs.

B. *The Argument of the Frontispiece.*

So that I may certainly conclude this strong conceit or imagination is *astrum hominis*, and the rudder of this our ship, which reason should steer, but overborne by fantasy cannot manage. B. p. 169

Thy soul is eclipsed for a time, I yield, as the sun is shadowed by a cloud; no doubt but those gracious beams of God's mercy will shine upon thee again, as they have formerly done. B. p. 736

I shall miss thee;
But yet thou shalt have freedom. So, so, so. V. 1, 95

And pity his case, that from the cradle to his old age beholds the same still; still, still the same, the same. B. p. 335

For you, most wicked sir, whom to call brother
Would even infect my mouth. V, 1, 130

. . . the vapour of the corrupt blood doth get in together with the rays, and so by the contagion the spectators' eyes are infected.
B. p. 520

I chose her when I could not ask my father
For his advice, nor thought I had one. V, 1, 190

So are all such matches made by those allurements of burning lust; where there is no respect of honesty, parentage, virtue, religion, education, and the like, they are extinguished in an instant, and instead of love comes hate; B. p. 530

I have inly wept,
Or should have spoke ere this. Look down, you gods,
And on this couple drop a blessed crown;
For it is you that have chalk'd forth the way
Which brought us hither. V, 1, 200

. . . when God sees his time, he will reveal these mysteries to mortal men, and show that to some few at last, which he hath concealed so long. For I am of his mind, that Columbus did not find out America by chance, but God directed him at that time to discover it: it was contingent to him, but necessary to God; he reveals and conceals to whom and when he will. B. p. 330

and all of us [found] ourselves
When no man was his own. V, 1, 212

. . . they should lead contented lives, and learning to know themselves would limit their ambition. B. p. 23

. . . and make them reflect and know themselves . B. p. 374

The Tempest

For all is but fortune. V, 1, 257

They supposed fortune alone gave kingdoms and empires, wealth, honours, offices. B. p. 709

He is as disproportion'd in his manners
As in his shape. V, 1, 290

They are, in brief, as disordered in their minds, as Thersites was in his body. B. p. 23

Gentle breath of yours my sails
Must fill, or else my project fails. Epilogue, line 11

. . . this one hath elegantly expressed by a windmill, still moved by the wind, which otherwise hath no motion of itself. *Sic tua ni spiret gratia, truncus ero*. He is wholly animated from her breath. B. p. 558

Which was to please. Epilogue, line 13

The comical poet . . . made this his only care and sole study to please the people, tickle the ear, and to delight; but mine earnest intent is as much to profit as to please. B. p. 469

The Two Gentlemen of Verona

Speed. You never saw her since she was deform'd.
Val. How long hath she been deform'd?
Speed. Ever since you lov'd her.
Val. I have lov'd her ever since I saw her, and still I see her beautiful.
Speed. If you love her, you cannot see her.
Val. Why?
Speed. Because Love is blind. II, 1, 56

Petrarch hath such another tale of a young gallant, that loved a wench with one eye, and for that cause by his parents was sent to travel into far countries, "after some years he returned, and meeting the maid for whose sake he was sent abroad, asked her how, and by what chance she lost her eye? no, said she, I have lost none, but you have found yours:" signifying thereby, that all lovers were blind, as Fabius saith, *Amantes de formâ judicare non possunt*, lovers cannot judge of beauty. B. p. 591

The Two Gentlemen of Verona

A man is never undone till he be hang'd — II, 5, 3

Divers have been recovered out of the very act of hanging and drowning themselves, and so brought *ad sanam mentem*. B. p. 723

Comfort thyself, no time is overpast, 'tis never too late. B. p. 728

Some are called at the eleventh hour. B. p. 732

If you wilt, go with me to the alehouse; if not, thou art an Hebrew, a Jew, and not worth the name of a Christian.
II, 5, 44

"How they love a man that will be drunk, crown him and honour him for it," hate him that will not pledge him, stab him, kill him; a most intolerable offence, and not to be forgiven. "He is a mortal enemy that will not drink with him," as Munster relates of the Saxons. B. p. 149

How use doth breed a habit in a man. — V, 4, 1

By art, discipline, custom, we get many bad habits. B. p. 107

Pro. . . . If hearty sorrow
Be a sufficient ransom for offence,
I tender't here; I do as truly suffer
As e'er I did commit.
Val. Then I am paid;
And once again I do receive thee honest.
Who by repentance is not satisfied
Is not of heaven nor of earth, for these are pleas'd;
By penitence th' Eternal's wrath's appeas'd. — V, 4, 74

Be penitent and heartily sorrow for thy sins. Repentance is a sovereign remedy for all sins, a spiritual wing to rear us, a charm for our miseries, a protecting amulet to expel sin's venom, an attractive loadstone to draw God's mercy and graces unto us.
B. p. 726

I will spare him because he hath not spared himself; I will pardon him because he doth acknowledge his offence. B. p. 735

Measure for Measure

Measure for Measure (title of play).

We have all our faults; *scimus, et hanc veniam*, &c.; thou censurest me, so have I done others, and may do thee. *Cedimus inque vicem*, &c., 'tis *lex talionis, quid pro quo*. B. p. 8

for if our virtues
Did not go forth of us, 'twere all alike
As if we had them not. I, 1, 34

I might be of Thucydides' opinion, "to know a thing and not to express it, is all one as if he knew it not." B. p. 5

Pom. All houses in the suburbs of Vienna must be pluck'd down. I, 2, 91

Mrs. Ov. But shall all our houses of resort in the suburbs be pull'd down. I, 2, 96

And this made the Romans, as Vitruvius relates, put Venus' temple in the suburbs, *extra murum, ne adolescentes venereis insuescant*, to avoid all occasions and objects. B. p. 535

As surfeit is the father of much fast,
So ever scope by the immoderate use
Turns to restraint. I, 2, 120

There is a loathing satiety of all things. B. p. 225

All excess, as Epictetus argues, will cause a dislike; sweet will be sour, which made that temperate Epicurus sometimes voluntarily fast. B. p. 390

. . . Lord Angelo, a man whose blood
Is very snow-broth, one who never feels
The wanton stings and motions of the sense,
But doth rebate and blunt his natural edge
With profits of the mind, study and fast. I, 4, 57

The second is contemplation, "which dries the brain and extinguisheth natural heat; for whilst the spirits are intent to meditation above in the head, the stomach and liver are left destitute . . ." B. p. 199

Sir, she came in great with child; and longing, saving your honour's reverence, for stew'd prunes. II, 1, 86

For the strange imagination of a woman works effectually upon her infant, that as Baptista Porta proves, *Physiog. coelestis l*, 5, *c.* 2, she leaves a mark upon it, which is most especially seen in such as prodigiously long for such and such meats, the child will love those meats, saith Fernelius, and be addicted to like-humours: "if a great-bellied woman see a hare, her child will often have a hare-lip." B. p. 139

This will last out a night in Russia,
When nights are longest there; II, 1, 128

In Muscovy, where they live in stoves and hot houses all winter long, come seldom or little abroad. B. p. 346

Merciful Heaven,
Thou rather, with thy sharp and sulphurous bolt,
Splits the unwedgeable and gnarled oak
Than the soft myrtle. II, 2, 114

Aerial spirits or devils, are such as keep quarter most part in the air, cause many tempests, thunder, and lightnings, tear oaks. B. p. 123

When as the lofty oak is blown down, the silly reed may stand. B. p. 395

but this virtuous maid
Subdues me quite. Ever till now,
When men were fond, I smil'd and wond'red how. II, 2, 185

. . . he was a severe woman-hater all his life . . . Yet this old doting fool was taken at last with that celestial and divine look of Myrilla. B. p. 515

and that there were
No earthly mean to save him but that either
You must lay down the treasures of your body
To this supposed, or else to let him suffer— II, 4, 94

One Archidamus, a Consul of Antioch, offered a hundred pounds of gold to a fair young wife, and besides to set her husband free, who was then *sub gravissimâ custodiâ*, a dark prisoner, *pro unius noctis concubitu:* but the chaste matron would not accept of it. B. p. 649

Sparrows must not build in his house-eaves because they are lecherous. III, 2, 164

Aristotle gives instance in sparrows, which are *parùm vivaces ob salacitatem*, short-lived because of their salacity. B. p. 313

Shame to him whose cruel striking
Kills for faults of his own liking!
Twice treble shame on Angelo,
To weed my vice and let his grow!
O, what may man within him hide,
Though angel on the outward side! III, 2, 249

Measure for Measure

Howsoever in public they pretend much zeal, seem to be very holy men, and bitterly preach against adultery, fornication, there are no verier bawds or whoremasters in a country. B. p. 548

'Tis good; though music oft hath such a charm
To make bad good and good provoke to harm. IV, I, 14

In a word, it [music] is so powerful a thing, that it ravisheth the soul, *regina sensuum*, the queen of the senses, by sweet pleasure (which is a happy cure), and corporal tunes pacify our incorporal soul, *sine ore loquens, dominatum in animan exercet*, and carries it beyond itself, helps, elevates, extends it. B. p. 367

For music enchants, as Menander holds, it will make such melancholy persons mad . . . Plato for this reason forbids music and wine to all young men . . . music makes some men mad as a tiger . . . it hath divers effects; and Theophrastus right well prophesied, that diseases were either procured by music or mitigated. B. p. 369

Nay, friar, I am a kind of burr; I shall stick. IV, 3, 173

They will stick together like burrs. B. p. 479

They say best men are moulded out of faults. V, I, 437

A denying Peter, a persecuting Paul, an adulterous cruel David, have been received. B. p. 731

We must endure sorrow and misery in this life. 'Tis no new thing this, God's best servants and dearest children have been so visited and tried. B. p. 735

Sirrah, thou art said to have a stubborn soul,
That apprehends no further than this world,
And squar'st thy life according. V, I, 478

Let them take heaven, paradise, and that future happiness that will, *bonum est esse hîc*, it is good being here: there is no talking to such, no hope of their conversion, they are in a reprobate sense, mere carnalists, fleshy-minded men. B. p. 706

Love's Labour's Lost

Love's Labour's Lost. [Title of play.]

His labours lost. B. p. 237

Therefore, brave conquerors—for so you are
That war against your own affections. I, I, 8

Have peace with all men, war with vice. B. p. 424

LOVE'S LABOUR'S LOST

> I am resolv'd; 'tis but a three years' fast.
> The mind shall banquet, though the body pine.
> Fat paunches have lean plates; and dainty bits
> Make rich the ribs, but bankrupt quite the wits. I, 1, 24

For it is held by some of them, as an axiom, that to keep them poor, will make them study; they must be dieted, as horses to a race, not pampered. B. p. 209

I could even live and die with such meditations, and take more delight, true content of mind in them, than thou hast in all thy wealth and sport, how rich soever thou art. B. p. 350

Virtue refuseth no stature, and commonly your great vast bodies, and fine features, are sottish, dull, and leaden spirits. B. p. 380

> Ay, that is study's god-like recompense. I, 1, 58

The delight is it, which I aim at, so great pleasure, such sweet content there is in study. B. p. 351

> Small have continual plodders ever won,
> Save base authority from others' books. I, 1, 86

Or else it [a book] is a thing of mere industry, a collection without wit or invention, a very toy. B. p. 9

> At Christmas I no more desire a rose
> Than wish a snow in May's new-fangled shows;
> But like of each thing that in season grows; I, 1, 105

Another must have roses in winter, *alieni temporis flores*, snow-water in summer, fruits before they can be or are usually ripe, artificial gardens and fishponds on the tops of houses, all things opposite to the vulgar sort, intricate and rare, or else they are nothing worth. B. p. 240

> So it is, besieged with sable-coloured melancholy, I did commend the black oppressing humour to the most wholesome physic of thy health-giving air; I, 1, 225

The medium must needs be good, where the air is temperate, serene, quiet, free from bogs, fens, mists, all manner of putrefaction, contagious and filthy noisome smells. . . . In Périgord in France the air is subtle, healthful, seldom any plague or contagious disease, but hilly and barren: B. p. 331

> *King.* Sir, I will pronounce your sentence: you shall fast a week with bran and water.
> *Cost.* I had rather pray a month with mutton and porridge.
> I, 1, 279

Guianerius therefore prescribes his patient "to go with hair-cloth next his skin, to go bare-footed, and bare-legged in cold weather, to whip himself now and then, as monks do, but above all to fast. Not with sweet wine, mutton and pottage, as many of those tender-bellies do, howsoever they put on Lenten faces, and whatsoever they pretend, but from all manner of meat. B. p. 585

> . . . There is no evil angel but Love. Yet was Samson so tempted, and he had an excellent strength; yet was Solomon so seduced, and he had a very good wit. Cupid's butt-shaft is too hard for Hercules' club. I, 2, 165

"Samson, David, Solomon, Hercules, Socrates," &c. are justly taxed of indiscretion in this point; B. p. 563

Let him now that so dotes meditate on this: let him see the event and success of others, Samson, Hercules, Holofernes, &c. B. p. 595

> Regent of love-rhymes, lord of folded arms, III, 1, 171

I' th' under column there doth stand
Inamorato with folded hand;
Down hangs his head, terse and polite
Some ditty sure he doth indite.

B. *The Argument of the Frontispiece*

> Fair payment for foul words is more than due. IV, 1, 19
> A giving hand, though foul, shall have fair praise.
> IV, 1, 23

. . . fair becomes foul, . . . fair or foul: B. p. 478

Let them be epicures, or atheists, libertines, machiavelians . . . they may be canonised for saints, they shall be honourably interred in mausolean tombs, commended by poets, registered in histories, have temples and statues erected to their names,—*è manibus illis—nascentur violæ.**—If he be bountiful in his life, and liberal at his death, he shall have one to swear, as he did by Claudius the Emperor in Tacitus, he saw his soul go to heaven, and be miserably lamented at his funeral. B. p. 229

* Shilleto gives "Pers. i, 38, 40. And from their ashes shall spring violets."

Love's Labour's Lost

Twice-sod simplicity, bis coctus! IV, 2, 19

cramben bis coctam apponere, B. p. 5

crambem bis coctam apponere, B. p. 248

These are begot in the ventricle of memory. IV, 2, 66

The fourth creek behind the head is common to the cerebel or little brain, and marrow of the back-bone, the last and most solid of all the rest, which receives the animal spirits from the other ventricles, and conveys them to the marrow in the back, and is the place where they say the memory is seated. B. p. 98

Vir sapit qui pauca loquitur. IV, 2, 76

vir sapit qui pauca loquitur; B. p. 70

King. In love, I hope; sweet fellowship in shame.
Ber. One drunkard loves another of the name. IV, 3, 45

With Rabelais, that French Lucian, drunkenness is better for the body than physic, because there be more old drunkards than old physicians. Many such frothy arguments they have, inviting and encouraging others to do as they do, and love them dearly for it (no glue like to that of good fellowship). B. p. 149

A wither'd hermit, five-score winters worn,
Might shake off fifty, looking in her eye,
Beauty doth varnish age, as if new-born,
And gives the crutch the cradle's infancy. IV, 3, 238

"Sweet Marian do not mine age disdain,
For thou canst make an old man young again." B. p. 578

Say, can you fast? Your stomachs are too young,
And abstinence engenders maladies. IV, 3, 290

Repletion and inanition may both do harm in two contrary extremes. B. p. 308

Why, universal plodding poisons up
The nimble spirits in the arteries, IV, 3, 301

Or else it is a thing of mere industry, a collection without art or invention, a very toy. B. p. 9

The vital spirits are made in the heart of the natural, which by the arteries are transported to all the other parts: B. p. 94

LOVE'S LABOUR'S LOST

"[Music] affecting not only the ears, but the very arteries, the vital and animal spirits, it erects the mind, and makes it nimble." Lemnius, *instit. cap.* 44. B. p. 367

> But love, first learned in a lady's eyes,
> Lives not alone immured in the brain,
> But with the motion of all elements,
> Courses as swift as thought in every power,
> And gives to every power a double power,
> Above their functions and their offices. IV, 3, 323

It adds spirits and makes them, otherwise soft and silly, generous and courageous, *Audacem faciebat amor.* Ariadne's love made Theseus so adventurous, and Medea's beauty Jason so victorious; *expectorat amor timorem.* B. p. 574

'Tis their chiefest study to sing, dance; and without question, so many gentlemen and gentlewomen would not be so well qualified in this kind, if love did not incite them. B. p. 577

> Never durst poet touch a pen to write
> Until his ink were temp'red with Love's sighs; IV, 3, 342

There never was any excellent poet that invented good fables, or made laudable verses, which was not in love himself; had he not taken a quill from Cupid's wings, he could never have written so amorously as he did. B. p. 580

> From women's eyes this doctrine I derive.
> They sparkle still the right Promethean fire;
> They are the books, the arts, the academes, IV, 3, 346

So think it [love] is the self-same fire Prometheus fetched from heaven. B. p. 490

> Ad dunghill . . . 'dunghill' for unguem. V, 1, 66–67

Ad haras aptius quam ad aras. B. p. 213

'tis not *conjugium* but *conjurgium.* B. p. 604

Si non casté, tamen cauté B. p. 648

> And so may you; for a light heart lives long. V, 2, 18

The merrier the heart the longer the life. B. p. 369

> Great reason; for 'past cure is still past care'. V, 2, 28

That which is past cannot be recalled. B. p. 422

Love's Labour's Lost

Cried 'Via! we will do't, come what will come'. V, 2, 112

A twelvemonth? Well, befall what will befall,
I'll jest a twelvemonth in an hospital. V, 2, 858

Come then what can come, befall what may befall. B. p. 402

If it cannot be helped, or amended, make the best of it. B. p. 402

A Midsummer Night's Dream

Thrice-blessed they that master so their blood
To undergo such maiden pilgrimage; I, 1, 74

Marriage replenisheth the earth, but virginity Paradise. B. p. 606

What an immortal crown belongs to virginity? B. p. 623

And make and mar
The foolish fates. I, 2, 31

'Tis opinion alone (saith Cardan), that makes or mars physicians.
B. p. 168

Either I mistake your shape and making quite,
Or else you are that shrewd and knavish sprite
Call'd Robin Goodfellow. II, 1, 32

A bigger kind there is of them called with us hobgoblins, and Robin Goodfellows, that would in those superstitious times grind corn for a mess of milk, cut wood, or do any manner of drudgery work.
B. p. 124

Thou speakest aright:
I am that merry wanderer of the night.
I jest to Oberon, and make him smile
When I a fat and bean-fed horse beguile,
Neighing in likeness of a filly foal;
And sometimes lurk I in a gossip's bowl
In very likeness of a roasted crab. II, 1, 42

[Spirits] sometimes appear in the likeness of hares, crows, black dogs, &c. B. p. 125

The ox hath therefore stretch'd his yoke in vain,
The ploughman lost his sweat, and the green corn
Hath rotted ere his youth attain'd a beard;
The fold stands empty in the drowned field,
And crows are fatted with the murrion flock; II, 1, 93

A MIDSUMMER NIGHT'S DREAM

Sigismund Scheretzius, *part.* 1. *cap.* 9. *de spect.*, reports confidently, that he conferred with sundry such, that had been so carried many miles, and that he heard witches themselves confess as much; hurt and infect men and beasts, vines, corn, cattle, plants. B. p. 131

I do but beg a little changeling boy
To be my henchman. II, 1, 120

. . . steal young children out of their cradles, *ministerio dæmonum*, and put deformed in their rooms, which we call changelings.
B. p. 131

And heard a mermaid on a dolphin's back II, 1, 150

The sea-nymphs half-naked, keeping time on dolphins' backs.
B. p. 577

It fell upon a little western flower,
Before milk-white, now purple with love's wound. II, 1, 166

The first step of love is sight, as Lilius Giraldus proves at large, *hist. deor. syntag.* 13. they as two sluices let in the influences of that divine, powerful, soul-ravishing, and captivating beauty, which, as one saith, "is sharper than any dart or needle, wounds deeper into the heart; and opens a gap through our eyes to that lovely wound, which pierceth the soul itself." B. p. 507

The juice of it on sleeping eyelids laid
Will make or man or woman madly dote. II, 1, 170

"It lies not in our power to love or hate,
For will in us is overrul'd by fate." B. p. 613

I'll put a girdle round about the earth
In forty minutes. II, 1, 175

That they [spirits] are most swift in motion, can pass many miles in an instant, and so likewise transform bodies of others into what shape they please, and with admirable celerity remove them from place to place. B. p. 117

An arrow out of a bow must go seven times about the earth whilst a man can say an Ave Maria. B. p. 325

Run when you will; the story shall be chang'd:
Apollo flies, and Daphne holds the chase;
The dove pursues the griffin; the mild hind
Makes speed to catch the tiger—bootless speed,
When cowardice pursues and valour flies. II, 1, 230

To see horses ride in a coach, men draw it; dogs devour their masters; towers build masons; children rule; old men go to school; women wear the breeches; sheep demolish towns, devour men, &c. B. p. 36

We should be woo'd, and were not made to woo. II, 1, 242

She should rather seem to be desired by a man, than to desire a man herself. B. p. 614

What thou seest when thou dost wake, II, 2, 27

Churl, upon thy eyes I throw
All the power this charm doth owe: II, 2, 78

In our times it is a common thing, saith Erastus, in his book *de Lamiis*, for witches to take upon them the making of these philters, "to force men and women to love and hate whom they will . . ." B. p. 549

good night, sweet friend.
Thy love ne'er alter till thy sweet life end! II, 2, 60

"Dear wife, let's live in love and die together,
As hitherto we have in all good will:
Let no day change or alter our affections,
But let's be young to one another still." B. p. 499

"No age shall part my love from thee, sweet wife,
Though I live Nestor or Tithonus' life." B. p. 499

For, as a surfeit of the sweetest things
The deepest loathing to the stomach brings, II, 2, 137

There is a loathing satiety of all things. B. p. 225

All excess, as Epictetus argues, will cause a dislike; sweet will be sour, which made that temperate Epicurus sometimes voluntarily fast. B. p. 390

What, a play toward! I'll be an auditor;
An actor too perhaps, if I see cause. III, 1, 70

Not to be an auditor only, or a spectator, but sometimes an actor himself. B. p. 371

The king was not a spectator only, but a principal actor himself. B. p. 540

He held it unfit to be a spectator, much less an actor. B. p. 541

Russet-pated choughs. III, 2, 21

They go in sheep's russet, many great men that might maintain themselves in cloth of gold. B. p. 196

Note—From this it would appear that the bird referred to was the jackdaw.

For methinks I am marvellous hairy about the face; and I am such a tender ass, if my hair do but tickle me I must scratch. IV, 1, 22

Besides, I might not well refrain, for *ubi dolor, ibi digitus*, one must needs scratch where it itches. B. p. 5

But, like in sickness, did I loathe this food;
But, as in health, come to my natural taste, IV, 1, 170

A sick man loseth his appetite, strength and ability, his disease prevaileth so far, that all his faculties are spent, hand and foot perform not their duties, his eyes are dim, hearing dull, tongue distastes things of pleasant relish. B. p. 736

Lovers and madmen have such seething brains,
Such shaping fantasies, that apprehend
More than cool reason ever comprehends.
The lunatic, the lover, and the poet,
Are of imagination all compact.
One sees more devils than vast hell can hold;
That is the madman. The lover, all as frantic,
Sees Helen's beauty in a brow of Egypt.
The poet's eye, in a fine frenzy rolling,
Doth glance from heaven to earth, from earth to heaven;
And as imagination bodies forth
The forms of things unknown, the poet's pen
Turns them to shapes, and gives to airy nothing
A local habitation and a name. V, 1, 4

Phantasy, or imagination, which some call estimative, or cogitative (confirmed, saith Fernelius, by frequent meditation), is an inner sense which doth more fully examine the species perceived by common sense, of things present or absent, and keeps them longer, recalling them to mind again, or making new of his own. In time of sleep this faculty is free, and many times conceives strange, stupend, absurd shapes, as in sick men we commonly observe. His organ is the middle cell of the brain; his objects all the species communicated to him by the common sense, by comparison of which he feigns infinite other unto himself. In melancholy men this faculty is most powerful and strong, and often hurts, producing many monstrous and prodigious things, especially if it be stirred up by some terrible object, presented to it from common sense or memory. In poets and painters imagination forcibly works, as appears by their several fictions, antics, images: as Ovid's house of sleep, Psyche's palace in Apuleius, &c. B. p. 101

> Or in the night, imagining some fear,
> How easy is a bush suppos'd a bear? V, 1, 21

What will not a fearful man conceive in the dark? What strange forms of bugbears, devils, witches, goblins? B. p. 167

Any object not well discerned in the dark, fear and phantasy will suspect to be a ghost, a devil, &c. B. p. 280

> *Wall.* This loam, this rough cast, and this stone, doth show
> That I am that same wall; the truth is so;
> And this the cranny is, right and sinister,
> Through which the fearful lovers are to whisper.
> *The.* Would you desire lime and hair to speak better?
> *Dem.* It is the wittiest partition that ever I heard discourse, my lord. V, 1, 160
>
> The wall is down that parted their fathers. V, 1, 341

Durum et durum non faciunt murum, as the diverb is, two refractory spirits will never agree, the only means to overcome is to relent, *obsequio vinces.* B. p. 417

> Marry, if he that writ it had played Pyramus, and hang'd himself in Thisby's garter, it would have been a fine tragedy. V, 1, 347

And it would not grieve him to be hanged, if he might be strangled in her garters. B. p. 572

> And the wolf behowls the moon; V, 1, 361

As a dog barks at the moon, to no purpose are your sayings. B. p. 207

Doth the moon care for the barking of a dog? B. p. 422

A Midsummer Night's Dream

Never mole, hare-lip, nor scar,
Nor mark prodigious, such as are
Despised in nativity. V, 1, 400

Great-bellied women, when they long, yield us prodigious examples in this kind, as moles, warts, scars, harelips, monsters, especially caused in their children by force of a depraved fantasy in them:
B. p. 167

The Merchant of Venice

In sooth, I know not why I am so sad.
It wearies me; you say it wearies you;
But how I caught it, found it, or came by it,
What stuff 'tis made of, whereof it is born,
I am to learn; I, 1, 1

Of the matter of melancholy, there is much question betwixt Avicen and Galen, as you may read in Cardan's Contradictions, Valesius' Controversies, Montanus, Prosper Calenus, Cappivaccius, Bright, Ficinus, that have written either whole tracts, or copiously of it, in their several treatises of this subject. "What this humour is, or whence it proceeds, how it is engendered in the body, neither Galen, nor any old writer, hath sufficiently discussed," as Jacchinus thinks.
B. p. 110

Grieving still, but why they cannot tell. B. p. 254

Saler. Your mind is tossing on the ocean;
There where your argosies, with portly sail—
Like signiors and rich burghers on the flood,
Or as it were the pageants of the sea—
Do overpeer the petty traffickers,
That curtsy to them, do them reverence,
As they fly by them with their woven wings.
Solan. Believe me, sir, had I such venture forth,
The better part of my affections would
Be with my hopes abroad. I should be still
Plucking the grass to know where sits the wind,
Peering in maps for ports, and piers, and roads;
And every object that might make me fear
Misfortune to my ventures, out of doubt,
Would make me sad. I, 1, 8

I laugh at all, only secure lest my suit go amiss, my ships perish, corn and cattle miscarry, trade decay. I have no wife nor children good or bad to provide for. A mere spectator of other men's fortunes and adventures, and how they act their parts, which methinks are diversely presented unto me as from a common theatre or scene. B. p. 3

> That therefore only are reputed wise
> For saying nothing. I, 1, 96

Vir sapit qui pauca loquitur. B. p. 70

> They are as sick that surfeit with too much as they that starve with nothing. It is no mean happiness, therefore, to be seated in the mean: superfluity comes sooner by white hairs, but competency lives longer. I, 2, 5

Repletion and inanition may both do harm in two contrary extremes. B. p. 308

Excess of meat breedeth sickness, and gluttony causeth choleric diseases: by surfeiting many perish, but he that dieteth himself prolongeth his life. B. p. 308

> *Port.* Good sentences, and well pronounc'd.
> *Ner.* They would be better, if well followed. I, 2, 9

So many preachers, so little practice. B. p. 26

Teach others to fast, and play the glutton themselves.
B. p. 27

> *Ner.* First, there is the Neapolitan prince.
> *Por.* Ay, that's a colt indeed, for he doth nothing but talk of his horse; I, 2, 35

We have a sprinkling of our gentry, here and there one, excellently well learned, . . . But they are but few in respect of the multitude, the major part (and some again excepted, that are indifferent) are wholly bent for hawks and hounds . . . their sole discourse is dogs, hawks, horses. B. p. 210

The ordinary sports which are used abroad are hawking, hunting, . . . 'tis all their study, their exercise, ordinary business, all their talk: and indeed some dote too much after it, they can do nothing else, discourse of nought else. B. p. 338

> *Ner.* How like you the young German, the Duke of Saxony's nephew?
> *Por.* Very vilely in the morning when he is sober; and most vilely in the afternoon when he is drunk. When he is best,

he is a little worse than a man, and when he is worst, he is little better than a beast. I, 2, 75

Germany hath not so many drunkards. B. p. 630

Thus they [drunkards] many times wilfully pervert the good temperature of their bodies, stifle their wits, strangle nature, and degenerate into beasts. B. p. 149

As good be melancholy still, as drunken beasts and beggars. B. p. 373

Let none presume
To wear an undeserved dignity. II, 9, 39

"And what is dignity to an unworthy man, but" (as Salvianus holds), "a gold ring in a swine's snout?" B. p. 417

To offend and judge are distinct offices
And of opposed natures. II, 9, 61

As the Reed and Fern in the Emblem, averse and opposite in nature. B. p. 604

The ancient saying is no heresy:
Hanging and wiving goes by destiny. II, 9, 82

As the saying is, marriage and hanging goes by destiny. B. p. 613

As You Like It

He lets me feed with his hinds, bars me the place of a brother. I, 1, 16

Such as live in prison, or some desert place, and cannot have company, as many of our country gentlemen do in solitary houses, they must either be alone without companions, or live beyond their means, and entertain all comers as so many hosts or else converse with their servants and hinds. B. p. 161

Oliver Now, sir! what make you here?
Orlando Nothing; I am not taught to make any thing.
Oliver What mar you then, sir?
Orlando Marry, sir, I am helping you to mar that which God made, a poor unworthy brother of yours, with idleness. . . .

> *Orlando* My father charg'd you in his will to give me good education: . . .
> *Oliver* And what wilt thou do? Beg, when that is spent?
> I, 1, 26–68

Many poor men, younger brothers, &c., by reason of bad policy and idle education (for they are likely brought up in no calling), are compelled to beg or steal, and then hanged for theft; B. p. 32

I will have several orders, degrees of nobility, and those hereditary, not rejecting younger brothers in the mean time, for they shall be sufficiently provided for by pensions, or so qualified, brought up in some honest calling, they shall be able to live of themselves.
B. p. 59

If I make nothing, as Montaigne said in like case,
I will mar nothing; B. p. 375

The one makes, the other mars. B. p. 684

> . . . Wert thou not my brother, I would not take this hand from thy throat till this other had pull'd out thy tongue for saying so. I, 1, 53

. . . they are ready to pull out one another's throats.
B. p. 33

> *Oliver* Get you with him, you old dog.
> *Adam* Is 'old dog' my reward? Most true. I have lost my teeth in your service. God be with my old master! He would not have spoke such a word. I, 1, 73

So long as they are behoveful, they love, or may bestead each other, but when there is no more good to be expected, as they do by an old dog, hang him up or cashier him: which Cato counts a great indecorum, to use men like old shoes or broken glasses, which are flung to the dunghill; he could not find in his heart to sell an old ox, much less to turn away an old servant. B. p. 33

> As they did in the golden world. I, 1, 109

In that golden age, *somnos dedit umbra salubres, potum quoque, lubricus amnis*, the tree gave wholesome shade to sleep under, and the clear rivers drink. B. p. 394

In the golden world men did so. B. p. 615

The dullness of the fool is the whetstone of the wits. I, 2, 50

Whetstones to make other tools cut, but cut not themselves.
B. p. 675

Come, where is this young gallant that is so desirous to lie with his mother earth? I, 1, 179

Great travail is created for all men, and an heavy yoke on the sons of Adam, from the day that they go out of their mother's womb, unto that day they return to the mother of all things. B. p. 81

Besides, *An terra sit animata?* which some so confidently believe, with Orpheus, Hermes, Averroes, from which all other souls of men, beasts, devils, plants, fishes, &c., are derived and into which again, after some revolutions, as Plato in his *Timæus*, Plotinus in his *Enneades*, more largely discuss, they return. B. p. 325

Sweet are the uses of adversity; II, 1, 12

That wise and virtuous lady, Queen Katherine, Dowager of England, in private talk, upon like occasion, said, that she would not willingly endure the extremity of either fortune; but if it were so, that of necessity she must undergo the one, she would be in adversity, because comfort was never wanting in it, but still counsel and government were defective in the other: they could not moderate themselves.
B. p. 198

Many philosophers have voluntarily sought adversity, and so much commend it in their precepts. Demetrius, in Seneca, esteemed it a great infelicity, that in his lifetime he had no misfortune. B. p. 404
(See, also, below, *Cymbeline*, III, 3, 19.)

And this our life, exempt from public haunt,
Finds tongues in trees, books in the running brooks,
Sermons in stones, and good in everything.
I would not change it. II, 1, 15

The waters ebb and flow to their conservation no doubt to teach us that we should ever be in action. B. p. 336

As a tree that is heavy laden with fruit breaks her own boughs, with their own greatness they ruin themselves. B. p. 388

This love is manifest, I say, in inanimate creatures. How comes a loadstone to draw iron to it? jet chaff? the ground to covet showers, but for love? No creature, S. Hierom concludes, is to be found, *quod non aliquid amat*, no stock, no stone, that hath not some feeling of love.
B. p. 474

Yet it [thy faith] may revive, as trees are dead in winter, but flourish in the spring! B. p. 727

> To the which place a poor sequest'red stag,
> That from the hunter's aim had ta'en a hurt,
> Did come to languish; II, 1, 33

As to a deer that is struck, whether he run, go, rest with the herd, or alone, this grief remains: B. p. 255

[Cato] could not find in his heart to sell an old ox. B. p. 33

> Did he not moralize this spectacle? II, 1, 44

Leon Hebreus gives many fabulous reasons, and moraliseth them withal. B. p. 474

Moralise this fable by thyself. B. p. 593

> First, for his weeping into the needless stream. II, 1, 46

O me miserum! Quis dabit in lachrymas fontem. B. p. 406

> 'Poor deer,' quoth he, 'thou mak'st a testament
> As worldlings do, giving thy sum of more
> To that which had too much'. Then, being there alone,
> Left and abandoned of his velvet friends:
> ''Tis right;' quoth he 'thus misery doth part
> The flux of company'. II, 1, 47

Our estate and *benè esse* ebbs and flows with our commodity; and, as we are endowed or enriched, so are we beloved and esteemed: it lasts no longer than our wealth; when that is gone, and the object removed, farewell friendship: as long as bounty, good cheer, and rewards were to be hoped, friends enough; they were tied to thee by the teeth, and would follow thee as crows do a carcass: but when thy goods are gone and spent, the lamp of their love is out, and thou shalt be contemned, scorned, hated, injured. B. p. 477

. . . as too many worldlings do. B. p. 394

> 'Sweep on, you fat and greasy citizens;
> 'Tis just the fashion. Wherefore do you look
> Upon that poor and broken bankrupt there?' II, 1, 55

"Show some pity for Christ's sake, pity a sick man, an old man," etc., he cares not, ride on . . . "Swear, protest, take God and all his angels to witness, *quære peregrinum*, thou art a counterfeit crank,

a cheater, he is not touched with it, *pauper ubique jacet*, ride on, he takes no notice of it." . . . Show him a decayed haven, a bridge, a school, a fortification, &c., or some public work, ride on; good your worship, your honour, for God's sake, your country's sake, ride on.
B. p. 487

. . . 'tis the common fashion of the world. B. p. 234

As it is with a man imprisoned for debt, if once in the goal, every creditor will bring his action against him, and there likely hold him. If any discontent seize upon a patient, in an instant all other perturbations (for—*quâ data porta ruunt*) will set upon him, and then like a lame dog or broken-winged goose he droops and pines away.
B. p. 92

I love to cope with him in these sullen fits, II, 1, 67

. . . their minds disquieted, dull heavy, &c., care, jealousy, fear of some disease, sullen fits, weeping fits seize too familiarly on them.
B. p. 160

Though I look old, yet I am strong and lusty;
For in my youth I never did apply
Hot and rebellious liquors in my blood,
Nor did not with unbashful forehead woo
The means of weakness and debility;
Therefore my age is as a lusty winter,
Frosty, but kindly. II, 3, 47

Tully holds, "better be a temperate old man than a lascivious youth." 'Tis the only sweet thing (which he adviseth) so to moderate ourselves, that we may have *senectutem in juventute, et in juventute senectutem*, be youthful in our old age, staid in our youth, discreet and temperate in both.
B. p. 310

Thou art not for the fashion of these times,
Where none will sweat but for promotion. III, 3, 59

He is a true geometrician, can measure out a good fortune to himself; a perfect astrologer that can cast the rise and fall of others, and mark their errant motions to his own use. The best optics are, to reflect the beams of some great men's favour and grace to shine upon him. He is a good engineer, that alone can make an instrument to get preferment.
B. p. 204

As You Like It

He that shall examine this iron age wherein we live, . . . He that shall see men swear and forswear, lie and bear false witness, to advantage themselves, prejudice others, . . . every man for himself, his own ends, the devil for all: B. pp. 488, 489

> *Jaq.* More, more, I prithee, more.
> *Ami.* It will make you melancholy, Monsieur Jaques.
> *Jaq.* I thank it. More, I prithee, more.
> I can suck melancholy out of a song, as a weasel sucks eggs.
> More, I prithee, more. II, 5, 9

Many men are melancholy by hearing music, but it is a pleasing melancholy that it causeth; and therefore to such as are discontent, in woe, fear, sorrow, or dejected, it is a most present remedy: it expels cares, alters their grieved minds, and easeth in an instant. B. p. 369

> Who doth ambition shun, II, 5, 34

I would not willingly be known. B. p. 1

Many that have refused honours, titles, and all this vain pomp and happiness, which others so ambitiously seek, and carefully study to compass and attain. B. p. 387

> If it do do come to pass II, 5, 46

By which means it comes to pass . . . B. p. 6

By which means it comes to pass . . . B. p. 30

> Here shall he see
> Gross fools as he,
> An if he will come to me. II, 5, 51

If any man shall ask in the meantime, who I am that so boldly censure others, *tu nullane habes vitia?* have I no faults? Yes, more than thou hast, whatsoever thou art. *Nos numerus sumus*, I confess it again, I am as foolish, as mad as any one. B. p. 71

> . . . comfort a little; cheer thyself a little. II, 6, 5

. . . comfort thyself, no time is overpast. B. p. 728

. . . comfort thyself then. B. p. 730

> We shall have shortly discord in the spheres. II, 7, 6

. . . music of the spheres. B. p. 542

And rail'd on Lady Fortune in good terms,
In good set terms—and yet a motley fool. II, 7, 16

He respects matter, thou art wholly for words; he loves a loose and free style, thou art all for neat composition. B. p. 9

Besides, it was the observation of that wise Seneca, "when you see a fellow careful about his words, and neat in his speech, know this for a certainty that man's mind is busied about toys, there's no solidity in him. B. p. 11

'Call me not fool till heaven hath sent me fortune.' II, 7, 19

Wealth and wisdom cannot dwell together, . . .
fools have fortune: B. p. 68

I must have liberty
Withal, as large a charter as the wind,
To blow on whom I please, for so fools have; II, 7, 47

It was written by an idle fellow, at idle times, about our Saturnalian or Dyonisian feasts, when as he said, *nullum libertati periculum est*, servants in old Rome had liberty to say and do what them list.
B. p. 73

And they that are most galled with my folly,
They most must laugh. And why, sir, must they so?
The why is plain as way to parish church:
He that a fool doth very wisely hit
Doth very foolishly, although he smart,
Not to seem senseless of the bob; if not,
The wise man's folly is anatomiz'd
Even by the squand'ring glances of the fool. II, 7, 50

If any be displeased, or take aught unto himself, let him not expostulate or cavil with him that said it (so did Erasmus excuse himself to Dorpius, *si parva licet componere magnis*) and so do I; "but let him be angry with himself, that so betrayed and opened his own faults in applying it to himself:" if he be guilty and deserve it, let him amend, whoever he is and not be angry. "He that hateth correction is a fool." *Prov.* xii. 1. If he be not guilty, it concerns him not; it is not my freeness of speech but a guilty conscience, a galled back of his own that makes him wince. B. p. 73

I have anatomized mine own folly. B. p. 73

If it be a natural impediment, as a red nose, squint eyes, crooked legs, or any such imperfection, infirmity, disgrace, reproach, the best way is to speak of it first thyself, and so thou shalt surely take away all occasions from others to jest at, or contemn, that they may perceive thee to be careless of it. Vatinius was wont to scoff at his own deformed feet, to prevent his enemies' obloquies and sarcasms in that kind. B. p. 423

> Most mischievous foul sin, in chiding sin;
> For thou thyself hast been a libertine. II, 7, 64

. . . teach others to fast, and play the gluttons themselves; like the watermen that row one way and look another. Vow virginity, talk of holiness, and yet indeed a notorious bawd, and famous fornicator, *lascivum pecus*, a very goat. B. p. 27

> Thou seest we are not all alone unhappy:
> This wide and universal theatre
> Presents more woeful pageants than the scene
> Wherein we play in. II, 7, 136

If thou alone wert distressed, it were indeed more irksome, and less to be endured; but when the calamity is common, comfort thyself with this, thou hast more fellows, *Solamen miseris socios habuisse doloris;* 'tis not thy sole case, and why shouldst thou be so impatient? B. p. 375

Yea, but thou thinkest thou art more miserable than the rest, other men are happy but in respect of thee, their miseries are but flea-bitings to thine, thou alone art unhappy, none so bad as thyself. B. p. 377

> All the world's a stage,
> And all the men and women merely players; II, 7, 139

A mere spectator of other men's fortunes and adventures, and how they act their parts, which methinks are diversely presented unto me as from a common theatre or scene. B. p. 3

> And one man in his time plays many parts. II, 7, 142

. . . and so for their own advantage can they play their parts. B. p. 676

> At first the infant,
> Mewling and puking in the nurse's arms; II, 7, 143

For to begin at the hour of his birth, as Pliny doth elegantly describe it, "he is born naked, and falls a whining at the very first, he is swaddled and bound up like a prisoner, cannot help himself, and so he continues to his life's end." B. p. 179

Then the whining school-boy, with his satchel
And shining morning face, creeping like snail
Unwillingly to school. II, 7, 145

We suffer our childhood in the grammar-school, which Austin calls *magnam tyrannidem, et grave malum*, and compares it to the torments of martyrdom. B. p. 205

Tyrannical, impatient, hare-brained schoolmasters, . . . make many children endure a martyrdom all the while they are at school . . . that they are *fracti animis*, moped many times weary of their lives, *nimia severitate deficiunt et desperant*, and think no slavery in the world (as once I did myself) like to that of a grammar scholar. B. p. 218

Seeking the bubble reputation
Even in the cannon's mouth. II, 7, 152

Void of all fear they run into imminent dangers, cannon's mouth, &c., *ut vulneribus suis ferrum hostium hebetent*, saith Barletius, to get a name of valour, honour and applause, which lasts not neither, for it is but a mere flash this fame, and like a rose, *intra diem unum extinguitur*, 'tis gone in an instant. B. p. 30

Childish bubbles of wealth. B. p. 350

Last scene of all,
That ends this strange eventful history,
Is second childishness and mere oblivion; II, 7, 163

. . . when old, a child again. B. p. 24

They dote at last (*senex bis puer*) . . . children again. B. p. 136

. . . a very child again, B. p. 501

Run, run, Orlando; carve on every tree,
The fair, the chaste, and unexpressive she. III, 2, 9

They have their wakes, Whitsun-ales, shepherd's feasts, meetings on holidays, country dances, roundelays, writing their names on trees, true lover's knots, pretty gifts. B. p. 580

It [life] is tedious. III, 2, 17

Our life is tedious. B. p. 407

Such a one is a natural philosopher. III, 2, 29

. . . that it is quite opposite to reason, to natural philosophy.
B. p. 326

> . . . and to betray a she-lamb of a twelvemonth to a crooked-pated, old, cuckoldy ram, out of all reasonable match.
> III, 2, 72

So on the other side, many a young lovely maid will cast away herself upon an old, doting, decrepit dizzard. B. p. 529

> For a taste. III, 2, 90

And who can speak of all? *Crimine ab uno disce omnes*, take this for a taste. B. p. 36

> If the cat will after kind, III, 2, 93

mali corvi malum ovum, cat to her kind. B. p. 657

> He that sweetest rose will find
> Must find love's prick and Rosalinde. III, 2, 101

. . . as in a rose, flowers and prickles; B. p. 91

> Truly, the tree yields bad fruit. III, 2, 106

If we may guess at the tree by the fruit, never so many as in these days; show me a plain-dealing true honest man: B. p. 712

> I'll graff it with you, and then I shall graff it with a medlar. III, 2, 107

What shall I say of Cincinnatus, Cato, Tully, and many such? how they have been pleased with it, to prune, plant, inoculate and graft, to show so many several kinds of pears, apples, plums, peaches, &c. B. pp. 342–343

> I was never so berhym'd since Pythagoras' time that I was an Irish rat, which I can hardly remember. III, 2, 163

Manichees hold that Pythagorean transmigration of souls from men to beasts. B. p. 696

> What did he when thou saw'st him? What said he? How look'd he? Wherein went he? What makes he here? Did he ask for me? Where remains he? How parted he with thee? And when shalt thou see him again? III, 2, 205

She is ill at ease, and sick till she see him again, peevish in the meantime; discontent, heavy, sad, and why comes he not? where is he? why breaks he promise? why tarries he so long? sure he is not well; sure he hath some mischance; sure he forgets himself and me; with infinite such. B. p. 555

> I will chide no breather in the world but myself, against whom I know most faults. III, 2, 263

Have I no faults? Yes, more than thou hast, whatsoever thou art. B. p. 71

> Time travels in divers paces with divers persons. III, 2, 290

Methinks the time runs very fleet . . .
Methinks the time moves very slow.
The Author's Abstract of Melancholy: B. Preface

> A beard neglected, which you have not; but I pardon you for that, for simply your having in beard is a younger brother's revenue. Then your hose should be ungarter'd, your bonnet unbanded, your sleeve unbutton'd, your shoe untied, and everything about you demonstrating a careless desolation. III, 2, 348

And 'tis the humour of them all, to be careless of their persons and their estates, as the shepherd in Theocritus, *et haec barba inculta est, squalidique capilli*, their beards flag, and they have no more care of pranking themselves or of any business, they care not, as they say, which end goes forward. [Symptoms of Love] B. p. 561

> Love is merely a madness. III, 2, 368

Love is madness. B. p. 68

Tully, in his *Tusculans*, defines it [love] a furious disease of the mind; Plato, madness itself. B. p. 501

> O knowledge ill-inhabited, worse than Jove in a thatch'd house. III, 3, 7

Hiero of Syracuse was a brave king, but wanted a kingdom; Perseus of Macedon had nothing of a king, but the bare name and title, for he could not govern it: so great places are often ill bestowed, worthy persons unrespected. B. p. 415

> Nor a man's good wit seconded with the forward child understanding. III, 3, 9

Pro captu lectoris habent sua fata libelli. B. p. 9

As You Like It

Is a single man therefore blessed? No. III, 3, 51

Let other men be averse, rail then and scoff at women, and say what they can to the contrary, *vir sine uxore malorum expers est*, etc., a single man is a happy man, etc., but this is a toy. B. p. 621

He that hath no wife wandereth to and fro mourning. B. p. 621

Sir Oliver Martext, you are well met. III, 3, 56

Sir Petronel Flash, a mere outside. B. p. 229

Sir Giles Goosecap, Sir Amorous La-Fool. B. p. 529

. . . as pigeons bill. III, 3, 71

Bill as doves. B. p. 536

The common executioner,
Whose heart th' accustom'd sight of death makes hard. . . .
III, 5, 3

Many at first cannot endure the sight of a green wound, a sick man, which afterward become good chirurgeons, bold empirics: a horse starts at a rotten post afar off, which coming near he quietly passeth. 'Tis much in the manner of making such kind of persons, be they never so averse from company, bashful, solitary, timorous, they may be made at last with those Roman matrons, to desire nothing more than, in a public show, to see a full company of gladiators breathe out their last. B. p. 364

That you insult, exult, and all at once,
Over the wretched. III, 5, 36

Insult over his betters. B. p. 35

He [the devil] insults and domineers in melancholy distempered fantasies and persons especially. B. p. 729

What though you have no beauty—
As, by my faith, I see no more in you
Than without candle may go dark to bed—
Must you be therefore proud and pitiless? III, 5, 37

It may be for all her costly tires she is bald, and though she seem so fair by dark, by candle-light, or afar off at such a distance, as Callicratides observed in Lucian, "If thou should see her near, or in a morning, she would appear more ugly than a beast;"
B. p. 596

'Tis not her glass, but you, that flatters her; III, 5, 54

Every lover admires his mistress, though she be very deformed of herself, ill-favoured, wrinkled, pimpled, [&c.]. B. p. 563

'Tis not nature so makes us, but most part the infirmity of the beholder. B. p. 598

But, mistress, know yourself. Down on your knees,
And thank heaven, fasting, for a good man's love;
For I must tell you friendly in your ear:
Sell when you can; you are not for all markets. III, 5, 57

. . . learning to know themselves, would limit their ambition. B. p. 23

"He that will not when he may,
When he will he shall have nay." B. p. 612

N.B.—For III, 5, 98 see *Addenda*, p. 334.

Jaq. Why, 'tis good to be sad and say nothing.
Ros. Why then, 'tis good to be a post. IV, 1, 8

To know a thing and not to express it, is all one as if he knew it not. B. p. 5

I have neither the scholar's melancholy, which is emulation. IV, 1, 10

A scholar's mind is busied about his studies, he applauds himself for what he hath done, or hopes to do, one while fearing to be out in his next exercise, another while contemning all censures; envies one, emulates another. B. p. 265

Note—This quotation is from section headed "Symptoms, or Signs of Melancholy in the Body."

Yes, I have gained my experience. IV, 1, 23

Something I can speak out of experience, *ærumnabilis experientia me docuit*. B. p. 5

A traveller! By my faith, you have great reason to be sad. I fear you have sold your own lands to see other men's, then to have seen much and to have nothing is to have rich eyes and poor hands. IV, 1, 19

Farewell, Monsieur Traveller; look you lisp and wear strange suits, disable all the benefits of your own country, be out of love with your nativity, and almost chide God for

> making you that countenance you are; or I will scarce think you have swam in a gondola. IV, I, 30

He took great content, exceeding delight in that his voyage, as who doth not that shall attempt the like, though his travel be *ad jactationem magis quam ad usum reipub*. (as one well observes) to crack, gaze, see fine sights and fashions, spend time, rather than for his own or public good? (as it is to many gallants that travel out their best days, together with their means, manners, honesty, religion) yet it availeth howsoever. B. p. 335

He travels into Europe, Africa, Asia, searcheth every creek, sea, city, mountain, gulf, to what end? See one promontory (said Socrates of old), one mountain, one sea, one river, and see all. B. pp. 239–240

> *Orl*. I would kiss before I spoke.
> *Ros*. Nay, you were better speak first; and when you were gravell'd for lack of matter, you might take occasion to kiss. Very good orators, when they are out, they will spit; and for lovers lacking—God warn us!—matter, the cleanliest shift is to kiss.
> *Orl*. How if the kiss be denied?
> *Ros*. Then she puts you to entreaty, and there begins new matter. IV, I, 64

First a word, and then a kiss, then some other compliment, and then a kiss, then an idle question, then a kiss, and when he had pumped his wits dry, can say no more, kissing and colling are never out of season. B. p. 553

> And the foolish chroniclers of that age found it was—Hero of Sestos. IV, I, 92

When Leander was drowned, the inhabitants of Sestos consecrated Hero's lantern to Anteros, *Anteroti sacrum*, and he that had good success in his love should light the candle: but never any man was found to light it; which I refer to nought, but the inconstancy and lightness of women. B. p. 601

> I will be more jealous of thee than a Barbary cock-pigeon over his hen. IV, I, 133

The Xeriffes of Barbary keep their courtezans in such a strict manner, that if any man come but in sight of them he dies for it. B. p. 642

> O, that woman that cannot make her fault her husband's occasion, let her never nurse her child herself, for she will breed it like a fool! IV, 1, 155

If she be a fool or dolt, the child she nurseth will take after her, or otherwise be misaffected; B. p. 217

> We must have your doublet and hose pluck'd over your head, and show the world what the bird hath done to her own nest. IV, 1, 181

In the other extreme some are too liberal, as the proverb is, *Turdus malum sibi cacat*, they make a rod for their own tails, as Candaules did to Gyges in Herodotus, commend his wife's beauty himself and besides would needs have him see her naked. B. p. 658

> No; that same wicked bastard of Venus, that was begot of thought, conceiv'd of spleen, and born of madness; that blind rascally boy, that abuses every one's eyes, because his own are out— IV, 1, 190

. . . like Æsop's fox, when he had lost his tail, would have all his fellow foxes cut off theirs. B. p. 37

Because he is damned himself, and in an error, he would have all the world participate of his errors, and be damned with him. B. p. 670

> I cannot be out of sight of Orlando. I'll go find a shadow and sigh till he come. IV, 1, 194

For when the daughter of Deburiades the Sycionian, was to take leave of her sweetheart now going to wars, *ut desiderio ejus minus tabesceret*, to comfort herself in his absence, she took his picture with coal upon a wall as the candle gave the shadow. B. p. 579

> *Touch.* Art rich?
> *Will.* Faith, sir, so so. V, 1, 23

I am not poor, I am not rich. B. p. 3

> The fool doth think he is wise, but the wise man knows himself to be a fool. V, 1, 28

"Surely I am more foolish than any man, and have not the understanding of a man in me," *Prov.* xxx. 2. B. p. 17

As You Like It

> *Touch.* Give me your hand. Art thou learned?
> *Will.* No, sir.
> *Touch.* Then learn this of me: to have is to have; for it is a figure in rhetoric that drink, being pour'd out of a cup into a glass, by filling the one doth empty the other; for all your writers do consent that ipse is he; now, you are not ipse, for I am he. V, 1, 35

As apothecaries we make new mixtures every day, pour out of one vessel into another; and as those old Romans robbed all the cities of the world, to set out their bad-sited Rome, we skim off the cream of other men's wits, pick the choice flowers of their tilled gardens to set out our own sterile plots. . . they pilfer out of old writers to stuff up their new comments, scrape Ennius' dung-hills, and out of Democritus' pit, as I have done. B. p. 6

> Therefore, you clown, abandon—which is in the vulgar leave—the society—which in the boorish is company—of this female— V, 1, 42

Enforced solitariness is commonly seen in students, monks, friars, anchorites, that by their order and course of life must abandon all company, society of other men, and betake themselves to a private cell; B. p. 161

> Rich honesty dwells like a miser, sir, in a poor house; as your pearl in your foul oyster. V, 4, 58

A mere madness, to live like a wretch, and die rich. B. p. 189

> He uses his folly like a stalking-horse, and under the presentation of that he shoots his wit. V, 4, 100

They make new laws, statutes, invent new religions, ceremonies, as so many stalking-horses, to their ends. B. p. 672

The Taming of the Shrew

> *The Taming of the Shrew.* [Title of play]

Every man, as the saying is, can tame a shrew but he that hath her. B. p. 360

Note—The outlines of the story of Sly are given as in the play. B. p. 347

It will be pastime passing excellent,
If it be husbanded with modesty. Induction I, 65

Dancing, singing, masking, mumming, stage plays, howsoever they be heavily censured by some severe Catos, yet if opportunely and soberly used, may justly be approved. B. p. 346

Paulus Jovius relates as much of Pope Leo Decimus, that he was a grave, discreet, staid man, yet sometimes most free, and too open in his sports. And 'tis not altogether unfit or misbeseeming the gravity of such a man, if that decorum of time, place, and such circumstances be observed. B. p. 371

Volateran gives the same testimony of this island, commending our jovial manner of entertainment and good mirth, and methinks he saith well, there is no harm in it; long may they use it, and all such modest sports. B. p. 372

1.*Serv.* Will't please your lordship drink a cup of sack?
2.*Serv.* Will't please your honour taste of these conserves?
3.*Serv.* What raiment will your honour wear to-day?
Induction, 2, 2

What dish will your good worship eat of? . . . What sport will your honour have? B. p. 228

And rail upon the hostess of the house,
And say you would present her at the leet,
Because she brought stone jugs and no seal'd quarts.
Induction, 2, 84

I will have no private monopolies, to enrich one man, and beggar a multitude, multiplicity of offices, of supplying by deputies, weights and measures the same throughout, and those rectified by the *Primum mobile*, and sun's motion, threescore miles to a degree according to observation, 1000 geometrical paces to a mile, five foot to a pace, twelve inches to a foot, etc. B. p. 63

Or, if not so, until the sun be set. Induction, 2, 118

For fasting, vows, religious orders, peregrinations, they [Mahometans] go far beyond any Papists, they fast a month together many times, and must not eat a bit till sun be set. B. p. 694

For your physicians have expressly charg'd,
In peril to incur your former malady,
That I should yet absent me from your bed.
Induction, 2, 119

Intemperate Venus is all but as bad in the other extreme. Galen *l.* 6. *de morbis popular. sect.* 5. *text.* 26, reckons up melancholy amongst those diseases which are "exasperated by venery:" B. p. 153

> Your honour's players, hearing your amendment,
> Are come to play a pleasant comedy;
> For so your doctors hold it very meet,
> Seeing too much sadness hath congeal'd your blood,
> And melancholy is the nurse of frenzy.
> Therefore they thought it good you hear a play
> And frame your mind to mirth and merriment,
> Which bars a thousand harms and lengthens life.
>
> Induction, 2, 126

Use honest and chaste sports, scenical shows, plays, games; . . . And this I enjoin you, not as a divine alone, but as a physician; for without this mirth, which is the life and quintessence of physic, medicines, and whatsoever is used and applied to prolong the life of man, is dull, dead, and of no force. B. p. 372

Prosper Calenus to that melancholy Cardinal Cæsius, "amidst thy serious studies and business, use jests and conceits, plays and toys, and whatsoever else may recreate thy mind." Nothing better than mirth and merry company in this malady. B. p. 373

> Or so devote to Aristotle's checks. I, 1, 32

Divines (for *Pythia Philippisat*), lawyers, physicians, philosophers, scholars are his, wholly devote to his service. B. p. 228

> Music and poesy use to quicken you. I, 1, 36

Amor mundum fecit, love built cities, *mundi anima*, invented arts, sciences, and all good things, incites us to virtue and humanity, combines and quickens. B. p. 475

> The mathematics and the metaphysics,
> Fall to them as you find your stomach serves you.
> No profit grows where is no pleasure ta'en;
> In brief, sir, study what you most affect. I, 1, 37

Now what so pleasing can there be as the speculation of these things, to read and examine such experiments, or if a man be more mathematically given, to calculate, or peruse Napier's Logarithms, . . . Or let him make an *ephemerides*, read Suisset, the calculator's works, Scaliger *de emendatione temporum*, and Petavius his adversary, till he understand them, peruse subtle Scotus and Suarez's metaphysics, . . . For, as he that plays for nothing will not heed his game; no more will voluntary employment so thoroughly affect a student, except he be very intent of himself, and take an extraordinary delight in the study, about which he is conversant. It should be of that nature his business, which *volens nolens* he must necessarily undergo, and without great loss, mulct, shame, or hindrance, he may not omit. B. p. 355

To comb your noddle with a three-legg'd stool, I, 1, 64

Like that of the thrush and swallow in Æsop, instead of mutual love, kind compellations, whore and thief is heard, they fling stools at one another's heads. B. p. 64

From all such devils, good Lord deliver us! I, 1, 66

As the proverb is, from heresy, jealousy and frenzy, good Lord deliver us. B. p. 660

And then have to't afresh. I, 1, 134

'Tis frequent with them to challenge the field for their lady and mistress' sake, to run a tilt,

"That either bears (so furiously they meet)
The other down under the horses' feet,"

and then up and to it again. B. p. 570

As are the swelling Adriatic seas. I, 2, 72

(See, below, *Othello*, III, 3, 457.)

Luc. Yea, and perhaps with more successful words
Than you, unless you were a scholar, sir.
Gre. O this learning, what a thing it is!
Gru. O this woodcock, what an ass it is! I, 2, 154

A mere scholar, a mere ass. B. p. 200

Hortensio, to what end are all these words? I, 2, 246

But what need many words? B. p. 591

ALL'S WELL THAT ENDS WELL

Our remedies oft in ourselves do lie,
Which we ascribe to heaven. The fated sky
Gives us free scope; only doth backward pull
Our slow designs when we ourselves are dull. I, 1, 202

"They seek that at God's hands which they may give unto themselves, if they could but refrain from those cares and perturbations, wherewith they continually macerate their minds." B. p. 170

"Every man's mind is stronger than fortune, and leads him to what side he will; a cause to himself each one is of his good or bad life." B. p. 403

"They supposed fortune alone gave kingdoms and empires, wealth, honours, offices; . . . but after, they began upon better advice to think otherwise, that every man made his own fortune." B. p. 709

All our quickest wits, as an owl's eyes at the sun's light, wax dull, and are not sufficient to apprehend them. B. p. 116

> 'Let me not live' quoth he
> 'After my flame lacks oil, to be the snuff
> Of younger spirits, whose apprehensive senses
> All but new things disdain;' I, 2, 58

After their death their memory stinks as a snuff of a candle put out. B. p. 484

> Your marriage comes by destiny I, 3, 59

Marriage and hanging goes by destiny, matches are made in heaven.

"It lies not in our power to love or hate
For will in us is overrul'd by fate." B. p. 613

> If ever we are nature's, these are ours; this thorn
> Doth to our rose of youth rightly belong; I, 3, 120

In general "as the heaven, so is our life, sometimes fair, sometimes overcast, tempestuous, and serene; as in a rose, flowers and prickles; . . ." B. p. 91

> O, will you eat
> No grapes, my royal fox? Yes, but you will
> My noble grapes, an if my royal fox
> Could reach them: II, 1, 68

The fox in the emblem would eat no grapes, but why? because he could not get them. B. p. 612

> It is like a barber's chair, that fits all buttocks—the pin buttock, the quatch buttock, the brawn buttock, or any buttock. II, 2, 16

Venus, a notorious strumpet, as common as a barber's chair. B. p. 689

> The web of our life is of a mingled yarn, good and ill together. Our virtues would be proud if our faults whipt them not; and our crimes would despair if they were not cherish'd by our virtues. IV, 3, 67

These concupiscible and irascible appetites are as the two twists of a rope, mutually mixed one with the other, and both twining about the heart: both good, as Austin holds, *l.* 14, *c.* 9, *de civ. Dei*, "if they be moderate; both pernicious if they be exorbitant." B. p. 184

And were it not for such gentle remembrances, men would have no moderation of themselves. B. p. 380

If every man might have what he would, we should all be deified, emperors, kings, princes. B. p. 415

"Therefore," saith Chrysostom, "good men do not always find grace and favour, lest they should be puffed up with turgent titles, grow insolent and proud." B. p. 417

> No, no, no, your son was misled with a snipt-taffeta fellow there, whose villainous saffron would have made all the unbak'd and doughy youth of a nation in his colour. IV, 5, 1

Bad companions have been their bane. For *malus malum vult ut sit sui similis;* one drunkard in a company, one thief, one whoremaster, will by his goodwill make all the rest as bad as himself . . . be of what complexion you will, inclination, love or hate, be it good or bad, if you come amongst them, you must do as they do. B. p. 374

> I am no great Nebuchadnezzar, sir; I have not much skill in grass. IV, 5, 18

Nebuchadnezzar did eat grass like an ox. B. p. 114

Nebuchadnezzar was really translated into a beast. B. p. 117

> I will henceforth eat no fish of Fortune's butt'ring. V, 2, 7

"Mine haven's found, fortune and hope adieu,
Mock others now, for I have done with you." B. p. 414

> I spake but by a metaphor. V, 2, 10

If it [jealousy] appear amongst bachelors, we commonly call them rivals, or co-rivals, a metaphor derived from a river, *rivales à rivo;* for as a river, saith Acron *in Hor. Art. Poet.* and Donat. *in* Ter.

ALL'S WELL THAT ENDS WELL

Eunuch. divides a common ground between two men, and both participate of it, so is a woman indifferent between two suitors, both likely to enjoy her. B. p. 629

> A paper from Fortune's close-stool to give to a nobleman! V, 2, 15

Not only libraries and shops are full of our putid papers, but every close-stool and jakes. B. p. 6

> *Par.* My lord, I am a man whom Fortune hath cruelly scratch'd.
> *Laf.* And what would you have me to do? 'Tis too late to pare her nails now. Wherein have you played the knave with Fortune, that she should scratch you, who of herself is a good lady and would not have knaves thrive long under her? V, 2, 26

Yet what I have formerly said of other melancholy, I will say again, it may be cured or mitigated at least by some contrary passion, good counsel and persuasion, if it be withstood in the beginning, maturely resisted, and as those ancients hold, "the nails of it be pared before they grow too long." B. p. 646

TWELFTH NIGHT

> If music be the food of love, play on. I, 1, 1

Et fugitare decet simulacra et pabula amoris. B. p. 588

> And my desires, like fell and cruel hounds,
> E'er since pursue me. I, 1, 22

But giving way to these violent passions of fear, grief, shame, revenge, hatred, malice, etc., they are torn in pieces as Actæon was with his dogs. B. p. 170

No such cruel affections, but by discipline they may be tamed. B. p. 361

> when liver, brain, and heart,
> Those sovereign thrones, . . . I, 1, 37

Languis, *med, epist, lib.* 1. *cap*, 24. will have this passion [love] seated in the liver, and to keep residence in the heart. . . . Jo. Frietagius, *cap*, 14. *noct. med.* supposeth all four affected, heart, liver, brain, blood. B. p. 502

Where, like Arion on the dolphin's back, I, 2, 15

Arion made fishes follow him. B. p. 368

The sea-nymphs half-naked, keeping time on dolphins' backs, . . . B. p. 577

There is a fair behaviour in thee, Captain;
And though that nature with a beauteous wall
Doth oft close in pollution, yet of thee
I will believe thou hast a mind that suits
With this thy fair and outward character. I, 2, 47

In fine, as Æneas Sylvius adds, "they are most part miserable, sottish, and filthy fellows, like the walls of their houses, fair without, foul within." B. p. 383

They are like painted walls, fair without, rotten within: B. p. 388

I am sure care's an enemy to life. I, 3, 2

Discontents, cares, crosses, miseries, . . . The common etymology will evince it, *Cura, quasi* cor uro, *Dementes curæ, insomnes curæ, damnosæ curæ, tristes, mordaces, carnifices, &c.*, biting, eating, gnawing, cruel, bitter, sick, sad, unquiet, pale, tetric, miserable, intolerable cares. B. pp. 178–179

He's a coward and a coystrill that will not drink to my niece till his brains turn o' th' toe like a parish-top. I, 3, 37

So in Poland, he is the best servitor, and the honestest fellow, saith Alexander Gaguinus, that drinketh most healths to the honour of his master. B. p. 149

Now, sir, thought is free. I, 3, 65

This roving humour (though not with like success) I have ever had, and like a ranging spaniel, that barks at every bird he sees, leaving his game, I have followed all, . . . I never travelled but in map or card, in which my unconfined thoughts have freely expatiated, as having ever been especially delighted with the study of Cosmography. B. pp. 2–3

. . . but I am a great eater of beef, and I believe that does harm to my wit. I, 3, 80

Beef, a strong and hearty meat (cold in the first degree, dry in the second, saith Gal. *l.* 3, *c.* 1., *de alim. fac.*) is condemned by him and all succeeding authors, to breed gross melancholy blood. B. p. 141

Sir To. Then hadst thou had an excellent head of hair.
Sir And. Why, would that have mended my hair?
Sir To. Past question; for thou seest it will not curl by nature.
Sir And. But it becomes me well enough, does't not?
Sir To. Excellent; it hangs like flax on a distaff, and I hope to see a huswife take thee between her legs and spin it off.
I, 3, 91

If once he be besotten on a wench, he must . . . mark above all things what hats, bands, doublets, breeches, are in fashion, how to cut his beard, . . . curl his head, . . . he may be scoffed at otherwise, as Julian that apostate emperor was for wearing a long hirsute goatish beard, fit to make ropes with. B. p. 576

I did think, by the excellent constitution of thy leg, it was form'd under the star of a galliard. I, 3, 124

Dancing a Greek galliard. B. p. 542

My mouse of virtue. I, 5, 59

(See, below, *Hamlet*, III, 4, 183.)

O, you are sick of self-love, Malvolio. I, 5, 85

I will only insist upon some few of the chief, and most noxious in their kind, as . . . self-love, pride, and inordinate desire of vain-glory. . . . B. p. 185

One of thy kin has a most weak pia mater. I, 5, 108

Therefore nature hath covered it with a skull of hard bone, and two skins or membranes, whereof the one is called *dura mater*, or meninx, the other *pia mater*. B. p. 97

A plague o' these pickle-herring! I, 5, 114

Invent new tricks, as sausages, anchovies, tobacco, caviare, pickled oysters, herrings, fumadoes, &c.; innumerable salt meats to increase their appetite. B. p. 148

Methinks I feel this youth's perfections
With an invisible and subtle stealth
To creep in at mine eyes. I, 5, 280

"To proceed first from the eyes so carried by our spirits, and kindled with imagination in the liver and heart;" *coget amare jecur*.
B. p. 502

> I do I know not what, and fear to find
> Mine eye too great a flatterer for my mind.
> Fate, show thy force: ourselves we do not owe;
> What is decreed must be; and be this so! I, 5, 292

Love cannot be compelled, they must affect as they may: *Fatum est in partibus illis quas sinus abscondit*, as the saying is, marriage and hanging goes by destiny, matches are made in heaven.

"It lies not in our power to love or hate,
For will in us is overrul'd by fate." B. p. 613

> If you can separate yourself and your misdemeanours, you are welcome to the house. II, 3, 93

I hate their vices, not their persons. B. p. 72

> *Mal.* My masters, are you mad? Or what are you? Have you no wit, manners, nor honesty, but to gabble like tinkers at this time of night? Do you make an ale-house of my lady's house, . . .
> *Sir To.* . . . Art any more than a steward?
> . . .
> *Mar.* Go shake your ears. II, 3, 83–118

As that stupid fellow put out the candle because the biting fleas should not find him; he shrouds himself in an unknown habit, borrowed titles, because nobody should discern him. Every man thinks with himself, *Egomet videor mihi sanus*, I am well, I am wise, and laughs at others. And 'tis a general fault amongst them all, that which our forefathers have approved, diet, apparel, opinions, humours, customs, manners, we deride and reject in our time as absurd. . . . So are we fools and ridiculous, absurd in our actions, carriages, diet, apparel, customs, and consultations; we scoff and point one at another, when as in conclusion all are fools, "and they the veriest asses that hide their ears most." B. p. 37

> Dost thou think, because thou art virtuous, there shall be no more cakes and ale? II, 3, 109

Some out of preposterous zeal object many times trivial arguments, and because of some abuse, will quite take away the good use, as if they should forbid wine because it makes men drunk; but in my judgment they are too stern: . . . I will subscribe to the king's declaration, and was ever of that mind, those May games, wakes, and Whitsun ales, &c., if they be not at unseasonable hours, may justly be permitted. B. p. 346

Now is the woodcock near the gin. II, 5, 77

'tis but a springe to catch woodcocks. B. p. 523

And, to inure thyself to what thou art like to be, cast thy humble slough and appear fresh. II, 5, 132

He shrouds himself in an unknown habit, borrowed titles. B. p. 37

This fellow is wise enough to play the fool;
And to do that well craves a kind of wit.
He must observe their mood on whom he jests,
The quality of persons, and the time;
And, like the haggard, check at every feather
That comes before his eye. This is a practice
As full of labour as a wise man's art;
For folly that he wisely shows is fit;
But wise men, folly-fall'n, quite taint their wit. III, 1, 57

Your greatest students are commonly no better, silly, soft fellows in their outward behaviour, absurd, ridiculous to others, and no whit experienced in worldly business. B. p. 201

I am as mad as he
If sad and merry madness equal be. III, 4, 14

That some are solitary, dull, heavy, churlish; some again blithe, buxom, light and merry, they ascribe wholly to the stars. As if Saturn be predominant in his nativity, and cause melancholy in his temperature then he shall be . . . sad. B. p. 260

Others . . . make madness and melancholy but one disease.
B. p. 88

I have lim'd her; but it is Jove's doing, III, 4, 69

It may not be learned, Ovid himself cannot teach us how to love.
B. p. 614

What, man, 'tis not for gravity to play at cherry-pit with Satan. Hang him, foul collier! III, 4, 110

From the devil can be no certainty, for he is a liar from the beginning; if he suggests any such thing, as too frequently he doth, reject him as a deceiver, an enemy of human kind, dispute not with him, give no credit to him, obstinately refuse him, as St. Antony did in the wilderness, whom the devil set upon in several shapes, or as the collier did, so do thou by him. For when the devil tempted him with the weakness of his faith, and told him he could not be saved, as being ignorant in the principles of religion, and urged him moreover to know what he believed, what he thought of such and such points and mysteries; the collier told him, he believed as the church did; but what (said the devil again) doth the church believe? as I do (said the collier); and what's that thou believest; as the church doth, etc., when the devil could get no other answer he left him. B. p. 731

> For it comes to pass oft that a terrible oath, with a swaggering accent sharply twanged off, gives manhood more approbation than ever proof itself would have earn'd him.
> III, 4, 170

As a cur that goes through a village, if he clap his tail between his legs, and run away, every cur will insult over him: but if he bristle up himself, and stand to it, give but a counter-snarl, there's not a dog dares meddle with him: much is in a man's courage and discreet carriage of himself. B. p. 423

> O, if it prove,
> Tempests are kind, and salt waves fresh in love! III, 4, 367

That seas and waters are enamoured with this our beauty, is all out as likely as that of the air and winds; for when Leander swam in the Hellespont, Neptune with his trident did beat down the waves, but

"They still mounted up intending to have kiss'd him,
And fell in drops like tears because they missed him." B. p. 511

> A very dishonest paltry boy, and more a coward than a hare.
> III, 4, 369

The Egyptians therefore in their hieroglyphics expressed a melancholy man by a hare sitting in her form, as being a most timorous and solitary creature. B. p. 259

> I am not tall enough to become the function well nor lean enough to be thought a good student. IV, 2, 6

For it is held by some of them, as an axiom, that to keep them poor, will make them study; they must be dieted, as horses to a race, not pampered, . . . a fat bird will not sing, a fat dog cannot hunt, . . .
B. p. 209

Twelfth Night

> *Clo.* What is the opinion of Pythagoras concerning wild fowl? IV, 2, 49

The Pythagoreans defend Metempsychosis; and Palingenesia, that souls go from one body to another, *epotâ prius Lethes undâ*, as men into wolves, bears, dogs, hogs, as they were inclined in their lives. B. p. 104

> Now my foes tell me plainly I am an ass; so that by my foes, sir, I profit in the knowledge of myself, and by my friends I am abused. V, 1, 16

We commonly love him best in this malady [vain-glory], that doth us most harm, and are very willing to be hurt. B. p. 193

The Winter's Tale

> *Arch.* You shall see, as I have said, great difference betwixt our Bohemia and your Sicilia.
> *Cam.* I think this coming summer the King of Sicilia means to pay Bohemia the visitation which he justly owes him. I, 1, 3

Bohemia is cold, for that it lies all along to the north. B. p. 322

Note—I think it can safely be concluded that the writer of these two passages would not give Bohemia a coast line and thus that another hand wrote Act III, Sc. 3, of this play.

> And therefore, like a cipher,
> Yet standing in rich place, I multiply
> With one 'We thank you' many thousands more
> That go before it. I, 2, 6

(See, below, *King Henry V, 1st Prologue*; lines 1–25.)

> *Her.* He'll stay, my lord. I, 2, 87
> *Leon.* This entertainment
> May a free face put on; derive a liberty
> From heartiness, from bounty, fertile bosom,
> And well become the agent. 'T may, I grant;
> But to be paddling palms and pinching fingers,
> As now they are, and making practis'd smiles
> As in a looking-glass; and then to sigh, as 'twere
> The mort o' th' deer. O, that is entertainment
> My bosom likes not, nor my brows! I, 2, 111

The indiscreet carriage of some lascivious gallant (*et è contra* of some light woman) by his often frequenting of a house, bold unseemly gestures, may make a breach, and by his over familiarity, if he be inclined to yellowness, colour him quite out. B. p. 639

And with his varying childness cures in me
Thoughts that would thick my blood. I, 2, 170

It [sorrow] hinders concoction, refrigerates the heart, takes away stomach, colour, and sleep, thickens the blood. B. p. 171

There have been,
Or I am much deceiv'd, cuckolds ere now;
And many a man there is, even at this present,
Now while I speak this, holds his wife by th' arm
That little thinks she has been sluic'd in's absence,
And his pond fish'd by his next neighbour, by
Sir Smile, his neighbour. I, 2, 190

"Stolen waters be more pleasant:" or as Vitellius the emperor was wont to say, *Jucundiores amores, qui cum periculo habentur*, like stolen venison, still the sweetest is that love which is most difficultly attained: they like better to hunt by stealth in another man's walk, than to have the fairest course that may be at game of their own.
B. p. 636

Should all despair
That have revolted wives, the tenth of mankind
Would hang themselves. Physic for't there's none;
I, 2, 198

Howsoever the best way is to contemn it, which Henry II. king of France advised a courtier of his, jealous of his wife, and complaining of her unchasteness, to reject it, and comfort himself; for he that suspects his wife's incontinency, and fears the Pope's curse, shall never live a merry hour, or sleep a quiet night: no remedy but patience. B. p. 651

Is there any remedy for this in physic? B. p. 24

My wife is slippery? I, 2, 273

All women are slippery, often unfaithful to their husbands.
B. p. 632

> Horsing foot on foot? I, 2, 288

She came and drank to him, and withal trod upon his toes, . . . B. p. 531

They cannot, I say, contain themselves, they will be still not only joining hands, kissing, but embracing, treading on their toes, &c. B. p. 553

> My father nam'd me Autolycus; who, being, as I am, litter'd under Mercury, was likewise a snapper-up of unconsidered trifles. With die and drab I purchas'd this caparison; and my revenue is the silly-cheat. IV, 3, 24

Or that of Autolicus, Mercury's son, that dwelt in Parnassus, who got so much treasure by cozenage and stealth. His father Mercury, because he could leave him no wealth, taught him many fine tricks to get means. B. p. 119

> If the springe hold, the cock's mine. IV, 3, 34

'tis but a springe to catch woodcocks. B. p. 523

> Not a more cowardly rogue in all Bohemia; if you had but look'd big and spit at him, he'd have run. IV, 3, 100

And withal acts a lord's part, takes upon him to be some statesman or magnifico, makes congés, gives entertainment, looks big, &c. B. p. 264

Preferred before his betters, because he can put himself forward, because he looks big. B .p. 415

> Jog on, jog on, the footpath way,
> And merrily hent the stile-a;
> A merry heart goes all the day,
> Your sad tires in a mile-a. IV, 3, 118

The merrier the heart the longer the life; "A merry heart is the life of the flesh," *Prov.* xiv. 30. B. p. 369

> The gods themselves,
> Humbling their deities to love, have taken
> The shapes of beasts upon them: Jupiter
> Became a bull and bellow'd; IV, 4, 25

Jupiter himself was turned into a satyr, shepherd, a bull, a swan, a golden shower, and what not, for love. B. p. 491

Fie, daughter! When my old wife liv'd, upon
This day she was both pantler, butler, cook;
Both dame and servant; welcom'd all; serv'd all;
Would sing her song and dance her turn; now here
At upper end o' th' table, now i' th' middle;
On his shoulder, and his; IV, 4, 55

. . . now stationary, now direct, now retrograde, now in *apogee*, then in *perigee*, now swift then slow, occidental, oriental, they turn round, jump and trace. . . . B. p. 542

the fairest flow'rs o' th' season
Are our carnations and streak'd gillyvors, IV, 4, 81

"The gilliflower, the rose is not so sweet,
As sugared kisses be when lovers meet:" B. p. 536

Their bath shall be the juice of gilliflowers. B. p. 544

Per. Of that kind
Our rustic garden's barren; and I care not
To get slips of them.
Pol. Wherefore, gentle maiden,
Do you neglect them?
Per. For I have heard it said
There is an art which in their piedness shares
With great creating nature.
Pol. So there be;
Yet nature is made better by no mean
But nature makes that mean; so over that art,
Which you say adds to nature, is an art
That nature makes. You see, sweet maid, we marry
A gentler scion to the wildest stock,
And make conceive a bark of baser kind
By bud of nobler race. *The Winter's Tale*, IV, 4, 83

Others again, in that opposite extreme, do as great harm by their too much remissness, they give them no bringing up, no calling to busy themselves about, or to live in, teach them no trade, or set them in any good course; . . . who is he of so little experience that knows not this of Fabius to be true? "Education is another nature, altering the mind and will, and I would to God (saith he) we ourselves did not spoil our children's manners, by our overmuch cockering and nice education, and weaken the strength of their bodies and minds, that causeth custom, custom nature," Etc. . . .

and spare for no cost, that they may be well nurtured and taught, it being a matter of so great consequence. B. p. 219

But these are improperly called jealousies, and by a metaphor, to show the care and solicitude they have of them. B. p. 627

This is an art
Which does mend nature—change it rather; but
The art itself is nature. IV, 4, 95

Est in nobis assuescere (as Plutarch saith), we may frame ourselves as we will. As he that useth an upright shoe, may correct the obliquity, or crookedness, by wearing it on the other side;
B. p. 361

Cam. I should leave grazing, were I of your flock,
And only live by gazing.
Per. Out, alas!
You'd be so lean that blasts of January
Would blow you through and through. IV, 4, 109

Hilarion, as Hierome reports in his life, and Athanasius of Antonius, was so bare with fasting, "that the skin did scarce stick to the bones; . . ." B. p. 681

nothing she does or seems
But smacks of something greater than herself,
Too noble for this place. IV, 4, 157

So much in the meantime I do attribute to Gentility, that if he be well-descended, of worshipful or noble parentage, he will express it in his conditions. B. p. 385

for never gaz'd the moon
Upon the water as he'll stand and read,
As 'twere, my daughter's eyes; IV, 4, 172

"They cannot look off whom they love," they will *impregnare eam ipsis oculis*, deflower her with their eyes, be still gazing, staring, stealing faces, smiling, glancing at her, as Apollo on Leucothoë, the moon on her Endymion, when she stood still in Caria, and at Latmos caused her chariot to be stayed. B. p. 554

Forewarn him that he use no scurrilous words in's tunes.
IV, 4, 210

To roar and sing scurrilous songs in base places. B. p. 373

Telling or hearing lascivious tales, scurrilous tunes. B. p. 579

Sooth, when I was young
And handed love as you do, I was wont
To load my she with knacks; IV, 4, 339

They will rain chickens, florins, crowns, angels, all manner of coins and stamps in her lap. B. p. 544

Flo. But come on,
Contract us fore these witnesses. . . .
Pol. Soft, swain, awhile, beseech you;
Have you a father?
Flo. I have, but what of him? IV, 4, 381

(See, above, *The Tempest*, V, 1, 190.)

we'll bar thee from succession;
Not hold thee of our blood, no, not our kin,
Farre than Deucalion off. IV, 4, 421

Or else they fetched their pedigree from those that were struck by Samson with the jaw-bone of an ass. Or from Deucalion and Pyrrha's stones. B. p. 70

Prosperity's the very bond of love,
Whose fresh complexion and whose heart together
Affliction alters. IV, 4, 565

So long as they are behoveful, they love, or may bestead each other, but when there is no more good to be expected, as they do by an old dog, hang him up or cashier him. B. p. 33
He shall be befriended, "for riches gather many friends," *Prov.* xix, 4. B. p. 227

I think affliction may subdue the cheek,
But not take in the mind. IV, 4, 568

A wound hurts not the soul. B. p. 380

The gout may hurt his hands, lameness his feet, convulsions may torture his joints, but not *rectam mentem*, his soul is free. B. p. 400

She [Fortune] can take away my means, but not my mind. B. p. 402

What a fool Honesty is. IV, 4, 587

Honesty is accounted folly. B. p. 34

Clo. We are but plain fellows, sir.
Aut. A lie: you are rough and hairy. Let me have no lying.
. . . Seest thou not the air of the court in these enfoldings? . . .
Receives not thy nose court-odour from me? IV, 4, 710–21

Note—This appears to me to refer to *Genesis*, XXV, 27 "and Jacob was a plain man"; XXVII, 11 "And Jacob said to Rebekah his mother, Behold, Esau my brother is a hairy man, and I am a smooth man"; XXVII, 27 "and he smelled the smell of his raiment." In the main plot Camillo is Rebekah; Florizel and, unawares, Perdita are Jacob; Polixenes and Leontes together are Isaac—"A sad tale's best for winter."

They have Esau's hands, and Jacob's voice. B. p. 712

Note: See Addenda (p. 334) for further notes on this passage and also for IV, 4, 734; IV, 4, 815, and IV, 4, 816.

He is gone aboard a new ship to purge melancholy and air himself. IV, 4, 751

. . . purgeth the brain of those anxious black melancholy fumes. B. p. 438

"Many other things helped, but change of air was that which wrought the cure [of melancholy], and did most good." B. p. 336

King John

Or if that surly spirit, melancholy. III, 3, 42

If hereafter anatomizing this surly humour [melancholy] B. p. 74

Hath bak'd thy blood and made it heavy-thick,
Which else runs tickling up and down the veins. III, 3, 43

"The melancholy juice is redundant all over", hirsute they are, and lean, they have broad veins, their blood is gross and thick. B. p. 271

I am not mad—I would to heaven I were!
For then 'tis like I should forget myself.
O, if I could, what grief should I forget! III, 4, 48

Madness is therefore defined to be a vehement dotage . . . without all fear and sorrow. B. p. 88

There's nothing in this world can make me joy.
Life is as tedious as a twice-told tale
Vexing the dull ear of a drowsy man. III, 4, 107

'Tis to no purpose in that vulgar phrase to use a company of obsolete sentences, and familiar sayings . . . either say something that I never read nor heard of before, or else hold thy peace.

B. p. 375

> A sceptre snatch'd with an unruly hand
> Must be as boisterously maintain'd as gain'd,
> And he that stands upon a slipp'ry place
> Makes nice of no vile hold to stay him up. III, 4, 135

Though they flourish many times, such hypocrites, such temporising foxes, and blear the world's eyes by flattery, bribery, dissembling their natures, or other men's weakness, that cannot so apprehend their tricks, yet in the end they will be discerned, and precipitated, in a moment: "surely", saith David, "thou hast set them in slippery places". B. p. 484

> Any annoyance in that precious sense! IV, 1, 94

Of these five senses, sight is held to be most precious. B. p. 100

> *Arth.* Lo, by my troth, the instrument is cold
> And would not harm me.
> *Hub.* I can heat it, boy.
> *Arth.* No, in good sooth; the fire is dead with grief,
> Being create for comfort, to be us'd
> In undeserved extremes. See else yourself:
> There is no malice in this burning coal;
> The breath of heaven hath blown his spirit out,
> And strew'd repentant ashes on his head.
> *Hub.* But with my breath I can revive it, boy.
> *Arth.* An if you do, you will but make it blush
> And glow with shame of your proceedings, Hubert.
> Nay, it perchance will sparkle in your eyes,
> And, like a dog that is compell'd to fight,
> Snatch at his master, that doth tarre him on. IV, 1, 104

Monsters of men, as we are, dogs, wolves, tigers, fiends, incarnate devils, we do not only contend, oppress, and tyrannize ourselves, but as so many firebrands, we set on, and animate others; our whole life is a perpetual combat, a conflict, a set battle, a snarling fit.

B. p. 487

Those embers of faith, hope and repentance, now buried in ashes, will flame out afresh and be fully revived. B. p. 736

O, when the last account 'twixt heaven and earth
Is to be made, then shall this hand and seal
Witness against us to damnation! IV, 2, 216

"Why do we contend and vex one another? Behold death is over our heads, and we must shortly give an account of all our uncharitable words and actions: think upon it and be wise."
B. p. 490

The seal of damnation. B. p. 666

How oft the sight of means to do ill deeds
Makes deeds ill done! IV, 2, 219

Nothing sooner revives, "or waxeth sore again" as Petrarch holds, "than love doth by sight." "As pomp renews ambition; the sight of gold, covetousness . . ." 'tis dangerous therefore to see. . . . For that cause belike Alexander discerning this inconvenience and danger that comes by seeing, "when he heard Darius' wife so much commended for her beauty, would scarce admit her to come in his sight." B. p. 589

And you have slander'd nature in my form,
Which, howsoever rude exteriorly,
Is yet the cover of a fairer mind
Than to be butcher of an innocent child. IV, 2, 256

Cornelius Mussus, that famous preacher in Italy, when he first came into the pulpit in Venice, was so much contemned by reason of his outside, a little, lean, poor, dejected person, that they were all ready to leave the church; but when they heard his voice they did admire him . . . A silly fellow to look to, may have more wit, learning, honesty, than he that struts it out . . . Æsop was crooked, Socrates purblind, long-legged, hairy; Democritus withered; Seneca lean and harsh, ugly to behold, yet show me so many flourishing wits, such divine spirits. B. p. 379

Away with me, all you whose souls abhor
Th' uncleanly savours of a slaughter-house;
For I am stifled with this smell of sin. IV, 3, 111

In each town these several tradesmen shall be so aptly disposed, as they shall free the rest from danger or offence . . . noisome or fulsome for bad smells, as butchers' slaughter-houses, chandlers, curriers, in remote places. B. p. 59

This sense is an organ of health . . . and that by avoiding bad smells, as by choosing good, which do as much alter and affect the body many times, as diet itself. B. p. 101

Where commonly carrion lies in the streets . . . and the streets uncleanly kept. B. p. 157

When the entrails were opened, and a noisome savour offended her nose. B. p. 221

> Withhold thine indignation, mighty heaven,
> And tempt us not to bear above our power! V, 6, 37

Though Cain cry out in the anguish of his soul, my punishment is greater than I can bear, 'tis not so; thou liest, Cain (saith Austin), "God's mercy is greater than thy sins." B. p. 725

He will not suffer thee to be tempted above measure. B. p. 735

> and his pure brain,
> Which some suppose the soul's frail dwelling-house,
> Doth by the idle comments that it makes
> Foretell the ending of mortality. V, 7, 2

In the upper region serving the animal faculties, the chief organ is the brain, which is a soft, marrowish, and white substance, engendered of the purest part of seed and spirits, included by many skins, and seated within the skull or brain pan; and it is the most noble organ under heaven, the dwelling-house and seat of the soul, the habitation of wisdom, memory, judgment, reason, and in which man is most like unto God. B. p. 97

> I am the cygnet to this pale faint swan
> Who chants a doleful hymn to his own death, V, 7, 21

"The jealous swanne against his death that singeth,
And eke the owle that of death bode bringeth." B. p. 629

> Be of good comfort, Prince; for you are born
> To set a form upon that indigest
> Which he hath left so shapeless and so rude. V, 7, 25

I must for that cause do my business myself, and was therefore enforced, as a bear doth her whelps, to bring forth this confused lump; I had not time to lick it into form, as she doth her young ones, . . . B. p. 11

King John

What surety of the world, what hope, what stay,
When this was now a king, and now is clay? V, 7, 68

The body is *domicilium animæ*, her house, abode, and stay. B. p. 245

Job aggravates this, iv. 18, "Behold he found no stedfastness in his servants, and laid folly upon his angels," 19. "How much more on them that dwell in houses of clay?" B. p. 20

King Richard The Second

Thou, now a-dying. II, 1, 90

One such a kiss alone would recover a man if he were a dying. B. p. 513

For sorrow's eye, glazed with blinding tears,
Divides one thing entire to many objects,
Like perspectives which . . . II, 2, 16

Multiplying glasses, perspectives, *ut unus homo apparet exercitus*. B. p. 354

Now comes the sick hour that his surfeit made. II, 2, 84

If I feed liberally, I am likely sick or surfeit. B. p. 408

And nothing can we call our own but death
And that small model of the barren earth
Which serves as paste and cover to our bones. III, 2, 152

Man, the most excellent and noble creature of the world, "the principal and mighty work of God, wonder of nature," as Zoroaster calls him; *audacis naturæ miraculum*, "the marvel of marvels" as Plato; "the abridgment and epitome of the world," as Pliny; Microcosmus a little world, a model of the world. B. p. 81

Go thou, and like an executioner
Cut off the heads of too fast growing sprays
That look too lofty in our commonwealth. III, 4, 43

Adrian the emperor was so galled with it [emulation] that he killed all his equals; so did Nero. B. p. 176

Now is this golden crown like a deep well
That owes two buckets, filling one another;
The emptier ever dancing in the air,
The other down, unseen, and full of water. IV, 1, 184

Like so many buckets in a well, as one riseth another falleth, one's empty, another's full. B. p. 33

Hence, villain! never more come in my sight. V, 2, 86

Out, villain, begone, come no more in my sight. B. p. 32

Our scene is alt'red from a serious thing,
And now chang'd to 'The Beggar and the King'. V, 3, 79

The scene is altered on a sudden, love is turned to hate, mirth to melancholy. B. p. 478

His words come from his mouth, ours from our breast. V, 3, 102

To see so much difference betwixt words and deeds, so many parasangs betwixt tongue and heart. B. p. 34

Where this true love is wanting, there can be no firm peace, friendship from teeth outward, counterfeit . . . B. p. 483

The better sort,
As thoughts of things divine, are intermix'd
With scruples, and do set the word itself
Against the word,
As thus: 'Come, little ones'; and then again,
'It is as hard to come as for a camel
To thread the postern of a small needle's eye'. V, 5, 11

Every small object affrights them, the very inconsiderate reading of Scripture itself, and misinterpretation of some places of it; as "Many are called, few are chosen. Not every one that saith Lord. Fear not little flock. He that stands let him take heed lest he fall." B. p. 717

What art thou? and how comest thou hither,
Where no man never comes but that sad dog
That brings me food to make misfortune live? V, 5, 69

He that gives a beggar an alms (as that comical poet saith) doth ill, because he doth but prolong his miseries. B. p. 287

K. Rich. How went he under him?
Groom. So proudly as if he disdain'd the ground. V, 5, 82

And why did Theogine's horse in Heliodorus curvet, prance, and go so proudly? B. p. 511

KING RICHARD THE SECOND

> For now the devil, that told me I did well,
> Says that this deed is chronicled in hell. V, 5, 115

And the devil that then told thee that it was a light sin, or no sin at all, now aggravates on the other side, and telleth thee, that it is a most irremissible offence. B. p. 719

KING HENRY THE FOURTH—PART ONE

> What, in thy quips and thy quiddities? I, 2, 44

Such quirks and quiddities, *quodlibetaries*, as Bale saith of Ferribrigge and Strode. B. p. 698

> What sayest thou to a hare, or the melancholy of Moor Ditch? I, 2, 76

The Egyptians therefore in their hieroglyphics expressed a melancholy man by a hare sitting in her form, as being a most timorous and solitary creature. B. p. 259

> For wisdom cries out in the streets. I, 2, 86

Wisdom cries out in the streets. B. p. 664

> Why, Hal, 'tis my vocation, Hal; 'tis no sin for a man to labour in his vocation. I, 2, 101

Labour in his vocation whatever it is. B. p. 595

> *Poins.* Then thou art damn'd for keeping thy word with the devil.
> *Prince.* Else he had been damn'd for cozening the devil. I, 2, 116

This conscience is that which approves good or evil, justifying or condemning our actions, and is the conclusion of the syllogism: as in that familiar example of Regulus the Roman, taken prisoner by the Carthaginians, and suffered to go to Rome, on that condition he should return again, or pay so much for his ransom. The synteresis proposeth the question; his word, oath, promise, is to be religiously kept, although to his enemy, and that by the law of nature. "Do not that to another which thou wouldest not have done to thyself." Dictamen applies it to him, and dictates this or the like: Regulus, thou wouldst not another man should falsify his oath, or break promise with thee: conscience concludes, therefore, Regulus, thou dost well to perform thy promise, and oughtest to keep thine oath. B. p. 106

> I prithee, Tom, beat Cut's saddle; put a few flocks in the point; poor jade is wrung in the withers out of all cess.
> II, 1, 5

A horse that tills the land fed with chaff, an idle jade have provender in abundance. B. p. 34

> No, ye fat chuffs; I would your store were here.
> On, bacons, on! What, ye knaves! young men must live.
> II, 2, 86

As they compel scholars in our times to complain of poverty, or crouch to a rich chuff for a meal's meat. B. p. 209

> My sword hack'd like a hand-saw. II, 4, 160

To fight so long "till their head-piece, bucklers be all broken, and swords hacked like so many saws". B. p. 570

> I deny your major II, 4, 478

This makes the major proposition in a practical syllogism.
B. p. 106

> I prithee tell me, doth he keep his bed? IV, 1, 21

And have more need of physic than many a man that keeps his bed. B. p. 700

KING HENRY THE FOURTH—PART TWO

> I, from the orient to the drooping west,
> Making the wind my post-horse, still unfold
> The acts commenced on this ball of earth.
> Induction, line 3

In the mean time, the world is tossed in a blanket amongst them, they hoist the earth up and down like a ball, make it stand and go at their pleasure: one saith the sun stands, another he moves.
B. p. 328

The times are wild, contention, like a horse
Full of high feeding, madly hath broke loose
And bears down all before him. I, 1, 9

If thine horse be too lusty, Hierome adviseth thee to take away some of his provender. B. p. 585

In poison there is physic. I, 1, 137

"Antimony is rather poison than a medicine." B. p. 441

Fal. Sirrah, you giant, what says the doctor to my water?
Page. He said, sir, the water itself was a good healthy water; but for the party that owed it, he might have moe diseases than he knew for. I, 2, 1

And for urine, that is *meretrix medicorum*, the most deceitful thing of all, as Forestus and some other physicians have proved at large. B. p. 428

Page. He's gone into Smithfield to buy your worship a horse.
Fal. I bought him in Paul's, and he'll buy me a horse in Smithfield. An I could get me but a wife in the stews, I were mann'd, hors'd, and wiv'd. I, 2, 46

He that marries a wife out of a suspected inn or alehouse, buys a horse in Smithfield, and hires a servant in Paul's, as the diverb is, shall likely have a jade to his horse, a knave for his man, an arrant honest woman to his wife. B. p. 657

He hath eaten me out of house and home. II, 1, 71

Thy wife's friends will eat thee out of house and home. B. p. 605

Marry, the immortal part needs a physician; but that moves not him. II, 2, 100

If our leg or arm offend us, we covet by all means possible to redress it; and if we labour of a bodily disease, we send for a physician; but for the diseases of the mind we take no notice of them. B. p. 36

Though that be sick, it dies not. II, 2, 102

Thy soul is eclipsed for a time, I yield, as the sun is shadowed by a cloud; no doubt but those gracious beams of God's mercy will shine upon thee again, as they have formerly done: those embers of faith, hope, and repentance, now buried in ashes, will flame out afresh, and be fully revived. B. p. 736

Even such kin as the parish heifers are to the town bull.
II, 2, 150

Thou rangest like a town bull, why art thou so incensed if she tread awry? B. p. 648

From a god to a bull? A heavy descension! It was Jove's case. II, 2, 167

Degenerate into dogs, hogs, asses, brutes; as Jupiter into a bull.
B. p. 563

I will toss the rogue in a blanket. II, 4, 212

(See above, this play, *Induction*, line 3.)

. . . and eats conger and fennel. II, 4, 235

Magninus rejects conger, sturgeon . . . Crato, *consil.* 21 *lib.* 2, speaks against all herbs and worts, except borage, bugloss, fennel . . .
B. p. 143

You see, my good wenches, how men of merit are sought after. II, 4, 361

Unheard, unsought for, or unseen.
Author's Abstract of Melancholy

O sleep, O gentle sleep,
Nature's soft nurse, how have I frighted thee,
That thou no more wilt weigh my eyelids down,
And steep my senses in forgetfulness? III, 1, 5

Sleep, rest of things, O pleasing deity,
Peace of the soul, which cares dost crucify,
Weary bodies refresh and mollify. B. p. 356

Uneasy lies the head that wears a crown. III, 1, 31

What king canst thou show me, not full of cares?
"Look not on his crown, but consider his afflictions . . ."
B. p. 183

Things that are mouldy lack use. III, 2, 108

A horse in a stable that never travels, a hawk in a mew that seldom flies, are both subject to diseases; which left unto themselves, are most free from any such incumbrances. An idle dog will be mangy . . . wit without employment is a disease *Ærugo animi, rubigo ingenii:* the rust of the soul. B. p. 159

We owe God a death. III, 2, 228

The Lord gives, the Lord takes, blessed be the name of the Lord. *Job*, I, 21. B. p. 735

Care I for the limb, the thews, the stature, bulk and big assemblance of a man! Give me the spirit. III, 2, 251

Virtue refuseth no stature, and commonly your great vast bodies, and fine features, are sottish, dull, and leaden spirits . . . What is Maximinus, Ajax, Caligula, and the rest of those great Zanzummins, or gigantical Anakims, heavy, vast, barbarous lubbers? B. p. 380

And sung those tunes to the overscutch'd huswifs that he heard the carmen whistle. III, 2, 305

A carman's whistle, a boy singing some ballad tune early in the street. B. p. 367

'Tis seldom when the bee doth leave her comb
In the dead carrion. IV, 4, 79

"A thing so common all over Europe at this day, and so generally abused, that many men are utterly undone by it," their means spent, patrimonies consumed, they and their posterity beggared; besides swearing, wrangling, drinking, loss of time, and such inconveniences, which are ordinary concomitants: "for when once they have got a haunt of such companies, and habit of gaming, they can hardly be drawn from it, but as an itch it will tickle them, and as it is with whoremasters, once entered, they cannot easily leave it off:" B. p. 345

"It is an easy passage down to hell,
But to come back, once there, you cannot well." B. p. 584

She either gives a stomach and no food—
Such are the poor, in health—or else a feast,
And takes away the stomach—such are the rich
That have abundance and enjoy it not. IV, 4, 105

Crœsus or rich Crassus cannot now command health, or get himself a stomach. "His worship," as Apuleius describes him, in all his plenty and great provision, is forbidden to eat, or else hath no appetite. B. p. 389

But wherefore did he take away the crown? IV, 5, 89

O my son,
God put it in thy mind to take it hence,
That thou mightst win the more thy father's love,
Pleading so wisely in excuse of it! IV, 5, 178

How jealous was our Henry the Fourth of King Richard the Second, so long as he lived, after he was deposed! and of his own son Henry in his later days! which the prince well perceiving, came to visit his father in his sickness, in a watchet velvet gown, full of eyelet holes, and with needles sticking in them (as an emblem of jealousy), and so pacified his suspicious father, after some speeches and protestations, which he had used to that purpose. B. p. 628

Prince. I never thought to hear you speak again.
King. Thy wish was father, Harry, to that thought.
I stay too long by thee, I weary thee.
Dost thou so hunger for mine empty chair
That thou wilt needs invest thee with my honours
Before thy hour be ripe? IV, 5, 92

It may be he was an hypocrite, as many are, and howsoever he spake thee fair, peradventure he prayed, amongst the rest that Icaro Menippus heard at Jupiter's whispering-place in Lucian, for his father's death, because he now kept him short, he was to inherit much goods, and many fair manors after his decease. B. p. 411

Therefore thou best of gold art worst of gold.
Other, less fine in carat, is more precious,
Preserving life in med'cine potable. IV, 5, 161

Matthiolus in the same place approves of potable gold. B. p. 435

But he and most commend *aurum potabile*. B. p. 438

God knows, my son,
By what by-paths and indirect crook'd ways
I met this crown; and I myself know well
How troublesome it sat upon my head:
To thee it shall descend with better quiet. IV, 5, 184

"No evil is to be done that good may come of it." B. p. 287

And had a purpose now
To lead out many to the Holy Land,
Lest rest and lying still might make them look

> Too near into my state. Therefore, my Harry,
> Be it thy course to busy giddy minds
> With foreign quarrels, that action, hence borne out,
> May waste the memory of the former days. IV, 5, 210

In a commonwealth, where there is no public enemy, there is likely civil wars, and they rage upon themselves: this body of ours, when it is idle, and knows not how to bestow itself, macerates and vexes itself with cares, griefs, false fears, discontents and suspicions.

B. p. 159

The ordinary recreations which we have in winter, and in most solitary times busy our minds with, are cards, tables . . .

B. p. 344

> *Davy.* Shall we sow the headland with wheat?
> *Shal.* With red wheat, Davy. V, 1, 14

Constantine wrote twenty books of husbandry. Lysander, when ambassadors came to see him, bragged of nothing more than of his orchard, *hi sunt ordines mei*. What shall I say of Cincinnatus, Cato, Tully, and many such? how they have been pleased with it, to prune, plant, inoculate and graft, to show so many several kinds of pears, apples, plums, peaches, etc. . . . Jucundus, in his preface to Cato, Varro, Columella, etc., put out by him, confesseth of himself, that he was mightily delighted with these husbandry studies, and took extraordinary pleasure in them: if the theory or speculation can so much affect, what shall the place and exercise itself: the practical part do? The same confession I find in Herbastien, Porta, Camerarius, and many others, which have written of that subject. If my testimony were aught worth, I could say as much of myself; I am *verè Saturnus*; no man took more delight in springs, woods, groves, gardens, walks, fishponds, rivers, etc. But

> "Tantalus à labri sitiens fugientia captat
> Flumina."

And so do I; *Velle licet, potiri non licet.* B. p. 342

(See also, below, *This Play*, V, 3, 1.)

> It is certain that either wise bearing or ignorant carriage is caught, as men take diseases, one of another; therefore let men take heed of their company. V, 1, 73

As Hermione lamented in Euripides, *malae mulieres me fecerunt malam.* Evil company marred her, may they justly complain bad companions have been their bane. For, *malus malum vult ut sit sui similis;* one drunkard in a company, one thief, one whoremaster, will by his goodwill make all the rest as bad as himself. B. p. 374

Now what these brain-sick heretics once broach, and impostors set on foot, be it never so absurd, false, and prodigious, the common people will follow and believe. It will run along like murrain in cattle, scab in sheep. B. p. 696

This is the English, not the Turkish court;
Not Amurath an Amurath succeeds,
But Harry Harry. V, 2, 47

Amurath the Turk. B. p. 54

Shal. Nay, you shall see my orchard, where, in an arbour, we shall eat a last year's pippin of mine own grafting, with a dish of caraways, and so forth. Come, cousin Silence. And then to bed.

Fal. Fore God, you have here a goodly dwelling and rich.

(See, above, *This Play*, V, 1, 14.) V, 3, 1

. . . the heart's all. V, 3, 29

. . . the mind is all. B. p. 397

And a merry heart lives long-a. V, 3, 47

(See, above, *Love's Labour's Lost*, V, 2, 18 and
The Winter's Tale, IV, 3, 118.)

Make less thy body hence, and more thy grace;
Leave gormandizing. V, 4, 53

"Meat and drink hath overcome as many, whilst they rather strive to please, satisfy their guts and belly, than to serve God and nature." B. p. 664

King Henry the Fifth

O for a muse of fire, that would ascend
The brightest heaven of invention
. . . .
. . . Can this cockpit hold
The vasty fields of France? Or may we cram
Within this wooden O the very casques

That did affright the air at Agincourt?
O, pardon! since a crooked figure may
Attest in little space a million;
And let us, ciphers to this great accompt,
On your imaginary forces work.
. . . .
Into a thousand parts divide one man,
And make imaginary puissance. 1*st Prologue*, lines 1–25

As a long-winged hawk, when he is first whistled off the fist, mounts aloft, and for his pleasure fetcheth many a circuit in the air, still soaring higher and higher till he be come to his full pitch, and in the end, when the game is sprung, comes down amain, and stoops upon a sudden: so will I, having now come at last into these ample fields of air, wherein I may freely expatiate and exercise myself for my creation, awhile rove, wander round about the world, mount aloft to those ethereal orbs and celestial spheres, and so descend to my former elements again. B. p. 313

Or let him demonstrate a proposition in Euclid, in his five last books, extract a square root, or study Algebra: than which, as Calvius holds, "in all human disciplines nothing can be more excellent and pleasant, so abstruse and recondite, so bewitching, so miraculous, so ravishing, so easy withal and full of delight," *omnem humanum captum superare videtur*. By this means you may define *ex ungue leonem*, as the diverb is, by his thumb alone the bigness of Hercules, or the true dimensions of the great Colossus, Solomon's temple, and Domitian's amphitheatre out of a little part. By this art you may contemplate the variation of the twenty-three letters, which may be so infinitely varied, that the words complicated and deduced thence will not be contained within the compass of the firmament; ten words may be varied 40,320 several ways: by this art you may examine how many men may stand one by another in the whole superficies of the earth, some say 148,456,800,000,000, *assignando singulis passum quadratum* (assigning a square foot to each), how many men, supposing all the world as habitable as France, as fruitful and so long-lived, may be born in 60,000 years, and so may you demonstrate with Archimedes how many sands the mass of the whole world might contain if all sandy, if you did but first know how much a small cube as big as a mustard-seed might hold, with infinite such. B. p. 353

If a man be more mathematically given, to calculate, or peruse Napier's logarithms. B. p. 355

It must be thought on. If it pass against us,
We lose the better half of our possession; I, 1, 7

Next to politicians, if I may distinguish them, are some of our priests (who make religion policy), if not far beyond them, for they domineer over princes and statesmen themselves. B. p. 674

And, to relief of lazars and weak age,
Of indigent faint souls, past corporal toil,
A hundred almshouses right well supplied. I, 1, 15

If they be impotent, lame, blind, and single, they shall be sufficiently maintained in several hospitals, built for that purpose; if married and infirm, past work . . . B. p. 61

Consideration like an angel came
And whipp'd th' offending Adam out of him,
Leaving his body as a paradise
T' envelop and contain celestial spirits.
Never was such a sudden scholar made;
Never came reformation in a flood,
With such a heady currance, scouring faults;
Nor never Hydra-headed wilfulness
So soon did lose his seat, and all at once,
As in this king. I, 1, 28

Consider of it . . . no such cruel affections, but by discipline they may be tamed; voluntarily thou wilt not do this or that, which thou oughtest to do, or refrain, etc., but when thou art lashed like a dull jade, thou wilt reform it; fear of a whip will make thee do, or not do. B. p. 361

Isæus, a philosopher of Assyria, was a most dissolute liver in his youth, *palàm lasciviens*, in love with all he met; but after he betook himself, by his friend's advice, to his study, and left women's company, he was so changed that he cared no more for plays, nor feasts, nor masks, nor songs, nor verses, fine clothes, nor no such love toys: he became a new man upon a sudden. B. p. 591

Recover thy credit by some noble exploit, as Themistocles did, for he was a most debauched and vicious youth, *sed juventæ maculas præclaris factis delevit*, but made the world amends by brave exploits; at last become a new man, and seek to be reformed. B. pp. 421–422

So that the art and practic part of life
Must be the mistress to this theoric. I, 1, 51

The common divisions are of the understanding, agent, and patient; speculative, and practical; . . . The agent is a doctor or teacher, the passive a scholar; B. pp. 105–106

If the theorick or speculation can so much affect, what shall the place and exercise itself, the practick part, do? B. p. 343

What more pleasing studies can there be than the mathematicks, theorick or practick parts? B. p. 350

N.B.—The Cowden Clarkes* interpret these two lines thus:—

"So that one would think the art of living, and the practical part of life, must have been that which taught him his theoretical knowledge."

And so the Prince obscur'd his contemplation
Under the veil of wildness; which, no doubt,
Grew like the summer grass, fastest by night,
Unseen, yet crescive in his faculty. I, 1, 63

Phantasy, or imagination, which some call estimative, or cogitative (confirmed, saith Fernelius, by frequent meditation), is an inner sense which doth more fully examine the species perceived by common sense, of things present or absent, and keeps them longer, recalling them to mind again, or making new of his own. In time of sleep this faculty is free. B. p. 101

"Sleep is a rest or binding of the outward senses, and of the common sense, for the preservation of body and soul" (as Scaliger defines it). . . . The phantasy alone is free, and his commander reason: as appeareth by those imaginary dreams. B. p. 102

Non eadem est ætas, non mens. B. p. 11

It must be so; for miracles are ceas'd;
And therefore we must needs admit the means
How things are perfected. I, 1, 67

There is nothing in the understanding, which was not first in the sense. (Footnote) *Nihil in intellectu, quod non prius fuerat in sensu.* Velcurio. B. p. 106

So sweet is the delight of study, the more learning they have (as he that hath a dropsy, the more he drinks the thirstier he is) the more they covet to learn, and the last day is *prioris discipulus*. B. p. 351

Note—I regard these Henry V passages as being among the most profound in the whole of "Shakespeare". It is interesting to note that they were not contained in the Quartos.

---

* *The Plays of Shakespeare*; Cassell, Petter and Galpin.

The King has kill'd his heart. II, 1, 85

No cut to unkindness. B. p. 242

'How now, Sir John!' quoth I, 'What, man, be o' good cheer.' So 'a cried out 'God, God, God!' three or four times. Now I, to comfort him, bid him 'a should not think of God; I hop'd there was no need to trouble himself with any such thoughts yet. II, 3, 17

Be of good cheer . . . comfort thyself. B. p. 728

Turn head and stop pursuit; for coward dogs
Most spend their mouths when what they seem to threaten
Runs far before them. Good my sovereign,
Take up the English short, and let them know
Of what a monarchy you are the head.
Self-love, my liege, is not so vile a sin
As self-neglecting. II, 4, 71

And sometimes again, so that it be discreetly and moderately done, it shall not be amiss to make resistance, to take down such a saucy companion, no better means to vindicate himself to purchase final peace: for he that suffers himself to be ridden, or through pusillanimity or sottishness will let every man baffle him, shall be a common laughing stock to flout at. As a cur that goes through a village, if he clap his tail between his legs, and runs away, every cur will insult over him: but if he bristle up himself, and stand to it, give but a counter-snarl, there's not a dog dares meddle with him: much is in a man's courage and discreet carriage of himself. B. p. 423

Undervalue not thyself. B. p. 424

Once more unto the breach, . . . III, 1, 1

Desire to enter upon breaches, lie sentinel, perdue, give the first onset, stand in the fore front of the battle. B. p. 30

I see you stand like greyhounds in the slips,
Straining upon the start. The game's afoot: III, 1, 31

As a long-winged hawk, . . . mounts aloft, . . . till he be come to his full pitch, and in the end, when the game is sprung, comes down amain, . . . B. p. 313

To the mines! . . . countermines. III, 2, 54–58

Minings and counterminings. B. p. 478

'Tis all our study, practice, and business how to plot mischief, mine, countermine. B. p. 186

Gow. Here 'a comes; and the Scots captain, Captain Jamy with him. III, 2, 71*

And now most happy in that fortunate union of England and Scotland, which our forefathers have laboured to effect, and desired to see. B. p. 49

And when the mind is quick'ned, out of doubt
The organs, though defunct and dead before,
Break up their drowsy grave and newly move
With casted slough and fresh legerity. IV, 1, 20

One Galeus de Rubeis, that being commended for refining of an instrument of Archimedes, for joy ran mad. B. p. 198

"Mirth" (saith Vives) "purgeth the blood, confirms health, causeth a fresh, pleasing and fine colour," prorogues life, whets the wit, makes the body young, lively and fit for any manner of employment. B. p. 369

No, not all these, thrice gorgeous ceremony,
Not all these, laid in bed majestical,
Can sleep so soundly as the wretched slave IV, 1, 262

"He sighs for grief of heart (as Cyprian hath it) and cannot sleep though it be upon a down bed; his wearish body takes no rest, troubled in his abundance, . . ." B. p. 188

the wretched slave
Who, with a body fill'd and vacant mind,
Gets him to rest, cramm'd with distressful bread.
IV, 1, 264

Husbandmen, and such as labour, can eat fat bacon, salt gross meat, hard cheese, etc. (*O dura messorum ilia*), coarse bread at all times, go to bed and labour upon a full stomach, which to some idle persons would be present death. B. p. 151

---

* See Verity, A. W., *King Henry V*, Cambridge University Press; *The Political Teaching of Henry V* in Introduction, p. xxiii.

and their poor jades
Lob down their heads, dropping the hides and hips,
The gum down-roping from their pale-dead eyes,
And in their pale dull mouths the gimmal'd bit
Lies foul with chaw'd grass, still and motionless;
And their executors, the knavish crows,
Fly o'er them, all impatient for their hour. IV, 2, 46

(See, above, *As You Like It*, II, 1, 33, and
King Henry The Fourth, pt. 1, II, 1, 5.)

West. Of fighting men they have full three-score thousand.
Exe. There's five to one; besides, they all are fresh. IV, 3, 3

Bodine excuseth his countrymen's overthrow at that famous battle at Agincourt, in Henry the Fifth his time (*cui simile*, saith Froissard, *tota historia producere non possit*, which no history can parallel almost, wherein one handful of Englishmen overthrew a royal army of Frenchmen), with this refuge of despair, *pauci desperati*, a few desperate fellows being compassed in by their enemies, past all hope of life, fought like so many devils. B. p. 713

By Jove, I am not covetous for gold,
Nor care I who doth feed upon my cost;
It yearns me not if men my garments wear; IV, 3, 24

I do not envy at their wealth, titles, offices. B. p. 396

Let them run, ride, strive as so many fishes for a crumb, scrape, climb, catch, snatch, cozen, collogue, temporise and fleire, take all amongst them, wealth, honour, and get what they can, it offends me not. B. p. 414

Or I will fetch thy rim out at thy throat. IV, 4, 14

This stomach is sustained by a large kell or kaull, called omentum; which some will have the same with peritoneum, or rim of the belly. B. p. 96

Gow. Alexander the Great.
Flu. Why, I pray you, is not 'pig' great? The pig, or the great, or the mighty, or the huge, or the magnanimous, are all one reckonings, save the phrase is a little variations. IV, 7, 14

I call a spade a spade, *animis haec scribo, non auribus*, I respect matter not words; remembering that of Cardan, *verba propter res, non res propter verba*. B. p. 11

King Henry the Fifth

> There is a river in Macedon; and there is also moreover a river at Monmouth; it is call'd Wye at Monmouth.
> IV, 7, 23

With us, navigable rivers are most part neglected; our streams are not great, I confess, . . . but calm and fair as Arar in France, Hebrus in Macedonia, Eurotas in Laconia, they gently glide along, and might as well be repaired many of them (I mean Wye, Trent, Ouse, Thamisis at Oxford, the defect of which we feel in the mean time) as the River of Lee from Ware to London. B. p. 55

> Alexander—God knows, and you know—in his rages, and his furies, and his wraths, and his cholers, and his moods, and his displeasures, and his indignations, and also being a little intoxicates in his prains, did, in his ales and his angers, look you, kill his best friend, Cleitus. IV, 7, 32

Alexander, a worthy man, but furious in his anger, overtaken in drink. B. p. 68

Alexander in his fury made Clitus his dear friend to be put to death. B. p. 628

"No cut to unkindness." B. p. 242

> Not for Cadwallader and all his goats. V, 1, 26

Cadwallader in Wales, Rollo in Normandy, Robin Hood and Little John, are as much renowned in Sherwood, as Cæsar in Rome.
B. p. 196

> But grow, like savages—as soldiers will,
> That nothing do but meditate on blood— V, 2, 59

They persecute beasts so long, till in the end they themselves degenerate into beasts. B. p. 190

King Henry the Sixth—Part Two

> Although by his sight his sin be multiplied. II, 1, 71

As pomp renews ambition; the sight of gold, covetousness; a beauteous object sets on fire this burning lust. *Et multum saliens incitat unda sitim.* The sight of drink makes one dry, and the sight of meat increaseth appetite. 'Tis dangerous therefore to see.
B. p. 589

If thou hadst been born blind, thou mightst as well have known all our names as thus to name the several colours we do wear. Sight may distinguish of colours; but suddenly to nominate them all, it is impossible. II, 1, 124

There is nothing in the understanding, which was not first in the sense. B. p. 106

A blind man cannot judge of colours. B. p. 300

Thus sometimes hath the brightest day a cloud. II, 4, 1

Or what so secure and pleasing a morning have we seen, that hath not been overcast before evening. B. p. 179

I must offend before I be attainted;
And had I twenty times so many foes,
And each of them had twenty times their power,
All these could not procure me any scathe
So long as I am loyal, true, and crimeless. II, 4, 59

Socrates was brought upon the stage by Aristophanes, and misused to his face, but he laughed as if it concerned him not: and as Ælian relates of him, whatsoever good or bad accident or fortune befell him, going in or coming out, Socrates still kept the same countenance; even so should a Christian do, as Hierom describes him, *per infamiam et bonam famam grassari ad immortalitatem*, march on through good and bad reports to immortality, not to be moved: for honesty is a sufficient reward, *probitas sibi præmium.* B. p. 420

The greatest help is quiet, gentle Nell.
I pray thee sort thy heart to patience;
These few days' wonder will be quickly worn. II, 4, 67

Thou shalt find greatest ease to be quiet. B. p. 420

I have been stigmatized, whipt at post, arraigned and condemned, I am a common obloquy, I have lost my ears, odious, execrable, abhorred of God and men. Be content, 'tis but a nine days' wonder. B. p. 421

Death, at whose name I oft have been afeard,
Because I wish'd this world's eternity. II, 4, 89

They start at the name of death, as a horse at a rotten post. Say what you can of that other world, Montezuma that Indian prince, *Bonum est esse hic*, they had rather be here. B. p. 406

KING HENRY THE SIXTH—PART TWO

Ah, Uncle Humphrey, in thy face I see
The map of honour, truth, and loyalty! III, 1, 202

As Eleonora, that exiled mournful duchess (in our English Ovid [Drayton]), laments to her noble husband Humphrey, duke of Glocester . . . B. p. 171

And as the butcher takes away the calf,
And binds the wretch and beats it when it strays,
Bearing it to the bloody slaughter-house,
Even so, remorseless, have they borne him hence;
And as the dam runs lowing up and down,
Looking the way her harmless young one went.
III, 1, 210

Some at the departure of friends only whom they shall shortly see again, weep and howl, and look after them as a cow lows after her calf. B. p. 234

Comb down his hair; look, look! it stands upright,
Like lime-twigs set to catch my winged soul! III, 3, 15

In a word, "the hairs are Cupid's nets, to catch all comers." (Footnote: Arandus. *Capilli retia Cupidinis.*) B. p. 517

Forbear to judge, for we are sinners all.
Close up his eyes, and draw the curtain close;
And let us all to meditation. III, 3, 31

Be justly offended with him as he was a murderer, but pity him now as a dead man . . . Who knows how he may be tempted? It was his case, it may be thine: *Quæ sua sors hodie est, cras fore vestra potest.* We ought not to be rash and rigorous in our censures, as some are; charity will judge and hope the best: God be merciful unto us all. B. p. 288

Spare none but such as go in clouted shoon. IV, 2, 180

To clout shoes upon a Sunday. B. p. 698

And henceforward all things shall be in common. IV, 7, 17

I will yet, to satisfy and please myself, make an Utopia of mine own, a new Atlantis, a poetical commonwealth of mine own.
B. p. 56

KING HENRY THE SIXTH—PART TWO

He is fled, my lord, and all his powers do yield,
And humbly thus, with halters on their necks,
Expect your Highness' doom of life or death. IV, 9, 10

P. Aemilius, *l.* 6, speaks of six senators of Calais, that came with halters in their hands to the king of England, to die for the rest.
B. p. 484

Oft have I seen a hot o'erweening cur
. . . .
Hath clapp'd his tail between his legs and cried.
V, 1, 151–154

As a cur, that goes through a village, if he clap his tail between his legs and run away, every cur will insult over him. B. p. 423

As crooked in thy manners as thy shape! V, 1, 158

(See, above, *The Tempest*, V, 1, 290.)

KING HENRY THE SIXTH—PART THREE

And to conclude: the shepherd's homely curds,
His cold thin drink out of his leather bottle,
His wonted sleep under a fresh tree's shade,
All which secure and sweetly he enjoys,
Is far beyond a prince's delicates— II, 5, 47

Let him be my lord, patron, baron, earl, and possess so many goodly castles, 'tis well for me that I have a poor house and a little wood, and a well by it. B. p. 396

Who's this? O God! It is my father's face,
Whom in this conflict I unwares have kill'd. II, 5, 61
Is this our foeman's face?
Ah, no, no, no, it is mine only son! II, 5, 82

Nothing so common as to have "father fight against the son, brother against brother, kinsman against kinsman, . . ."
B. p. 28

So abominable a thing is war . . . the late civil wars in France, those abominable wars . . . so many myriads of the commons butchered up with sword, famine, war . . . or at our late Pharsalian fields in the time of Henry the Sixth, betwixt the houses of Lancaster and York, a hundred thousand men slain. B. p. 29

King Henry The Sixth—Part Three

Let me embrace thee, sour adversity,
For wise men say it is the wisest course. III, 1, 24

Many philosophers have voluntarily sought adversity, and so much commend it in their precepts. Demetrius, in Seneca, esteemed it great infelicity that in his lifetime he had no misfortune. B. p. 404
This is the safest course, and thou shalt find greatest ease to be quiet. B. p. 420

Ah, simple men, you know not what you swear!
Look, as I blow this feather from my face,
And as the air blows it to me again,
Obeying with my wind when I do blow,
And yielding to another when it blows,
Commanded always by the greater gust,
Such is the lightness of you common men. III, 1, 83

For the common people are as a flock of sheep, a rude, illiterate rout, void many times of common sense, a mere beast, *bellua multorum capitum*, will go whithersoever they are led: as you lead a ram over a gap by the horns, all the rest will follow. B. p. 678

Good day, my lord! What, at your book so hard? V, 6, 1

Ptolemeus . . . became Strato's scholar, fell hard to his book. B. p. 405

Suspicion always haunts the guilty mind:
The thief doth fear each bush an officer. V, 6, 11

Fear makes our imagination conceive what it list, invites the devil to come to us, as Agrippa and Cardan avouch, and tyrannizeth over our fantasy more than all other affections, especially in the dark. B. p. 172

The bird that hath been limed in a bush
With trembling wings misdoubteth every bush; V, 6, 13

"Like travellers and seamen," saith Plutarch, "that when they have been sanded, or dashed on a rock, for ever after fear not that mischance only, but all such dangers whatsoever." B. p. 222

King Richard The Third

That trudge betwixt the King and Mistress Shore. I, 1, 73

Shore's wife by this engine overcame Edward the Fourth. B. p. 534

More pity that the eagles should be mew'd
While kites and buzzards prey at liberty. I, 1, 132

Not eagles, but kites. B. p. 19

And leave the world for me to bustle in. I, 1, 152

Because he looks big, can bustle in the world. B. p. 415

Thou hadst but power over his mortal body,
His soul thou canst not have. I, 2, 47

Mens immota manet, though the body be torn in pieces with wild horses, broken on the wheel, pinched with fiery tongs, the soul cannot be distracted. B. p. 418

For thou hast made the happy earth thy hell. I, 2, 51

Before blessed and happy, now miserable and accursed. B. p. 81

O, gentlemen, see, see! Dead Henry's wounds
Open their congeal'd mouths and bleed afresh.
Blush, blush, thou lump of foul deformity,
For 'tis thy presence that exhales this blood
From cold and empty veins where no blood dwells.
I, 2, 55

Why doth a carcass bleed, when the murderer is brought before it, some weeks after the murder hath been done? B. p. 169

And we may manifestly perceive a strange eduction of spirits, by such as bleed at nose after they be dead, at the presence of the murderer. B. p. 521

And by despairing shalt thou stand excused
For doing worthy vengeance on thyself
That didst unworthy slaughter upon others. I, 2, 86

Tacitus the historian, Plutarch the philosopher, much approve a voluntary departure, and Aust. *de civ. Dei, l.* 1. *c.* 29. defends a violent death, so that it be undertaken in a good cause. B. p. 287

Out of my sight! Thou dost infect mine eyes. I, 2, 148

Among so many thousand authors you shall scarce find one, by reading of whom you shall be any whit better, but rather much worse, *quibus inficitur potiùs quàm perficitur*, by which he is rather infected than any way perfected. B. p. 7

Lo here I lend thee this sharp-pointed sword;
Which if thou please to hide in this true breast
And let the soul forth that adoreth thee,
I lay it naked to the deadly stroke,
And humbly beg the death upon my knee. I, 2, 174

Polienus, when his mistress Circe did but frown upon him in Petronius, drew his sword, and bade her kill, stab, or whip him to death, he would strip himself naked and not resist. B. p. 568

'Tis a point of wisdom. I, 4, 98

When thou art once in love, to moderate thyself (as he saith) is a singular point of wisdom. B. p. 590

1 *Murd.* When he opens his purse to give us our reward, thy conscience flies out.
2 *Murd.* 'Tis no matter; let it go; there's few or none will entertain it.
1 *Murd.* What if it come to thee again? I, 4, 128

Our conscience, which is a great ledger book, wherein are written all our offences, a register to lay them up, (which those Egyptians in their hieroglyphics expressed by a mill, as well for the continuance, as for the torture of it,) grinds our souls with the remembrance of some precedent sins, makes us reflect upon, accuse and condemn our ownselves. B. p. 718

So do not I. Go, coward as thou art. I, 4, 277

Thou sayest as much of me, stomachosus as thou art. B. p. 13

Then go like a beggar as thou art. B. p. 415

Comfort, dear mother. God is much displeas'd
That you take with unthankfulness his doing.
In common worldly things 'tis call'd ungrateful
With dull unwillingness to repay a debt
Which with a bounteous hand was kindly lent;
Much more to be thus opposite with heaven,
For it required the royal debt it lent you. II, 2, 89

"The Lord gives, the Lord takes, blessed be the name of the Lord." *Job*, I, 21. B. p. 735

Grandam, this would have been a biting jest. II, 4, 30

Biting jests, *mordentes et aculeati*. B. p. 225

Sweet Prince, the untainted virtue of your years
Hath not yet div'd into the world's deceit;
Nor more can you distinguish of a man
Than of his outward show; which, God He knows,
Seldom or never jumpeth with the heart. III, I, 7

If every man had a window in his breast, which Momus would have had in Vulcan's man, or that which Tully so much wished it were written in every man's forehead, *Quid quisque de republicâ sentiret*, what he thought. B. p. 36

That Julius Cæsar was a famous man;
With what his valour did enrich his wit,
His wit set down to make his valour live.
Death makes no conquest of this conqueror;
For now he lives in fame, though not in life. III, I, 84

Cosmo de Medici, that rich citizen of Florence, ingenuously confessed to a near friend of his, that would know of him why he built so many public and magnificent palaces, and bestowed so liberally on scholars, not that he loved learning more than others, "but to eternize his own name, to be immortal by the benefit of scholars; for when his friends were dead, walls decayed, and all inscriptions gone, books would remain to the world's end." The lanthorn in Athens was built by Zenocles, the theatre by Pericles, the famous port Pyræum by Musicles, Pallas Palladium by Phidias, the Pantheon by Callicratidas; but these brave monuments are decayed all, and ruined long since, their builders' names alone flourish by meditation of writers. And as he said of that Marian oak, now cut down and dead, *nullius Agricolæ manu culta stirps tam diuturna quam quæ poetæ versu seminari potest*, no plant can grow so long as that which is *ingenio sata*, set and manured by such ever-living wits.
B. p. 488

York. Because that I am little, like an ape,
He thinks that you should bear me on your shoulders.
Buck. With what a sharp-provided wit he reasons!
To mitigate the scorn he gives his uncle
He prettily and aptly taunts himself. III, I, 130

If it be a natural impediment, as a red nose, squint eyes, crooked legs, or any such imperfection, infirmity, disgrace, reproach, the best way is to speak of it first thyself, and so thou shalt surely take away all occasions from others to jest at, or contemn, that they may perceive thee to be careless of it. B. p. 423

A knot you are of damned blood-suckers. III, 3, 6

As a hen and chickens, all of a knot. B. p. 479

We know each other's faces; for our hearts,
He knows no more of mine than I of yours. III, 4, 11

(See, above, this play, III, 1, 7.)

Tut, I can counterfeit the deep tragedian
Speak and look back, and pry on every side. III, 5, 5

As a heron when she fishes, still prying on all sides. B. p. 641

Th' insatiate greediness of his desire. III, 7, 7

Looked wistfully and steadily on her, *inconnivo aspectu*, with much eagerness and greediness. B. p. 554

And look you get a prayer-book in your hand,
And stand between two churchmen, good my lord.
III, 7, 47

Captain Machiavel will have a prince by all means to counterfeit religion, to be superstitious in show at least, to seem to be devout, frequent holy exercises, honour divines, love the church. B. p. 672

When holy and devout religious men
Are at their beads, 'tis much to draw them thence,
So sweet is zealous contemplation. III, 7, 92

Such contemplations, and fantastical meditations, which are like unto dreams, and they will hardly be drawn from them. B. p. 161

Ea suavitas (one holds) *ut cum quis ea degustaverit, quasi poculis Circeis captus, non possit unquam ab illis divelli;* the like sweetness, which as Circe's cup bewitcheth a student, he cannot leave off. B. p. 350

Such sweet content there is in study. B. p. 351

But at hand, at hand,
Ensues his piteous and unpitied end. IV, 4, 73

Erit, erit, it shall be so. *Nemesis* comes after, *serò sed seriò,* stay but a little and thou shalt see God's just judgment overtake him.
B. p. 419

Note—The repetition "at hand, at hand"; "*erit, erit.*"

Now thy proud neck bears half my burden'd yoke,
From which even here I slip my weary head
And leave the burden of it all on thee. IV, 4, 111

But as the ox tired, told the camel (both serving one master), that refused to carry some part of his burden, before it were long he should be compelled to carry all his pack, and skin to boot (which by and by, the ox being dead, fell out). B. p. 356

Duch. Why should calamity be full of words?
Q. Eliz. Windy attorneys to their client woes,
Aery succeeders of intestate joys,
Poor breathing orators of miseries,
Let them have scope; though what they will impart
Help nothing else, yet do they ease the heart. IV, 4, 126

"All adversity finds ease in complaining (as Isidore holds), and 'tis a solace to relate it" . . . good words are cheerful and powerful of themselves, but much more from friends, as so many props, mutually sustaining each other like ivy and a wall, which Camerarius hath well illustrated in an emblem. *Lenit animum simplex vel saepè narratio*, the simple narration many times easeth our distressed minds. B. p. 362

Give me another horse. Bind up my wounds.
Have mercy, Jesu! Soft! I did but dream.
O coward conscience, how dost thou afflict me! V, 3, 177

Why had Richard the Third such fearful dreams, saith Polydore, but for his frequent murders? B. p. 719

Kennetus, King of Scotland, when he had murdered his nephew Malcom, King Duffe's son, Prince of Cumberland, and with counterfeit tears and protestations dissembled the matter a long time, "at last his conscience accused him, his unquiet soul could not rest day or night, he was terrified with fearful dreams, visions, and so miserably tormented all his life." B. p. 719

My conscience hath a thousand several tongues,
And every tongue brings in a several tale,
And every tale condemns me for a villain. V, 3, 193

The scrupulous conscience (as Peter Forestus calls it) which tortures so many, that either out of a deep apprehension of their unworthiness, and consideration of their own dissolute life, "accuse themselves and aggravate every small offence . . ." B. p. 718

King Richard The Third

Not shine today! Why, what is that to me
More than to Richmond? For the self same heaven
That frowns on me looks sadly upon him. V, 3, 285

As the rain falls on both sorts, so are riches given to good and bad, *sed bonis in bonum*, but they are good only to the godly. B. p. 387

Conscience is but a word that cowards use,
Devis'd at first to keep the strong in awe. V, 3, 309

No way better to curb than superstition, to terrify men's consciences, and to keep them in awe: they make new laws, statutes, invent new religions, ceremonies, as so many stalking horses, to their ends. B. p. 672

Troilus and Cressida

strong as the axle-tree
On which heaven rides. I, 3, 66

And as Helisæus Rœslin contends, [comets] have poles, axle-trees, circles of their own, and regular motions. B. p. 324

For if the earth be the centre of the world, stand still, and the heavens move, as the most received opinion is, which they call *inordinatem cœli dispositionem*, though stiffly maintained by Tycho, Ptolemeus, and their adherents, *quis ille furor?* etc., what fury is that, saith Dr. Gilbert, *satis animosè*, as Cabeus notes, that shall drive the heavens about with such incomprehensible celerity in twenty-four hours. B. p. 325

Degree being vizarded,
Th' unworthiest shows as fairly in the mask. I, 3, 83

Utopian parity is a kind of government, to be wished for, rather than effected, . . . I will have several orders, degrees of nobility. B. pp. 58–59

or, rather, right and wrong—
Between whose endless jar justice resides— I, 3, 116

Our love in spiritual things is too defective, in worldly things too excessive, there is a jar in both. B. p. 665

But that Achilles, were his brain as barren
As banks of Libya. I, 3, 327

. . . in a barren place, as the desert of Libya. B. p. 44

Blockish Ajax. I, 3, 375

They are sleepy, saith Savenarola, dull, slow, cold, blockish, ass-like. B. p. 261

Ajax. Thou bitch-wolf's son, canst thou not hear?
Feel, then. (*Strikes him.*) II, 1, 10

Ther. Ajax goes up and down the field asking for himself.
III, 3, 245

Mantanus, *consil.* 21, had a melancholy Jew to his patient, he ascribes this for a principal cause: *Irascebatur levibus de causis*, he was easily moved to anger. Ajax had no other beginning of his madness.
B. p. 178

Pia mater. II, 1, 68

(See, above, *Twelfth Night*, I, 5, 108.)

Who wears his wit in his belly and his guts in his head.
II, 1, 71

To see a man wear his brains in his belly, his guts in his head. (Footnote—Agrippa, *Ep.* 28, *l*, 7. *Quorum cerebrum est in ventre, ingenium in patinis.*) B. p. 35

Have ears more deaf than adders. II, 2, 172

As the enchanted adder, they stop their ears. B. p. 207

. . . for that, methinks, is the curse depending on those that war for a placket. II, 3, 18

What would he have said to see, hear, and read so many bloody battles, so many thousands slain at once, such streams of blood able to turn mills: *unius ob noxam furiasque*, or to make sport for princes, without any just cause, "for vain titles (saith Austin), precedency, some wench, or such like toy. . . ." B. p. 27

Heaven bless thee from a tutor, and discipline come not near thee! Let thy blood be thy direction till thy death.
II, 3, 25

Satan is their guide, the flesh is their instructor. B. p. 705

That were to enlard his fat already pride. II, 3, 190

They brag inwardly, and feed themselves fat with a self-conceit of sanctity. B. p. 196

Bull-bearing Milo his addition yield
To sinewy Ajax. II, 3, 241

Hadst thou Sampsons hair, Milo's strength . . . B. p. 182

He eats nothing but doves, love; and that breeds hot blood, and hot blood begets hot thoughts, and hot thoughts beget hot deeds, and hot deeds is love. III, 1, 122

. . . they are fatally driven on, and by reason of their hot blood, idle life, full diet, &c. are forced to dote upon them that come next. B. p. 531

Pruriens corpus, pruriens anima. B. p. 579

Pan. You'll remember your brother's excuse?
Par. To a hair. III, 1, 136

Bulco Opiliensis, sometime Duke of Silesia, was such a one to a hair; he lived (saith Æneas Sylvius) at Uratislavia, "and was so mad to satisfy his lust." B. p. 706

Helen. Commend me to your niece. III, 1, 139

"Birds of a feather will gather together." B. p. 479

Pan. She's making her ready, she'll come straight; you must be witty now. She does so blush, and fetches her wind so short, as if she were fray'd with a sprite. I'll fetch her. It is the prettiest villian; she fetches her breath as short as a new-ta'en sparrow.
Tro. Even such a passion doth embrace my bosom.
My heart beats thicker than the feverous pulse. III, 2, 29

"Her pulse began to vary, and to beat swifter, and so by often feeling her pulse, he perceived what the matter was." Apollonius, *Argonaut, lib.* 4. poetically setting down the meeting of Jason and Medea, makes them both to blush at one another's sight, and at the first they were not able to speak . . . Phædria trembled at the sight of Thais, others sweat, blow short. B. p. 552

Achilles stands i' th' entrance of his tent.
Please it our general pass strangely by him,
As if he were forgot; and, Princes all,
Lay negligent and loose regard upon him. III, 3, 38

Achilles left all his friends for Polyxena's sake, his enemy's daughter.
B. p. 512

> And better would it fit Achilles much
> To throw down Hector than Polyxena.
> But it must grieve young Pyrrhus now at home,

III, 3, 207

Plutarch, in his book *contra Coleten*, rails downright at such kind of marriages which are attempted by old men . . . *funerata est hæc pars jam fuit olim Achillea* . . . and as many doting sires do to their own shame, their children's undoing, and their families' confusion.

B. p. 654

> Sweet, rouse yourself; and the weak wanton Cupid
> Shall from off your neck unloose his amorous fold,
> And, like a dew-drop from the lion's mane,
> Be shook to airy air.

III, 3, 222

Rule thyself then with reason, satisfy thyself, accustom thyself, wean thyself from such fond conceits, vain fears, strong imaginations, restless thoughts. Thou mayest do it: *Est in nobis assuescere* (as Plutarch saith), we may frame ourselves as we will. As he that useth an upright shoe, may correct the obliquity, or crookedness, by wearing it on the other side; we may overcome passions if we will.

B. p. 361

He must wisely withstand the beginnings, rouse up reason.

B. p. 588

> Ajax goes up and down the field asking for himself.

III, 3, 245

(See, above, this play, II, 1, 10.)

> *Ther.* I said 'Good morrow, Ajax'; and he replies 'Thanks, Agamemnon'. What think you of this man that takes me for the general?

III, 3, 260

Marcellus Donatus knew such a gentlewoman in Mantua called Elionora Meliorina, that constantly believed she was married to a king, and "would kneel down and talk with him, as if he had been there present with his associates."

B. p. 265

> There's language in her eye, her cheek, her lip,
> Nay, her foot speaks; her wanton spirits look out
> At every joint and motive of her body.

IV, 5, 55

Chrysostom telleth them downright: "though they say nothing with their mouths, they speak in their gait, they speak with their eyes, they speak in the carriage of their bodies."

B. p. 524

Ther. Thou art said to be Achilles' male varlet.
Patr. Male varlet, you rogue! What's that?
Ther. Why, his masculine whore. V, 1, 14

Yet either out of their own weakness, a depraved nature, or love's tyranny, which so furiously rageth, they suffer themselves to be led like an ox to the slaughter: (*Facilis descensus Averni*) they go down headlong to their own perdition, they will commit folly with beasts, men "leaving the natural use of women", as Paul saith, "burned in lust one towards another, and man with man wrought filthiness."
B. p. 497

Now, the rotten diseases of the south, the guts-griping ruptures, catarrhs, . . . (&c.). V, 1, 16

Division of Diseases. If you require a more exact division of these ordinary diseases which are incident to men, I refer you to physicians; they will tell you of acute and chronic, first and secondary, lethales, salutares, errant, fixed, simple, compound, connexed, or consequent, belonging to parts or the whole. B. p. 86

Plagues, apoplexies, leprosies, wounds, sores, tetters, pox, pestilent agues. B. p. 407

He has not so much brain as ear-wax. V, 1, 50

These men . . . had no more brains than so many beetles. B. p. 20
Ear-wax of a dog. B. p. 457

Ask me not what I would be, if I were not Thersites. V, 1, 60

King James, 1605, when he came to see our University of Oxford, and amongst other edifices now went to view that famous library, renewed by Sir Thomas Bodley, in imitation of Alexander, at his departure brake out into that noble speech, If I were not a king, I would be a university man. B. p. 351

Good night and welcome, both at once, to those
That go or tarry. V, 1, 74

They can hardly be pleased or eased, though in other men's opinion most happy, go, tarry, run, ride. B. p. 255

Troilus, farewell! One eye yet looks on thee;
But with my heart the other eye doth see. V, 2, 105

Tro. O Cressid! O false Cressid! false, false, false! V, 2, 176

Cressida forsook Troilus by conversing with Diomede. B. p. 592

Troilus and Cressida

Sleeve-less errand. V, 4, 7

Make sleeveless errands to see her. B. p. 555

Sleeveless errands. B. p. 567

Ajax hath lost a friend
And foams at mouth, and he is armed and at it,
Roaring for Troilus; who hath done today
Mad and fantastic execution,
Engaging and redeeming of himself
With such a careless force and forceless care
As if that luck, in very spite of cunning,
Bade him win all. V, 5, 35

Fortune and Virtue, Wisdom and Folly, their seconds, upon a time contended in the Olympics; every man thought that Fortune and Folly would have the worst, and pitied their cases; but it fell out otherwise. Fortune was blind and cared not where she stroke, nor whom, without laws, *Andabatarum instar*, etc. Folly, rash and inconsiderate, esteemed as little what she said or did. Virtue and Wisdom gave place, were hissed out and exploded by the common people. B. p. 18

Coriolanus

Menenius Agrippa. There was a time when all the body's members
Rebell'd against the belly. I, 1, 94

As (footnote: Liv. *lib.* 1) Menenius Agrippa well satisfied the tumultous rout of Rome, in his elegant apologue of the belly and the rest of the members. B. p. 403

Trust ye?
With every minute you do change a mind
And call him noble that was now your hate. I, 1, 179

Go get you home, you fragments. I, 1, 221

(See, above, *King Henry the Sixth*, pt. 3, III, 1, 83.)

And were I anything but what I am,
I would wish me only he. I, 1, 229

(See, above, *Troilus and Cressida*, V, 1, 60.)

> I saw him run after a gilded butterfly; and when he caught it he let it go again, and after it again, and over and over he comes, and up again, catch'd it again. I, 3, 60

"As children do by a bird or a butterfly in a string, pull in and let him out as they list . . ." B. p. 212

> One on's father's moods. I, 3, 66

"And where the complexion and constitution of the father is corrupt, there (saith Roger Bacon) the complexion and constitution of the son must needs be corrupt, and so the corruption is derived from the father to the son." Now this doth not so much appear in the composition of the body, according to that of Hippocrates, "in habit, proportion, scars, and other lineaments; but in manners and conditions of the mind, *Et patrum in natos abeunt cum semine mores*." B. p. 137

> Indeed, no, by your patience; I'll not over the threshold till my head return from the wars. I, 3, 74

Virtuous women should keep house; and 'twas well performed and ordered by the Greeks,

—"mulier ne qua in publicum
Spectandam se sine arbitro præbeat viro:" B. p. 658

> Nature teaches beasts to know their friends. II, 1, 5

Put a bird in a cage, he will die for sullenness, or a beast in a pen, or take his young ones or companions from him, and see what effect it will cause. B. p. 43

> What I think I utter. II, 1, 48

As I do commonly all other exercises, *effudi quicquid dictavit genius meus*, out of a confused company of notes, and writ with as small deliberation as I do ordinarily speak. B. p. 11

> I cannot call you Lycurguses. II, 1, 50

It is not with us, as amongst those Lacedemonian senators of Lycurgus in Plutarch, "He preferred that deserved best, was most virtuous and worthy of the place, not swiftness, or strength, or wealth, or friends carried it in those days:" B. p. 229

They may as well, with Lycurgus and Mahomet, cut down all vines, forbid the drinking of wine, for that it makes some men drunk. B. p. 542

> If you see this in the map of my microcosm, follows it that I am known well enough too? II, 1, 57

As a purly hunter, I have hitherto beaten about the circuit of the forest of this microcosm, and followed only those outward adventitious causes. I will now break into the inner rooms, and rip up the antecedent immediate causes which are there to be found.
B. p. 244

> You know neither me, yourselves, nor anything. II, 1, 62

So that if men would attempt no more than what they can bear, they should lead contented lives, and learning to know themselves, would limit their ambition. B. p. 23

Know thyself, acknowledge thy present misery, and make right use of it. B. p. 249

> You wear out a good wholesome forenoon in hearing a cause between an orange-wife and a fosset-seller, and then rejourn the controversy of threepence to a second day of audience.
> II, 1, 64

No controversy to depend above a year, but without all delays and further appeals to be speedily despatched, and finally concluded in that time allotted. These and all other inferior magistrates to be chosen as the *literati* in China, or by those exact suffrages of the Venetians, and such again not to be eligible, or capable of magistracies, honours, offices, except they be sufficiently qualified for learning, manners, and that by the strict approbation of reputed examiners. B. p. 60

> Dismiss the controversy bleeding. II, 1, 71

Whereas the princes or great men are malicious, envious, factious, ambitious, emulators, they tear a commonwealth asunder . . . and with mutual murders let it bleed to death. B. p. 45

> Yet you must be saying Marcius is proud; who, in a cheap estimation, is worth all your predecessors since Deucalion.
> II, 1, 85

(See, above, *The Winter's Tale*, IV, 4, 421.)

> More of your conversation would infect my brain, being the herdsmen of the beastly plebeians. II, 1, 87

(See, above, *The Tempest*, V, 1, 130.)

> A letter for me! It gives me an estate of seven years' health; in which time I will make a lip at the physician. The most sovereign prescription in Galen is but empiricutic and, to this preservative, of no better report than a horse-drench.
>
> II, 1, 107

A letter sent or read will do as much; *multum allevor quum tuas literas lego*, I am much eased, as Tully wrote to Pomponius Atticus, when I read thy letters, and as Julianus the Apostate once signified to Maximus the philosopher; as Alexander slept with Homer's works, so do I with thine epistles, *tanquam Pæoniis medicamentis, easque assiduè tanquam recentes et novas iteramus; scribe ergo, et assiduè scribe*, or else come thyself; *amicus ad amicum venies*. Assuredly a wise and well-spoken man may do what he will in such a case; a good orator alone, as Tully holds, can alter affections by power of his eloquence, "comfort such as are afflicted, erect such as are depressed, expel and mitigate fear, lust, anger," &c. And how powerful is the charm of a discreet and dear friend? B. p. 365

Those loathsome and fulsome filthy potions, heteroclitical pills (so he calls them), horse medicines. B. p. 435

A medicine fitter for a horse than a man. B. p. 440

Repentance is a sovereign remedy for all sins. B. p. 726

> We call a nettle but a nettle, and
> The faults of fools but folly. II, 1, 181

. . . . a loose, plain, rude writer, *ficum voco ficum, et ligonem ligonem*, and as free, as loose, *idem calamo quod in mente*, I call a spade a spade. B. p. 11

> our veil'd dames
> Commit the war of white and damask in
> Their nicely gawded cheeks to th' wanton spoil
> Of Phœbus' burning kisses. II, 1, 205

Women keep in all winter, and most part of summer, to preserve their beauties. B. p. 405

> that to's power he would
> Have made them mules, silenc'd their pleaders, and
> Dispropertied their freedoms; holding them
> In human action and capacity
> Of no more soul nor fitness for the world

Than camels in their war, who have their provand
Only for bearing burdens, and sore blows
For sinking under them. II, 1, 236

Like an ass, he wears out his time for provender. B. p. 202

The common muck of the world. II, 2, 124

This earth itself the muck-hill of the world. B. p. 729

And manhood is call'd foolery when it stands
Against a falling fabric. III, 1, 246

Like those Celtes in Damascen, with ridiculous valour, *ut dedecorosum putarent muro ruenti se subducere*, a disgrace to run away for a rotten wall, now ready to fall on their heads. B. p. 31

The beast
With many heads butts me away. IV, 1, 1

For the common people are as a flock of sheep, a rude, illiterate rout, void many times of common sense, a mere beast, *bellua multorum capitum.* B. p. 678

'Tis fond to wail inevitable strokes. IV, 1, 26

Fear not that which cannot be avoided. B. p. 424

Cats that can judge as fitly of his worth
As I can of those mysteries which heaven
Will not have earth to know. IV, 2, 34

When God sees his time, he will reveal these mysteries to mortal men, and show that to some few at last, which he hath concealed so long. B. p. 330

Anger's my meat; I sup upon myself,
And so shall starve with feeding. IV, 2, 50

Homer, *Iliad*, 1, brings in Achilles eating of his own heart in his idleness. B. p. 158

In a commonwealth, where is no public enemy, there is likely civil wars, and they rage upon themselves; this body of ours, when it is idle, and knows not how to bestow itself, macerates and vexeth itself with cares, griefs, false fears, discontents, and suspicions; it tortures and preys upon his own bowels, and is never at rest.
B. p. 159

It [Envy] is "a moth of the soul, a consumption to make another man's happiness his misery, to torture, crucify, and execute himself, to eat his own heart. Meat and drink can do such men no good. . . ."

B. pp. 175–176

They live solitary, alone, sequestered from all company but heart-eating melancholy; and for want of meat, must eat that bread of affliction, prey upon themselves. B. p. 226

The present peace
And quietness of the people, which before
Were in wild hurry, here do make his friends
Blush that the world goes well; who rather had,
Though they themselves did suffer by't, behold
Dissentious numbers pest'ring streets than see
Our tradesmen singing in their shops, and going
About their functions friendly. IV, 6, 2

As he did in Æsop, lose one eye willingly, that his fellow might lose both, or that rich man in Quintilian that poisoned the flowers in his garden, because his neighbour's bees should get no more honey from them. His whole life is sorrow, and every word he speaks a satire: nothing fats him but other men's ruins. B. p. 174

and they follow him
Against us brats with no less confidence
Than boys pursuing summer butterflies,
Or butchers killing flies. IV, 6, 93

(See, above, this play, I, 3, 60.)

Whether 'twas pride,
Which out of daily fortune ever taints
The happy man. IV, 7, 37

So many men, if any new honour, office, preferment, booty, treasure, possession, or patrimony, *ex insperato* fall unto them, for immoderate joy, and continual meditation of it, cannot sleep or tell what they say or do, they are so ravished on a sudden; and with vain conceits transported, there is no rule with them. Epaminondas, therefore, the next day after his Leuctrian victory, "came abroad all squalid and submiss," and gave no other reason to his friends of so doing, than that he perceived himself the day before, by reason of his good fortune, to be too insolent, overmuch joyed.

B. p. 198

One fire drives out one fire; one nail, one nail. IV, 7, 54

One fire drives out another. . . . "Heathen philosophers drive out one love with another, as they do a peg, or pin with a pin. . . ." B. p. 593

and my young boy
Hath an aspect of intercession which
Great nature cries 'Deny not.' V, 3, 31

Nature binds all creatures to love their young ones. B. p. 484

These eyes are not the same I wore in Rome. V, 3, 38

He became a new man upon a sudden, *tanquam si priores oculos amisisset* (saith mine author), as if he had lost his former eyes. B. p. 591

Like a dull actor now
I have forgot my part and I am out,
Even to a full disgrace. V, 3, 40

. . . and are so dejected many times for some public injury, disgrace, as a box on the ear by their inferior, to be overcome of their adversary, foiled in the field, to be out in a speech, some foul fact committed or disclosed, &c., that they dare not come abroad all their lives after. B. p. 173

"Apollonius Rhodius wilfully banished himself, forsaking his country, and all his dear friends, because he was out in reciting his poems." B. p. 173

This is a poor epitome of yours. V, 3, 68

"The abridgment and epitome of the world" as Pliny; Microcosmus, a little world, a model of the world. B. p. 81

Ay, and mine,
That brought you forth this boy to keep your name
Living to time. V, 3, 125

Saith Nevisanus, matrimony makes us immortal. B. p. 622

Auf. [*Aside*] I am glad thou hast set thy mercy and thy honour
At difference in thee. Out of that I'll work
Myself a former fortune. V, 3, 200

Take heed of a reconciled enemy. B. p. 424

Coriolanus

Ladies, you deserve
To have a temple built you. All the swords
In Italy, and her confederate arms,
Could not have made this peace. V, 3, 206

The matrons of Rome, as Dionysius Halicarnassæus relates, because at their entreaty Coriolanus desisted from his wars, consecrated a church *Fortunæ muliebri.* B. p. 689

Sic. Is't possible that so short a time can alter the condition of a man?
Men. There is differency between a grub and a butterfly; yet your butterfly was a grub. V, 4, 10

A monster by stupend metamorphosis, a fox, a dog, a hog, what not? *Quantum mutatus ab illo?* How much altered from that he was. B. p. 81
"They hurt his feet in the stocks, the iron entered his soul." B. p. 226

At a few drops of women's rheum, which are
As cheap as lies, he sold the blood and labour
Of our great action. V, 6, 46

And as much pity is to be taken of a woman weeping, as of a goose going barefoot. B. p. 546

Romeo and Juliet

What's in a name? That which we call a rose
By any other name would smell as sweet. II, 2, 43

Her very name (let it be what it will) is a most pretty, pleasing name. B. p. 566

The orchard walls are high and hard to climb;
And the place death, considering who thou art,
If any of my kinsmen find thee here. II, 2, 63

How they will venture their lives, creep in at windows, gutters, climb over walls to come to their sweethearts. B. p. 568

Thou knowest the mask of night is on my face,
Else would a maiden blush bepaint my cheek
For that which thou hast heard me speak tonight. II, 2, 85

. . . any object heard or seen, for blind men never blush, as Dandinus observes, the night and darkness make men impudent. B. p. 278

Dost thou love me? I know thou wilt say ay,
And I will take thy word; yet, if thou swear'st,
Thou mayst prove false; at lovers' perjuries
They say Jove laughs. II, 2, 90

For when lovers swear, Venus laughs, *Venus hæc perjura ridet*, Jupiter himself smiles, and pardons it withal, as grave Plato gives out; of all perjury, that alone for love matters is forgiven by the gods.
B. p. 544

O, swear not by the moon, th' inconstant moon,
That monthly changes in her circled orb. II, 2, 109

Maginus makes eleven heavens, subdivided into their orbs and circles. B. p. 324

The sun immoveable in the centre of the whole world, the earth centre of the moon. B. p. 325

Love goes toward love as school-boys from their books;
But love from love, toward school with heavy looks.
II, 2, 156

(See, above, *As You Like It*, II, 7, 145.)

'Tis almost morning. I would have thee gone;
And yet no farther than a wanton's bird,
That lets it hop a little from her hand,
Like a poor prisoner in his twisted gyves,
And with a silk thread plucks it back again,
So loving-jealous of his liberty. II, 2, 177

(See, above, *Coriolanus*, I, 3, 60.)

And fleckel'd darkness like a drunkard reels. II, 3, 3

Let's all be mad and drunk. But we commonly mistake, and go beyond our commission, we reel to the opposite part. B. p. 42

O, mickle is the powerful grace that lies
In plants, herbs, stones, and their true qualities;
For naught so vile that on the earth doth live
But to the earth some special good doth give. II, 3, 15

Some herbs provoke lust, some again, as agnus castus, water-lily, quite extinguisheth seed; poppy causeth sleep, cabbage resisteth drunkenness, etc., and that which is more to be admired, that such and such plants should have a peculiar virtue to such particular parts, as to the head, aniseeds, foalfoot, betony, calamint, eyebright, lavender, bays, roses, rue, sage, marjoram, peony, etc. For the lungs, calamint, liquorice, enula campana, hyssop, horehound, water germander, etc. For the heart, borage, bugloss, saffron, balm, basil, rosemary, violet, roses, etc. For the stomach, wormwood, mints, betony, balm, centaury, sorrel, purslain. For the liver, darthspine . . . B. p. 431

Timon of Athens

A thing slipp'd idly from me.
Our poesy is as a gum, which oozes
From whence 'tis nourished. The fire 'i th' flint
Shows not till it be struck: our gentle flame
Provokes itself, and like the current flies
Each bound it chafes. I, 1, 22

And as by the striking of a flint fire is enforced, so by the vehement motion of spirits, they do *elicere voces inauditas*, compel strange speeches to be spoken. B. p. 281

Imagination . . . doth more fully examine the species perceived by common sense, of things present or absent, and keeps them longer, recalling them to mind again, or making new of his own. B. p. 101

In melancholy men this faculty [imagination] . . . often hurts . . . especially if it be stirred up by some terrible object. . . . In poets and painters imagination forcibly works. B. p. 102

(See, above, *A Midsummer Night's Dream*, V, 1, 4, for these two latter passages in full.)

Such a one was old Sophocles, and Democritus himself had *hilare delirium* . . . melancholy men of all others are most witty, which causeth many times a divine ravishment, and a kind of *enthusiasmus*, which stirreth them up to be excellent philosophers, poets, prophets, etc. B. p. 262

Sir, I have upon a high and pleasant hill
Feign'd Fortune to be thron'd. The base o' th' mount . . .
I, 1, 66

Lucian in his tract *de Mercede conductis*, hath excellent well deciphered such men's [prodigals] proceedings in his picture of Opulentia, whom he feigns to dwell on the top of a high mount, much sought after by many suitors. B p. 190

A thousand moral paintings I can show
That shall demonstrate those quick blows of Fortune's
More pregnantly than words. I, 1, 93

A good picture is *falsa veritas, et muta poesis.* B. p. 348

Yet you do well
To show Lord Timon that mean eyes have seen
The foot above the head. I, 1, 95

Now such a man (saith Austin) "that is so led [by passion], in a wise man's eye, is no better than he that stands upon his head."
B. p. 165

'Tis not enough to help the feeble up,
But to support him after. I, 1, 110

If married and infirm, past work, or by inevitable loss, or some such like misfortune cast behind, by distribution of corn, house-rent free, annual pensions or money, they shall be relieved.
B. p. 61

For since dishonour traffics with man's nature,
He is but outside. I, 1, 161

An outside, a glow-worm, a proud fool, an arrant ass. B. p. 383

He that loves to be flattered is worthy o' the flatterer.
I, 1, 228

Such are many sottish princes, brought into a fool's paradise by their parasites, 'tis a common humour, incident to all men, when they are in great places, or come to the solstice of honour, have done, or deserved well, to applaud and flatter themselves.
B. p. 197

They say, my lords, Ira furor brevis est; but yond man is ever angry. I, 2, 28

Ira furor brevis est, "anger is temporary madness". B. p. 177

Here's that which is too weak to be a sinner, honest water, which ne'er left man i' th' mire. I, 2, 56

I am *aquæ potor,* drink no wine at all. B. p. 11

Rich men sin, and I eat root. I, 2, 69

"A small thing that the righteous hath, is better than the riches of the ungodly." *Psal.* XXXVII, 16. B. p. 396

We are born to do benefits; and what better or properer can we call our own than the riches of our friends?
I, 2, 96

I will spend my time and knowledge, which are my greatest fortunes, for the common good of all. B. p. 5

Men shut their doors against a setting sun. I, 2, 139

We adore the rising sun most part. B. p. 383

Alcibiades,
Thou art a soldier, therefore seldom rich.
It comes in charity to thee; for all thy living
Is 'mongst the dead, and all the lands thou hast
Lie in a pitch'd field. I, 2, 221

Or if we do applaud, honour and admire, *quota pars*, how small a part, in respect of the whole world, never so much as hears our names, how few take notice of us, how slender a tract, as scant as Alcibiades' land in a map! B. p. 195

Large-handed robbers your grave masters are, and pill by law.
IV, 1, 11

A great man in office may securely rob whole provinces, undo thousands, pill and poll, oppress *ad libitum*, flea, grind, tyrannize, enrich himself by spoils of the commons, be uncontrollable in his actions, and after all be recompensed with turgent titles, honoured for his good service. B. p. 31

Rob Peter and pay Paul; scrape unjust sums with one hand, purchase great manors by corruption, fraud and cozenage, and liberally to distribute to the poor with the other, give a remnant to pious uses, etc. B. p. 35

Gouty benefactors . . . steal a goose, and stick down a feather, rob a thousand to relieve ten. B. p. 57

Timon will to the woods, where he shall find
Th' unkindest beast more kinder than mankind.
IV, 1, 35

To descend to more particulars, how many creatures are at deadly feud with men? Lions, wolves, bears, &c. Some with hoofs, horns, tusks, teeth, nails: how many noxious serpents and venomous creatures, ready to offend us with stings, breath, sight, or quite kill us? How many pernicious fishes, plants, gums, fruits, seeds,

flowers, &c., could I reckon up on a sudden, which by their very smell many of them, touch, taste, cause some grievous malady, if not death itself? Some make mention of a thousand several poisons: but these are but trifles in respect. The greatest enemy to man, is man.
B. p. 84

> Rich only to be wretched—thy great fortunes
> Are made thy chief afflictions. IV, 2, 43

Riches do not so much exhilarate us with their possession, as they torment us with their loss.
B. p. 238

In a word, "to get wealth is a great trouble, anxiety to keep, grief to lose it."
B. p. 391

And as the Moon when she is fuller of light is still farthest from the Sun, the more wealth they have, the farther they are commonly from God.
B. p. 389

> Earth, yield me roots.
> Who seeks for better of thee, sauce his palate
> With thy most operant poison. IV, 3, 23

Agellius, out of Euripedes, accounts bread and water enough to satisfy nature, "of which there is no surfeit, the rest is not a feast but a riot" . . . he that is not satisfied with a little will never have enough.
B. p. 395

> Clear heavens. IV, 3, 27

Clear light of sun and moon.
B. p. 392

> This is it that makes the wappen'd widow wed again—
> IV, 3, 37

. . . an old widow, a mother so long since (in Pliny's opinion), she doth very unseemly seek to marry, yet whilst she is so old a crone, a beldam, she can neither see, nor hear, go nor stand, a mere carcase, a witch, and scarce feel; she catterwauls, and must have a stallion, a champion, she must and will marry again, and betroth herself to some young man, that hates to look on, but for her goods.
B. p. 501

> She whom the spittal-house and ulcerous sores
> Would cast the gorge at, this [gold] embalms and spices
> To th' April day again. IV, 3, 38

Gomesius *lib.* 3. *de sale gen. c.*22. gives instance in a Florentine gentleman, that was so deceived with a wife, she was so radiantly set out with rings and jewels, lawns, scarfs, laces, gold, spangles, and gaudy devices that the young man took her to be a goddess (for he never saw her but by torchlight); but after the wedding solemnities, when as he viewed her the next morning without her tires and in a clear day, she was so deformed, a lean, yellow, shrivelled, etc., such a beastly creature in his eyes, that he could not endure to look upon her. B. p. 532

I am Misanthropos, and hate mankind. IV, 3, 52

These wretches do frequently degenerate from men, and of sociable creatures become beasts, monsters, inhumane, ugly to behold, *Misanthropi*; they do even loathe themselves and hate the company of men, as so many Timons, Nebuchadnezzars, by too much indulging to these pleasing humours, and through their own default. B. p. 163

But when his gold was spent, his fair possessions gone, farewell Timon; none so ugly, none so deformed, so odious an object as Timon. B. p. 477

This fell whore of thine
Hath in her more destruction than thy sword. IV, 3, 60

The board consumes more than the sword. B. p. 85

Alcib. How came the noble Timon to this change?
Tim. As the moon does, by wanting light to give.
But then renew I could not, like the moon;
There were no suns to borrow of.
Alcib. Noble Timon,
What friendship may I do thee? IV, 3, 65

Tully, as I remember, in an epistle to his dear friend Atticus, much condoles the defect of such a friend. I live here (saith he) in a great city, where I have a multitude of acquaintance, but not a man of all that company with whom I dare familiarly breathe, or freely jest . . . He or he, or whosoever then labours of this malady, by all means let him get some trusty friend, *Semper habens Pylademque aliquem qui curet Orestem*, a Pylades, to whom freely and securely he may open himself. For as in all other occurrences, so it is in this, *Si quis in cœlum ascendisset*, &c., as he said in Tully, if a man had gone to heaven, "seen the beauty of the skies," stars errant, fixed, &c., *insuavis erit admiratio*, it will do him no pleasure, except he have somebody to impart what he hath seen. B. p. 362

Consumptions sow
In hollow bones of man; . . . &c. IV, 3, 150

(See, above, *Troilus and Cressida*, V, 1, 16.)

Common mother, thou,
Whose womb unmeasurable and infinite breast
Teems and feeds all. IV, 3, 176

(See, above, *As You Like It*, I, 2, 179.)

Dry up thy marrows, vines, and plough-torn leas,
Whereof ingrateful man, with liquorish draughts
And morsels unctuous, greases his pure mind,
That from it all consideration slips— IV, 3, 192

For when they come to be in great place, rich, they that were most temperate, sober, and discreet in their private fortunes, as Nero, Otho, Vitellius, Heliogabalus (*optimi imperatores nisi imperâssent*) degenerate on a sudden into brute beasts, so prodigious in lust, such tyrannical oppressors. B. p. 404

Will these moist trees,
That have outliv'd the eagle, page thy heels
And skip when thou point'st out? IV, 3, 222

Pancrates in Lucian, wanting a servant as he went from Memphis to Coptus in Egypt, took a door bar, and after some superstitious words pronounced (Eucrates the relator was then present) made it stand up like a serving-man, fetch him water, turn the spit, serve in supper, and what work he would besides; and when he had done that service he desired, turned his man to a stick again. B. p. 11

If thou didst put this sour-cold habit on
To castigate thy pride, 'twere well; but thou
Dost it enforcedly. Thou'dst courtier be again
Wert thou not beggar. Willing misery
Outlives incertain pomp, is crown'd before. IV, 3, 238

Apem. Art thou proud yet?
Tim. Ay, that I am not thee.
Apem. I, that I was no prodigal.
Tim. I, that I am one now. IV, 3, 275

Another kind of mad men there is opposite to these, that are insensibly mad, and know not of it, such as contemn all praise and glory, think themselves most free, when as indeed they are most mad: *calcant sed alio fastu*: a company of cynics, such as are monks, hermits, anachorites, that contemn the world, contemn themselves, contemn all titles, honours, offices: and yet in that contempt are more proud than any man living whatsoever. They are proud in humility, proud in that they are not proud, *sæpe homo de vanæ gloriæ contemptu, vaniùs gloriatur*, as Austin hath it, *confess. lib.* 10. *cap.* 38, like Diogenes, *intus gloriantur*, they brag inwardly, and feed themselves fat with a self-conceit of sanctity, which is no better than hypocrisy. They go in sheep's russet, many great men that might maintain themselves in cloth of gold, and seem to be dejected, humble by their outward carriage, when as inwardly they are swoln full of pride, arrogancy, and self-conceit. B. p. 196

If thou wilt curse, thy father, that poor rag,
Must be thy subject; who, in spite, put stuff
To some she-beggar and compounded thee
Poor rogue hereditary. IV, 3, 270

Hyginus, *fab.* 220, to this purpose hath a pleasant tale. Dame Cura by chance went over a brook, and taking up some of the dirty slime, made an image of it; Jupiter eftsoons coming by, put life to it, but Cura and Jupiter could not agree what name to give him, or who should own him; the matter was referred to Saturn as judge, he gave this arbitrement: his name shall be *Homo ab humo, Cura eum possideat quamdiu vivat*, Care shall have him whilst he lives, Jupiter his soul, and Tellus his body when he dies. B. p. 179

[*Looks at the gold*] O thou sweet king-killer, and dear divorce
'Twixt natural son and sire! thou bright defiler
Of Hymen's purest bed! IV, 3, 378

And 'tis a general fault amongst most parents in bestowing of their children, the father wholly respects wealth, when through his folly, riot, indiscretion, he hath embezzled his estate, to recover himself, he confines and prostitutes his eldest son's love and affection to some fool, or ancient, or deformed piece for money. B. p. 613

The moon's an arrant thief,
And her pale fire she snatches from the sun. IV, 3, 435

If the earth move, it is a planet, and shines to them in the moon, and to the other planetary inhabitants, as the moon and they do to us upon the earth. B. p. 326

What! know you not,
Being mechanical, you ought not to walk
Upon a labouring day without the sign
Of your profession? I, 1, 2

The same attire shall be kept, and that proper to several callings, by which, they shall be distinguished. B. p. 62

I meddle with no tradesman's matters nor women's matters, but with awl. I, 1, 22

I am a bachelor myself, and lead a monastic life in a college. B. p. 274

Meddle not with other men's matters. B. p. 424

To get myself into more work. I, 1, 30

They will make more work for themselves. B. p. 46

O you hard hearts, you cruel men of Rome,
Knew you not Pompey? . . .
And do you now strew flowers in his way
That comes in triumph over Pompey's blood? I, 1, 37–51

(See, above, *King Henry the Sixth*, pt. 3, III, 1, 83.)

These growing feathers pluck'd from Cæsar's wing
Will make him fly an ordinary pitch,
Who else would soar above the view of men,
And keep us all in servile fearfulness. I, 1, 73

I was born as free as Cæsar; so were you. I, 2, 97

Of the same nature is oppression, *Eccles.* vii. 7, "surely oppression makes a man mad," loss of liberty, which made Brutus venture his life. B. p. 242

Nor construe any further my neglect
Than that poor Brutus, with himself at war,
Forgets the shows of love to other men. I, 2, 45

Friends and companions get you gone,
'Tis my desire to be alone;
Ne'er well but when my thoughts and I
Do domineer in privacy. *The Author's Abstract of Melancholy*

Why, man, he doth bestride the narrow world
Like a Colossus. I, 2, 135

A great stentorian Democritus, as big as that Rhodian Colossus.
B. p. 25

Men at some time are masters of their fates:
The fault, dear Brutus, is not in our stars,
But in ourselves, that we are underlings. I, 2, 139

Yet oftentimes, I may not deny it, the main fault is in ourselves.
B. p. 209

'Tis in our power, as they say, to make or mar ourselves.
B. p. 402

Faber quisque fortunæ suæ, and in some sort I may truly say, prosperity and adversity are in our own hands. *Nemo læditur nisi à seipso*, and which Seneca confirms out of his judgment and experience. "Every man's mind is stronger than fortune, and leads him to what side he will; a cause to himself each one is of his good or bad life."
B. p. 403

He is a great observer. I, 2, 202

The prophet Isaiah, a courtier himself, and a great observer.
B. p. 523

Cas. But soft, I pray you. What, did Cæsar swoon?
Casca. He fell down in the market-place, and foam'd at mouth, and was speechless.
Bru. 'Tis very like. He hath the falling sickness. I, 2, 250

To fall into a swoon, and oftentimes fits of the falling sickness.
B. p. 89

Cassius from bondage will deliver Cassius. I, 3, 90

Cas. But life, being weary of these worldly bars,
Never lacks power to dismiss itself.
If I know this, know all the world besides,
That part of tyranny that I do bear,
I can shake off at pleasure.
Casca. So can I;
So every bondman in his own hand bears
The power to cancel his captivity. I, 3, 96

There remains no more to such persons, if that heavenly Physician, by his assisting grace and mercy alone do not prevent (for no human persuasion or art can help), but to be their own butchers, and execute themselves. Socrates his *cicuta*, Lucretia's dagger, Timon's halter, are yet to be had; Cato's knife, and Nero's sword are left behind them, as so many fatal engines, bequeathed to posterity, and will be used to the world's end, by such distressed souls.

B. p. 284

> It is the bright day that brings forth the adder,
> And that craves wary walking. II, 1, 14

Yet in the midst of his prosperity, let him remember that *caveat* of Moses, "Beware that he do not forget the Lord his God;" that he be not puffed up, but acknowledge them to be his good gifts and benefits. B. p. 83

SPERATE, MISERI.
CAVETE, FŒLICES. B. p. 739

> Looks in the clouds, scorning the base degrees
> By which he did ascend. II, 1, 26

Baseness of birth is a great disparagement to some men, especially if they be wealthy, bear office, and come to promotion in a commonwealth; then (as he—footnote: Boeth. *lib.* 2 *pr.* 4—observes), if their birth be not answerable to their calling, and to their fellows, they are much abashed and ashamed of themselves. Some scorn their own father and mother, deny brothers and sisters, with the rest of their kindred and friends, and will not suffer them to come near them, when they are in their pomp, accounting it a scandal to their greatness to have such beggarly beginnings. Simon in Lucian, having now got a little wealth, changed his name from Simon to Simonides, for that there were so many beggars of his kin, and set the house on fire where he was born, because nobody should point at it. B. p. 381

> For in the engrafted love he bears to Cæsar. II, 1, 184

If we desire to be ingrafted into him, leave all and follow him.

B. p. 665

> Enjoy the honey-heavy dew of slumber.
> Thou hast no figures nor no fantasies
> Which busy care draws in the brains of men;
> Therefore thou sleep'st so sound. II, 1, 230

(See, above, *King Henry the Fourth*, pt. 2, III, 1, 5.)

Dwell I but in the suburbs
Of your good pleasure? If it be no more,
Portia is Brutus' harlot, not his wife. II, 1, 285

And this made the Romans, as Vitruvius relates, put Venus' temple in the suburbs, *extra murum, ne adolescentes venereis insuescant.* B. p. 535

When beggars die there are no comets seen;
The heavens themselves blaze forth the death of princes. II, 2, 30

Prodigies frequently occur at the deaths of illustrious men. B. p. 125

Cowards die many times before their deaths:
The valiant never taste of death but once. II, 2, 32

An old soldier in the world methinks should not be disquieted, but ready to receive all fortunes, encounters, and with that resolute captain, come what may come, to make answer,
No labour comes at unawares to me,
For I have long before cast what may be. B. p. 413

Of all the wonders that I yet have heard,
It seems to me most strange that men should fear,
Seeing that death, a necessary end,
Will come when it will come. II, 2, 34

Necessary concomitants or affections of this vegetal faculty are life and his privation death. B. p. 99

'Tis an inevitable chance, the first statute in *Magna Charta*, an everlasting Act of Parliament, all must die. B. p. 409

'Tis a folly to fear that which cannot be avoided B. p. 412

But I am constant as the northern star III, 1, 60

And the pole-star, which to our thinking, scarce moveth out of its place B. p. 325

The skies are painted with unnumb'red sparks,
They are all fire, and every one doth shine III, 1, 63

Whether they [the stars] be hot by themselves, or by accident cause heat? B p 324

If our world be small in respect, why may we not suppose a plurality of worlds, those infinite stars visible in the firmament to be so many suns, with particular fixed centres. B. p. 327

Cas. How many ages hence
Shall this our lofty scene be acted over
In states unborn and accents yet unknown!
Bru. How many times shall Cæsar bleed in sport. . . !

III, 1, 112

To see one of Cæsar's triumphs in old Rome revived, or the like.

B. p. 341

The very reading of feasts, triumphs, interviews, nuptials, tilts, tournaments, combats, and monomachies, is most acceptable and pleasant. . . . The rare workmanship of those ancient Greeks, in theatres, obelisks, temples, statues, gold, silver, ivory, marble images, *non minore fermè quum leguntur, quam quum cernuntur, animum delectatione complent,* affect one as much by reading almost as by sight.

B. p. 342

Pindarus of Thebes, is as much renowned for his poems, as Epaminondas, Pelopidas, Hercules or Bacchus, his fellow citizens, for their warlike actions; *et si famam respicias, non pauciores Aristotelis quam Alexandri meminerunt* (as Cardan notes), Aristotle is more known than Alexander; for we have a bare relation of Alexander's deeds, but Aristotle, *totus vivit in monumentis,* is whole in his works.

B. pp. 350–351

Whate'er men do, vows, fears, in ire, in sport,
Joys, wand'rings, are the sum of my report.

B. p. 1

So oft as that shall be,
So often shall the knot of us be call'd
The men that gave their country liberty.

III, 1, 117

As a hen and chickens, all of a knot.

B. p. 479

O world, thou wast the forest to this hart;
And this indeed, O world, the heart of thee!

III, 1, 208

Alexander, Cæsar, Trajan, Adrian, were as so many land-leapers, now in the east, now in the west, little at home.

B. p. 406

As a purly hunter, I have hitherto beaten about the circuit of the forest of this microcosm, and followed only those outward adventitious causes. I will now break into the inner rooms, and rip up the antecedent immediate causes which are there to be found.

B. p. 244

—as he was ambitious, I slew him.

III, 2, 26

. . . and death for his ambition.

III, 2, 28

The noble Brutus

Hath told you Cæsar was ambitious. III, 2, 77

Cæsar and Scipio valiant and wise, but vain-glorious, ambitious. B. p. 68

All. Live, Brutus! live, live!
1 *Pleb.* Bring him with triumph home unto his house.
2 *Pleb.* Give him a statue with his ancestors.
3 *Pleb.* Let him be Cæsar. III, 2, 47

1 *Pleb.* This Cæsar was a tyrant. III, 2, 69

4 *Pleb.* They were traitors. Honourable men!
All. The will! the testament!
2 *Pleb.* They were villains, murderers. The will!
Read the will. III, 2, 153

(See, above, *King Henry the Sixth*, pt. 3, III, 1, 83.)

This was the most unkindest cut of all. III, 2, 183

"No cut to unkindness," as the saying is. B. p. 242

But, as you know me all, a plain blunt man. III, 2, 218

I am . . . a loose, plain, rude writer. B. p. 11

Ant. Moreover, he hath left you all his walks,
His private arbours, and new-planted orchards,
On this side Tiber; he hath left them you,
And to your heirs for ever—common pleasures,
To walk abroad and recreate yourselves.
Here was a Cæsar! When comes such another?
1 *Pleb.* Never, never! III, 2, 248

If he be bountiful in his life, and liberal at his death, he shall have one to swear, as he did by Claudius the Emperor in Tacitus, he saw his soul go to heaven, and be miserably lamented at his funeral. B. p. 229

Wisely, I say I am a bachelor. III, 3, 16

I am a bachelor myself, and lead a monastic life in a college. B. p. 274

Like to an empty ass. IV, 1, 26

His daughter is in the same predicament forsooth, as an empty boat she must carry what, where, when, and whom her father will. B. p. 613

Have not you love enough to bear with me,
When that rash humour which my mother gave me
Makes me forgetful? IV, 3, 117

Such a mother, such a daughter. B. p. 137

Poet. For shame, you generals! What do you mean?
Love, and be friends, as two such men should be;
For I have seen more years, I'm sure, than ye.
Cas. Ha, ha! How vilely doth this cynic rhyme!
Bru. Get you hence, sirrah; saucy fellow, hence!
Cas. Bear with him, Brutus: 'tis his fashion.
Bru. I'll know his humour when he knows his time.
What should the wars do with these jigging fools?
IV, 3, 128

Let them approve themselves worthy first, sufficiently qualified for learning and manners, before they presume or impudently intrude and put themselves on great men as too many do, with such base flattery, parasitical colloguing, such hyperbolical elogies they do usually insinuate, that it is a shame to hear and see. B. p. 210

Bru. O Cassius, I am sick of many griefs!
Cas. Of your philosophy you make no use,
If you give place to accidental evils. IV, 3, 142

As ivy doth an oak, these miseries encompass our life. And it is most absurd and ridiculous for any mortal man to look for a perpetual tenure of happiness in this life. B. p. 91

For triumphs, lamentations: for joy, tears. "So it is and so it was, and so it ever will be. He that refuseth to see and hear, to suffer this, is not fit to live in this world, and knows not the common condition of all men, to whom so long as they live, with a reciprocal course, joys and sorrows are annexed, and succeed one another.
B. pp. 375–376

Deformities and imperfections of our bodies, as lameness, crookedness, deafness, blindness, be they innate or accidental, torture many men. B. p. 379

Why, farewell, Portia. We must die, Messala.
With meditating that she must die once,
I have the patience to endure it now. IV, 3, 188

Why dost thou so macerate thyself? 'Tis an inevitable chance, the first statute in *Magna Charta*, an everlasting Act of Parliament, all must die. B. p. 409

JULIUS CÆSAR

> Omitted, all the voyage of their life
> Is bound in shallows and in miseries. IV, 3, 218

But on the contrary, if he be poor, *Prov.* xv. 15, "all his days are miserable," he is under hatches, dejected, rejected and forsaken, poor in purse, poor in spirit. B. p. 229

> This was the noblest Roman of them all. V, 5, 68

"I have ever loved as thou knowest (so Tully wrote to Dolabella) Marcus Brutus for his great wit, singular honesty, constancy, sweet conditions . . ." B. p. 481

> He only in a general honest thought
> And common good to all made one of them. V, 5, 71

I will spend my time and knowledge, which are my greatest fortunes for the common good of all. B. p. 5

MACBETH

> Doubtful it stood,
> As two spent swimmers that do cling together
> And choke their art. I, 1, 7

As a man desperately swimming drowns him that comes to help him. B. p. 192

> 1 *Witch.* Where hast thou been, sister? . . . &c. [to]
> So, all hail, Macbeth and Banquo! I, 3, 1–68

Water-devils are those Naiads or water nymphs which have been heretofore conversant about waters and rivers. The water (as Paracelsus thinks) is their chaos, wherein they live; some call them fairies, and say that Habundia is their queen; these cause inundations, many times shipwrecks, and deceive men divers ways, as Succuba, or otherwise, appearing most part (saith Tritemius) in women's shapes. Paracelsus hath several stories of them that have lived and been married to mortal men, and so continued for certain years with them, and after, upon some dislike, have forsaken them. Such a one as Ægeria, with whom Numa was so familiar, Diana, Ceres, &c. Olaus Magnus hath a long narration of one Hotherus, a king of Sweden, that having lost his company, as he was hunting one day, met with these water nymphs or fairies, and was feasted by them; and Hector Boethius, of Macbeth, and Banquo, two Scottish lords, that as they were wandering in the woods, had their fortunes told them by three strange women. B. p. 124

> And the very ports they blow,
> All the quarters that they know
> I' th' shipman's card. I, 3, 15

As the lines of several sea-cards cut each other in a globe or map. B. p. 181

As our new cards inform us that California is not a cape, but an island. B. p. 314

> Good sir, why do you start, and seem to fear
> Things that do sound so fair? I, 3, 51

The devil commonly suggests things opposite to nature, opposite to God and his word, impious, absurd, such as a man would never of himself, or could not conceive, they strike terror and horror into the parties' own hearts. For if he or they be asked whether they do approve of such like thoughts or no, they answer (and their own souls truly dictate as much) they abhor them as hell and the devil himself, they would fain think otherwise if they could; he hath thought otherwise, and with all his soul desires so to think again; he doth resist, and hath some good motions intermixed now and then: so that such blasphemous, impious, unclean thoughts, are not his own, but the devil's; they proceed not from him, but from a crazed phantasy, distempered humours, black fumes which offend his brain: they are thy crosses, the devil's sins, and he shall answer for them, he doth enforce thee to do that which thou dost abhor, and didst never give consent to: and although he hath sometimes so slily set upon thee, and so far prevailed, as to make thee in some sort to assent to such wicked thoughts, to delight in, yet they have not proceeded from a confirmed will in thee, but are of that nature which thou dost afterwards reject and abhor. B. pp. 729–730

> Thou shalt get kings. I, 3, 67

Valens the emperor in Constantinople, when as he left no man alive of quality in his kingdom that had his name begun with Theo; Theodoti, Theognosti, Theodosii, Theoduli, &c. They went all to their long home, because a wizard told him that name should succeed in his empire. B. p. 628

If chance will have me king

. . . .

Time and the hour runs through the roughest day.

I, 3, 143–147

Time and chance comes to all. B. p. 707

Come what come may. I, 3, 146

Come what may come. B. p. 413

There's no art

To find the mind's construction in the face. I, 4, 11

His mind no art can well express.

The Argument of the Frontispiece, Verse X

If every man had a window in his breast, which Momus would have had in Vulcan's man, or that which Tully so much wished it were written in everyman's forehead, *Quid quisque de republicâ sentiret*, what he thought. B. p. 36

We will establish our estate upon

Our eldest, Malcolm, whom we name hereafter

The Prince of Cumberland; I, 4, 37

Kennetus, King of Scotland, when he had murdered his nephew Malcolm, King Duffe's son, Prince of Cumberland, and . . .

B. p. 719

Stars, hide your fires;

Let not light see my black and deep desires. I, 4, 50

They will endure any misery, any trouble, suffer and do that which the sunbeams will not endure to see. B. p. 686

(See, also, *Julius Cæsar*, III, 1, 63.)

Stop up th' access and passage to remorse. I, 5, 41

This ligation of senses [during sleep] proceeds from an inhibition of spirits, the way being stopped by which they should come; this stopping is caused of vapours arising out of the stomach, filling the nerves, by which the spirits should be conveyed. When these vapours are spent, the passage is open, and the spirits perform their accustomed duties. B. p. 102

Dun. This castle hath a pleasant seat; the air

Nimbly and sweetly recommends itself

Unto our gentle senses.

Ban. This guest of summer,
The temple-haunting martlet, does approve
By his lov'd mansionry that the heaven's breath
Smells wooingly here; no jutty, frieze,
Buttress, nor coign of vantage, but this bird
Hath made her pendent bed and procreant cradle.
Where they most breed and haunt, I have observ'd
The air is delicate. I, 6, 1

Note—I consider that "the heaven's breath" is used in the same sense as is "The breath of heaven" in *King John*, IV, 1, 110.

Wadley in Berkshire is situate in a vale, though not so fertile a soil as some vales afford, yet a most commodious site, wholesome, in a delicious air, a rich and pleasant seat. So Segrave in Leicestershire (which town I am now bound to remember) is situated in a champaign, at the edge of the wolds, and more barren than the villages about it, yet no place likely yields a better air. B. p. 332
. . . in Egypt, he saw swallows, Spanish kites, and many such other European birds, in December and January. B. p. 316

This beauty and "splendour of the divine majesty", is it that draws all creatures to it, to seek it, love, admire, and adore it. . . . he woos us by his beauty, gifts, promises, to come unto him. B. p. 662

I live and breathe under that glorious heaven, that august capitol of nature, enjoy the brightness of stars, that clear light of sun and moon, those infinite creatures, plants, birds, beasts, fishes, herbs, all that sea and land can afford, far surpassing all that art and *opulentia* can give. B. p. 392

Thou covetous wretch, as Austin expostulates, "why dost thou stand gaping on this dross, muck-hills, filthy excrements? behold a far fairer object, God himself woos thee; behold him, enjoy him, he is sick for love", *Cant.* V. He invites thee to his sight, to come into his fair garden, to eat and drink with him, to be merry with him, to enjoy his presence for ever. B. p. 664

Note—I disagree with Bradley when he says* these lines are ironical. I prefer to see in them Macbeth's garden, beautiful before his fall, and to compare them with Milton's passage beginning:—
"Now, when as sacred light began to dawn"†

---

* *Shakespearean Tragedy;* Macmillan; pp. 334 and 339.
† *Paradise Lost,* Book IX, 192.

But in these cases
We still have judgment here. I, 7, 7

They supposed fortune alone gave kingdoms and empires, wealth, honours, offices . . . but after, they began upon better advice to to think otherwise, that everyman made his own fortune. The last of Necessity was Seneca's tenet that God . . . could alter nothing that was once decreed. B. p. 709

I have no spur
To prick the sides of my intent, but only
Vaulting ambition, which o'er-leaps itself,
And falls on th' other. I, 7, 25

This concupiscible appetite [ambition], howsoever it may seem to carry with it a show of pleasure and delight, and our concupiscences most part affect us with content and a pleasing object, yet if they be in extremes, they rack and wring us on the other side. B. p. 184
If he chance to miss, and have a canvass, he is in a hell on the other side. B. p. 186

Mine eyes are made the fools o' th' other senses,
Or else worth all the rest. I see thee still;
And on thy blade and dudgeon gouts of blood,
Which was not so before. There's no such thing;
It is the bloody business which informs
Thus to mine eyes. Now o'er the one half-world
Nature seems dead, and wicked dreams abuse
The curtain'd sleep. II, 1, 44

As the saying is, they dream of that they desire. Like Sarmiento the Spaniard, who when he was sent to discover the straits of Magellan, and confine places, by the Prorex of Peru, standing on the top of a hill, *Amœnissimam planitiem despicere sibi visus fuit, ædificia magnifica, quamplurimos Pagos, altas Turres, splendida Templa*, and brave cities, built like ours in Europe, not, saith mine author, that there was any such thing, but that he was *vanissimus et nimis credulus*, and would fain have had it so. Or as Lod. Mercatus proves, by reason of inward vapours, and humours from blood, choler, etc., diversely mixed, they apprehend and see outwardly, as they suppose, divers images, which indeed are not. B. p. 279

Thou sure and firm-set earth,
Hear not my steps which way they walk, for fear
Thy very stones prate of my whereabout. II, 1, 56

Or to omit all smaller controversies, as matters of less moment, and examine that main paradox, of the earth's motion, now so much in question. B. p. 325

Fracastorius will have the earth stand still, as before. B. p. 328
(See, also, *As You Like It*, II, 1, 15.)

> But wherefore could not I pronounce 'Amen'?
> I had most need of blessing, and 'Amen' stuck in my throat. II, 2, 31

The last and greatest cause of this malady, is our own conscience, sense of our sins, and God's anger justly deserved, a guilty conscience for some foul offence formerly committed. B. p. 718

> Methought I heard a voice cry 'Sleep no more; . . .' II, 2, 35

Tully makes it an argument of Roscius Amerinus' innocency, that he killed not his father, because he so securely slept. B. p. 721

> —the innocent sleep,
> Sleep that knits up the ravell'd sleave of care,
> The death of each day's life, sore labour's bath,
> Balm of hurt minds, great nature's second course,
> Chief nourisher in life's feast. II, 2, 36

(See, above, *King Henry the Fourth*, pt. 2, III, 1, 5.)

Sore laboured. B. p. 445

> Will all great Neptune's ocean wash this blood
> Clean from my hand. II, 2, 60

She died *tantâ* (saith mine author) *fœtissimi puris copiâ*, of so fulsome a disease, that no water could wash her clean. B. p. 306

> Here's an English tailor come hither for stealing out of a French hose. II, 3, 12

A tailor, a thief. B. p. 184

> *Macd.* What three things does drink especially provoke?
> *Port.* Marry, sir, nose-painting, sleep, and urine.
> Lechery, sir, it . . . II, 3, 26

The bottom [of the bladder] holds the water, the neck is constringed with a muscle, which, as a porter, keeps the water from running out against our will. Members of generation are common to both sexes, or peculiar to one. B. p. 97

Amber provokes urine. B. p. 454

Most sacrilegous murder hath broke ope
The Lord's anointed temple and stole thence
The Life o' th' building. II, 3, 65

[Referring to the anatomy of the human body] "Suppose you were now brought into some sacred temple or majestical palace (as Melancthon saith) to behold not the matter only, but the singular art, workmanship, and counsel of this our great Creator. B. p. 96

Shake off this downy sleep, death's counterfeit. II, 3, 74

Death is but a perpetual sleep. B. p. 407

The wine of life is drawn, and the mere lees
Is left this vault to brag of. II, 3, 93

And Babylon, the greatest city that ever the sun shone on, hath now nothing but walls and rubbish left. B. p. 410

The expedition of my violent love
Outran the pauser, reason. II, 3, 109

Reason is overborne by passion: *Fertur equis auriga, nec audit currus habenas*, as so many wild horses run away with a chariot, and will not be curbed. B. p. 107

Nor our strong sorrow
Upon the foot of motion. II, 3, 123

Why was Hecuba said to be turned to a dog? Niobe into a stone? but that for grief she was senseless and stupid. B. p. 171

Fears and scruples shake us. II, 3, 128

And Jason Pratensis "that the devil . . . can . . . terrify our souls with fearful dreams, and shake our minds with furies." B. p. 129

They are troubled with scruples of conscience. B. p. 252

Cares and contentions attend me all day long, fears and suspicions all my life. B. p. 408

Let him . . . submit himself to the advice of good physicians and divines, which is *contraventio scrupulorum*, as he [Navarrus] calls it, hear them speak to whom the Lord hath given the tongue of the learned, to be able to minister a word to him that is weary, whose words are as flagons of wine. B. p. 736

In the great hand of God I stand. II, 3, 129

"We must submit ourselves unto the mighty hand of God."
B. p. 115

"Humble thyself, therefore, under the mighty hand of God," 1 *Peter*, v. 6. B. p. 249

To be thus is nothing,
But to be safely thus. Our fears in Banquo
Stick deep. III, 1, 47

A true saying it is, "Desire hath no rest;" is infinite in itself, endless; and as one calls it, a perpetual rack, or horse-mill, according to Austin, still going round as in a ring. . . . I will only insist upon some few of the chief, and most noxious in their kind, as that exorbitant appetite and desire of honour, which we commonly call ambition. B. pp. 184–185

He hath a wisdom that doth guide his valour
To act in safety. There is none but he
Whose being I do fear; and under him
My Genius is rebuk'd, as it is said
Mark Antony's was by Cæsar. III, 1, 52

Saul envied David; Domitian Agricola, because he did excel him, obscure his honour, as he thought, eclipse his fame. B. p. 627

Are you so gospell'd
To pray for this good man and for his issue,
Whose heavy hand hath bow'd you to the grave
And beggar'd yours for ever. III, 1, 87

Poverty begets sedition and villany. B. p. 46

Ay, in the catalogue ye go for men. III, 1, 91

This catalogue of wise men. B. p. 42

In the catalogue of Ignoramus. B. p. 351

I am one, my liege,
Whom the vile blows and buffets of the world
Hath so incens'd that I am reckless what
I do to spite the world. III, 1, 107

We will turn parasites and slaves, prostitute ourselves, swear and lie, damn our bodies and souls, forsake God, abjure religion, steal, rob, murder, rather than endure this insufferable yoke of poverty.
B. p. 227

Things without all remedy
Should be without regard. What's done is done.
III, 2, 11

Grieve not for that which cannot be recalled. B. p. 424

We have scotch'd the snake, not kill'd it;
She'll close, and be herself. III, 2, 13

If their [devils'] bodies be cut, with admirable celerity they come together again. B. p. 117

In the affliction of these terrible dreams
That shake us nightly. III, 2, 18

(See, above, *King Richard The Third*, V, 3, 177.)

And make our faces vizards to our hearts,
Disguising what they are. III, 2, 34

(See, above, this play, I, 4, 11.)

Thou mayst revenge. O slave! III, 3, 18

Mancipia gulæ, slaves to their several lusts and appetite, they precipitate and plunge themselves into a labyrinth of cares blinded with lust, blinded with ambition. B. p. 170

Lovers are slaves to their mistresses, rich men to their gold, courtiers generally to lust and ambition, and all slaves to our affections.
B. p. 404

Then comes my fit again. I had else been perfect.
III, 4, 21

They [the ambitious] will contend, they may not cease, but as a dog in a wheel, a bird in a cage, or a squirrel in a chain, so Budæus compares them; they climb and climb still, with much labour, but never make an end, never at the top. B. p. 186

Now good digestion wait on appetite,
And health on both! III, 4, 38

The like, *consil.* 229, or not to eat till he be an hungry, which rule Berengarius did most strictly observe, as Hilbertus, *Cenomecensis Episc.* writes in his life;
— "cui non fuit unquam
Ante sitim potus, nec cibus ante famem,"
and which all temperate men do constantly keep. B. p. 309

It will have blood; they say blood will have blood.
Stones have been known to move, and trees to speak.

III, 4, 122

Nemesis comes after, *serò sed seriò* B. p. 419

Every small circumstance before neglected and contemned, will now amplify itself, rise up in judgment, and accuse the dust of their shoes, dumb creatures, as to Lucian's tyrant, *lectus et candela*, the bed and candle did bear witness, to torment their souls for their sins past. B. p. 719

There's not a one of them but in his house
I keep a servant fee'd. III, 4, 131

One servant is set in his absence to watch another. B. p. 641

And you all know security
Is mortals' chiefest enemy. III, 5, 32

Be not secure then, "be sober and watch." B. p. 250

In the other extreme or in defect, march those impious epicures, libertines, atheists, hypocrites, infidels, worldly, secure, impenitent. B. p. 666

Many a carnal man is lulled asleep in perverse security. B. p. 734

Round about the cauldron go;
In the poison'd entrails throw. . . .
Then the charm is firm and good. IV, 1, 4–38

Sacks of wormwood, mandrake, henbane, roses made like pillows and laid under the patient's head, are mentioned by Cardan and Mizaldus, "to anoint the soles of the feet with the fat of a dormouse, the teeth with the ear wax of a dog, swine's gall, hare's ears:" charms, &c. B. p. 457

Pour in sow's blood that hath eaten
Her nine farrow. IV, 1, 64

"Paglarensis was amazed, and said his farmer had surely cozened him, when he heard him tell that his sow had eleven pigs, and his ass had but one foal." B. p. 201

When was it she last walk'd? V, 1, 2

This is likewise evident in such as walk in the night in their sleep, and do strange feats: these vapours move the fantasy, the fantasy the appetite, which moving the animal spirits causeth the body to walk up and down as if they were awake. B. p. 166

Bayerus, *lib.* 2. *c.* 13. sets down some remedies against fearful dreams, and such as walk and talk in their sleep. B. p. 457

> *Doct.* You see her eyes are open.
> *Gent.* Ay, but their sense is shut. V, I, 23

"Sleep is a rest or binding of the outward senses, and of the common sense, for the preservation of body and soul" (as Scaliger defines it); . . . This ligation of the senses proceeds from the inhibition of spirits, the way being stopped by which they should come. B. p. 102

> All the perfumes of Arabia will not sweeten this little hand. V, I, 49

All Arabia will not serve to perfume her hair. B. p. 605

> Yet I have known those which have walk'd in their sleep who have died holily in their beds. V, I, 58

Experience teacheth us, that though many die obstinate and wilful in this malady, yet multitudes again are able to resist and overcome, seek for help and find comfort, are taken *é faucibus Erebi*, from the chops of hell, out of the devil's paws, though they have by obligation given themselves to him. B. p. 723

> Infected minds
> To their deaf pillows will discharge their secrets. V, I, 70

The bed and candle did bear witness, to torment their souls for their sins past. B. p. 719

> More needs she the divine than the physician. V, I, 72

And this I enjoin you, not as a divine alone, but as a physician. B. p. 372

> *Ment.* What does the tyrant?
> *Caith.* Great Dunsinane he strongly fortifies.
> Some say he's mad; others, that lesser hate him,
> Do call it valiant fury; but for certain
> He cannot buckle his distemper'd cause
> Within the belt of rule.
> *Ang.* Now does he feel
> His secret murders sticking on his hands;
> Now minutely revolts upbraid his faith-breach;
> Those he commands move only in command,

> Nothing in love. Now does he feel his title
> Hang loose about him, like a giant's robe
> Upon a dwarfish thief.

V, 2, 11

And those men which have no other object of their love, than greatness, wealth, authority, &c., are rather feared than beloved.

B. p. 483

But it is most grievous when it is for a kingdom itself, or matters of commodity, it produceth lamentable effects, especially amongst tyrants, *in despotico Imperio*, and such as are more feared than beloved of their subjects, that get and keep their sovereignity by force and fear.

B. p. 627

It may be thou art not fit; but a child that puts on his father's shoes, hat, headpiece, breastplate, breeches, or holds his spear, but is neither able to wield the one, or wear the other; so wouldst thou do by such an office, place, or magistracy: thou art unfit: "And what is dignity to an unworthy man, but" (as Salvianus holds) "a gold ring in a swine's snout?"

B. p. 417

> I have liv'd long enough.

V, 3, 22

Adrian, Galba, Nero, Otho, Vitellius, Caracalla, were in such horror of conscience for their offences committed, murders, rapes, extortions, injuries, that they were weary of their lives, and could get nobody to kill them. Kennetus, King of Scotland, when he had murdered his nephew Malcolm, King Duffe's son, Prince of Cumberland, and with counterfeit tears and protestations dissembled the matter for a long time, "at last his conscience accused him, his unquiet soul could not rest day or night, he was terrified with fearful dreams, visions, and so miserably tormented all his life."

B. p. 719

> Curses not loud but deep, mouth-honour, breath,
> Which the poor heart would fain deny, and dare not.

V, 3, 27

A great man in office may securely rob whole provinces, undo thousands, pill and poll, oppress *ad libitum*, flea, grind, tyrannise, enrich himself by spoils of the commons, be uncontrollable in his actions, and after all, be recompensed with turgent titles, honoured for his good service, and no man dare find fault, or mutter at it.

B. p. 31

Where this true love is wanting, there can be no firm peace, friendship from teeth outward, counterfeit.

B. p. 483

Not so sick, my lord,
As she is troubled with thick-coming fancies
That keep her from her rest. V, 3, 37

Tossed in a sea, and that continually without rest or intermission, they can think of nought that is pleasant, "their conscience will not let them be quiet." B. p. 721

Cure her of that.
Canst thou not minister to a mind diseas'd,
Pluck from the memory a rooted sorrow,
Raze out the written troubles of the brain,
And with some sweet oblivious antidote
Cleanse the stuff'd bosom of that perilous stuff
Which weighs upon the heart? V, 3, 39

There is no sickness almost but physic provideth a remedy for it: to every sore chirurgery will provide a salve; friendship helps poverty; hope of liberty easeth imprisonment; suit and favour revoke banishment; authority and time wear away reproach; but what physic, what chirurgery, what wealth, favour, authority can relieve, bear out, assuage, or expel a troubled conscience? B. p. 721

" . . . and the black blood drawn from the spleen, and diffused under the ribs, on the left side, makes those perilous hypochondriacal convulsions, which happen to them that are troubled with sorrow." B. p. 171

Two main antidotes, Hemmingius observes, opposite to despair. B. p. 724

Irremissible sins, sins of the first magnitude, written with a pen of iron, engraven with the point of a diamond. B. p. 728

To be able to minister a word to him that is weary. B. p. 739

Doct. Therein the patient
Must minister to himself.
Macb. Throw physic to the dogs—I'll none of it. V, 3, 45

Another thing is, that out of bashfulness he do not conceal his grief; if aught trouble his mind, let him freely disclose it, "*Stultorum incurata pudor malus ulcera celat:*" by that means he procures to himself much mischief, and runs into a greater inconvenience; he must be willing to be cured, and earnestly desire it. B. p. 301

And often out of prejudice, a loathing and distaste of physic, they had rather die, or do worse, than take any of it. B. p. 302

From the patient himself the first and chiefest remedy must be had; for if he be averse, peevish, waspish, give way wholly to his passions, will not seek to be helped, or be ruled by his friends, how is it possible he should be cured? B. p. 359

Out, out, brief candle!
Life's but a walking shadow. V, 5, 23

Our life is but short, a very dream, and while we look about, *immortalitas adest*, eternity is at hand. B. p. 378

a poor player,
That struts and frets his hour upon the stage,
And then is heard no more; it is a tale
Told by an idiot, full of sound and fury,
Signifying nothing. V, 5, 24

A lascivious *inamorato* plots all the day long to please his mistress, acts and struts, and carries himself as if she were in presence.

B. p. 265

"This question of the immortality of the soul, is diversely and wonderfully impugned and disputed, especially among the Italians of late," saith Jab. Colerus, *lib. de immort. animæ, cap.* 1. The popes themselves have doubted of it: Leo Decimus, that Epicurean pope, as some record of him, caused this question to be discussed *pro* and *con* before him, and concluded at last, as a prophane and atheistical moderator, with that verse of Cornelius Gallus, *Et redit in nihilum, quod fuit ante nihil.* It began of nothing, and in nothing it ends. Zeno and his Stoics, as Austin quotes him, supposed the soul so long to continue, till the body was fully putrefied, and resolved into *materia prima:* but after that, *in fumos evanescere*, to be extinguished and vanished. B. p. 104

"We shall be hereafter as though we had never been; for the breath is as smoke in our nostrils, etc., and the spirit vanisheth as the soft air." B. p. 705

Blow wind, come wrack;
At least we'll die with harness on our back. V, 5, 51

Let the devil himself, and all the plagues of Egypt come upon thee at once, *Ne tu cede malis, sed contra audentior ito*, be of good courage.

B. p. 399

Macb. I bear a charmed life, which must not yield
To one of woman born.
Macd. Despair thy charm;
And let the angel whom thou still hast serv'd
Tell thee Macduff was from his mother's womb
Untimely ripp'd.
Macb. Accursed be that tongue that tells me so,
For it hath cow'd my better part of man;
And be these juggling fiends no more believ'd.

. . . .

Though Birnam wood be come to Dunsinane,
And thou oppos'd, being of no woman born,
Yet I will try the last. Before my body
I throw my warlike shield. Lay on, Macduff;
And damn'd be him that first cries 'Hold, enough!'

V, 8, 12–34

Mine haven's found, fortune and hope adieu,
Mock others now, for I have done with you. B. p. 414

Siw. Had he his hurts before?
Ross. Ay, on the front.
Siw. Why, then, God's soldier be he!

V, 8, 46

We are sent as so many soldiers into this world to strive with it, the flesh, the devil; our life is a warfare, and who knows it not? . . .

Ite nunc fortes, ubi celsa magni
Ducit exempli via: cur inertes
Terga nudatis? superata tellus
Sidera domat. B. p. 378

Shilleto translates this thus: "Go now, brave fellows, where the lofty path of a great example leads. Why do you stupidly expose your backs? The earth brings the stars to subjection."

N.B.—The manner of death of Siward's son is similarly recorded in Holinshed (Nicoll, pp. 223–4) but with the omission of

"Why, then, God's soldier be he!"

and here we have an example of how Burton could transform his borrowed material. Let my reader contrast this kind of borrowing with Shakespeare's extensive mere copying to which attention was drawn in Chapter V, above. For another such example see, below, *Antony and Cleopatra*, IV, 15, 34.

Thou know'st 'tis common—all that lives must die,
Passing through nature to eternity. I, 2, 72

'Tis an inevitable chance, the first statute in *Magna Charta*, an everlasting Act of Parliament, all must die. B. p. 409

But to persever
In obstinate condolement is a course
Of impious stubbornness. I, 2, 92

'Twas Germanicus' advice of old, that we should not dwell too long upon our passions, to be desperately sad, immoderate grievers.
B. p. 409

For what we know must be, and is as common
As any the most vulgar thing to sense,
Why should we in our peevish opposition
Take it to heart? I, 2, 98

'This must be so.' I, 2, 106

If thou alone wert distressed, it were indeed more irksome, and less to be endured; but when the calamity is common, comfort thyself with this, thou hast more fellows, *Solamen miseris socios habuisse doloris;* 'tis not thy sole case, and why shouldst thou be so impatient? . . . "So it is and so it was, and so it ever will be. . . ."
B. pp. 375–376

If it were his case alone, it were hard; but being as it is almost a common calamity, 'tis not so grievously to be taken. B. p. 647

Or that the Everlasting had not fix'd
His canon 'gainst self-slaughter! I, 2, 131

God, and all good men are against it: He that stabs another can kill his body; but he that stabs himself, kills his own soul.
B. p. 287

But two months dead! I, 2, 138

If one die, the other party shall not marry till six months after.
B. p. 62

O God! a beast that wants discourse of reason
Would have mourn'd longer. I, 2, 150

In men it [the imagination] is subject and governed by reason, or at least should be; but in brutes it hath no superior, and is *ratio brutorum*, all the reason they have. B. p. 102

Thirdly, brutes cannot reflect upon themselves. Bees indeed make neat and curious works, and many other creatures besides; but when they have done, they cannot judge of them. B. p. 105

Think it no more;
For nature crescent does not grow alone
In thews and bulk, but as this temple waxes,
The inward service of the mind and soul
Grows wide withal. I, 3, 10

Many things I disallow at this present, which when I writ, *Non eadem est ætas, non mens;* I would willingly retract much, &c., but 'tis too late, I can only crave pardon now for what is amiss. B. p. 11

[Dealing with the anatomy of the human body, Burton writes] "Suppose you were now brought into some sacred temple, or majestical palace (as Melancthon saith), to behold not the matter only, but the singular art, workmanship, and counsel of this our great Creator." B. p. 96

But, good my brother,
Do not, as some ungracious pastors do,
Show me the steep and thorny way to heaven,
Whiles, like a puff'd and reckless libertine,
Himself the primrose path of dalliance treads
And recks not his own rede. I, 3, 46

Had he more particularly examined a Jesuit's life amongst the rest, he should have seen an hypocrite profess poverty, and yet possess more goods and lands than many princes, to have infinite treasures and revenues; teach others to fast, and play the gluttons themselves; like the water men that row one way and look another. Vow virginity, talk of holiness, and yet indeed a notorious bawd, and famous fornicator, *lascivum pecus*, a very goat. Monks by profession, such as give over the world and the vanities of it, and yet a *Machiavelian* rout interested in all manner of state: holy men, peace makers, and yet composed of envy, lust, ambition, hatred, and malice. B. p. 27

Give every man thy ear, but few thy voice. I, 3, 68

Hear much, speak little. B. p. 424

Ay, springes to catch woodcocks! I, 3, 115

'Tis but a springe to catch woodcocks. B, p. 523

I do know,
When the blood burns, how prodigal the soul
Lends the tongue vows. I, 3, 115

Oaths, vows, promises, are much protested;
But when their mind and lust is satisfied,
Oaths, vows, promises, are quite neglected. B. p. 544

This heavy-headed revel east and west
Makes us traduc'd and tax'd of other nations;
They clepe us drunkards. I, 4, 17

Danes, Dutchmen, Polanders and Bohemians drink it [grief] down. B. p. 412

The dram of eale
Doth all the noble substance of a doubt
To his own scandal. I, 4, 36

These ill-gotten goods, as an eagle's feathers, will consume the rest of their substance. . . . A little gain evil-gotten will subvert the rest of their goods. B. p. 208

Ham. I say, away! Go on; I'll follow thee.
Hor. He waxes desperate with imagination. I, 4, 86

Yet again, many of them desperate hare-brains, rash, careless, fit to be assassins, as being void of all fear and sorrow, according to Hercules *de Saxoniâ*, "Most audacious, and such as dare walk alone in the night, through deserts and dangerous places, fearing none." B. p. 257

O villain, villain, smiling, damned villain!
My tables—meet it is I set it down
That one may smile, and smile, and be a villain. I, 5, 106

To see a man protest friendship, kiss his hand, *quem mallet truncatum videre*, smile with an intent to do mischief, or cozen him whom he salutes. B. p. 34

The time is out of joint. O cursed spite,
That ever I was born to set it right! I, 5, 189

We had need of some general visitor in our age, that should reform what is amiss. B. p. 55

He falls to such perusal of my face
As 'a would draw it. Long stay'd he so. II, 1, 90

Many lovers confess when they came in their mistress' presence, they could not hold off their eyes, but looked wistfully and steadily on her, *inconnivo aspectu*, with much eagerness and greediness, as if they would look through, or should never have enough sight of her. B. p. 554

Pol. What do you read, my lord?
Ham. Words, words, words.
Pol. What is the matter, my lord?
Ham. Between who?
Pol. I mean, the matter that you read, my lord.
II, 2, 190

I respect matter not words; remembering that of Cardan, *verba propter res, non res propter verba.* B. p. 11

The satirical rogue says here that old men . . . II, 2, 195

Note—Highet*, referring to this passage, writes "Hamlet was reading Juvenal: the Tenth Satire, which tells of the weakness, folly, and ugliness of old age."

Burton, in *The Anatomy*, frequently refers to Juvenal.

For you yourself, sir, shall grow old as I am, if, like a crab, you could go backwards. II, 2, 201

Senex bis puer. B. p. 20

When old, a child again. B. p. 24

In the secret parts of Fortune? O, most true; she is a strumpet. II, 2, 234

He calls her on a sudden all to naught, she is a strumpet, a light housewife, a bitch, an arrant whore. B. p. 641

Ham. Denmark's a prison.
Ros. Then is the world one. II, 2, 242

What is our life but a prison? B. p. 405

This earth itself the muck-hill of the world, a prison, a house of correction. B. p. 729

---

* *Juvenal the Satirist;* Oxford at the Clarendon Press; 1954–5; p. 213.

Ros. We think not so, my lord.
Ham. Why, then, 'tis none to you; for there is nothing either good or bad, but thinking makes it so. To me it is a prison.
Ros. Why, then your ambition makes it one; 'tis too narrow for your mind. II, 2, 247

It is not another man's opinion can make me happy: but as Seneca well hath it, "He is a miserable wretch that doth not account himself happy; though he be sovereign lord of a world, he is not happy, if he think himself not to be so; for what availeth it what thine estate is, or seems to others, if thou thyself dislike it?" B. p. 181

This most excellent canopy the air, look you, this brave o'erhanging firmament. II, 2, 298

I live and breathe under that glorious heaven, that august capitol of nature, enjoy the brightness of stars, that clear light of sun and moon. B. p. 392

What a piece of work is a man! How noble in reason! II, 2, 301

Man, the most excellent and noble creature of the world. B. p. 81

And yet, to me, what is this quintessence of dust? II, 2, 307

But this most noble creature, *Heu tristis, et lachrymosa commutatio* (one exclaims) O pitiful change! is fallen from that he was. B. p. 81

Quintessence of wisdom. B. p. 71

The quintessence of all love. B. p. 485

The quintessence of beauty. B. p. 663

I am but mad north-north-west; when the wind is southerly I know a hawk from a handsaw. II, 2, 374

As they write of heat and cold, we may say of this humour, one is *melancholicus ad octo*, a second two degrees less, a third half-way. 'Tis superparticular, *sesquialtera*, *sesquitertia*, and *superbipartiens tertias, quintas Melancholiæ, &c.*, all those geometrical proportions are too little to express it. It comes to many by fits, and goes; to others it is continuate: many (saith Faventinus) in spring and fall only are molested, some once a year. B. p. 265

For they say an old man is twice a child. II, 2, 381

(See this play, II, 2, 201.)

> The best actors in the world, either for tragedy, comedy, history, pastoral, pastoral-comical [&c.] II, 2, 392

In this tragi-comedy of love, to act several parts, some satirically, some comically, some in a mixed tone, as the subject I have in hand gives occasion, and present scene shall require or offer itself.
B. p. 471

> For look where my abridgment comes. II, 2, 415

Man . . . "the abridgment and epitome of the world," as Pliny.
B. p. 81

> *Ham.* . . . Good my lord, will you see the players well bestowed? . . .
> *Pol.* My lord, I will use them according to their desert.
> II, 2, 516–521

For that cause, plays, masks, jesters, gladiators, tumblers, jugglers, &c., and all that crew is admitted and winked at: . . . So that as Tacitus said of the astrologers in Rome, we may say of them, *genus hominum est quod in civitate nostra et vitabitur semper et retinebitur*, they are a debauched company most part, still spoken against, as well they deserve some of them (for I so relish and distinguish them as fiddlers, and musicians), and yet ever retained. B. p. 346

> Tears in his eyes, distraction in's aspect,
> A broken voice, and his whole function suiting
> With forms to his conceit? And all for nothing!
> For Hecuba!
> What's Hecuba to him or he to Hecuba,
> That he should weep for her? II, 2, 548

So when she heard her son was slain, she abruptly broke off her work, changed countenance and colour . . . Many years after, the remembrance of such friends, of such accidents, is most grievous unto us, to see or hear of it, though it concern not ourselves but others. Scaliger saith of himself, that he never read Socrates' death, in Plato's *Phædon*, but he wept: Austin shed tears when he read the destruction of Troy. B. p. 407

> The very faculties of eyes and ears. II, 2, 559

The apprehensive faculty is subdivided into two parts, inward and outward. Outward, as the five senses, of touching, hearing, seeing, smelling, tasting. B. p. 100

I have heard
That guilty creatures, sitting at a play,
Have by the very cunning of the scene
Been struck so to the soul that presently
They have proclaim'd their malefactions;
For murder, though it have no tongue, will speak
With most miraculous organ. II, 2, 584

If the party be sad, or otherwise affected, "consider (saith Trallianus) the manner of it, all circumstances, and forthwith make a sudden alteration," by removing the occasions, avoid all terrible objects, heard or seen, "monstrous and prodigious aspects," tales of devils, spirits, ghosts, tragical stories; to such as are in fear they strike a great impression, renewed many times, and recall such chimeras and terrible fictions into their minds. "Make not so much as mention of them in private talk, or a dumb show tending to that purpose; such things (saith Galateus) are offensive to their imaginations." B. pp. 363–364

To be, or not to be— . . . III, 1, 56

Another doubt is made by some philosophers, whether it be lawful for a man, in such extremity of pain and grief, to make away himself. B. p. 285

When we have shuffled off this mortal coil. III, 1, 67

Plato in *Timæo*, and in his *Phædon* (for ought I can perceive) differs not much from this opinion, that it [the soul] was from God at first, and knew all, but being inclosed in the body, it forgets, and learns anew, which he calls *reminiscentia*, or recalling, and that it was put into the body for a punishment. B. p. 104

Note—According to this reading the word "coil" does not mean "turmoil," as given by at least some authorities, but the coil of the body around the soul.

. . . the law's delay. III, 1, 72

And continue causes so long, *lustra aliquot*, I know not how many years before the cause is heard. B. p. 47

When he himself might his quietus make
With a bare bodkin? III, 1, 75

There's no necessity for a man to live in misery. B. p. 285

> The undiscover'd country, from whose bourn
> No traveller returns. III, 1, 79

But what shall become of their souls, God alone can tell. B. p. 288
"Our life is short and tedious, and in the death of a man there is no recovery, neither was any man known that hath returned from the grave. . . ." B. p. 705

> And thus the native hue of resolution
> Is sicklied o'er with the pale cast of thought,
> And enterprises of great pitch and moment,
> With this regard, their currents turn awry
> And lose the name of action. III, 1, 84

Inconstant they [melancholy persons] are in all their actions, vertiginous, restless, unapt to resolve of any business, they will and will not, persuaded to and fro upon every small occasion, or word spoken. B. p. 256

> Lady, shall I lie in your lap?
> I mean, my head upon your lap?
> Do you think I meant country matters?
> O God, your only jig-maker! III, 2, 110–120

There be many others, which will of themselves intend this passion of burning lust, amongst which, dancing is not the least; . . . Owen Tudor won Queen Catherine's affection in a dance, falling by chance with his head in her lap. B. pp. 540–541

> Then there's hope a great man's memory may outlive his life half a year; but by'r lady, 'a must build churches, then; or else shall 'a suffer not thinking on, with the hobby-horse, whose epitaph is 'For O, for O, the hobby-horse is forgot!' III, 2, 126

This puffing humour it is, that hath produced so many great tomes, built such famous monuments, strong castles, and Mausolean tombs, to have their acts eternised. B. p. 195

> Let the galled jade wince, our withers are unwrung. III, 2, 236

It is not my freeness of speech but a guilty conscience, a galled back of his own that makes him wince. B. p. 73

> Why, let the strucken deer go weep,
> The hart ungalled play. III, 2, 265

As to a deer that is struck, whether he run, go, rest with the herd, or alone, this grief remains. B. p. 255

> You do surely bar the door upon your own liberty, if you deny your griefs to your friend. III, 2, 329

Grief concealed strangles the soul; but when as we shall but impart it to some discreet, trusty, loving friend, it is instantly removed, by his counsel happily, wisdom, persuasion, advice, his good means, which we could not otherwise apply unto ourselves. B. p. 361

> Sir, I lack advancement. III, 2, 331

I was once so mad to bustle abroad, and seek about for preferment. B. p. 414

> Ay, sir, but 'While the grass grows'—the proverb is something musty. III, 2, 334

A good hour may come upon a sudden; expect a little.

Yea, but this expectation is it which tortures me in the mean time; *futura expectans præsentibus angor*, whilst the grass grows the horse starves. B. pp. 400–401

> *Ham.* . . .
> Govern these ventages with your fingers and thumb, give it breath with your mouth, and it will discourse most eloquent music. Look you, these are the stops.
> *Guil.* But these cannot I command to any utterance of harmony; I have not the skill.
> *Ham.* Why, look you now, how unworthy a thing you make of me! You would play upon me; you would seem to know my stops; you would pluck out the heart of my mystery; you would sound me from my lowest note to the top of my compass; and there is much music, excellent voice, in this little organ, yet cannot you make it speak. III, 2, 348

So that, I hope, I may justly conclude with Cajetan, *Cœlum est vehiculum divinæ virtutis, &c.*, that the heaven is God's instrument, by mediation of which he governs and disposeth these elementary bodies; or a great book, whose letters are the stars (as one calls it), wherein are written many strange things for such as can read, "or an excellent harp, made by an eminent workman, on which, he that can but play, will make most admirable music." B. p. 133

O, my offence is rank, it smells to heaven;
It hath the primal eldest curse upon't—
A brother's murder! III, 3, 36

'Tis by reason of their sins: which like the blood of Abel cry loud to heaven for vengeance, *Lam.* v. 15. B. p. 82

But, O, what form of prayer
Can serve my turn? 'Forgive me my foul murder!'
That cannot be; since I am still possess'd
Of those effects for which I did the murder—
My crown, mine own ambition, and my queen.
May one be pardon'd and retain th' offence? III, 3, 51

Theodoret, out of Plotinus the Platonist, "holds it a ridiculous thing for a man to live after his own laws, to do that which is offensive to God, and yet to hope that He should save him. . . ." B. p. 40

O limed soul, that, struggling to be free,
Art more engag'd! III, 3, 68

Yea, but this meditation is that mars all, and mistaken makes many men far worse, misconceiving all they read or hear, to their own overthrow; the more they search and read scriptures, or divine treatises, the more they puzzle themselves, as a bird in a net, the more they are entangled and precipitated into this preposterous gulf. B. p. 730

And let me wring your heart; for so I shall,
If it be made of penetrable stuff;
If damned custom have not braz'd it so
That it be proof and bulwark against sense. III, 4, 35

According to that of Hippocrates 2, *Aphoris.* 50, "Such things as we have been long accustomed to, though they be evil in their own nature yet they are less offensive." B. p. 150

You cannot call it love; for at your age
The heyday in the blood is tame. III, 4, 68

Worse it is in women than in men, when she is *ætate declivis, diu vidua, mater olim, parum decorè matrimonium sequi videtur*, an old widow, a mother so long since (in Pliny's opinion) she doth very unseemly seek to marry. B. p. 501

Sense, sure, you have,
Else you could not have motion. III, 4, 71

This sensible soul is divided into two parts, apprehending or moving. By the apprehensive power we perceive the species of sensible things present, or absent, and retain them as wax doth the print of a seal. By the moving, the body is outwardly carried from one place to another; or inwardly moved by spirits and pulse. The apprehensive faculty is subdivided into two parts, inward or outward. Outward, as the five senses, of touching, hearing, seeing, smelling, tasting.
B. p. 100

This power [the appetite] is inseparable from sense, for where sense is, there are likewise pleasure and pain. B. p. 102

Moving from place to place, is a faculty necessarily following the other [the appetite]. For in vain were it otherwise to desire and to abhor, if we had not likewise power to prosecute or eschew, by moving the body from place to place. B. p. 103

And reason panders will. III, 4, 88

Will is the other power of the rational soul, "which covets or avoids such things as have been before judged and apprehended by the understanding." If good, it approves; if evil, it abhors it: so that his object is either good or evil. Aristotle calls this our rational appetite; for as, in the sensitive, we are moved to good or bad by our appetite, ruled and directed by sense; so in this we are carried by reason. B. p. 106

It [the will] was (as I said) once well agreeing with reason, and there was an excellent consent and harmony between them, but that is now dissolved, they often jar, reason is overborne by passion: . . . Lust counsels one thing, reason another. B. p. 107

Conceit in weakest bodies strongest works. III, 4, 114

Another was sick of the plague with conceit. One seeing his fellow let blood falls down in a swoon. Another (saith Cardan out of Aristotle) fell down dead (which is familiar to women at any ghastly sight), seeing but a man hanged. B. p. 168

And 'tis strange what women and children will conceive unto themselves, if they go over a churchyard in the night, lie or be alone in a dark room, how they sweat and tremble on a sudden.
B. p. 172

That monster custom, who all sense doth eat,
Of habits devil, is angel yet in this,
That to the use of actions fair and good
He likewise gives a frock or livery
That aptly is put on. III, 4, 161

As a horse that starts at a drum or trumpet, and will not endure the shooting of a piece, may be so manned by art, and animated that he can not only endure, but is much more generous at the hearing of such things, much more courageous than before, and much delighteth in it: they must not be reformed, *ex abrupto*, but by all art and insinuation, made to such companies, aspects, objects they could not formerly away with. B. p. 364

For this same lord
I do repent. III, 4, 172

Ægesippus, *de excid. urbis Hieros. l.* 1. *c.* 37. hath such a story of Herod, that out of an angry fit, became mad, leaping out of his bed, he killed Josippus, and played many such bedlam pranks, the whole court could not rule him for a long time after: sometimes he was sorry and repented, much grieved for what he had done, *Postquam deferbuit ira*, by and by outrageous again. B. p. 178

. . . call you his mouse. III, 4, 183

All the bombast epithets, pathetical adjuncts, incomparably fair, curiously neat, divine, sweet, dainty, delicious, &c., pretty diminutives, *corculum*, *suaviolum*, &c., pleasant names may be invented, bird, mouse, lamb, puss, pigeon, pigsney, kid, honey, love, dove, chicken, &c. he puts on her. B. p. 566

For 'tis the sport to have the engineer
Hoist with his own petar. III, 4, 206

Those strange fire-works, devilish petards, and such like warlike machinations derived hence, of which read Tartalea and others.
B. p. 354

They shall be recompensed according to the works of their hands, as Haman was hanged on the gallows he provided for Mordecai.
B. p. 419

But I will delve one yard below their mines
And blow them at the moon. III, 4, 208

(See, above, *King Henry the Fifth*, II, 2, 54–58.)

Truly to speak, and with no addition,
We go to gain a little patch of ground
That hath in it no profit but the name. IV, 4, 17

"Neither Sicily nor Sardinia are worth such cost and pains, so many fleets and armies, or so many famous Captains' lives."
B. p. 63

Cudgel thy brains no more about it, for your dull ass will not mend his pace with beating. V, 1, 56

By this means [fasting] Hilarion "made his ass, as he called his own body, leave kicking (so Hierome relates of him in his life), when the devil tempted him to any such foul offence." B. p. 585

Custom hath made it in him a property of easiness.
V, 1, 67

(See this play, III, 4, 161.)

Ham. Ay, marry, why was he sent into England?
1 *Clo.* Why, because 'a was mad: 'a shall recover his wits there; or, if 'a do not, 'tis no great matter there.
Ham. Why?
1 *Clo.* 'Twill not be seen in him there: there the men are as mad as he. V, 1, 145

When all are mad, where all are like opprest
Who can discern one mad man from the rest? B. p. 38

Her obsequies have been as far enlarg'd
As we have warrantise. Her death was doubtful;
And, but that great command o'ersways the order,
She should in ground unsanctified have lodg'd
Till the last trumpet. V, 1, 220

P. Forestus hath a story of two melancholy brethren, that made away themselves, and for so foul a fact, were accordingly censured to be infamously buried, as in such cases they use, to terrify others, as it did the Milesian virgins of old, but upon farther examination of their misery and madness, the censure was revoked, and they were solemnly interred. B. p. 288

A minist'ring angel shall my sister be
When thou liest howling. V, 1, 235

Poor Lazarus lies howling at his gates for a few crumbs. B. p. 487

Now pile your dust upon the quick and dead,
Till of this flat a mountain you have made
T' o'er-top old Pelion or the skyish head
Of blue Olympus. V, 1, 245

Make Ossa like a wart! V, 1, 277

Whether Mount Athos, Pelion, Olympus, Ossa, Caucasus, Atlas, be so high as Pliny, Solinus, Mela relate, above clouds, meteors.
B. p. 315

This is mere madness;
And thus awhile the fit will work on him;
Anon, as patient as the female dove
When that her golden couplets are disclos'd,
His silence will sit drooping. V, 1, 278

(See this play, III, 4, 172.)
—"*et nidos avium scrutari.*" B. p. 343

*Our indiscretion sometime serves us well,
When our deep plots do pall; and that should learn us
There's a divinity that shapes our ends,
Rough-hew them how we will. V, 2, 8

(See, above, *The Tempest*, V, 1, 200.)

For know this, in conclusion, *Non est volentis nec currentis, sed miserentis Dei*, 'tis not as men, but as God will. "The Lord maketh poor and maketh rich, bringeth low, and exalteth (1 *Sam.* ii. ver. 7, 8), he lifteth the poor from the dust, and raiseth the beggar from the dunghill, to set them amongst princes, and make them inherit the seat of glory;" 'tis all as he pleaseth, how, and when, and whom; he that appoints the end (though to us unknown) appoints the means likewise subordinate to the end. B. p. 394

Thou art wise in thine own conceit, but in other more mature judgment altogether unfit to manage such a business. Or be it thou art more deserving than any of thy rank, God in his providence hath reserved thee for some other fortunes, *sic superis visum.*
B. p. 417

An earnest conjuration from the King,
As England was his faithful tributary,
As love between them like the palm might flourish,
As peace should still her wheaten garland wear
And stand . . . V, 2, 39

* See Note 1 at end of this Chapter.

When our Thame and Isis meet
"Oscula mille sonant, connexu brachia pallent,
Mutuaque explicitis connectunt colla lacertis."
Inachus and Pineus, and how many loving rivers can I reckon up, whom beauty hath enthralled! B. p. 511

Constantine *de Agric. lib.* 10. *cap.* 4. gives an instance out of Florentius his Georgics, of a palm-tree that loved most fervently, "and would not be comforted until such time her love applied herself unto her; you might see the two trees bend, and of their own accords stretch out their boughs to embrace and kiss each other; they will give manifest signs of mutual love." . . . which the husbandmen perceiving . . . tying the leaves and branches of the one to the stem of the other, will make them both flourish and prosper a great deal better. B. p. 492

What plague, what fury brought so devilish, so brutish a thing as war first into men's minds? B. p. 28

For by the image of my cause I see
The portraiture of his. V, 2, 77

Observe him; for as in a glass
Thine angry portraiture it was.

The Argument of The Frontispiece, Verse VII

Thy state is the more gracious; for 'tis a vice to know him.
V, 2, 85

As Hermione lamented in Euripides, *malæ mulieres me fecerunt malam*, evil company marred her, may they justly complain, bad companions have been their bane. B. p. 374

If it be now, 'tis not to come; if it be not to come, it will be now; if it be not now, yet it will come—the readiness is all. V, 2, 213

(See, above, *Julius Cæsar*, II, 2, 32.)

If Hamlet from himself be ta'en away,
And when he's not himself does wrong Lærtes,
Then Hamlet does it not, Hamlet denies it. V, 2, 226

Paul himself confesseth, *Rom.* vii. 19, "He did not the good he would do, but the evil which he would not do; 'tis not I, but sin that dwelleth in me." B. p. 730

HAMLET, PRINCE OF DENMARK

> Absent thee from felicity awhile,
> And in this harsh world draw thy breath in pain,
> To tell my story. V, 2, 339

Death makes an end of our miseries. B. p. 407

The Thracians wept still when a child was born, feasted and made mirth when any man was buried: and so should we rather be glad for such as die well, that they are so happily freed from the miseries of this life. B. p. 412

KING LEAR

> I have so often blush'd to acknowledge him that now I am braz'd to't. I, 1, 9

(See, above, *As You Like It*, III, 5, 3.)

> There was good sport at his making. I, 1, 22

That impious and carnal crew of worldly-minded men, impenitent sinners, that go to hell in a lethargy. B. p. 711

> Nothing will come of nothing. I, 1, 89

As, 'Out of nothing, nothing can be brought;
And that which is, can ne'er be turn'd to nought.'

B. p. 200

> She is herself a dowry. I, 1, 241

Beauty is a dowry of itself all sufficient. B. p. 613

Good education and beauty is a competent dowry, stand not upon money. B. p. 615

> You see how full of changes his age is . . . The best and soundest of his time hath been but rash; then must we look from his age to receive not alone the imperfections of long-engraffed condition, but therewithal the unruly waywardness that infirm and choleric years bring with them.

I, 1, 287–298

We see this in old men, children, Europeans; Asians, hot and cold climes; sanguine are merry; melancholy, sad; phlegmatic, dull; by reason of abundance of those humours, and they cannot resist such passions which are inflicted by them. For in this infirmity of human nature, as Melancthon declares, the understanding is so tied to, and captivated by his inferior senses, that without their help he cannot exercise his functions, and the will being weakened, hath but a small power to restrain those outward parts, but suffers herself to be overruled by them; that I must needs conclude with Lemnius, *spiritus et humores maximum nocumentum obtinet*, spirits and humours do most harm in troubling the soul. How should a man choose but be choleric and angry, that hath his body so clogged with abundance of gross humours? or melancholy, that is so inwardly disposed? That thence comes then this malady, madness, apoplexies, lethargies, &c., it may not be denied. B. p. 245

Why bastard? Wherefore base?
When my dimensions are as well compact,
My mind as generous, and my shape as true
As honest madam's issue? Why brand they us
With base? with baseness? bastardy? base, base?
Who, in the lusty stealth of nature, take
More composition and fierce quality
Than doth, within a dull, stale, tired bed,
Go to th' creating a whole tribe of fops. I, 2, 6

Hercules, Romulus, Alexander (by Olympia's confession), Themistocles, Jugurtha, King Arthur, William the Conqueror, Homer, Demosthenes, P. Lumbard, P. Comestor, Bartholus, Adrian the fourth Pope, &c., bastards; and almost in every kingdom, the most ancient families have been at first princes' bastards; their worthiest captains, best wits, greatest scholars, bravest spirits in all our annals, have been base. Cardan*, in his Subtleties, gives a reason why they are most part better able than others in body and mind, and so, *per consequens*, more fortunate . . . and why then should baseness of birth be objected to any man. B. p. 384

* *Footnote:—Corpore sunt et animo fortiores spurii, plerumque ob amoris vehementiam seminis crass., etc.*

This is the excellent foppery of the world. I, 2, 115

Mere fopperies and illusions. B. p. 705

They are fopperies and fictions. B. p. 738

As if we were villains on necessity; fools by heavenly compulsion. I, 2, 117

"Men were diversely affected: some said they were God's just judgments for the execution of that good man, some referred all to natural causes, some to stars, some thought they came by chance, some by necessity," decreed *ab initio*, and could not be altered. The two last opinions of necessity and chance were, it seems, of greater note than the rest. B. p. 709

The hedge-sparrow fed the cuckoo . . . I, 4, 214

. . . a bitch bring up a kid, a hen ducklings, a hedge-sparrow a cuckoo. B. p. 475

But where the greater malady is fix'd,
The lesser is scarce felt. Thou'dst shun a bear;
But if thy flight lay toward the roaring sea,
Thou'dst meet the bear i' th' mouth. When the mind's free
The body's delicate; this tempest in my mind
Doth from my senses take all feeling else,
Save what beats there. Filial ingratitude! III, 4, 8

When grief appears, all other passions vanish. B. p. 170

"By some greater sorrow to drive out the less." B. p. 591

As those old Britons, oppressed by the Picts, *mare ad barbaros, barbari ad mare*, the barbarians drove them to the sea, the sea drove them back to the barbarians. B. p. 398

The other parts cannot perform their functions, having the spirits drawn from them by vehement passion, but fail in sense and motion; so we look upon a thing, and see it not; hear, and observe not; which otherwise would much affect us, had we been free.
B. p. 165

Poor naked wretches, wheresoe'er you are,
That bide the pelting of this pitiless storm,
How shall your houseless heads and unfed sides,
Your loop'd and window'd raggedness, defend you
From seasons such as these? O, I have ta'en
Too little care of this! Take physic, pomp;
Expose thyself to feel what wretches feel,
That thou mayst shake the superflux to them,
And show the heavens more just. III, 4, 28

He feasts, revels, and profusely spends, hath variety of robes, sweet music, ease, and all the pleasures the world can afford, whilst many an hunger-starved poor creature pines in the street, wants clothes to cover him, labours hard all day long, runs, rides for a trifle, fights peradventure from sun to sun, sick and ill, weary, full of pain and grief, is in great distress and sorrow of heart. B. p. 183

> Away! the foul fiend follows me. III, 4, 45

This foul fiend of fear was worshipped heretofore as a god by the Lacedæmonians. B. pp. 171–172

> Is it the fashion that discarded fathers
> Should have thus little mercy on their flesh?
> Judicious punishment! 'twas this flesh begot
> Those pelican daughters. III, 4, 71

"Vengeance is mine and I will repay, saith the Lord." B. p. 418
Erit, erit, it shall be so. *Nemesis* comes after, *serò sed seriò*, stay but a little and thou shalt see God's just judgment overtake him.
B. p. 419

> Take heed o' th' foul fiend; obey thy parents. III, 4, 78

Have peace with all men, war with vice. . . . Honour thy parents.
B. p. 424

> Wine lov'd I deeply, dice dearly; and in woman out-paramour'd the Turk. False of heart, light of ear, bloody of hand; hog in sloth, fox in stealth, wolf in greediness, dog in madness, lion in prey. III, 4, 89

"For how (saith he) shall I know thee to be a man, when thou kickest like an ass, neighest like a horse after women, ravest in lust like a bull, ravenest like a bear, stingest like a scorpion, rakest like a wolf, as subtle as a fox, as impudent as a dog? Shall I say thou art a man, that hast all the symptoms of a beast? . . ." B. p. 40

> Let not the creaking of shoes nor the rustling of silks betray thy poor heart to woman. III, 4, 93

"She walks along, and with the ruffling of her clothes, makes men look at her, her shoes creak . . ." B. p. 533

"O Venus, thou knowest my poor heart." B. p. 557

> Thou art the thing itself. III, 4, 104

I hasten to the thing itself. B. p. 141

To speak *ad rem.* B. p. 40

Unaccommodated man is no more but such a poor, bare, forked animal as thou art. Off, off, you lendings!

III, 4, 106

"We are by nature all as one, all alike, if you see us naked; let us wear theirs and they our clothes, and what is the difference?"

B. p. 384

This is the foul fiend Flibbertigibbet; he begins at curfew, and walks till the first cock; he gives the web and the pin, squenes the eye, and makes the hare-lip. III, 4, 113

(See, above, *A Midsummer Night's Dream*, V, 1, 400.)

*No; he's a yeoman that has a gentleman to his son; for he's a mad yeoman that sees his son a gentleman before him.

III, 6, 12

*All which Livy exemplifies, *dec.* 1. *lib.* 4. a gentleman and a yeoman wooed a wench in Rome (contrary to that statute that the gentry and commonalty must not match together); . . .

B. p. 613

If a yeoman have one sole daughter, he must overmatch her above her birth and calling, to a gentleman forsooth, because of her great portion, too good for one of her own rank, as he supposeth: a gentleman's daughter and heir must be married to a knight baronet's eldest son at least; and a knight's only daughter to a baron himself, or an earl, and so upwards, her great dower deserves it. B. p. 616

**Edg.* Come o'er the bourn, Bessy, to me.
Fool. Her boat hath a leak,
And she must not speak,
Why she dares not come over to thee. III, 6, 25

*And 'tis a general fault amongst most parents in bestowing of their children, the father wholly respects wealth, when through his folly, riot, indiscretion, he hath embezzled his estate, to recover himself, he confines and prostitutes his eldest son's love and affection to some fool, or ancient, or deformed piece for money. . . . His daughter is in the same predicament forsooth, as an empty boat she must carry what, where, when, and whom her father will.

B. p. 613

---

* It is noteworthy that these two passages appear together both in *King Lear* and in *The Anatomy* respectively.

How do you sir? Stand you not so amazed. III, 6, 33
Tear his hair in commiseration, stand amazed. B. p. 29

O pity! Sir, where is the patience now
That you so oft have boasted to retain? III, 6, 57
"Where is all your boasted virtue now, my friend?" B. p. 239

Only I do not like the fashion of your garments.
You will say they are Persian, but let them be chang'd.
III, 6, 78
'Tis very good to wash his hands and face often, to shift his clothes, to have fair linen about him, to be decently and comely attired, for *sordes vitiant*, nastiness defiles and dejects any man that is so voluntarily, or compelled by want, it dulleth the spirits. B. p. 310

Yet better thus and known to be contemn'd,
Than still contemn'd and flatter'd. To be worst,
The lowest and most dejected thing of fortune,
Stands still in esperance, lives not in fear.
The lamentable change is from the best;
The worst returns to laughter. Welcome, then,
Thou unsubstantial air that I embrace!
The wretch that thou hast blown unto the worst
Owes nothing to thy blasts. IV, 1, 1
I am in the extremity of human adversity; and as a shadow leaves the body when the sun is gone, I am now left and lost, and quite forsaken of the world. *Qui jacet in terra, non habet unde cadat;* comfort thyself with this yet, thou art at the worst, and before it be long it will either overcome thee or thou it. B. p. 399
Poverty and want are generally corrosives to all kind of men, especially to such as have been in good and flourishing estate, are suddenly distressed, nobly born, liberally brought up, and by some disaster and casualty miserably dejected. B. p. 231
I confess it is a great misery to have been happy, the quintessence of infelicity, to have been honourable and rich, but yet easily to be endured. B. p. 401

I have no way, and therefore want no eyes;
I stumbled when I saw: full oft 'tis seen
Our means secure us, and our mere defects
Prove our commodities. IV, 1, 19
'Tis for thy good, *Periisses nisi periisses:* hadst thou not been so visited, thou hadst been utterly undone. B. p. 378

Deformities and imperfections of our bodies, as lameness, crookedness, deafness, blindness, be they innate or accidental, torture many men; yet this may comfort them, that those imperfections of the body do not a whit blemish the soul, or hinder the operations of it, but rather help and much increase it. B. p. 379

When our bodily eyes are at worst, generally the eyes of our soul see best. Some philosophers and divines have evirated themselves, and put out their eyes voluntarily, the better to contemplate. B. p. 379

"Before I was afflicted I went astray." B. p. 734

> As flies to wanton boys are we to th' gods—
> They kill us for their sport. IV, 1, 37

(See, above, *Coriolanus*, I, 3, 60.)

> Let the superfluous and lust-dieted man
> That slaves your ordinance, that will not see
> Because he does not feel, feel your power quickly;
> So distribution should undo excess,
> And each man have enough. IV, 1, 68

Men in prosperity forget God and themselves, they are besotted with their wealth, as birds with henbane; miserable if fortune forsake them, but more miserable if she tarry and overwhelm them: for when they come to be in great place, rich, they that were most temperate, sober, and discreet in their private fortunes, as Nero, Otho, Vitellius, Heliogabalus (*optimi imperatores nisi imperâssent*) degenerate on a sudden into brute beasts, so prodigious in lust, such tyrannical oppressors. B. pp. 403–404

They have cauterized consciences, and are indeed in a reprobate sense, "past all feeling, have given themselves over to wantonness. . . ." B. p. 711

I was much moved to see that abuse which I could not mend. B. p. 4

> There is a cliff whose high and bending head
> Looks fearfully in the confined deep:
> Bring me but to the very brim of it
> And I'll repair the misery thou dost bear
> With something rich about me. From that place
> I shall no leading need. IV, 1, 74

Dost thou see that steep place, that river, that pit, that tree, there's liberty at hand. B. p. 285

I must change arms at home, and give the distaff
Into my husband's hands. IV, 2, 17

Sophia the empress, Justinian's wife, broke a bitter jest upon Narsetes the eunuch, a famous captain then disquieted for an overthrow which he lately had: that he was fitter for a distaff and to keep women company, than to wield a sword, or to be a general of an army. B. p. 224

As some birds hatch eggs by turns, they do all women's offices. B. p. 633

It is the stars,
The stars above us, govern our conditions,
Else one self mate and make could not beget
Such different issues. IV, 3, 32

The physicians refer this to their temperament, astrologers to trine and sextile aspects, or opposite of their several ascendants, lords of their genitures, love and hatred of planets. B. pp. 478–479

There be those that think they are necessitated by fate, their stars have so decreed. B. p. 617

Alas poor soul, I pity thee,
What stars incline thee so to be?

The Argument of the Frontispiece, Verse VI

Doctor. There is means, madam.
Our foster-nurse of nature is repose,
The which he lacks; that to provoke in him
Are many simples positive, whose power
Will close the eye of anguish. IV, 4, 11

The means to procure it [sleep] are inward or outward. Inwardly taken, are simples, or compounds; simples, as poppy, nymphea, violets, roses, lettuce, mandrake, henbane, nightshade or solanum, saffron, hemp-seed, nutmegs, willows, with their seeds, juice, decoctions, distilled waters, &c. Compounds are syrups, or opiates, syrup of poppy, violets, verbasco, which are commonly taken with distilled waters. B. pp. 456–457

O you mighty gods!
This world I do renounce, and in your sights
Shake patiently my great affliction off.
If I could bear it longer, and not fall

To quarrel with your great opposeless wills,
My snuff and loathed part of nature should
Burn itself out. IV, 6, 34

It is controverted by some, whether a man so offering violence to himself, dying desperate, may be saved, ay or no? If they die so obstinately and suddenly, that they cannot so much as wish for mercy, the worst is to be suspected, because they die impenitent. If their death had been a little more lingering, wherein they might have some leisure in their hearts to cry for mercy, charity may judge the best; divers have been recovered out of the very act of hanging and drowning themselves, and so brought *ad sanam mentem*, they have been very penitent, much abhorred their former act, confessed that they have repented in an instant, and cried for mercy in their hearts. B. p. 723

Yet after their death their memory stinks as a snuff of a candle put out. B. p. 484

And yet I know not how conceit may rob
The treasury of life, when life itself
Yields to the theft. IV, 6, 42

Some die suddenly, as she that saw her son come from the battle at Cannæ. B. p. 167

Sometimes death itself is caused by force of fantasy. I have heard of one that coming by chance in company of him that was thought to be sick of the plague (which was not so) fell down suddenly dead. Another was sick of the plague with conceit. One seeing his fellow let blood falls down in a swoon. Another (saith Cardan out of Aristotle) fell down dead (which is familiar to women at any ghastly sight), seeing but a man hanged. B. p. 168

Edg. It was some fiend; therefore, thou happy father,
Think that the clearest gods, who make them honours
Of men's impossibilities, have preserved thee.
Glo. I do remember now. Henceforth I'll bear
Affliction till it do cry out itself
'Enough, enough' and die. That thing you speak of
I took it for a man; often 'twould say,
'The fiend, the fiend'. He led me to that place.
Edg. Bear free and patient thoughts. IV, 6, 72

"When I speak of despair," saith Zanchie, "I speak not of every kind, but of that alone which concerns God. It is opposite to hope, and a most pernicious sin, wherewith the devil seeks to entrap men." . . . This pernicious kind of desperation is the subject of our discourse, *homicida animæ*, the murderer of the soul, as Austin terms it, a fearful passion, wherein the party oppressed thinks he can get no ease but by death, and is fully resolved to offer violence unto himself; so sensible of his burden, and impatient of his cross, that he hopes by death alone to be freed of his calamity (though it prove otherwise), and chooseth with *Job* vi. 8. 9. vii. 15. "Rather to be strangled and die, than to be in his bonds." The part affected is the whole soul, and all the faculties of it; there is a privation of joy, hope, trust, confidence, of present and future good, and in their place succeed fear, sorrow, &c., as in the symptoms shall be shown. The heart is grieved, the conscience wounded, the mind eclipsed with black fumes arising from those perpetual terrors.

B. p. 714

Lazarus was poor and full of boils, and yet still he relied upon God, Abraham did hope beyond hope. B. p. 736

Let him not be obstinate, headstrong, peevish, wilful, self-conceited (as in this malady they are), but give ear to good advice, be ruled and persuaded; and no doubt but such good counsel may prove as prosperous to his soul, as the angel was to Peter, that opened the iron gates, loosed his bands, brought him out of prison, and delivered him from bodily thraldom; they may ease his afflicted mind, relieve his wounded soul, and take him out of the jaws of hell itself.

B. p. 737

> When the rain came to wet me once, and the wind to make me chatter; when the thunder would not peace at my bidding; there I found 'em, there I smelt 'em out. Go to, they are not men o' their words. They told me I was everything; 'tis a lie—I am not ague-proof. IV, 6, 99

"What more ridiculous," as Lactantius urges, "than to hear how Xerxes whipped the Hellespont," threatened the Mountain Athos, and the like? To speak *ad rem*, who is free from passion? *Mortalis nemo est quem non attingat dolor, morbusve*, as Tully determines out of an old poem, no mortal men can avoid sorrow and sickness, and sorrow is an inseparable companion from melancholy.

B. p. 40

Great Alexander in the midst of all his prosperity, by a company of parasites deified, and now made a god, when he saw one of his wounds bleed, remembered that he was but a man, and remitted of his pride. B. p. 83

Such a one was Xerxes, that would whip the sea, fetter Neptune *stultâ jactantiâ*, and send a challenge to Mount Athos; and such are many sottish princes, brought into a fool's paradise by their parasites, 'tis a common humour, incident to all men, when they are in great places, or come to the solstice of honour, have done, or deserved well, to applaud and flatter themselves. B. p. 197

"Claudius the emperor was angry with Heaven, because it thundered, and challenged Jupiter into the field; with what madness! saith Seneca; he thought Jupiter could not hurt him, but he could hurt Jupiter." B. p. 710

> Thou shalt not die. Die for adultery? No.
> The wren goes to't, and the small gilded fly
> Does lecher in my sight. IV, 6, 111

The silly wren, the titmouse also,
The little redbreast have their election,
They fly I saw and together gone,
Whereas hem list, about environ
As they of kinde have inclination,
And as nature impress and guide,
Of everything list to provide.

But man alone, alas the hard stond,
Full cruelly by kinds ordinance
Constrained is, and by statutes bound,
And debarred from all such pleasance;
What meaneth this, what is this pretence
Of laws, I wis, against all right of kinde,
Without a cause, so narrow men to binde? B. p. 619

> O ruin'd piece of nature! This great world
> Shall so wear out to nought. IV, 6, 134

The world itself must have an end; and every part of it. B. p. 410

> I see it feelingly. IV, 6, 149

We see with the eyes of our understanding. B. p. 507
It is the eye of contemplation by which we must behold it. B. p. 664

> See how yond justice rails upon yond simple thief. Hark, in thine ear: change places and, handy-dandy, which is the justice, which is the thief? IV, 6, 151

Magistrates make laws against thieves, and are the veriest thieves themselves. B. p. 24

There thou mightst behold the great image of authority: a dog's obey'd in office. IV, 6, 158

A magistrate commends a quiet life; a quiet man would be in his office, and obeyed as he is. B. p. 24

Thou rascal beadle, hold thy bloody hand. IV, 6, 160

It [true religion] adds courage, boldness, and begets generous spirits: although tyrants rage, persecute, and that bloody Lictor, or sergeant be ready to martyr them. B. p. 666

we came crying hither.
Thou know'st the first time that we smell the air
We wawl and cry. IV, 6, 179

For to begin at the hour of his birth, as Pliny doth elegantly describe it, "he is born naked, and falls a whining at the very first. . . ." B. p. 179

A most poor man, made tame to fortune's blows,
Who, by the art of known and feeling sorrows,
Am pregnant to good pity. Give me your hand;
I'll lead you to some biding. IV, 6, 223

Something I can speak out of experience, *ærumnabilis experientia me docuit;* and with her in the poet, *Haud ignara mali miseris succurrere disco;* I would help others out of a fellow feeling. B. p. 5

The King is mad; how stiff is my vile sense,
That I stand up, and have ingenious feeling
Of my huge sorrows! Better I were distract;
So should my thoughts be severed from my griefs,
And woes by wrong imagination lose
The knowledge of themselves. IV, 6, 279

Madness is therefore defined to be a vehement dotage; or raving without a fever, far more violent than melancholy, full of anger and clamour, horrible looks, actions, gestures, troubling the patients with far greater vehemency both of body and mind, without all fear and sorrow, with such impetuous force and boldness, that sometimes three or four men cannot hold them. B. p. 88

But see the madman rage downright
With furious looks, a ghastly sight.
Naked in chains bound doth he lie,
And roars amain he knows not why!

The Argument of the Frontispiece, Verse VII

I had rather lose the battle than that sister
Should loosen him and me. V, 1, 18

"For I cannot be without thy company," mournful Amyntas, painful Amyntas, careful Amyntas; better a metropolitan city were sacked, a royal army overcome, an invincible armada sunk, and twenty thousand kings should perish, than her little finger ache, so zealous are they, and so tender of her good. B. p. 558

Nereus' wife, a widow, and lady of Athens, for the love of a Venetian gentleman, betrayed the city. . . . Leucophria betrayed the city where she dwelt, for her sweetheart's sake, that was in the enemies' camp. B. p. 584

Men must endure
Their going hence, even as their coming hither;
Ripeness is all. V, 2, 9

The term of life is set to every man,
Which is but short, and pass it no one can. B. p. 99

Come what can come, I am prepared. B. p. 414

The mind is all. B. p. 397

"'Tis a misery to be born, a pain to live, a trouble to die."
B. p. 407

The gods are just, and of our pleasant vices
Make instruments to plague us:
The dark and vicious place where thee he got
Cost him his eyes. V, 3, 170

(See this play, III, 4, 71 and IV, 1, 19.)

Vex not his ghost. O, let him pass!
He hates him
That would upon the rack of this tough world
Stretch him out longer. V, 3, 313

"Wilt thou have him crazed and sickly still," like a tired traveller that comes weary to his inn, begin his journey afresh, "or to be freed from his miseries: thou hast more need rejoice that he is gone." B. p. 410

Three great ones of the city,
In personal suit to make me his lieutenant,
Off-capp'd to him. I, 1, 8

Still cogging and collogueing, embracing, capping, cringing, applauding, flattering. B. p. 185

We cannot all be masters. I, 1, 43

They that are scarce auditors, *vix auditores*, must be masters and teachers, before they be capable and fit hearers. B. p. 6

We may not be all gentlemen, all Catos, or Lælii, as Tully telleth us, all honourable, illustrious, and serene, all rich. B. p. 402

You shall mark
Many a duteous and knee-crooking knave
That, doting on his own obsequious bondage,
Wears out his time, much like his master's ass,
For nought but provender; and when he's old, cashier'd.
I, 1, 44

Like an ass, he wears out his time for provender. B. p. 202

So long as they are behoveful, they love, or may bestead each other, but when there is no more good to be expected, as they do by an old dog, hang him up or cashier him. B. p. 33

Others there are
Who, trimm'd in forms and visages of duty,
Keep yet their hearts attending on themselves;
And, throwing but shows of service on their lords,
Do well thrive by 'em and, when they have lin'd their coats,
Do themselves homage. I, 1, 49

Obsequious parasites, says Erasmus, teach, say, write, admire, approve, contrary to their conviction, anything you please, not to benefit the people but to improve their own fortunes. They subscribe to any opinions and decisions contrary to the word of God, that they may not offend their patron but retain the favour of the great, the applause of the multitude, and thereby acquire riches for themselves. B. p. 215

(*Note*—This is a translation of Burton's Latin passage.)

In following him I follow but myself—
Heaven is my judge, not I for love and duty,
But seeming so for my peculiar end. I, 1, 59

In a word every man for his own ends. B. p. 33

Nor sociable as they ought to be, but counterfeit, dissemblers, ambidexters, all for their own ends. B. p. 182

We love the world too much; God too little; our neighbour not at all, or for our own ends. B. p. 665

> To the gross clasps of a lascivious Moor. I, 1, 127

Bodine, *cap*. 5. *meth. hist.*, ascribes a great cause to the country or clime, and discourseth largely there of this subject, saying that southern men are more hot, lascivious, and jealous, than such as live in the north. B. p. 630

> Farewell; for I must leave you.
> It seems not meet nor wholesome to my place
> To be producted—as if I stay I shall—
> Against the Moor. I, 1, 145

(See, below, *Othello*, I, 2, 30.)

> Is there not charms
> By which the property of youth and maidhood
> May be abus'd? I, 1, 172

In the kingdom of Malabar, and about Goa in the East Indies, the women are so subtile that, with a certain drink they give them to drive away cares as they say, "they will make them sleep for twenty-four hours, or so intoxicate them that they can remember nought of that they saw done, or heard, and, by washing of their feet, restore them again, and so make their husbands cuckolds to their faces." B. pp. 638–639

> For know, Iago,
> But that I love the gentle Desdemona,
> I would not my unhoused free condition
> Put into circumscription and confine
> For the seas' worth. I, 2, 24

Like those birds in the Emblem, that fed about a cage, so long as they could fly away at their pleasure liked well of it . . . "So long as we are wooers, may kiss and coll at our pleasure, nothing is so sweet, we are in heaven as we think; but when we are once tied, and have lost our liberty, marriage is an hell," "give me my yellow hose again:" a mouse in a trap lives as merrily. B. p. 602

Not I; I must be found.
My parts, my title, and my perfect soul
Shall manifest me rightly. I, 2, 30

Go as thou wouldest be met, sit as thou wouldest be found.
B. p. 424

for my particular grief
Is of so flood-gate and o'erbearing nature
That it engluts and swallows other sorrows,
And it is still itself. I, 3, 55

His wealth increaseth, and the more he hath, the more he wants: like Pharaoh's lean kine, which devoured the fat, and were not satisfied. B. p. 188

Rude am I in my speech,
And little blest with the soft phrase of peace;
For since these arms of mine had seven years' pith,
Till now some nine moons wasted, they have us'd
Their dearest action in the tented field;
And little of this great world can I speak
More than pertains to feats of broil and battle. I, 3, 81

He holds me well;
The better shall my purpose work on him. I, 3, 384

So some said this, some that, as they conceived themselves, which the devil perceiving, led them further out (as Lemnius observes) and made them worship him as their God with stocks and stones, and torture themselves to their own destruction, as he thought fit himself, inspired his priests and ministers with lies and fictions to prosecute the same, which they for their own ends were as willing to undergo, taking advantage of their simplicity, fear and ignorance.
B. p. 678

And of the Cannibals that each other eat,
The Anthropophagi. I, 3, 143

Or as those anthropophagi, to eat one another. B. p. 35

For thy escape would teach me tyranny,
To hang clogs on them. I, 3, 197

Those Italian and Spanish dames, that are mewed up like hawks, and locked up by their jealous husbands? B. p. 226

"Those jealous Italians do very ill to lock up their wives. . . ."
B. p. 649

When remedies are past, the griefs are ended
By seeing the worst, which late on hopes depended.
To mourn a mischief that is past and gone
Is the next way to draw new mischief on. I, 3, 202

(See, above, *The Winter's Tale*, III, 2, 219.)

"Sorrow on the other side refrigerates the body, and extinguisheth natural heat, overthrows appetite, hinders concoction, dries up the temperature, and perverts the understanding." B. p. 359

So many things are offensive to us, not of themselves, but out of our corrupt judgment, jealousy, suspicion, and the like; we pull these mischiefs upon our own heads. B. p. 361

I never yet did hear
That the bruis'd heart was pierced through the ear.
I, 3, 218

For it [love] wounds and cannot be perceived how, when it came, where it pierced. B. p. 560

Not to be too rash and precipitate in his election, to run upon the first he meets, or dote upon every stout fair piece he sees, but to choose her as much by his ears as eyes, to be well-advised whom he takes, of what age, &c., and cautelous in his proceedings. An old man should not marry a young woman, nor a young woman an old man. B. p. 654

The tyrant custom. I, 3, 229

But custom, that tyrant, so prevails. B. p. 307

A moth of peace. I, 3, 256

"A moth of the soul." B. p. 175

The moth of holiness. B. p. 185

No, when light-wing'd toys
Of feather'd Cupid seel with wanton dullness
My speculative and offic'd instruments. I, 3, 268

Only scholars neglect that instrument, their brain and spirits (I mean) which they daily use. B. p. 199

Now this body of ours is most part distempered by some precedent diseases, which molest his inward organs and instruments. B. p. 245

The body works upon the mind, by obfuscating the spirits and corrupted instruments. B. p. 715

Look to her, Moor, if thou hast eyes to see:
She has deceiv'd her father, and may thee. I, 3, 292

(See, above, *The Tempest*, V, 1, 190.)

*'Tis in ourselves that we are thus or thus. Our bodies are our gardens to which our wills are gardeners. I, 3, 319

(See, above, *Julius Cæsar*, I, 2, 139.)

The actions of the will are *velle* and *nolle*, to will and nill; which two words comprehend all, and they are good or bad, accordingly as they are directed. B. p. 107

As fern grows in untilled grounds and all manner of weeds, so do gross humours in an idle body. B. p. 159

Why, the power and corrigible authority of this lies in our wills. If the balance of our lives had not one scale of reason to poise another of sensuality, the blood and baseness of our natures would conduct us to most preposterous conclusions. I, 3, 326

And the devil is still ready at hand with his evil suggestions, to tempt our depraved will to some ill-disposed action, to precipitate us to destruction, except our will be swayed and counterpoised again with some divine precepts, and good motions of the spirit, which many times restrain, hinder and check us, when we are in the full career of our dissolute courses. B. p. 107

But this appetite is many times rebellious in us, and will not be contained within the lists of sobriety and temperance. It was (as I said) once well agreeing with reason, and there was an excellent consent and harmony between them, but that is now dissolved, they often jar, reason is overborne by passion. B. p. 107

It was a violent commencement in her, and thou shalt see an answerable sequestration. I, 3, 340

Yet what is the event of all such matches, that are so made for money, goods, by deceit, or for burning lust, *quos fœda libido conjunxit*, what follows? they are almost mad at first, but 'tis a mere flash; as chaff and straw soon fired, burn vehemently for a while, yet out in a moment; so are all such matches made by those allurements of burning lust; where there is no respect of honesty, parentage, virtue, religion, education, and the like, they are extinguished in an instant and instead of love comes hate. B. p. 530

---

* See note I at end of this Chapter.

Therefore put money in thy purse. If thou wilt needs damn thyself, do it a more delicate way than drowning. Make all the money thou canst. I, 3, 350

And for a little momentary pelf, damn his own soul! B. p. 188

Some are so busied about merchandise to get money, they lose their own souls, whilst covetously carried, and with an insatiable desire of gain, they forget God. B. p. 664

I have told thee often, and I retell thee again and again I hate the Moor. I, 3, 362

'Tis a patient and quiet mind (I say it again and again), gives true peace and content. B. p. 403

How often shall I say it? thou mayest perform . . . B. p. 736

There are many events in the womb of time which will be delivered. I, 3, 367

Beyond all hope and expectation many things fall out, and who knows what may happen? B. p. 401

The wind-shak'd surge, with high and monstrous mane,
Seems to cast water on the burning bear
And quench the guards of the ever-fixed pole. II, 1, 13

And the pole-star which to our thinking, scarce moveth out of its place. B. p. 325

Tempests themselves . . .
As having sense of beauty, do omit
Their mortal natures, letting go safely by
The divine Desdemona. II, 1, 68

That seas and waters are enamoured with this our beauty is all out as likely as that of the air and winds; for when Leander swam in the Hellespont, Neptune with his trident beat down the waves.
B. p. 511

O most lame and impotent conclusion. II, 1, 160

Those cures must be imperfect, lame and to no purpose, wherein the causes have not first been searched. B. p. 114

By reason of ill tools his work must needs be lame and imperfect.
B. p. 715

> If thou be'st valiant—as they say base men being in love have then a nobility in their natures more than is native to them—list me. II, 1, 212

In brief he [Cymon] became, from an idiot and a clown, to be one of the most complete gentlemen in Cyprus, did many valorous exploits, and all for the love of mistress Iphigenia. B. p. 575

> Mark me with what violence she first lov'd the Moor.

(See this play, I, 3, 340.) II, 1, 218

> Her eye must be fed; and what delight shall she have to look on the devil? When the blood is made dull with the act of sport, there should be—again to inflame it, and to give satiety a fresh appetite—loveliness in favour, sympathy in years, manners, and beauties—all which the Moor is defective in. II, 1, 221

He that marries a wife that is snowy fair alone, let him look, saith Barbarus, for no better success than Vulcan had with Venus, or Claudius with Messalina. And 'tis impossible almost in such cases the wife should contain, or the good man not be jealous; for when he is so defective, weak, ill-proportioned, unpleasing in those parts which women most affect, and she most absolutely fair and able on the other side, if she be not very virtuously given, how can she love him? and although she be not fair, yet if he admire her and think her so, in his conceit she is absolute, he holds it impossible for any man living not to dote as he doth, to look on her and not lust, not to covet, and if he be in company with her, not to lay seige to her honesty: or else out of a deep apprehension of his infirmities, deformities, and other men's good parts, out of his own little worth and desert, he distrusts himself (for what is jealousy but distrust?) he suspects she cannot affect him, or be not so kind and loving as she should, she certainly loves some other man better than himself. B. p. 635

Or if they be not equal in years, the like mischief happens.
B. p. 241

> Or failing so, yet that I put the Moor
> At least into a jealousy so strong
> That judgment cannot cure. II, 1, 294

If then our judgment be so depraved, our reason overruled, will precipitated, that we cannot seek our own good, or moderate ourselves. . . . B. p. 361

I have very poor and unhappy brains for drinking;
I could well wish courtesy would invent some other custom of entertainment. II, 3, 30

It is a frequent solemnity still used with us, when friends meet, to go to the alehouse or tavern, they are not sociable otherwise: and if they visit one another's houses, they must both eat and drink. I reprehend it not, moderately used; but to some men nothing can be more offensive; they had better, I speak it with Saint Ambrose, pour so much water in their shoes. B. p. 309

Cassio. I'll do't; but it dislikes me. II, 3, 43

I am *aquæ potor*, drink no wine at all. B. p. 11

And let me the canakin clink, clink. II, 3, 64

Let drums beat on, trumpets sound taratantarra. B. p. 419

He gives your Hollander a vomit ere the next pottle can be fill'd. II, 3, 77

"And when nought else serves, they will go forth, or be conveyed out, to empty their gorge, that they may return to drink afresh."
B. p. 148

There be souls must be saved, and there be souls must not be saved. II, 3, 95

How many shall be saved, damned? B. p. 239

"Or have they souls to be saved? . . ." B. p. 327

How many shall be saved and who damned in a parish. B. p. 699

He is a soldier fit to stand by Cæsar
And give direction; and do but see his vice;
'Tis to his virtue a just equinox. II, 3, 114

They are the causes of our infirmities, our surfeiting, and drunkenness, . . . All which that prince of poets observed of Agamemnon, that when he was well pleased, and could moderate his passion, he was—*os oculosque Jovi par:* like Jupiter in feature, Mars in valour, Pallas in wisdom, another god; but when he became angry, he was a lion, a tiger, a dog, *etc.*, there appeared no sign or likeness of Jupiter in him . . . a just and deserved punishment of our sins.
B. p. 85

> Reputation, reputation, reputation! O, I have lost my reputation! I have lost the immortal part of myself, and what remains is bestial. My reputation, Iago, my reputation!
> II, 3, 254

Yet a modest man, one that hath grace, a generous spirit, tender of his reputation, will be deeply wounded, and so grievously affected with it, that he had rather give myriads of crowns, lose his life, than suffer the least defamation of honour, or blot in his good name. B. p. 174

Drink causeth mirth, and drink causeth sorrow, drink causeth "poverty and want," (*Prov.* xxi.) shame and disgrace. B. p. 192
My good name's lost. B. p. 421

> O thou invisible spirit of wine, if thou hast no name to be known by, let us call thee devil! . . . That we should with joy, pleasance, revel and applause, transform ourselves into beasts! II, 3, 272–283

They are the causes of our infirmities, our surfeiting, and drunkenness, our immoderate insatiable lust, and prodigious riot . . . by which means we metamorphose ourselves and degenerate into beasts. B. p. 85

> It hath pleas'd the devil drunkenness to give place to the devil wrath. One unperfectness shows me another.
> II, 3, 286

Those which are jealous, most part, if they be not otherwise relieved, "proceed from suspicion to hatred, from hatred to frenzy, madness, injury, murder and despair." B. p. 644

> Come, you are too severe a moraller. II, 3, 289
>
> Come, come, good wine is a good familiar creature if it be well us'd; exclaim no more against it. II, 3, 298

Let's drive down care with a cup of wine: and so say I too (though I drink none myself), for all this may be done, so that it may be modestly, soberly, opportunely used. B. p. 453

As if they should forbid wine because it makes men drunk; but in my judgment they are too stern. B. p. 346

> This crack of your love. II, 3, 315

Scarce any conveyance so accurately penned by one, which another will not find a crack in. B. p. 48

When devils will their blackest sins put on,
They do suggest at first with heavenly shows. II, 3, 340

The "Devil rangeth abroad like a roaring lion, still seeking whom he may devour:" and as in several shapes, so by several engines and devices he goeth about to seduce us; sometimes he transforms himself into an angel of light. B. p. 669

And when I love thee not
Chaos is come again. III, 3, 92

And therefore this is true love indeed, the cause of all good to mortal men, that reconciles all creatures, and glues them together in perpetual amity and firm league; and can no more abide bitterness, hate, malice, than fair and foul weather, light and darkness, sterility and plenty may be together; as the sun in the firmament (I say), so is love in the world . . . the world itself composed, and all that is in it conjoined in God, and reduced to one. B. p. 485

I prithee speak to me as to thy thinkings,
As thou dost ruminate; and give thy worst of thoughts
The worst of words. III, 3, 135

I had . . . even so to publish it [*The Anatomy*], as it was first written *quicquid in buccam venit*, . . . a loose, plain, rude writer, *ficum voco ficum, et ligonem ligonem*, and as free, as loose, *idem calamo quod in mente*, I call a spade a spade. B. p. 11

O, beware, my lord, of jealousy. III, 3, 169

Jealousy, saith Vives, "begets unquietness in the mind, night and day: he hunts after every word he hears, every whisper, and amplifies it to himself (as all melancholy men do in other matters) with a most unjust calumny of others, he misinterprets everything is said or done, most apt to mistake or misconstrue," he pries into every corner, follows close, observes to a hair. B. p. 640

But riches fineless is as poor as winter
To him that ever fears he shall be poor. III, 3, 177

Apicius the Roman, when he cast up his accounts, and found but 100,000 crowns left, murdered himself for fear he should be famished to death. . . . Another of a merchant, learned, wise otherwise and discreet, but, out of a deep apprehension he had of a loss at seas, would not be persuaded but, as Ventidius in the poet, he should die a beggar. B. p. 233

In Venice they do let God see the pranks
They dare not show their husbands; their best conscience
Is not to leave't undone, but keep't unknown. III, 3, 206

Or had he been present with Icaromenippus in Lucian at Jupiter's whispering place, and heard one pray for rain, another for fair weather; one for his wife's, another for his father's death, &c.; "to ask that at God's hand which they are abashed any man should hear." B. p. 36

Thus can they cunningly counterfeit, as Platina describes their customs, "kiss their husbands, whom they had rather see hanging on a gallows, and swear they love him dearer than their own lives, whose soul they would not ransom for their little dog's." B. p. 638
Like Alexander VI, so cunning dissemblers, that what they think, they never speak. B. p. 711

She did deceive her father, marrying you. III, 3, 210

(See, above, *The Tempest*, V, 1, 190.)

But I am much to blame. III, 3, 215

But they are much to blame in it. B. p. 218

These men are too distrustful and much to blame, to use such speeches. B. p. 621

If I do prove her haggard,
Though that her jesses were my dear heartstrings,
I'd whistle her off and let her down the wind
To prey at fortune. III, 3, 264

As a long-winged hawk, when he is first whistled off the fist, mounts aloft . . . B. p. 313

Haply, for I am black
And have not those soft parts of conversation
That chamberers have, or for I am declin'd
Into the vale of years. III, 3, 267

The devil is still ready at hand with his evil suggestions to tempt our depraved will to some ill-disposed action. B. p. 107

To these advantages of hope and fear, ignorance and simplicity, he hath several engines, traps, devices, to batter and enthral, omitting no opportunities, according to men's several inclinations, abilities, to circumvent and humour them, to maintain his superstitions, sometimes to stupify, besot them. B. p. 679

O, now for ever
Farewell the tranquil mind! farewell content! III, 3, 351

This jealousy, which I am to treat of, is that which belongs to married men, in respect of their own wives; to whose estate, as no sweetness, pleasure, happiness can be compared in the world, if they live quietly and lovingly together; so if they disagree or be jealous those bitter pills of sorrow and grief, disastrous mischiefs, mischances, tortures, gripings, discontents, are not to be separated from them. A most violent passion it is where it taketh place, an unspeakable torment, a hellish torture, an infernal plague, as Ariosto calls it, "a fury, a continual fever, full of suspicion, fear, and sorrow, a martyrdom, a mirth-marring monster. . . ."

B. p. 630

And O ye mortal engines whose rude throats
Th' immortal Jove's dread clamours counterfeit.

III, 3, 359

Hope and fear, those two battering cannons and principal engines.

B. p. 677

It were a tedious difficulty, I think,
To bring them to that prospect. Damn them, then,
If ever mortal eyes do see them bolster
More than their own! What then? How then?

III, 3, 401

What shall a man do now in such a case? What remedy is to be had? how shall he be eased? By suing a divorce? this is hard to be effected: *si non castè, tamen cautè*, they carry the matter so cunningly, that though it be as common as simony, as clear and as manifest as the nose in a man's face, yet it cannot be evidently proved, or they likely taken in the fact: they will have a knave Gallus to watch, or with that Roman Sulpitia, all made fast and sure,

"Ne se Cadurcis destitutam fasciis,
Nudam Caleno concumbentem videat."

"she will hardly be surprised by her husband, be he never so wary." B. p. 648

Let us be wary, let us hide our loves. III, 3, 424

(See this play, III, 3, 401.)

Antony and Cleopatra

> I am fire and air; my other elements
> I give to baser life. V, 2, 287

The four elements. B. pp. 83, 120 & 122

And as Peter Nonius will have it, the air be so august, what proportion is there betwixt the other three elements and it?
B. p. 323

That element of fire. B. p. 323

Cymbeline

> *Cym.* Thou took'st a beggar, wouldst have made my throne
> A seat for baseness.
> *Imo.* No; I rather added
> A lustre to it.
> *Cym.* O thou vile one!
> *Imo.* Sir,
> It is your fault that I have lov'd Posthumus.
> You bred him as my playfellow, and he is
> A man worth any woman; overbuys me
> Almost the sum he pays.
> *Cym.* What, art thou mad?
> *Imo.* Almost, sir. Heaven restore me! Would I were
> A neat-herd's daughter, and my Leonatus
> Our neighbour shepherd's son! I, 1, 141

Some are so curious in this behalf, as those old Romans, our modern Venetians, Dutch and French, that if two parties dearly love, the one noble, the other ignoble, they may not by their laws match, though equal otherwise in years, fortunes, education, and all good affection. In Germany, except they can prove their gentility by three descents, they scorn to match with them. A nobleman must marry a noblewoman; a baron, a baron's daughter; a knight a knight's; a gentleman a gentleman's; as slaters sort their slates, do they degrees and families. If she be never so rich, fair, well qualified otherwise, they will make him forsake her. The Spaniards abhor all widows; the Turks repute them old women, if past five-and-twenty. But these are too severe laws, and strict customs, *dandum aliquid amori*, we are all the sons of Adam, 'tis opposite to nature, it ought not to be so. B. p. 610

> Senseless linen, happier therein than I! I, 3, 7

O happy ground on which she treads. B. p. 571

Hast thou not learn'd me how
To make perfumes? distil? preserve? yea, so
That our great king himself doth woo me oft
For my confections? I, 5, 12

Confections, conserves, distillations. B. p. 355

I will try the forces
Of these thy compounds on such creatures as
We count not worth the hanging—but none human—
To try the vigour of them, and apply
Allayments to their act, and by them gather
Their several virtues and effects. I, 5, 18

The same author hath another tract of Mumia (all out as vain and prodigious as the first) by which he will cure most diseases, and transfer them from a man to a beast, by drawing blood from one, and applying it to the other, *vel in plantam derivare*, and an *Alexipharmacum*, of which Roger Bacon of old in his *Tract. de retardanda senectute*, to make a man young again, live three or four hundred years. B. p. 354

Your Highness
Shall from this practice but make hard your heart;
Besides, the seeing of these effects will be
Both noisome and infectious. I, 5, 23

(See, above, *As You Like It*, III, 5, 3.)

Some men are much to blame. I, 6, 76

(See, above, *Othello*, III, 3, 215.)

How far it is
To this same blessed Milford. And by th' way
Tell me how Wales was made so happy as
T' inherit such a haven. III, 2, 57

We have many excellent havens, royal havens, Falmouth, Portsmouth, Milford, &c. B. p. 55

Accessible is none but Milford way. III, 2, 81

Ubi dolor, ibi digitus. One must needs scratch where it itches.
B. p. 5

The gates of monarchs
Are arch'd so high that giants may jet through
And keep their impious turbans on without
Good morrow to the sun. III, 3, 4

A silly fellow to look to, may have more wit, learning, honesty, than he that struts it out *Ampullis jactans*, etc., *grandia gradiens*. B. p. 379

N.B.—Burton is using the word "jet" as being derived from the Latin *jactare*, to boast of.

And often to our comfort shall we find
The sharded beetle in a safer hold
Than is the full-wing'd eagle. III, 3, 19

Deformities and imperfections of our bodies, as lameness, crookedness, deafness, blindness, be they innate or accidental, torment many men: yet this may comfort them, that these imperfections of the body do not a whit blemish the soul, or hinder the operations of it, but rather help and much increase it. B. p. 379

Sickness is the mother of modesty, putteth us in mind of our mortality; and when we are in the full career of worldly pomp and jollity, she pulleth us by the ear, and maketh us know ourselves. (See, also, above, *As You Like It*, II, 1, 12.) B. p. 380

Bel. . . . No life to ours!
Gui. Out of your proof you speak. We, poor unfledg'd,
Have never wing'd from view o' th' nest, nor know not
What air's from home. Haply this life is best,
If quiet life be best; sweeter to you
That have a sharper known. III, 3, 26

And when they are once past, this commodity comes of infelicity, it makes the rest of our life sweeter unto us. B. p. 376

Cato told his soldiers marching in the deserts of Libya, "Thirst, heat, sands, serpents, were pleasant to a valiant man;" honourable enterprises are accompanied with dangers and damages, as experience evinceth; they will make the rest of thy life relish the better. B. p. 399

And though train'd up thus meanly
I' th' cave wherein they bow, their thoughts do hit
The roofs of palaces, and nature prompts them
In simple and low things to prince it much
Beyond the trick of others. III, 3, 82

If he retain those ancient characters of true gentry, he will be more affable, courteous, gently disposed, of fairer carriage, better temper, or a more magnanimous, heroical, and generous spirit, than that *vulgus hominum*, those ordinary boors and peasants. B. p. 386

Stomacher. III, 4, 82

Stomacher B. p. 522

Why, good fellow,
What shall I do the while? where bide? how live?
Or in my life what comfort, when I am
Dead to my husband? III, 4, 126

And inquire with Epicurus, what God did before the world was made? was he idle? Where did he bide? What did he make the world of? Why did he then make it and not before? B. p. 330

I see a man's life is a tedious one. III, 6, 1

(See, above, *As You Like It*, III, 2, 17.)

To lapse in fulness
Is sorer than to lie for need; and falsehood
Is worse in kings than beggars. III, 6, 12

A poor sheep-stealer is hanged for stealing of victuals, compelled peradventure by necessity of that intolerable cold, hunger, and thirst, to save himself from starving; but a great man in office may securely rob whole provinces. B. p. 31

Weariness
Can snore upon the flint, when resty sloth
Finds the down pillow hard. III, 6, 33

(See, above, *King Henry V*, IV, 1, 262.)

Gui. I do note
That grief and patience, rooted in him both,
Mingle their spurs together.
Ary. Grow patience!
And let the stinking elder, grief, untwine
His perishing root with the increasing vine! IV, 2, 58

As you may read at large in Constantine's husbandry, that antipathy betwixt the vine and the cabbage, vine and oil. B. p. 43

As between the vine and the elm a great sympathy, between the vine and the cabbage, between the vine and the olive, *Virgo fugit Bromium*, between the vine and bays a great antipathy, the vine loves not the bay, "nor his smell, and will kill him, if he grow near him."
B. p. 474

Clo. Thou villain base,
Know'st me not by my clothes?
Gui. No, nor thy tailor, rascal,
Who is thy grandfather; he made those clothes,
Which, as it seems, make thee. IV, 2, 81

You shall likely know them by their clothes. B. p. 204

A tailor-like spruceness, a peculiar garb in all their proceedings.
B. p. 386

Being scarce made up,
I mean to man, he had not apprehension
Of roaring terrors; for defect of judgment
Is oft the cease of fear. IV, 2, 110

Erasmus vindicates fools from this melancholy catalogue, because they have most part moist brains and light hearts; they are free from ambition, envy, shame and fear; they are neither troubled in conscience, nor macerated with cares, to which our whole life is most subject.
B. p. 110

Triumphs for nothing and lamenting toys
Is jollity for apes and grief for boys. IV, 2, 194

Then of sweet sports let no occasion 'scape,
But be as wanton, toying as an ape. B. p. 371

O melancholy!
Who ever yet could sound thy bottom? find
The ooze to show what coast thy sluggish crare
Might'st easiliest harbour in? IV, 2, 204

To anatomize this humour [melancholy] aright, through all the members of this our Microcosmus, is as great a task, as to reconcile those chronological errors of the Assyrian monarchy, find out the quadrature of a circle, the creeks and sounds of the north-east, or north-west passages.
B. p. 15

Of the matter of melancholy there is much question betwixt Avicen and Galen, as you may read in Cardan's Contradictions,

Valesius' Controversies, Montanus, Prosper Calenus, Cappivaccius, Bright, Ficinus, that have written either whole tracts, or copiously of it, in their several treatises of this subject. "What this humour is, or whence it proceeds, how it is engendered in the body, neither Galen, nor any old writer, hath sufficiently discussed," as Jacchinus thinks: the Neoterics cannot agree. B. p. 110

Thou diedst, a most rare boy, of melancholy. IV, 2, 209

"Generally," saith Rhasis, "the finest wits and most generous spirits, are before other obnoxious to it [melancholy]." B. p. 110

Pray you fetch him hither.
Thersites' body is as good as Ajax',
When neither are alive. IV, 2, 252

Be justly offended with him as he was a murderer, but pity him now as a dead man. B. p. 288

Golden lads and girls all must,
As chimney-sweepers, come to dust. IV, 2, 263

Ladislaus, king of Bohemia, eighteen years of age, in the flower of his youth, so potent, rich, fortunate and happy, in the midst of all his friends, amongst so many physicians, now ready to be married, in thirty-six hours sickened and died. We must so be gone sooner or later all, and as Calliopeius in the comedy took leave of his spectators and auditors, *Vos valete et plaudite, Calliopeius recensui*, must we bid the world farewell (*Exit* Calliopeius), and having now played our parts, for ever be gone. B. p. 409

Thou art past the tyrant's stroke. IV, 2, 266

"You had more need rejoice that I am freed from diseases, agues, cares, anxieties, livor, love, covetousness, hatred, envy, malice, that I fear no more thieves, tyrants, enemies, as you do." B. p. 411

Care no more to clothe and eat. IV, 2, 267

Is it not much better not to hunger at all than to eat: not to thirst than to drink to satisfy thirst: not to be cold than to put on clothes to drive away cold? B. p. 411

To thee the reed is as the oak. IV, 2, 268

And when as the lofty oak is blown down, the silly reed may stand. B. p. 395

The sceptre, learning, physic, must
All follow this and come to dust. IV, 2, 269

(See, above, *The Tempest*, IV, 1, 152.)

The ground that gave them first has them again.
IV, 2, 290

(See, above, *As You Like It*, I, 2, 179.)

Our very eyes
Are sometimes like our judgments, blind. IV, 2, 302

The other parts cannot perform their functions, having the spirits drawn from them by vehement passion, but fail in sense and motion; so we look upon a thing, and see it not; hear, and observe not; which otherwise would much affect us, had we been free.
B. p. 165

Some falls are means the happier to arise. IV, 2, 406

If he be in sorrow, need, sickness, or any other adversity, seriously to recount with himself, why this or that malady, misery, this or that incurable disease is inflicted upon him; it may be for his good, *sic expedit*, as Peter said of his daughter's ague. Bodily sickness is for his soul's health, *periisset nisi periisset*, had he not been visited, he had utterly perished; for "the Lord correcteth him whom he loveth, even as a father doth his child in whom he delighteth." B. p. 83

Than be so,
Better to cease to be. IV, 4, 30

. . .: than which, as Clavius holds, "in all human disciplines nothing can be more excellent . . ." B. p. 353

. . .; than which what can be more ridiculous? B. p. 690

To shame the guise o' the world, I will begin
The fashion—less without and more within. V, 1, 32

Fair without, foul within. B. p. 383

Admire him for his brave apparel, horses, dogs, fine houses, manors, orchards, gardens, walks? Why? a fool may be the possessor of this as well as he. B. p. 383

To darkness fleet souls that fly backwards! V, 3, 25

(See, above, *Macbeth*, V, 8, 46.)

Yet am I better
Than one that's sick o' th' gout, since he had rather
Groan so in perpetuity than be cur'd
By th' sure physician death, who is the key
T' unbar these locks. V, 4, 4

To wish and hope for immortality, desire to be happy, and yet by all means avoid death, a necessary passage to bring him to it.
B. p. 35

And though we hope for a better life, eternal happiness, after these painful and miserable days, yet we cannot compose ourselves willingly to die. B. p. 406

Must I repent,
I cannot do it better than in gyves,
Desir'd more than constrain'd. V, 4, 13

Condemned to the mines, quarries, to gyves, in dungeons. B. p. 397

Art in prison? Make right use of it and mortify thyself;
"Where may a man contemplate better than in solitariness?"
B. p. 405

No more, you petty spirits of region low. V, 4, 93

Lipsius will have all places full of Angels, Spirits, and Devils, above and beneath the Moon . . . The celestial Devils above, and aerial beneath . . . though Anthony Rusca in his book *de Inferno, lib. V, cap.* 7. would confine them in the middle Region. B. p. 121

Poor shadows of Elysium, hence, and rest
Upon your never-withering banks of flow'rs. V, 4, 97

We must all go, *non à deliciis ad delicias*, but from the cross to the crown. B. p. 735

No care of yours it is; you know 'tis ours. V, 4, 100

Howsoever as Martianus foolishly supposeth, *Ætherii Dæmones non curant res humanas*, they care not for us, do not attend our actions, or look for us, those ætherial spirits have other worlds to reign in belike or business to follow. B. p. 122

Or put case thou art forsaken of the world, dejected, condemned, yet comfort thyself, as it was said to Agar in the wilderness, "God sees thee, he takes notice of thee." B. p. 378

Jup. Whom best I love I cross; to make my gift,
The more delay'd, delighted. V, 4, 101*

(See this play, IV, 2, 406.)

Mount, eagle, to my palace crystalline. V, 4, 113

Besides those other heavens, whether they be crystalline or watery.
B. p. 122

His royal bird,
Prunes the immortal wing, and cloys his beak,
As when his god is pleas'd. V, 4, 117

The gods are well pleased, when they see great men contending with adversity. B. p. 378

Poor wretches, that depend
On greatness' favour, dream as I have done;
Wake and find nothing. V, 4, 127

I was once so mad to bustle abroad, and seek about for preferment, tire myself, and trouble all my friends, *sed nihil labor tantus profecit.*
B. p. 414

'Tis still a dream, or else such stuff as madmen
Tongue, and brain not. V, 4, 144

But see the madman rage downright
. . . .
And roars amain he knows not why.
The Argument of the Frontispiece, Verse VII

O, the charity of a penny cord! V, 4, 166

They gave him a penny to buy a rope. B. p. 477

SONNETS

From fairest creatures we desire increase. I, 1

For to what end is a man born? why lives he, but to increase the world? B. p. 622

* Wilson Knight; *The Crown of Life;* Methuen; prefaces his chapter, *The Vision of Jupiter*, by quoting *Proverbs*, III, 11 and 12.

Thyself thy foe, to thy sweet self too cruel. I, 8

Without a wife, . . . he is false, an enemy to the commonwealth, injurious to himself. B. p. 622

This were to be new made when thou art old. 2, 13

Matrimony makes us immortal. B. p. 622

But flowers distill'd, though they with winter meet,
Leese but their show: their substance still lives sweet. 5, 13

Wither away as a flower ungathered in a garden. B. p. 212

Seeking that beauteous roof to ruinate
Which to repair should be thy chief desire. 10, 7

"A young man is like a fair new house, the carpenter leaves it well built, in good repair, of solid stuff; but a bad tenant lets it rain in, and for want of reparation, fall to decay, etc." B. p. 160

If all were minded so, the times should cease,
And threescore year would make the world away. 11, 7

Procreation of children is as necessary as that finding out of truth. B. p. 473

When in eternal lines to time thou grow'st.
So long as men can breathe or eyes can see,
So long lives this, and this gives life to thee. 18, 12

But these brave monuments are decayed all, and ruined long since, their builders' names alone flourish by meditation of writers. . . . Allon Bachuth, that weeping oak, under which Deborah, Rebecca's nurse died, and was buried, may not survive the memory of such everlasting monuments. B. p. 488

As an unperfect actor on the stage
Who with his fear is put beside his part. 23, 1

(See, above, *Coriolanus*, V, 3, 40.)

They draw but what they see, know not the heart. 24, 14

What, therefore, Timanthes did in his picture of Iphigenia, now ready to be sacrificed, when he had painted Chalcas mourning, Ulysses sad, but most sorrowful Menelaüs; and showed all his art in expressing a variety of affections, he covered the maid's father Agamemnon's head with a veil, and left it to every spectator to conceive what he would himself. B. p. 720

Let those who are in favour with their stars
Of public honour and proud titles boast,
Whilst I, whom fortune of such triumph bars,
Unlook'd for joy in that I honour most. 25, 1

By a brook side or wood so green,
Unheard, unsought for, or unseen.
The Author's Abstract of Melancholy

When in disgrace with Fortune and men's eyes,
I all alone beweep my outcast state . . .
For thy sweet love rememb'red such wealth brings
That then I scorn to change my state with kings. 29, 1–14

N.B.—This alternation of sorrow and joy is paralleled in *The Author's Abstract of Melancholy*, e.g.:—

I'll not change life with any King
I ravisht am. Verse 11

I'll change my state with any wretch,
Thou canst from goal or dunghill fetch. Verse 12

And with old woes new wail my dear time's waste,
Then can I drown an eye unus'd to flow,
For precious friends hid in death's dateless night,
And weep afresh love's long since cancell'd woe,
And moan th' expense of many a vanish'd sight. 30, 5

Loss of time, loss of honour, office, of good name, of labour, frustrate hopes, will much torment. B. p. 236

Lamentable, tragical, and fearful those symptoms are, that they should be so far forth affrighted with their fictitious gods, as to spend the goods, lives, fortunes, precious time, best days in their honour. B. p. 690

Many years after, the remembrance of such friends, of such accidents, is most grievous unto us. B. p. 407

Full many a glorious morning have I seen
. . . .
Anon permit the basest clouds to ride
With ugly rack on his celestial face. 33, 1–6

Or what so secure and pleasing a morning have we seen, that hath not been overcast before the evening? B. p. 179

A fair morning turns to a lowering afternoon. B. p. 182

No more be griev'd at that which thou hast done:
Roses have thorns, and silver fountains mud;
Clouds and eclipses stain both moon and sun,
And loathsome canker lives in sweetest bud.
All men make faults, . . . 35, 1

We must all go, not *à deliciis ad delicias*, but from the cross to the crown, by hell to heaven, as the old Romans put Virtue's temple in the way to that of Honour: we must endure sorrow and misery in this life. 'Tis no new thing this, God's best servants and dearest children have been so visited and tried. B. p. 735

When most I wink, then do mine eyes best see,
For all the day they view things unrespected;
But when I sleep, in dreams they look on thee,
And darkly bright, are bright in dark directed. 43, 1

When our bodily eyes are at worst, generally the eyes of our soul see best. B. p. 379

We see with the eyes of our understanding. B. p. 507

In time of sleep this faculty [the phantasy] is free, and many times conceives strange, stupend, absurd shapes. B. p. 101

But that, so much of earth and water wrought. 44, 11

The other two, slight air and purging fire. 45, 1

(See, above, *Antony and Cleopatra*, V, 2, 287.)

Betwixt mine eye and heart a league is took. 47, 1

Make a league with thine eyes, as Job did. B. p. 589

How heavy do I journey on the way,
When what I seek—my weary travel's end— 50, 1

(See, above, *King Lear*, V, 3, 313.)

The beast that bears me, tired with my woe,
Plods dully on, to bear that weight in me. 50, 5

(See, above, *Hamlet*, V, 1, 56.)

Sweet roses do not so:
Of their sweet deaths are sweetest odours made. 54, 11

(See, above, *Sonnet* 5, lines 13–14.)

Or call it winter, which, being full of care,
Makes summer's welcome thrice more wish'd, more rare.

56, 13

"This commodity comes of infelicity, it makes the rest of our life sweeter unto us." B. p. 376

If there be nothing new, but that which is
Hath been before, how are our brains beguil'd,
Which labouring for invention bear amiss
The second burthen of a former child! 59, 1

Yea, but you will infer that this is *actum agere*, an unnecessary work, *cramben bis coctam apponere*, the same again and again in other words. B. p. 5

Nihil dictum quod non dictum prius. B. p. 8

Sin of self-love possesseth all mine eye. 62, 1

(See, above, *Twelfth Night*, I, 5, 85.)

Robbing no old to dress his beauty new. 68, 12

They pilfer out of old writers to stuff up their new comments.

B. p. 6

So are you to my thoughts as food to life,
Or as sweet-season'd showers are to the ground. 75, 1

This love is manifest, I say, in inanimate creatures. How comes a loadstone to draw iron to it? jet chaff? the ground to covet showers, but for love? B. p. 474

Why write I still all one, ever the same,
And keep invention in a noted weed. 76, 5

But we weave the same web still, twist the same rope again and again; or if it be a new invention, 'tis but some bauble or toy which idle fellows write, for as idle fellows to read, and who so cannot invent? B. p. 7

(See also *Sonnet*, 59, 1.)

Your name from hence immortal life shall have,
Though I, once gone, to all the world must die. 81, 5

Though I be gone. B. p. 16

"My time is now come to be gone. I to my death, you to live on...." B. p. 408

We must so be gone sooner or later all. B. p. 409

I think good thoughts, whilst other write good words.

85, 5

I respect matter not words; remembering that of Cardan, *verba propter res, non res propter verba:* and seeking with Seneca, *quid scribam, non quemadmodum*, rather *what* than *how* to write. B. p. 11

Some glory in their birth, some in their skill,

. . . .

Some in their hawks and hounds, some in their horse.

91, 1–4

(See, above, *The Merchant of Venice*, I, 2, 35.)

And every humour hath his adjunct pleasure. 91, 5

They have most part some gullish humour or other, by which they are led; one is an Epicure, an Atheist, a second a gamester, a third a whoremaster . . . one is mad of hawking, hunting, cocking; another of carousing, horse-riding, spending. B. p. 68

For sweetest things turn sourest by their deeds:
Lilies that fester smell far worse than weeds. 94, 13

"As a posy she smells sweet, is most fresh and fair one day, but dried up, withered, and stinks another." B. p. 596

Aristo, the son of Agasicles, married a Spartan lass, the fairest lady in all Greece next to Helen, but for her conditions the most abominable and beastly creature of the world. B. p. 597

Whilst, like a willing patient, I will drink
Potions of eisel, 'gainst my strong infection. 111, 9

Health indeed is a precious thing, to recover and preserve which we will undergo any misery, drink bitter potions. B. p. 476

Those lines that I before have writ do lie;
Even those that said I could not love you dearer;
Yet then my judgment knew no reason why
My most full flame should afterwards burn clearer. 115, 1

(See, above, *Hamlet*, I, 3, 10.)

Love is not love
Which alters when it alteration finds. 116, 2

(See, above, *A Midsummer Night's Dream*, II, 2, 60.)

Sonnets 118 and 119. See B. pp. 426–445, in which Burton deals with medicinal physic.

O benefit of ill! Now I find true
That better is by evil still made better. 119, 9

(See, above, *As You Like It*, II, 1, 12.)

Two loves I have, of comfort and despair,
Which like two spirits do suggest me still;
The better angel is a man right fair,
The worser spirit a woman colour'd ill. . . .
Till my bad angel fire my good one out. 144, 1–14

"One Venus is ancient without a mother, and descended from heaven, whom we call celestial; the younger, begotten of Jupiter and Dione, whom commonly we call Venus." Ficinus, in his comment upon this place, *cap*. 8, following Plato, calls these two loves, two devils, or good and bad angels according to us, which are still hovering about our souls. B. p. 473

Is this thy body's end?
Then, soul, live thou upon thy servant's loss,
And let that pine to aggravate thy store. 146, 9

The second is contemplation, "which dries the brain and extinguisheth natural heat; for whilst the spirits are intent to meditation above in the head, the stomach and liver are left destitute." B. p. 199

My love is as a fever, longing still
For that which longer nurseth the disease;
Feeding on that which doth preserve the ill,
Th' uncertain sickly appetite to please.
My Reason, the physician to my Love,
Angry that his prescriptions are not kept,
Hath left me, and I desperate now approve
Desire is death, which physic did except. 147, 1

"As in a city (saith Melancthon) they do by stubborn rebellious rogues, that will not submit themselves to political judgment, compel them by force; so must we do by our affections. If the heart will not lay aside those vicious motions, and the fantasy those fond imaginations, we have another form of government to enforce and refrain our outward members, that they be not led by our passions." If appetite will not obey, let the moving faculty overrule her, let her resist and compel her to do otherwise. In an ague the appetite would drink; sore eyes that itch would be rubbed; but reason saith no, and therefore the moving faculty will not do it. Our fantasy would intrude a thousand fears, suspicions, chimeras upon us, but we have reason to resist, yet we let it be overborne by our appetite. B. p. 361

Sonnets 153 and 154

I could tell you such another story of a spindle that was fired by a fair lady's looks, or fingers, some say, I know not well whether, but fired it was by report, and of a cold bath that suddenly smoked, and was very hot when naked Cœlia came into it. B. p. 511

Of as much virtue as that fountain Salmacis in Vitruvius, Ovid, Strabo, that made all such mad for love that drank of it, or that hot bath at Aix in Germany, wherein Cupid once dipt his arrows, which ever since hath a peculiar virtue to make them lovers all that wash in it. B. p. 550

Note 1:—Comment seems desirable on two of the above passages which seem to contradict one another. They are:—

"There's a divinity that shapes our ends,
Rough-hew them how we will." *Hamlet*, V, 2, 10

"Our bodies are our gardens to the which our wills are gardeners." *Othello*, I, 3, 319

This contradiction appears to me to be adequately explained by Burton thus:—

"The actions of the will are *velle* and *nolle*, to will and nill: which two words comprehend all, and they are good or bad, accordingly as they are directed, and some of them freely performed by himself; although the Stoics absolutely deny it, and will have all things inevitably done by destiny, imposing a fatal necessity upon us, which we may not resist; yet we say that our will is free in respect of us, and things contingent, howsoever, in respect of God's determinate counsel, they are inevitable and necessary." B. p. 107

Note 2:—This chapter makes abundantly clear the fact that the mind of the author of "Shakespeare's" Works was learning-sensitized. That "Shakespeare" himself admitted this is shown in the parallel passages at *As You Like It*, V, 1, 35, and at *Sonnet*, 59, 1.

Chapter XII

EPILOGUE

From the foregoing chapters the reader will have gathered that Robert Burton was a poet, a dramatist, a man with a great command of language and one with a knowledge of and interest in the same themes as are dealt with by "Shakespeare" in the great plays. One remaining difficulty, admittedly a major one, is that nowhere in *The Anatomy of Melancholy* does Burton write Shakespearean blank verse. Burton's own reason for this could well have been his enunciation in the words from *The Tempest*, IV, 1, 148, "Our revels now are ended", which could be taken to indicate that their author had done with that random revelling of the spirit suitable for dramatic poetry and wanted a medium of expression more fitted to convey the details of his philosophy; hence the systematic prose work, *The Anatomy of Melancholy*. Moreover, need we doubt Burton's ability to write such verse? Take this passage (B. p. 106): "The conscience is that which approves good or evil, justifying or condemning our actions, and is the conclusion of the syllogism: as in that familiar example of Regulus the Roman, taken prisoner by the Carthaginians, and suffered to go to Rome, on that condition he should return again, or pay so much for his ransom. The synteresis proposeth the question: his word, oath, promise, is to be religiously kept, although to his enemy, and that by the law of nature. 'Do not that to another which thou wouldest not have done to thyself'. Dictamen applies it to him, and dictates this or the like: Regulus, thou wouldst not another man should falsify his oath, or break promise with thee: conscience concludes, therefore, Regulus, thou dost well to perform thy promise, and oughtest to keep thine oath". To this power to write logical and informed prose, add the power to write logical and informed, musical and pleasing verse as shown in the Burton's two poems already given in full in Chapter IX. Then the requisites for the great verse are at hand and the result is a passage like the following one:—

> It must be so; for miracles are ceas'd;
> And therefore we must needs admit the means
> How things are perfected. *King Henry V*, I, 1, 67

These are three wonderful lines showing profound understanding of the mode of operation of the human mind and I am strongly of the opinion that they come from the same hand which wrote the wonderful chapter on the "Anatomy of the Soul" (B. pp. 98–108) which gives their burden *in extenso*. Jonson said Shakespeare was for all time and undoubtedly these lines are as fresh today as when they were first written. I should think that my medically-minded readers will recognize a like freshness in the following words from Burton (B. p. 137): ". . . instance of a young man that was so affected *ex matre melancholica*, had a melancholy mother, *et victu melancholico*, and bad diet together. . . . And that which is more to be wondered at, it skips in some families the father, and goes to the son, 'or takes every other, and sometimes every third in a lineal descent, and doth not always produce the same, but some like, and a symbolizing disease'." Burton does not claim this as original and gives his authorities, but the vital point is that he had the ability to recognize what was important, what was "for all time".

I claim that one person, Robert Burton, wrote that passage from *King Henry V* and many others of a consistently high calibre. Another person, William Shakespeare, wrote on a much lower plane; he was quite content, even late in his career, to cause King Cymbeline and his step-son, Cloten, to converse in the following terms:—

> *Cym.* Attend you here the door of our stern daughter?
> Will she not forth?
> *Clo.* I have assailed her with musics, but she vouchsafes no notice.
> *Cym.* The exile of her minion is too new;
> She hath not yet forgot him; some more time
> Must wear the print of his remembrance out,
> And then she's yours. *Cymbeline*, II, 3, 37

It should be abundantly clear that the characters of these two quotations from Shakespeare are poles apart. In Chapter V I detailed many reasons for believing that at least two authors contributed to the "Shakespeare" canon. Another important, such reason can well be given here:—In *Othello*, III, 3, 281 *et seq.*, Desdemona enters to accompany Othello to a dinner given in his honour. She drops her handkerchief and *exeunt* Othello and Desdemona (line 293). At line 333 Othello returns, having stayed at the dinner, where presumably he was chief guest, for about two minutes, the time estimated for the speaking of the intervening forty lines. Moreover, three of these lines show, perhaps better than any others in the whole of "Shakespeare", how poor an author the inferior contributor was capable of being, even in this late play to boot:—

> *Iago:* Hast stole it from her?
> *Emil.* No, faith; she let it drop by negligence,
> And to the advantage, I, being here, took't up.

Yet in this same *Othello*, we find this most powerful passage:—

He is a soldier fit to stand by Cæsar
And give direction; and do but see his vice;
'Tis to his virtue a just equinox,
The one as long as th'other II, 3, 113

which surely was not written by the same hand, but which could well have been by the hand which penned:—"Hannibal, as he had mighty virtues, so had he many vices; *unam virtutem mille vitia comitantur*, as Machiavel of Cosmo de Medici, he had two distinct persons in him." B. p. 68.

Thus here and elsewhere in this book I have stressed the defects in those writings which I consider to be by the inferior author, Shakespeare. I would, however, weaken my case by not also stressing that this inferior author did have good points and Shakespeare must have had these, else he would not have been able to impress his colleagues and contemporaries, as evidence shows he did do. In Chapter V, I drew attention to some of Shakespeare's merits and, here, I credit him with:—

But look, the morn, in russet mantle clad,
Walks o'er the dew of yon high eastward hill.

Hamlet, I, 1, 166

The barge she sat in, like a burnish'd throne,
Burn'd on the water. The poop was beaten gold;
Purple the sails, and so perfumed that
The winds were love-sick with them; the oars were silver,
Which to the tune of flutes kept stroke, and made
The water which they beat to follow faster,
As amorous of their strokes. *Antony and Cleopatra*, II, 2, 195

These two passages constitute examples of fine descriptive poetry and the person who wrote them must have had a very considerable command of language and a keen appreciation of poetic fancy. The crucial question to be asked, therefore, is whether or not such poetry merges into the undoubtedly great passages without any dividing line and my answer is, that it does not. The quality of the first passage is not sustained but is followed by two examples of poor arrangement of words:—

Break we our watch up; Line 168

and I this morning know
Where we shall find him most convenient. Lines 174–5

Any praise for the second passage must be tempered by the fact that its essence, with many of its actual words, is taken from North's translation of Plutarch, Shakespeare admittedly adding some fanciful touches of his own as "The barge . . . like a burnish'd throne, burn'd on the water"; "The winds were love sick . . .";

"and made the water to follow faster as amorous . . ." As in the first passage so also here the quality is not sustained:—

For her own person,
It beggar'd all description. Lines 201–2

is just padding.

Upon her landing, Antony sent to her,
Invited her to supper. She replied
It should be better he became her guest; Lines 223–5

is not poetry at all but prose (copied practically word for word from Plutarch) in verse form.

Being barber'd ten times o'er, Line 228

is commonplace fancy. It is worth while also to examine the metre of certain of the lines:—

It beggar'd all description. She did lie Line 202

is an irregular line if one give "description" four syllables and then make a pause to accord with the sense, or it is a regular line if one give "description" three syllables and carry the beat over to "She", thereby reading contrary to the sense. I think the latter is what the author intended as not only is it unusual to give "description" four syllables but also there occur, in this same passage, lines in which there is no alternative but to scan them in a manner contrary to the sense, for example:—

And made their bends adornings. At the helm Line 212
That yarely frame the office. From the barge Line 215
Invited her to supper. She replied Line 224

He speaks of the fancy out-working nature (line 205) and, in my discussion, the terms "fanciful touches" and "commonplace fancy" are used; I maintain that much of Shakespeare's work dealt with the fanciful whereas Burton, both in *The Anatomy* and in his parts of the "Shakespeare" canon, strove after reality. The verbose, fanciful descriptions of the horse in *Venus and Adonis* (lines 271–306), of the picture in *The Rape of Lucrece* (lines 1366–1442) and that of Queen Mab's waggon in *Romeo and Juliet*, I, 4, 53–94, all already referred to in Chapter V, might just as well never have been written for all the meaning they convey or for all their value in furthering the action of the poem or play; admittedly they are from early works but how futile also is the fanciful statue scene at the end of the late *The Winter's Tale*!

Shakespeare had an aptitude for making verses and had also great powers of assimilating the work of other authors; he was one content with the physical, the commonplace and the fanciful, and he had no message of his own to deliver. These qualities enabled him as a young man to spin out the old stories of *Venus and Adonis* and *The Rape of Lucrece*, to retell *The Taming of a Shrew* and *The Troublesome Raigne* and to assimilate and then versify *Holinshed.*

Towards the end of his career we find him versifying and padding out Holinshed's account of King Henry VIII, versifying *Plutarch* in *Antony and Cleopatra* and repeating what had already been told in *Cymbeline*. Having no message of his own he would find the fanciful well suited to his purpose as being easier to write but probably this easy path it was that led him to perpetrate discrepancies such as:—

(1) Lucrece, whilst contemplating suicide, is in line 1365:—

Pausing for means to mourn some newer way.

(2) Portia saying in *The Merchant of Venice*, IV, 1, 179,

The quality of mercy is not strain'd

only to demand later (in poorly arranged words be it noted) that old-man Shylock sign a deed willing his money to the nefarious, yet fanciful, Lorenzo and Jessica who had robbed and deserted him:—

Inquire the Jew's house out, give him this deed,
And let him sign it; we'll away tonight,
And be a day before our husbands home.
This deed will be well welcome to Lorenzo. IV, 2, 1

(3) After all of Antonio's vessels had been declared lost (III, 2, 273), three return safely (V, 1, 276).

(4) Failure to depict consistently Margaret, Emilia and Macbeth, etc.

Thus, although the inferior author shows considerable poetic and dramatic skill, the quality is never high enough or consistent enough to merit his being designated a master. Even the two early poems, where the flow of language and of thought is not interrupted by dialogue, show inconsistencies, with good lines and very poor lines appearing on a background of general mediocrity. The author shows great ingenuity in assembling ideas and words to express them but the ideas often appear as if forced into the piece and the words are often inaccurately employed, giving as result an unpleasing and sometimes meaningless verse, as the following illustrates:—

Whereat her tears began to turn their tide,
Being prison'd in her eye like pearls in glass;
Yet sometimes falls an orient drop beside,
Which her cheek melts, as scorning it should pass
To wash the foul face of the sluttish ground,
Who is but drunken when she seemeth drown'd.

Venus and Adonis, 979–984

Other faults in *Venus and Adonis* and *The Rape of Lucrece* and in the plays or parts of plays by the inferior author have been pointed out in Chapter V. Each of the two poems was prefaced with a dedication signed "William Shakespeare" and the whole of *The*

First Folio was attributed to William Shakespeare. However, the inaccurate, unpleasing, repetitious, commonplace character of the former corresponds only with certain parts of the latter, and thus, logically, the authorship of the great parts was not accounted for. Shakespeare never claimed in writing that the plays were his own and it was seven years after his death that Heminge and Condell made their publication. What agreement, if any, was reached between Shakespeare and Burton regarding authorship claims is not known and Shakespeare probably never discussed publication with Heminge and Condell. Thus the latter probably acted in good faith in attributing the whole of the folio to Shakespeare. As to why Burton did not remonstrate I offer two possible reasons: (i) Burton did not want publicity ("I would not willingly be known". B. p. 1), and (ii) the message of the plays is re-incorporated and amplified in *The Anatomy of Melancholy*.

To attempt to summarize Shakespeare's qualities as an author: Shakespeare had strong powers of assimilation of other writers' work and his original material consisted largely of the physical, the commonplace and the fanciful; he had a ready, yet superficial, skill in composing narrative, rhymed or blank verse; he had at his command many words which he did not use always accurately and appropriately; he had no message to convey; he was relatively insensitive and unsympathetic. His having no message corresponds with Hazlitt's remarking that, in the two early poems, Shakespeare thought of his verses and not of his subject; his insensitiveness accounts for his poor ear for rhythm or for rhyme and for his being content with poor wit and with his many repetitions; Hazlitt's finding also, that Shakespeare, in these poems, thought not of what his characters would feel but of what he shall say, is consistent with my finding in him a lack of true sympathy. This feature explains the altogether misplaced word-play exchanges between King Richard and Queen Elizabeth, as it does also the lack of sympathy with nature, both dealt with in Chapter V. What could indicate less sympathy with nature than:—

> These blue-vein'd violets whereon we lean
> Never can blab, nor know not what we mean?

What could indicate more than Burton's:—

> And this our life, exempt from public haunt
> Finds tongues in trees, books in the running brooks?

He assimilated Holinshed, Plutarch and old plays. Another book he made great use of was *Ovid's Metamorphoses*. Knowledge of it enabled him to refer to the story of Venus and Adonis in his poem of that name; to Philemon in *Much Ado About Nothing*, II, 1, 82; to Scylla and Charybdis in *The Merchant of Venice*, III, 5, 14; to Thisbe, to Dido and to Medea and Æson in *The Merchant of Venice*,

V, 1, 6–14; to Orpheus in *The Merchant of Venice*, V, 1, 80; to Althæa and Calydon in *King Henry VI*, pt. 2, I, 1, 229; to Actæon in *The Merry Wives of Windsor*, II, 1, 106 and III, 2, 36 and *Titus Andronicus*, II, 3, 63; to Europa in *The Merry Wives of Windsor*, V, 5, 3 and *Much Ado About Nothing*, V, 4, 45 and 46; to Phaethon and Merops in *The Two Gentlemen of Verona*, III, 1, 153; probably the fate of Itys supplied the ideas for the three lines—*Titus Andronicus*, V, 3, 60–62. He actually names *Ovid's Metamorphoses* in *Titus Andronicus*, IV, 1, 42, and in the same passage refers to Tereus and Philomela as he does again in *Cymbeline*, II, 2, 45. I see no reason why *Venus and Adonis*, *Much Ado About Nothing*, etc., could not well have been written by a person with such limited book learning.

I credit Shakespeare with a very considerable share of the canon; some others give him no share whatever. A Cambridge graduate writes*: "Genius can do much, but it is far from being able to make a man *omnibus numeris absolutus*, or 'complete' in the sense that Shakespeare was. Genius alone can undoubtedly lift a man to a purer and a larger æther than ordinary mortals can breathe in. Instances are numerous enough in the annals of many a cottage home and lowly birthplace, but these self-same favoured mortals, even if, as with Milton, they could hope to soar

'Above the flight of Pegasean wing,'

still would find that their wings of genius are sadly clipped, confined, and weakened unless they are taught to rise and fly by the knowledge that is in books and by the varied wisdom that has descended from the ages of the past. Without these helps they may indeed rise somewhat from the brute earth of ordinary humanity, but they will never be able to make those glorious circling swoops in the lofty 'circumambient air' which are ever the wonder of the earth-bound crowd below, the marvel of an admiring world.

"Such an ever-living *stupor mundi* is Shakespeare—but not Keats, nor yet Burns, nor James Ferguson, as *Notes and Queries* would suggest when their critic remarks, 'It is only in degree that Shakespeare is more of a miracle than Burns or than James Ferguson.' I cannot accept such a statement as this. The miracle of the Shakespeare Works is a different *kind* of miracle from that of Burns, or Ferguson, or Keats. Theirs is really after all no miracle, for *they* only went where their genius led them. But Shakespeare went where no natural genius ever did or ever could lead a man, and that is the miracle we are asked to believe. Put Bacon in Shakespeare's place, the miracle disappears, and a much easier problem awaits us." If 'A Graduate of Cambridge' had replaced the name

* *Is It Shakespeare?* by A Graduate of Cambridge, John Murray, London, 1903, p. 126.

Bacon by that of Burton I would have agreed with what he said, with the proviso that he can be referring only to the great works of the "Shakespeare" canon.

Blanks occur in the life-histories both of Shakespeare and of Burton. Assuming that the hypothesis advanced in this book be a correct one, it is interesting to speculate on where the two authors first met. They were born in neighbouring counties and Burton tells us (B. p. xi, Introductory data, and B. p. 332) he was a grammar scholar at Nuneaton and at Sutton Coldfield (both in Warwickshire), so they posssibly were acquainted quite early in Burton's life. The next operative point of contact would be Oxford, which Shakespeare appears to have visited upon a number of occasions and where Burton studied and resided from 1593 onwards. Bergen Evans* suggests that the unusually long time taken by Burton to obtain his degree might have been due to an illness; I suggest that he neglected his academic studies in order to write his plays. From what is known we can be certain that their modes of life differed very much. Shakespeare was busy with the affairs of the theatre and as an actor, using his earnings to purchase estate in Stratford and London. Evidently he looked after his gains well even to the extent of going to law should he consider he was being wronged. Burton on the other hand appears to have been of a very studious and retiring disposition, spending much time in "mine own library" and in the Bodleian. It is interesting to compare their aims as shown in passages from their respective writings which might be taken as autobiographical. Shakespeare wrote thus:—

> The aim of all is but to nurse the life
> With honour, wealth, and ease in waning age;
> And in this aim there is such thwarting strife
> That one for all or all for one we gage:
> As life for honour in fell battle's rage;
> Honour for wealth; and oft that wealth doth cost
> The death of all, and all together lost.
>
> *The Rape of Lucrece*, 141–147

and it would appear that he did achieve this aim and was able to retire to Stratford to enjoy "wealth and ease in waning age". Burton (B. p. 5) writes: "I will spend my time and knowledge, which are my greatest fortunes, for the common good of all." He also achieved his aim for his plays and *The Anatomy* have enriched the lives of many. How much money he got from his writings is not known; he said (B. p. 3) "I am not poor, I am not rich." His Will is copied in the preface to modern editions of *The Anatomy*. In it he gives instructions concerning what he wished done with

* *The Psychiatry of Robert Burton*; Columbia Univ. Press, p. 7.

his books. The author of *The Tempest* loved his books:—

> Knowing I lov'd my books, he furnish'd me
> From mine own library with volumes that
> I prize above my dukedom. I, 2, 166
>
> Burn but his books.
> He has brave utensils—for so he calls them—
> Which, when he has a house, he'll deck withal. III, 2, 91

Burton never had a house of his own, so that "when he has a house" is autobiographical. If Shakespeare possessed and loved many books, why did he not deck New Place with them or mention them in his Will?

The implied meaning of Burton's words "*Paucis notus, paucioribus ignotus*" is not clear. Possibly they were intended to convey that he was known to few because of his secluded life, yet known to many through his writings and through the performance of his plays.

It is generally accepted that the last of "Shakespeare's" plays was written about 1611 and thus, if the thesis maintained in this book prove to be valid, the great contributor did live for some twenty-nine years after that date. During this period he wrote, and continued to make additions to, *The Anatomy of Melancholy* and, therefore, all estimations of "Shakespeare" as an author would require revision. It would be quite beyond the scope of this book to attempt this task here; the reader should recall the high praise accorded by Samuel Johnson and others to *The Anatomy*. Several points only I wish to touch on before ending. *The Sonnets* were published in 1609 and thus were written then or before; the poem entitled *The Argument of the Frontispiece* occurs in the Fourth Edition (1632) and, as the engraved frontispiece, without the verse commentary, occurs in the Third Edition (1628), it would appear that this poem was written between 1628 and 1632. Wilson Knight* observes that Hamlet thought only of himself, whereas Lear had regard for the suffering of others. So also it may be said that *The Sonnets* express selfish thought, whereas *The Argument* deals with the trials of others; for its combination of knowledge, insight, pity and humour the verse on the madman must have been surpassed but rarely, if ever. In my opinion these two contrasts indicate an increasing maturity thereby bearing out Burton's quotation from Horace, "*Non eadem est ætas, non mens*", already referred to in Chapter V. In Chapter V also I said that Shakespeare, in contrast to Burton, did not evolve, and in this present chapter that Shakespeare had no message to deliver. These two characteristics of Shakespeare's writings are important as they might well be the answer to F. E. Halliday's

---

* *The Crown of Life*; Methuen & Co., 1952, p. 12.

questioning of why Shakespeare retired so early in life: he had nothing new to say and no message to deliver so, when the financial motive was satisfied, he was content. The real "Shakespeare", on the other hand, kept on adding to *The Anatomy of Melancholy* until his death. Students of "Shakespeare" will agree that with each reading of the great plays something new strikes one's mind. This sure sign of great profundity shows itself also in *The Anatomy*, a phenomenon not to be wondered at as, being the product of a life-time study, the full flowering of the author's genius is there displayed; little surprise then that Samuel Johnson, John Keats* and Charles Lamb†, all great students of Shakespeare, were captivated by *The Anatomy* also.

Middleton Murry‡ compares Shakespeare and Keats and quotes Keats' view on poetry: " 'If poetry come not as naturally as the leaves of a tree, it had better not come at all.' This is what Keats meant by the poetry of 'sensation'; for him it *was* sensation: the outcome of some mysterious and total surrender of the personal self. It produced Keats' odes and Keats felt that it had produced Shakespeare's poetry." I am certain that this is exactly what Burton meant when he wrote (B. p. 5), "Besides, I might not well refrain, *ubi dolor, ibi digitus*, one must needs scratch where it itches ... Concerning myself I can peradventure affirm with Marius in Sallust, 'that which others hear or read of, I felt and practiced myself; they get their knowledge by books; I mine by melancholizing'." Moreover, Burton further elaborates this theme: "For I am of that nobleman's mind, 'Melancholy advanceth men's conceits, more than any humour whatsoever', improves their meditations more than any strong drink or sack" (B. p. 257). "Such a one was old Sophocles, and Democritus himself had *hilare delirium*, much in this vein. Laurentius, *cap.* 3 *de melan.*, thinks this kind of melancholy, which is a little adust with some mixture of blood, to be that which Aristotle meant when he said melancholy men of all others are most witty, which causeth many times a divine ravishment, and a kind of *enthusiasmus*, which stirreth them up to be excellent philosophers, poets, prophets, etc." B. p. 262. The corresponding lines in "Shakespeare" are:—

Our poesy is a gum, which oozes
From whence 'tis nourish'd. *Timon of Athens*, I, 1, 22

Burton's language is noble, thought-provoking and apt—"Come then what can come, befall what may befall" (B. p. 402); "Wise from his cradle" (B. p. 18); "An old torn gown, an ensign of

---

* *John Keats. The Living Year*, by Robert Gittings; Heinemann, 1954.
† *Dictionary of National Biography*, edited by Leslie Stevens; Smith, Elder & Co., 1886.
‡ *Shakespeare*; Jonathan Cape, 1948, p. 15.

his [a student's] infelicity" (B. p. 202); "Doth the moon care for the barking of a dog? They detract, scoff and rail, saith one, and bark at me on every side; but I, like that Albanian dog sometime given to Alexander for a present, *vindico me ab illis solo contemptu*, I lie still and sleep, vindicate myself by contempt alone" (B. p. 422). The utterness and the nobility expressed in the first and fourth of these quotations have their parallel in this, from the last words of Macbeth:—

> Though Birnam wood be come to Dunsinane,
> And thou oppos'd, being of no woman born,
> Yet I will try the last.

He was a great lover of the beautiful both in life and literature. He quotes many beautiful passages:—"As the mountains are about Jerusalem, so is the Lord about his people, from henceforth and for ever" (B. p. 379), and his own language is often very beautiful:— "We must so be gone sooner or later all, and as Calliopeius in his comedy took his leave of his spectators and auditors, *Vos valete et plaudite, Calliopeius recensui*, must we bid the world farewell (*Exit* Calliopeius), and having now played our parts, for ever be gone" (B. p. 409). His favourite word used in describing beautiful objects was "fair"; on B. p. 662 we read ". . . a fair house, a fair horse . . . so fair a body, so fair a face . . . all fair and lovely to behold . . . if heaven be so fair, the sun so fair, how much fairer shall he be that made them fair? 'For by the greatness and beauty of the creatures proportionally the maker of them is seen'. *Wisd.* XIII, 5." We find similar thought and similar words in:—

> Stoop, boys; this gate
> Instructs you how t'adore the heavens, and bows you
> To a morning's holy office. The gates of monarchs
> Are arch'd so high that giants may jet through
> And keep their impious turbans on without
> Good morrow to the sun. Hail, thou fair heaven!
>
> *Cymbeline*, III, 3, 2

The use of certain words which make us pause to consider their full significance adds to the beauty of "Shakespeare's" language and reading *The Anatomy* helps us to understand their connotations. We read (B. p. 236): "In a word, as he [Footnote Mat. Paris] saith of Edward the First at the news of Edward of Caernarvon his son's birth, *immortaliter gavisus*, he was immortally glad, may we say on the contrary of friends' deaths, *immortaliter gementes*, we are diverse of us as so many turtles, eternally dejected with it." and when we read (*Antony and Cleopatra*, V, 2, 278),

> Give me my robe, put on my crown; I have
> Immortal longings in me

we see how the word "immortal" would be associated in the

author's mind with the death of Antony. We pause on reading "this ample third of our fair kingdom" (*King Lear*, I, 1, 79) to consider the author's etymological accuracy in the use of the word "ample"; this word is used in similar context in B. p. 394: ". . . how many sumptuous palaces had they, what provinces and cities, ample territories, fields, rivers, fountains, parks, forests, lawns, woods, cells, etc.?" For the second time, I contrast such language with that of the author of "fishify".

His love for the beautiful in life is well shown in his contempt for all that is base; my mind sees a striking similarity, in each's expression of love of abiding values, between:—

All gold and silver rather turn to dirt,
As 'tis no better reckon'd but of those
Who worship dirty gods. *Cymbeline*, III, 6, 53

and "Let them take wealth, *Stercora stercus amet*" (B. p. 395). The beauty of his mind is also shown in his enlightened suggestions for improving the lot of humanity, as set forth in his description of an imaginary commonwealth (B. p. 56 *et seq.*). He would have fire-fighting engines, state-aided legal and medical services and state-maintained hospitals, full utilization of land, long leases at a known rent, no exclusion of plebeians from honours, tax on luxuries and little or none on necessities, set times of recreation and holidays, annual pensions for the deserving old and indigent. We hear *King Lear* echo approval. The kindliness of the author of the great plays is well shown in Brutus' care for the boy Lucius and for Varro and Claudius (*Julius Cæsar*, IV, 3, 238–270). It is of interest also to observe, in this same passage, the author's love of music as indicated by the words of Brutus:—

Brut. Canst thou hold up thy heavy eyes awhile,
And touch thy instrument a strain or two?
Luc. Ay, my lord, an't please you.
Brut. It does, my boy.

and to read in *The Anatomy* a passage of similar context: ". . . many times the sound of a trumpet on a sudden, bells ringing, a carman's whistle, a boy singing some ballad tune early in the street, alters, revives, recreates a restless patient that cannot sleep in the night". B. p. 367.

Like the great plays, *The Anatomy* shows a great interest in human character. Sections deal with ambition, love, jealousy, envy, etc., and *The Argument of the Frontispiece* describes the jealous man, the solitary, the Inamorato, the hypochondriac, the superstitious and the mad; here, as in the plays, effective use is made of imagery.

Burton was a great teacher; no one has taught me more; not only did he deal in worthy subjects but, also, his genius could extract from his learning-sensitized mind the fitting, concrete example, which replaced woolly abstractions. He, himself, enunciates the role played by learning in the evolution of the educated mind, saying (B. p. 6) "We skim off the cream of other men's wits, pick the choice flowers of their tilled gardens to set out our own sterile plots", and (B. pp. 7–8) "The matter is theirs most part, and yet mine . . . which nature doth with the aliment of our bodies incorporate, digest, assimilate, I do *concoquere quod hausi*, dispose of what I take. I make them pay tribute, to set out this my Maceronicon, the method only is mine own, I must usurp that of Wecker *è* Ter. *nihil dictum quod non dictum prius, methodus sola artificem ostendit*, we can say nothing but what hath been said, the composition and method is ours only, and shows a scholar." Emerson writes (*Spiritual Laws*): "No man can learn what he has not preparation for learning, however near to his eyes is the object. A chemist may tell his most precious secrets to a carpenter, and he shall be never the wiser—the secrets he would not utter to a chemist for an estate. God screens us evermore from premature ideas. Our eyes are holden that we cannot see things that stare us in the face, until the hour arrives when the mind is ripened; then we behold them, and the time when we saw them not is like a dream," and in his essay on *Intellect*: "Then in a moment, and unannounced, the truth appears. A certain wandering light glimmers, and is the distinction, the principle, we wanted. But the oracle comes, because we had previously laid seige to the shrine." Shakespeare had not laid seige to the shrine of great learning as evidenced by his often empty, commonplace, repetitive or borrowed writings. That the art and practic part of life must be the mistress of this theoric and that the last day is *prioris discipulus* did apply to him, as indeed to all men, is well illustrated by his ability to make use of, in his plays, data acquired during the course of his work as a butcher (so traditionally recorded) and by his failing to employ correctly a knowledge of astronomy, which knowledge he appears not to have possessed. Contrariwise, Burton's wide net in study provided his imagination with ample data "to keep", "to recall to mind again" and "by comparison of which to feign infinite other unto himself". The great importance of what he said about the powers of the imagination or phantasy justifies requoting (B. p. 101):—"phantasy . . . is an inner sense which doth more fully examine the species perceived by common sense, of things present or absent, and keeps them longer, recalling them to mind again, or making new of his own. In time of sleep this faculty is free, and many times conceives strange, stupend, absurd shapes, as in sick men we commonly observe. His organ is the middle cell of the brain; his objects all the species communicated to him by the common sense, by comparison of which he feigns infinite other unto himself". Undoubtedly

"Shakespeare" is referring to the activity of the unconscious mind when he wrote "fastest by night, unseen yet crescive in his faculty" and one asks whether "fastest by night" is in reference to that phenomenon which, according to Beveridge (*loc. cit.* p. 74), is not uncommon, namely that the time when one is most likely to receive intuitive impressions is on first awakening in the morning. I can say in passing that this has been my own experience. From what Burton has said it is probable that he experienced his own unconscious mind "making new of his own", as in dreams, and "by comparison of" newly arrived impressions with impressions received in the past, perhaps the quite distant past; he writes (B. p. 100) "By the apprehensive power we perceive the species of sensible things present, or absent, and retain them *as wax doth the print of a seal*", and (B. p. 102) "Memory lays up all the species which the senses have brought in, and records them *as a good register*, that they may be forthcoming when they are called for by *phantasy* and reason." [Italics mine.] The parallel passage in "Shakespeare" is:—

> By what? By any other house, or person?
> Of any thing the image, tell me, that
> Hath kept with thy remembrance?
> . . . .
> But how is it
> That this lives in thy mind? What seest thou else
> In the dark backward and abyss of time?
>
> *The Tempest*, I, 2, 42–50

"Image" in the "Shakespeare" passage and "as the print of a seal" in *The Anatomy* convey the same idea and coincidence would appear an unlikely explanation of its occurring in two passages each dealing with memory. My reader will also observe that not only do these passages from "Shakespeare" and from Burton deal with similar psychological phenomena but also they resemble one another in being expressed in the barest skeleton terms—no verbosity here.

Examples of association of ideas, at first glance appearing alien, occur in *The Anatomy of Melancholy:*—"Industry is a loadstone to draw all good things; as the dog barks at the moon, to no purpose are your sayings; as a tree that is heavy laden with fruit breaks her own boughs, with their own greatness they ruin themselves." The greater contributor to the "Shakespeare" canon had similar powers:—"Antony, like a doting mallard; Cleopatra, like a cow in June; young Pyrrhus now at home; dwell I but in the suburbs?; the moon's an arrant thief." Such imagery does serve to irradiate the mind through all her powers and it is my opinion that Milton was referring, at least in part, to this shining inward, this power of the inward, unconscious mind to associate ideas, when he wrote (*Paradise Lost*, Book III, lines 51–55):—

So much the rather thou, celestial Light,
Shine inward, and the mind through all her powers
Irradiate, there plant eyes, all mists from thence
Purge and disperse, that I may see and tell
Of things invisible to mortal sight.

and that he believed this power to vary with differing emotional states. Burton wrote:—

To clear our brain of misty fogs,
Which dull our senses, and Soul clogs.

The Argument of the Frontispiece

and on B. p. 165: "The other parts cannot perform their functions, having the spirits drawn from them by vehement passion, but fail in sense and motion; so we look upon a thing and see it not; hear, and observe not; which would much affect us, had we been free", and on B. p. 379: "Homer was blind, yet who (saith he) made more accurate, lively, or better descriptions, with both his eyes? Democritus was blind, yet as Laertius writes of him, he saw more than all Greece besides." Burton suffered from melancholy and thus was from the cheerful ways of men cut off, but he was enabled to write:—

Sweet are the uses of adversity;
Which, like the toad, ugly and venomous,
Wears yet a precious jewel in his head,

which, in my opinion, is a rendering of "It is good for me that I have been afflicted", which he quotes on B. p. 734. Emerson (*Intellect*) writes in similar vein:—"A self-denial, no less austere than the saint's, is demanded of the scholar." Burton also says: "I neglect phrases, and labour wholly to inform my reader's understanding" (B. p. 12), and "*Non oculi sed mens videt*, we see with the eyes of our understanding" (B. p. 507); "We are wiser than we know" is Emerson's rendering (*The Over-soul*) of the burden of the latter. Like Milton* and Emerson, Burton sensed the great value of the wandering or celestial light and that it could be bright or dim, and one grasps something of the secret of his power on realizing that in him Light and Learning joined forces.

* F. E. Hutchinson closes his book, *Milton and the English Mind*, Hodder & Stoughton, on a note similar to that on which I have closed mine.

1. Add to foot of p. 96:—Two excellent examples of "Shakespeare's" interest in ecology occur in this passage:—

   Ros. . . . here in the skirts of the forest, like fringe upon a petticoat.

   Orl. Are you native of this place?

   Ros. As the coney that you see dwell where she is kindled.

   As You Like It, III, 2, 315

2. To be considered as at *As You Like It*, III, 5, 98, on p. 165 and to be compared with *The Winter's Tale*, IV, 4, 710-21, on p. 186:—

   So holy and so perfect is my love,
   And I in such a poverty of grace,
   That I shall think it a most plenteous crop
   To glean the broken ears after the man
   That the main harvest reaps; loose now and then
   A scatt'red smile, and that I'll live upon.

   This is clearly a reference to:—"And Ruth the Moabitess said unto Naomi, Let me now go to the field, and glean ears of corn after him in whose sight I shall find grace." *Ruth*, II, 2. "And let fall also some of the handfuls of purpose for her, and leave them, that she may glean them." *Ruth*, II, 16.

   If those outward ornaments were not of such force, why doth Naomi give Ruth counsel how to please Boaz? B. p. 527

3. To be considered as at *The Winter's Tale*, IV, 4, 710-21 (p. 186):— The Arbuthnot Bible (1579) and the Barker Bible (1597) both give "Behold, Esau my brother is rough and I am smooth." The Barker Bible (1591) gives "Behold, Esau my brother is a hairy man and I am smooth."

   How blessed are we that are not simple men! IV, 4, 734

   The Barker Bibles (1582 and 1588) give, as alternative to "plaine" in "but Jacob was a plaine man," "simple and innocent."

   We are blest in this man, as I may say, even blest. IV, 4, 815

"Bless me, *even* me also, O my father." *Gen.*, xxvii, 38

   He was provided to do us good. IV, 4, 816

   "And in thee [Jacob] and in thy seed shall all the families of the earth be blessed." *Gen.*, xxviii, 14

KEY TO PAGE NUMBERS

according to Partitions, Sections, Members and Subsections as they appear in the Chatto & Windus Edition of *The Anatomy of Melancholy*, 1883. In this present book these page numbers are referred to as B. p. . . .

Democritus Junior to the Reader B. Pages 1–74

Part.	Sec.	Mem.	Subs.	B. Pages
1	1	1	1	81–86
1	1	1	2	86–87
1	1	1	3	87
1	1	1	4	87–90
1	1	1	5	90–92
1	1	2	1	92–93
1	1	2	2	93–94
1	1	2	3	94–95
1	1	2	4	95–98
1	1	2	5	98–100
1	1	2	6	100–101
1	1	2	7	101–102
1	1	2	8	102–103
1	1	2	9	103–105
1	1	2	10	105–106
1	1	2	11	106–108
1	1	3	1	108–109
1	1	3	2	109–110
1	1	3	3	110–112
1	1	3	4	112–114
1	2	1	1	114–115
1	2	1	2	115–130
1	2	1	3	130–133
1	2	1	4	133–135
1	2	1	5	136
1	2	1	6	136–140
1	2	2	1	140–146
1	2	2	2	146–150
1	2	2	3	150–152
1	2	2	4	152–155
1	2	2	5	155–158
1	2	2	6	158–163
1	2	2	7	163
1	2	3	1	164–166
1	2	3	2	166–169
1	2	3	3	169–170
1	2	3	4	170–171
1	2	3	5	171–172
1	2	3	6	173–174
1	2	3	7	174–175
1	2	3	8	175–177
1	2	3	9	177–178
1	2	3	10	178–184
1	2	3	11	184–186
1	2	3	12	186–189
1	2	3	13	189–193

Part.	Sec.	Mem.	Subs.	B. Pages
1	2	3	14	193–198
1	2	3	15	198–216
1	2	4	1	216–218
1	2	4	2	218–219
1	2	4	3	219–222
1	2	4	4	222–225
1	2	4	5	225–227
1	2	4	6	227–234
1	2	4	7	234–244
1	2	5	1	244–246
1	2	5	2	246–247
1	2	5	3	247–248
1	2	5	4	248–249
1	2	5	5	249–250
1	3	1	1	250–252
1	3	1	2	252–260
1	3	1	3	260–264
1	3	1	4	264–268
1	3	2	1	268–269
1	3	2	2	269–271
1	3	2	3	271
1	3	2	4	271–275
1	3	3		275–281
1	4	1		281–288
2	1	1		293–295
2	1	2		295–297
2	1	3		297–299
2	1	4	1	299–301
2	1	4	2	301–303
2	1	4	3	303–304
2	2	1	1	304–307
2	2	1	2	307–310
2	2	2		310–313
2	2	3		313–336
2	2	4		336–356
2	2	5		356–358
2	2	6	1	358–362
2	2	6	2	363–367
2	2	6	3	367–369
2	2	6	4	369–374
2	3	1	1	374–379
2	3	2		379–387
2	3	3		387–404
2	3	4		404–406
2	3	5		406–412
2	3	6		412–414

Part.	Sec.	Mem.	Subs.	B. Pages
2	3	7		414–425
2	3	8		425–426
2	4	1	1	426–429
2	4	1	2	429–431
2	4	1	3	431–433
2	4	1	4	433–435
2	4	1	5	436–439
2	4	2	1	439–441
2	4	2	2	441–444
2	4	2	3	444–445
2	4	3		445
2	5	1	1	446
2	5	1	2	446–447
2	5	1	3	447–450
2	5	1	4	450–451
2	5	1	5	451–456
2	5	1	6	456–459
2	5	2		459–460
2	5	3	1	460–462
2	5	3	2	462–463
3	1	1	1	466–471
3	1	1	2	471–475
3	1	2	1	476–478
3	1	2	2	478–479
3	1	2	3	480–484
3	1	3		484–490
3	2	1	1	490–496
3	2	1	2	496–502
3	2	2	1	502–506
3	2	2	2	506–521
3	2	2	3	521–530
3	2	2	4	530–546
3	2	2	5	546–550
3	2	3		550–581
3	2	4		581–584
3	2	5	1	584–587
3	2	5	2	588–593
3	2	5	3	594–607
3	2	5	4	607–608
3	2	5	5	609–626
3	3	1	1	626–630
3	3	1	2	630–640
3	3	2	1	640–644
3	3	3		644–646
3	3	4	1	646–652
3	3	4	2	652–660
3	4	1	1	660–669
3	4	1	2	669–683
3	4	1	3	683–700
3	4	1	4	700–702
3	4	1	5	702–704
3	4	2	1	704–713
3	4	2	2	713–714
3	4	2	3	714–720
3	4	2	4	720–723
3	4	2	5	723
3	4	2	6	723–739

N.B.—The chapter beginning "Natural Beauty is a stronger loadstone" is indicated in the Fifth Edition of *The Anatomy* as

Part. 3 Sec. 2 Mem. 3 Subsect. 3

instead of ,, 3 ,, 2 ,, 2 ,, 3 as occurs in the Fourth Edition. The Fifth Edition rectifies its mistake before the beginning of the true Mem. 3; the Sixth Edition, however, continues the error, giving Mem. 3 as Mem. 4, Mem. 4 as Mem. 5, Mem. 5 as Mem. 6, until about half-way through "Mem. 6" Subsect. 5, when it reverts to the correct Mem. 5 Subsect. 5.

The Seventh and Eighth Editions and at least some subsequent editions follow the mistakes of the Sixth Edition and in addition keep in error right to the end of Part. 3 Sect. 2 "Mem. 6" Subsect. 5.

INDEX OF AUTHORS

OTHER THAN SHAKESPEARE AND BURTON